W9-CDA-646

1 THE YOUNG STALIN

THE YOUNG

the early years of an elusi

EDWARD ELLIS SMIT

TALIN

volutionary ☆

, Straus and Giroux | *New York*

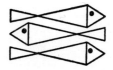

WINGATE COLLEGE LIBRARY
WINGATE, N. C.

Copyright © 1967 by
Edward Ellis Smith
Library of Congress catalog card number 67–26488
All rights reserved
First printing, 1967
Published simultaneously in Canada by
Ambassador Books, Ltd., Rexdale, Ontario
Printed in the United States of America

Contents

36754

AUTHOR'S PREFACE

No one may write comprehensively about the events preceding the 1917 upheaval in Russia without having studied the Okhrana Collection at The Hoover Institution on War, Revolution and Peace at Stanford University. Its primary source materials include thousands of original documents of the tsarist Department of Police from the latter part of the nineteenth century to 1917. These have been described as a "phantom file" of the Russian secret police. Basil Maklakov, who was the Russian Ambassador to Paris when the bolsheviks seized power, secretly shipped these files from Paris to Stanford. As The Hoover Institution explains, "Because the truth would have placed his life in jeopardy, Maklakov stipulated in a contract with The Hoover Institution that the sixteen large wooden packing crates were to remain sealed until his death and the contents not shown to the public until at least three months thereafter." In any event, this incomparable Okhrana Collection was of major importance in reconstructing Stalin's early life. The tsarist police (whose role in revolutionary events and operations has been vastly underestimated) was a highly professional outfit that keenly and carefully observed revolutionary parties and personalities.

Stalin's biographer must acknowledge a debt for Boris Souvarine whose *Staline: aperçu historique du bolshevisme,* published in 1935, remains authoritative and formidable even today. That Souvarine lacked the benefit of later source materials does not detract from his well-documented work. I should add that he was very helpful in replying to my queries about sources he utilized in his book.

Although Iremashvili, Vereshchak, Uratadze, and Zhordania have passed away, their individual reminiscences of Stalin in his

youth and pre-revolutionary manhood, which the reader will encounter, contributed much to my assessment of Stalin. Arsenidze, an
important witness to Stalin's life in the Transcaucasus, died in Paris
while I was *en route* to talk with him; nonetheless, he left valuable
memoirs about Stalin's early life. To all of these I give grateful
acknowledgment.

Isaac Don Levine pioneered in his biography of Stalin (1931),
which H. G. Wells described as a "godsend" and Albert Einstein as
a "symphony on a theme: violence breeds violence." Later, in his
essay *Stalin's Great Secret* (1956), Levine tried to pry open the
Kremlin vaults and, although he did not succeed, he opened the
eyes of many to the possibility of Stalin's collusion with the tsarist
Department of Police. My conversations with him and with Eugene
Lyons, another outstanding biographer of Stalin, were highly re-
warding in connection with Stalin's pre-revolutionary life. I am also
grateful to Bertram D. Wolfe not only because his book, *Three Who
Made a Revolution,* broke new ground in the life of Stalin but also
because of his kind disposition to discuss with me certain episodes
in Stalin's early life.

Trotsky's bitter biography, *Stalin: an Appraisal of the Man and
His Influence* (1941), which was in preparation when Stalin's assassin murdered the author in Mexico, is valuable and deserves
study even though Trotsky was sometimes inaccurate and allowed
prejudices to cloud his judgment. Although he was not fully successful as a chronicler of important dates and events in Stalin's pre-
revolutionary life, he was an astute observer. The late Charles
Malamuth, translator and editor of Trotsky's book, volunteered
helpful suggestions for my own work.

My correspondence with George Kennan, who has long studied
Stalin's early life, was stimulating. I am grateful to V. J. Nanuashvili
of San Francisco for his assistance in explaining some of the intricacies of the Georgian language. Eddy Gilmore aided me in obtaining London newspaper accounts of the 1907 Congress of the
Russian Social-Democratic Workers' Party and provided personal
reminiscences about persons who figure in these pages.

Ladis K. D. Kristof, Research Fellow at The Hoover Institution, kindly reconstructed from the materials about Boris Ivanovich Nicolaevsky heretofore unpublished information concerning Stalin.

Arline Paul and Marina Tinkoff of The Hoover Institution's reference staff were of great assistance. Michael Futrell and Francis B. Randall were generous in answering my requests for sources of information. Sidney C. Graves, Stephen Johnsson, Robert C. Tucker, Richard Wraga and Captain J. J. Zarriello, U.S.N. (MC) kindly discussed with me various aspects of the book. The expertise of Irene Hoggan in research and the verification of source materials was indispensable to my writing. I extend my deep thanks for the friendly and unerringly incisive editorial advice of Robert Giroux.

I owe a special debt of gratitude to my friend Dr. Stefan T. Possony, Director of The International Studies Program at The Hoover Institution. His counsel regarding those passages concerning Lenin and his reading of the manuscript were of enormous value.

I hasten to add, however, that I bear sole responsibility for the contents of the narrative. I have tried to obviate errors but perhaps they have crept in, much as I have tried to shut them out. One is tempted to blame Stalin, who is guilty of obfuscating history but not of my errors.

Finally, without the uncommon forebearance and assistance of my wife, Olga, this work would have been impossible.

E.E.S.

I THE YOUNG STALIN

INTRODUCTION

May, 1907 in London; the rains were chilly, and Spring seemed reluctant to arrive. Carrying umbrellas and wearing heavy coats, detectives from Scotland Yard congregated in Whitechapel to keep an eye on Brotherhood Church. Inside this dingy building secret police agents of France, England and Russia mingled in disguise among the Poles, Jews, Letts, Georgians, Tartars and Russians, numbering almost four hundred, who had assembled there. The smell of the place, on this occasion recognizably Russian, arose from a combination of unbathed bodies, unwashed clothes and cheap tobacco smoke. On the floor of the assembly, solemn pronouncements and pedantic marxist hair-splitting were intermingled with un-English shouting. London—placid, prosperous and unconcerned—was host to the Fifth Congress of the Russian Socialist-Democratic Workers Party, the last before the Russian Revolution of 1917.

On this particular morning—Tuesday, May 21, 1907—the Congress was in its eighth day and it was the turn of a small, balding, red-bearded man named Lenin to be chairman. After nervously calling the delegates to order, he proposed that a young Georgian, along with three others, be given a deliberative or consultative delegate's right at the revolutionary meeting. The Georgian proposed by Lenin was twenty-seven years old and of swarthy complexion; his name was Joseph Vissarionovich Dzhugashvili. Suddenly there was a shout from the floor. Lenin was startled as Martov, his menshevik opponent at the Congress, demanded to know who was being proposed and in what status. "Who are these people, where do they come from?" Martov asked. And Lenin meekly replied, "I really don't know. . . ."

The young man proposed as a deliberative delegate was later known as Joseph Stalin. Where he came from and how he happened to be in London are elements in an astounding saga that spans his seventy-four years from 1879 to 1953, beginning in a small, obscure Caucasian town and ending in the Kremlin. However, no one at the London Congress of 1907 or anywhere else had the faintest notion that he would someday become one of the most powerful dictators of all time. Anyone who might have suggested in 1907 that thirty-six years later this man would parley with chiefs of state, including the First Minister of the British sovereign to whose capital he had travelled, might well have been thought insane. Eventually the fate of many people would rest uneasily in the hands of the delegate—an unkempt, disagreeable-looking little man with a crippled left arm. To the question "Who is he?" history would give the answer, "Perhaps the most influential person of the twentieth century."

For almost a quarter of a century, from 1929 to 1953, Stalin had absolute power over the people of Soviet Russia and at the apogee of his dictatorship, after World War II, he virtually ruled more than a sixth of the earth's surface, the vast territory from Central Europe to the Pacific Ocean and from the Arctic Circle to the Black Sea. During this twenty-five year period he caused millions of people in Russia and its satellites to die of starvation, to perish in his concentration camps, or to be executed by his police. As the Iron Curtain descended around three hundred million people, he extended the tentacles of his subversive and imperialistic apparatus into the most remote areas of the world. Not only in Soviet Russia but even abroad his assassins killed, with uncommon impunity, known or suspected political adversaries.

He exerted an enormous influence on international affairs. His assistance in advancing the careers of Hitler and Mussolini, both of whom later turned against him, was a crucial factor leading to World War II. Personally or by proxy he played a major role in almost every armed conflict during the twenty-five years he was the undisputed *vozhd,* or leader, of the Soviet Union. His deeds continue to exert an immense effect on the human race, and in all probability his influence will be felt in many succeeding decades. He manipulated statesmen, politicians, generals, and intellectuals on a stage that was no less than worldwide, and as a result the historians of the world have not slighted him. The number of articles, essays and books about Stalin—a great many of which were written under his personal direction—may equal that of any other person who ever lived. Sheer quantity, of course, has never guaranteed accuracy, and as the volume of literature about Stalin has multiplied, one point has stood out in sharp relief: the more that became available, the more confusing became the story of his life and the more difficult it became to be sure of the facts. It is easy to explain this muddle, for Stalin himself planned it over a period of years and he was to some degree successful, as the historian searching for truth is reluctantly forced to admit. Why did Stalin do it? This is a troublesome question, the answer to which is undoubtedly bound up with the nature of his personal psychopathology.

Before Stalin's hireling drove an alpine pickaxe through Trotsky's skull in Mexico City, the victim had recorded a trenchant observation in his unfinished biography of the dictator. "Our epoch is above all an epoch of lies." Trotsky's comment might well apply to Stalin himself, who created a whole fabric of lies about his life— especially the early period. Of course, it was not an easy matter for Stalin to falsify his post-1917 life, although he was able to disorient a legion of persons from all walks of life and from many nations concerning even that period. Fortunately, the available records and the many people who had dealings with the dictator prevented him from distorting the facts of his later life. Nonetheless, he had a success of sorts even at this, for Soviet sources are still remarkably silent about scores of highly significant events in which he was all-important. The contemporary Kremlin rulers, having locked up in Moscow vaults data of vital importance to everyone, remain co-conspirators with the dead Stalin.

While precise information in many areas of Stalin's post-revolutionary life is lacking, the outlines of his activities are often clearly discernible. Moreover, the numerous dark corners of his dictatorship are slowly, almost imperceptibly, being illuminated, though at the present rate it might be another century before all the facts see the light of day. Much of the reluctance of Soviet authorities to disclose information is easily explained by their close connection with Stalin's rise to power and dictatorship. Some of those still in prominent positions were his protégés and are tied, even after his death, to his bloody past.

His life from 1917 to 1953 has a comparatively well-defined configuration, and careful observation and study yield more information about it year by year. The earlier portion, representing the years from his birth to 1917, however, has remained largely a mystery. Strangely enough, no work has dealt exclusively with the first half of his life, although numerous accounts concern in part what were doubtless the years during which his character and personality were molded and in which the explanations for his later tyranny and his predilection for gross inhumanity to man may be found. It would be a boon to history if the few remaining, aging bolsheviks who knew Stalin before 1917 would record what they know about the dictator's early life. Unfortunately, they are silent for the time being and there are not many of them left. So, while innumerable persons still alive will probably write in relative freedom about his post-1917 life, a reconstruction of his first thirty-seven years must perforce rely on what is already known. To that period—from his birth in 1879 to the year 1917, the most cataclysmic year in Russian history—this narrative is addressed.

Stalin's drive to obliterate the record of his pre-1917 life assumed the dimensions of a fully mounted military campaign replete with regiments of psychological warfare experts, trumpeters sounding false notes, and scores of writers acting as battering-rams to destroy the fortress of truth. Such an enormous effort to confound history indicates that he was striving to conceal matters the disclosure of which would have been politically disastrous or personally shameful to him and might also have placed his life in jeopardy. Here he was successful only to the degree that he made it exceedingly difficult to establish a given fact, forcing the biographer to use what has been described as the archeological method of historical excavation, where the failure to discover a particular artifact at a given level of diggings is often as important as a real find.

After 1917, Stalin publicly mentioned his first thirty-seven years on only five—possibly six—occasions, in a few paragraphs of a few hundred words that were more noteworthy for their falsehoods than for their accuracy. His reluctance to speak or write about his pre-revolutionary life is not surprising, for he probably had more important skeletons in his closet then than later. It is not surprising that Stalin, by twisting the story of his early life, created difficulties for writers dealing with this period. What *is* surprising was his success in inducing biographers of this period, in many instances, to follow the lead of his court historians. During the last twenty-five years of his life scores of sycophants were persuaded, by subtle and not too subtle threats, to write fanciful untruths. More than a few biographers repeated and perpetuated this pap even when they were skeptical of its validity. A few authors, silently cursing the mumbo-jumbo about Stalin, read the standard works and finally succumbed to what someone else had written; more often than not, it was of Stalinist origin. "Established" dates, places, and events in his pre-1917 life thus found an easy route to the stronghold of the writ, because of the difficulties of disproving them or an apparent unwillingness or inability to hack away at the mythology surrounding his early life.

In addition to Stalin's distortion of his early life and the need to weigh each assertion in his official works, there are a number of paradoxes confronting the biographer: the more that has been written about Stalin's pre-revolutionary life, the less clarity has emerged; the more details that have been supplied, the deeper one must dig for facts; and the closer the writer has been to Stalin, the greater has been the twisting of data, unintentional in the writing of some yet deliberate in that of others. The more important the writer was in the Stalinist hierarchy, the greater was his falsification of the story of Stalin's first thirty-seven years; and the older he became, if he was in the upper reaches of the Soviet power structure, the more his reminiscences of pre-1917 events were subject to rewriting and editing, particularly during the period of Stalin's purges. As if this were not enough to plague the chronicler of Stalin's early life, he is beset by the irony that most of the people who had personal knowledge about Stalin's first thirty-seven years were executed after being forced to write adulatory and falsified accounts of that knowledge. Few survived. Those who did are suspect because they varnished the information they released on behalf of the dictator. Stalin made it mandatory that writings about his early life exclude the slightest human frailty or fault; otherwise the hapless writers, labelled "enemies of the people," might end up in Siberia or perish in the cellar of a prison.

Five brief and vapid statements about the first half of his life serve as noteworthy companion pieces to the labored articles and speeches in his autobiographical *Collected Works,* which are heavily laden with nonsense and misinformation. In thirty-seven years, moreover, he wrote only a few letters of which we are aware. Three were published under Soviet auspices; two survive only in police archives, although the tsarist secret service intercepted and read six. Not one letter or postcard to his mother, wife, son, or any other relative has turned up from these years in prison and exile or his extensive travels in Russia and Europe. Only one letter with his future parents-in-law has been published. Since the record includes no more, it may be assumed that he destroyed many others that might reveal explosive or embarrassing facts about his pre-1917 life. Apparently for the same reason, he kept no diary. He did not have a collection of personal papers or, if he did, it has not appeared to date. Other revolutionaries, of course, amassed copious files of personal recollections. Soviet agents even today are alert throughout the world to the appearance of writing by Lenin, each paragraph of which is considered historically significant. But no one seems greatly interested in recovering what Stalin penned before the revolution. The collectors of memorabilia, whether in the Free World or behind the Iron Curtain, know that his letters and papers do not exist except perhaps in Kremlin vaults. Even that is doubtful, for after his rise to power it would have been an easy matter for him to destroy what he had composed earlier.

Rarely in modern history does a major political figure fail to mention his forebears or his family. Stalin, however, wrote not a word about any blood relative for public attention. Only once, during the course of an interview with Emil Ludwig, did he refer to his parents. It was a brief remark to the effect that they had not treated him badly. But in all his writing and speaking he ignored his children and his two wives with a persistence that could not have been accidental. Indeed if history had to depend on Stalin as its only source, we would not know that he had been married and had fathered three legitimate children, let alone the names of his wives and children. No photographs of Stalin with his parents, with first wife, or with his first child survive. When Yasha, his first-born son, perished in a Nazi prisoner-of-war camp during World War II, he said not a word and wrote not even a sentence of eulogy. And while wartime security might explain his silence at the time, it does not explain why he ignored his own son while causing thousands of eulogies to be written about other war heroes. Was it because Stalin—concerned lest his order be disobeyed that no one was to be taken prisoner by the Nazis—put his role of generalissimo above fatherly concern for a valiant son?

Hitler's diabolical life included a faithful dog, a mistress whom he married in a mad scenario before his suicide, and a group of weird friends. Stalin once alluded to his Siberian dog, Tishka, but he never referred to a mistress, a wife, or a friend in his early life. The staunch friendships one normally enjoys in childhood and youth, and which often thrive throughout later life, were largely absent from his early years. Even as a young man, he seemed to take a macabre pleasure in betraying persons who trusted him or who tried to assist him. Throughout his seventy-four years, it is difficult to find one person whom he really befriended. Frequently, those who were helpful or friendly to Stalin before 1917 later found themselves in a tsarist jail; after he became dictator, they sometimes faced his firing squads or landed in one of his concentration camps.

Stalin ushered into history the era of the total dictator who not only tried to obliterate all opposition to his rule but every trace of his past except an incomplete "official" version. He tried to construct for himself a thoroughly new fabricated past, based on his own falsifications and the coerced writings of people who had ostensibly known him before the revolution. In many respects Stalin was extraordinary, but in this respect he made a unique and indelible imprint on the story of our time.

However, the truth will out. Just as Sherlock Holmes found conclusive evidence in the quietness of a dog at night, much of the interesting and vital information about Stalin's early life must be learned from the silences. These, together with the writings and recollections of often obscure persons and the tsarist police records, have made it possible to reconstruct the story of Stalin's life that Stalin himself tried so mightily to suppress, to see that life more clearly even than some of his contemporaries did, and to become acquainted with its changeable motivations.

In a rare moment of candor during 1913, Stalin achieved a high place among cynics when he wrote, "Paper will put up with anything that is written on it." For the next four decades he and his sycophants expanded on this theme and managed to deceive millions of persons concerning the facts of his early life. His propaganda and writings swirled from continent to continent overwhelming many of good persuasion and sometimes even those who were skeptical of his assertions. He managed to confuse millions of people, among them some of the greatest names in modern history. It is probable that he may have deluded himself with the thought that he had cheated history of its rightful knowledge about his past. If, as the Soviet poet Evgeniy Evtushenko claims, he is only "pretending to be dead" and his ghost still stalks unhappy Russia, he, as well as those who would profit from further trickery, will perceive that the deception is over. When (or if) the Kremlin opens its archives, of course, or when new information ultimately comes to light elsewhere, the extent of Stalin's secrets will be enlarged, not diminished. For the time being, however, it is hoped that these pages will help to expose his well-designed fraud.

1 | BACKGROUND AND EARLY LIFE

Stalin was the adopted pseudonym of Iosif (Joseph) Vissariono-vich Dzhugashvili. The only child of Vissarion (Beso) Dzhugashvili and Ekaterina (Keke) Geladze, he was born in 1879 in Gori, a small and ancient town nestled in the mountains of Georgia. His parents were the children of serfs; they and their ancestors lived and died in Georgia, part of the land of Caucasia.

Georgia, as well as the rest of Transcaucasia (the area south of the Caucasus Mountains), is enveloped in mythology and legend that often blend with recorded history. At many points, however, the myth and the legend fuse into a sort of romantic fairy tale, important nonetheless as a mirror in which latter-day Georgians saw themselves. It would appear that the Georgians are descend-ants of Japheth, the son of Noah, and his great-great grandson Kar-thlos, the second son of Thargamos (see Genesis, x, 3). From Kar-thlos, tradition has it that Georgia was originally called Karthli. His son, Mtskethos, founded the ancient city of Mtskhetha (now Mtsket) as the capital of his kingdom. Some scholars believe it was the mythical Colchis, where Jason and his Argonauts obtained the celebrated Golden Fleece. The ancient Greeks found Georgia an awesome but beautiful land where Prometheus supposedly was chained to one of its mountain peaks. To the Persians Georgia was Gurjistar, to the Romans and Greeks it was Iberia, to the Armeni-ans, Vrastan. The Russians continue to call it Gruzia.

The legions of Alexander the Great conquered Georgia, but in the third century B.C. a Georgian prince, Pharnavaz, managed to liberate his countrymen from Alexander's domination. Geographi-cal and cultural closeness with Armenia to the south brought vexatious problems to the Georgian princelings. The Roman General Pompey, at war with the Armenians in 65 B.C., invaded Georgia that year, but shortly thereafter withdrew. Romans were last seen in Georgia as an invasion force led by Emperor Trajan in A.D. 114. In addition to the Greeks, Romans, and Armenians, who as friends or invaders had great impact on Georgia, the Jews and the Genoese left their imprint either as traders or colonizers. During the reign of King Mirian (265-342 A.D.), son of a Persian king, he and many of his subjects were converted to Christianity by an Armenian nun, St. Nino (*Nuno*), and under his auspices the first Christian church was built at Mtsket. In the last decades of 300, Persian invaders built the fort Tphilis (Tiflis or Tbilisi), which remains Georgia's capital. From this time the Persians, Armenians, and Turks menaced Georgia until its leaders discovered a redeeming formula in 571, when they appealed to the Byzantine Emperor Justine II to provide them with a king. He appointed Guaram, the first of the royal Bagratid family that reigned in Georgia until 1803.

In 1492, when Columbus was discovering a new world, the Georgians, witnessing one of the frequent wars between Persia and the Turks, asked the powerful Russian Tsar for assistance. It was granted. The Persians threatened Georgia in 1619 and an appeal was reluctantly directed to Michael, the first Romanov Tsar. It is unclear whether he extended aid. In the early part of the eighteenth century, King Vakhtang declared allegiance to Peter the Great, and placed himself under his protection. This arrangement, which the Georgians hoped would shield them from their traditional enemies, was a failure; the Turks captured Tiflis, and in 1795 Shah Agha Mohammed of Persia left the city in ruins. This experience caused King George XIII in 1799 to renounce his kingdom in favor of the Tsar of Russia. In 1801, Georgia became a part of Russia—adding a million people (five hundred years earlier it had seven million) to the Russian Empire.[1] As the United States of America consolidated its independence, Georgia voluntarily became a vassalage from which it has never emerged except for the years 1918-21.[2] The Russians developed Georgia to protect the southern flank of the Empire. They built roads over and through the Caucasian Mountains. Foreseeing economic benefits, they encouraged the cultivation of noncompetitive crops and fostered Russian colonization. The nineteenth century thus brought an infusion of Russian troops, bureaucrats, tourists, settlers, traders and priests. This, of course, was a variation on an old theme that Georgia knew well.[3]

Georgia absorbed numerous alien cultural intrusions during its two thousand years of recorded history, but failed to escape their influences. Kurds, Armenians, Persians, Tartars, Jews, Mongols, Greeks, Romans and Slavs left cultural traces, and by the time Stalin was born in 1879, Georgia bore marks, often almost imperceptible, of Eastern and Western mores. Its language, with at least fourteen clearly defined dialects, had an Indo-European grammar. Its art and architecture leaned toward Byzantium and the Judeo-Christian tradition. It constituted a bridge between East and West, North and South. It nonetheless remained agriculturally and industrially backward compared to Russia and Europe. Farm implements were primitive; peasant homes were frequently roofed with mud and branches. Modern industry and transportation, which were to take root later, were then nonexistent. Perhaps most important, serfdom had been abolished only fifteen years earlier. Wretched as its history had been, and primitive as its economics appeared in the last decades of the nineteenth century, Georgia with Russian assistance was pulling itself out of its past while maintaining its peculiar brand of culture from both Occident and Orient.[4]

The Georgians are small in stature by Western standards. The men are usually little more than five feet tall and are generally of swarthy complexion. An abundance of black hair is characteristic of men and women. They have an incredible record of longevity. One may read in the press today of Georgians who live to a hundred years or more. No scientific explanation has been offered for this phenomenon, although folklore says that the secret reposes in the goat's milk and red wine that many of them consider essential to their diet. Certain traits may be mentioned as having been ascribed to the Georgians over the centuries. They are quick to re-

WINGATE COLLEGE LIBRARY
WINGATE, N. C.

venge a familial insult. Blood brothers are said to be as common as the vendetta. Observers have described Georgians as quick-tempered, intensely emotional and religious.

Joseph Dzhugashvili was a true child of Georgian history and culture. The myriad influences of Mongol and Slav, of Byzantium and Samarkand, contributed to the shaping of his character and personality. Georgian was his mother tongue. From a legendary hero in Georgian literature he adopted his nickname "Koba." [5] He never ventured outside Georgian territory until he was twenty-six. His boyhood chums and his first wife were Georgians. Hs second wife was also half-Georgian. In short, if one is to understand his life, it must be within the Georgian milieu.

He was born near Tiflis in Gori, one of Georgia's most beautiful and appealing towns, located at the confluence of the rivers Liakhva, Medzhuda, and Kura. Its ancient and remarkable buildings included the church of Anskia Bogomateria and an old Armenian cathedral of Gothic design. A strong fort, in the finest tradition of the American Wild West, was situated some five miles away on the left bank of the Kura at the cave city of Uplis-Tsikhe; it was at the foot of a conical hill surmounted by the ruins of the castle of Goris-Tsikhe. The small town of Gori took pride in its gardens and vineyards. Its wine, Khedistav, was "very light and pleasant to the taste." Celebrated for its sheep herds, dairies and beehives, in 1879 it boasted sidewalks, bridges, lampposts, various stores, hotels, plumbing, a telegraph and several educational institutions, including a teachers' school and elementary schools for Russians, Georgians, Armenians, and Moslems. It ranked after Tiflis as a cultural center. The townspeople had few complaints about their surroundings, although they bitterly resented the Armenian domination of commerce and light industry. Armenians were unpopular throughout Georgia.

Gori was not economically depressed. Its few slums existed only in the town's Oriental quarter. Handicrafts and light industry combined to produce brisk trade and commerce. Records of the period 1880-1917 fail to suggest the serious shortage of food and drink that troubled Russia and Eastern Europe. The mild Gori climate, and the clear mountain air, smiled on the town's residents.[6]

Joseph Vissarionovich Dzhugashvili was born December 9, 1879, in this comparatively affluent town. Two impressive sources, the Russian Department of Police and Keke Dzhugashvili, his mother, dispute this date, which became an occasion for gala celebrations after he became dictator of Soviet Russia. However, both were understandably mistaken. An official tsarist police circular, No. 5500, issued May 1, 1904, asserts that he was born in 1881.[7] Either this was a clerical error or Dzhugashvili misinformed his interrogators after his first arrest with deliberate intent to confuse the gendarmes. In her old age, his mother insisted her son Joseph was born in 1880. In 1930, she excitedly told the American journalist H. R. Knickerbocker, of the New York *Evening Post,* in Tiflis:

"He will be fifty-one eight days after Christmas old style. I don't know what date it would be by this new way of reckoning. I never could learn it. I only know I was twenty years old then and he was my fourth son."

Keke Dzhugashvili referred to the Old Style calendar, the only one she could understand, and used it to calculate the birth date for her only surviving son, whom she "treasured above everything in the world." [8] That date would not have been easily wrenched from her mind. If her memory served her correctly, Stalin was born on January 14, 1880. The Russian Orthodox Christmas was celebrated twelve days after the Western Christian date during the nineteenth century. (It became thirteen days in the twentieth century.) Keke probably muddled Stalin's birthday with his baptismal date, which would have been vastly more important to her. "Eight days after Christmas" her son would have been five weeks old—just about the age for baptism and christening.

The Georgian Orthodox Church considered the birth of a male child of major significance. Unlike the practice in rural America at the same time, when the name and birth date of the child were normally placed in the family Bible, pious Georgians—and Stalin's mother was a most religious person—deemed the Holy Writ far too sacred to be inscribed, except for a "dedication" entry. A few weeks after birth the newborn child was taken to church, where the parish priest ceremonially baptized him, entering his own name, the name of the child, the names of his parents, and those of witnessing godparents (sometimes nobles represented by proxy) in a special *Baptismal Record Book* (*Metricheskaya Kniga*). This entry in the form of a certificate was afterward issued to the child's parents, henceforth to serve as an official birth and baptismal certificate. Stalin's godparents remain unidentified, the priest who baptized and consecrated him is unknown, and his birth record has not survived.

Until 1939, when Stalin celebrated his sixtieth birthday, only meager information was available concerning his forebears, his birth, and his childhood. However, in the spate of literature hailing his achievements and glorifying his person that year, a book called *The Childhood and Youth of the Leader* was published in Moscow.[9] This was a compendium of personal reminiscences by several persons claiming they had knowledge of his lineage, and it represented the first serious attempt to establish a Dzhugashvili family tree. Although the book is scantily documented, it is important not only because it indicates the family picture Stalin wanted to present for posterity but also because it probably included as much data as could be assembled with a great deal of effort about his forebears.

There is little doubt that his parents had been serfs whose owners were not accustomed to maintaining genealogical records of their chattels. Stalin's paternal ancestors lived in the village of Ger, near Gori, for as long as anyone could remember. "As were all peasants of that ravine, they were serfs of Prince Machabeli," according to A. M. Tsikhitatrishvili, a childhood acquaintance, who added that "one of the major peasant uprisings took place in the mid-19th century in Ananuri," a small county seat near Ger on the Aragva River. Tsarist military forces quickly crushed the insurrection and arrested ten insurgents, including the peasant Zaza Dzhugashvili, Stalin's paternal great-grandfather. Before he was imprisoned, Zaza escaped his guard and hid out near Gori, where he was soon seized and remanded as a serf to a Prince Eristavi. He was again involved in a peasant uprising on the Eristavi estate. When it was promptly repressed, Zaza ran away and became a shepherd for some time and then went to Didi-Lilo, a village near Tiflis. If this account is accurate, Zaza Dzhugashvili was in rebellion against established authority more than half a century before his great-grandson became a revolutionary.

Considering the celebrated longevity of Georgians, Zaza was probably born no later than 1800. Although no certain information exists concerning all the children of Zaza and his unknown wife, we know that he sired Stalin's grandfather, Vano Dzhugashvili, a cultivator of vineyards in Didi-Lilo. Vano had two sons, Vissarion (Beso) and Georgy. After Vano's death (presumably about 1850) Georgy died in Kakhetia probably the victim of a rival bandit gang. Iosif Dzhugashvili's maternal grandparents were Glakh (Georgy) and Melania Geladze, whose birth dates are unknown. Grandmother Melania's maiden name is unrecorded.

It is not surprising that little or nothing is known about the maternal grandparents: women were not highly regarded in nineteenth-century Georgia. However, it is perplexing that no information exists concerning uncles, aunts, cousins, nephews, or nieces. While this would be understandable with an ordinary Georgian peasant family, it is less so with Stalin's. The name Dzhugashvili was somewhat rare and Stalin as a dictator had every opportunity to determine his ancestry with some precision over a period of more than twenty-five years. The lack of information raises questions, probably unanswerable, about his lineage. Whatever the reasons for the lack of information, however, speculation is useless, for the record is apparently lost to history.

More, but not a great deal, is known about his parents. His father, Vissarion (Beso) Ivanovich Dzhugashvili, was in turn a peasant, a serf, and a cobbler, who came from the village of Didi-Lilo, near Gori.[10] The few accounts that mention him fail to provide his birth date, but all agree that he was overly fond of the Georgian wine and some assert that he was a drunkard.[11] He married Ekaterina (Keke) Georgievna Geladze (born near Gori in 1856) in

1874, when she was barely eighteen years of age. It is probable that Vissarion was some years older than his bride; Georgian males traditionally married when they were in their twenties. Thus he was probably born into a family of serfs about 1850. He apparently died in 1890 in his native Georgia from natural causes, his death hastened by alcohol. Keke died in her native Georgia in 1937.[12] There is some evidence that she had two brothers; if so, they join the group of Stalin's relatives without names or birth dates. From the marriage of Vissarion, the cobbler, and Keke, who became a seamstress of sorts, three (or four) sons were born. Only one, Joseph, survived. We do not know whether the others died at birth or later. Stalin made no known mention of them publicly or privately to the end of his days.

As already noted, the wedding of Vissarion and Keke took place in 1874. We may be sure that the pious Keke insisted that her marriage to Vissarion conform to Church regulations. Shortly thereafter the newlyweds moved into the house where Joseph was born five years later.[13] Whether Vissarion had purchased or rented it is unknown. It was like many homes built in Gori about that time in the 19th century. Whatever the method, he could not have imagined that it would become a national shrine. It still survives surrounded by magnificent marble walls and columns, and a memorial plaque on the façade reads, "Here the great Stalin was born December 21, 1879, and spent his childhood until 1883."

The "little house" (*domik*) was at No. 10 Cathedral (Soborovaya) Street, in the former quarter of Rusis-Ubani where Russian military units were garrisoned. A comfortable, though somewhat cheerless dwelling, it was located in a respectable part of town near Gori's main cathedral. Wooden steps lead to a primitively ornate front porch beyond which is a solid two-room brick house with brick floors and a basement. A sparsely furnished main room and an adequately equipped kitchen provide at least twice the living space alloted to a Soviet family today and tend to arouse envy in contemporary Russian tourists.

At No. 10 Cathedral Street, Vissarion plied his cobbler's trade and Keke reared young Soso (the Georgian diminutive for Joseph

—"Little Joe") until he was four years old. In his fifth year a major change occurred: his father, Vissarion, left his home for Tiflis, some sixty miles away, and obtained work in the Adelkhanov shoe factory. The wife and son remained in Gori.[14]

No explanation has been advanced for Vissarion's departure from Gori, but it probably had something to do with his drinking. Perhaps his customers found him unreliable or his wife found him insufferable. Until he died in 1890, further details of Vissarion's life are almost unknown. He must have returned from Tiflis to Gori for periodic visits. His wife insisted many years later that he attempted to take young Soso from school in order to make a cobbler of him.[15] But this period of Vissarion's life is shrouded in comparative silence.

Keke was exceedingly busy during her husband's absence, sewing, baking bread, working as a maid—anything to increase the family income. Semen P. Goglichidze, a teacher at the Gori school, who had known her for many years, said, "Everyone in Gori knew this lively woman who loved to work." Marya Abramidze, another friend, recalls that Keke kept Soso clean and neat, thus disputing other claims that he was reared in squalidness. A warm blue coat clothed him in winter. As she often sang folk songs to him, Keke discovered that her son had inherited her love for music and good voice. His schoolmates Z. A. Davitashvili and Doremidont Gogokhiya confirm that he was vocally talented during childhood. Apparently he discontinued his singing in later years; no one remembers hearing him sing after 1917.[16]

We know that Keke and Soso ate well during Vissarion's absence, even though G. I. Elisabedashvili, a friend of the Dzhugashvilis', writing under pressure in 1939, asserted that the family ate poorly. This contradiction is easily discernible in his description of the usual "dishes" for the poor people of Gori; red beans, boiled potatoes, Georgan greens, or vegetables with ground meat and tomatoes with rice or roasted meat. "They snacked on bread with onions." This diet of the poorer Georgians certainly compared favorably with Russian victuals of the same period. That young Soso excelled in physical activity is evidence that he was well nourished.

Many of his childhood acquaintances have glowingly described his early physical prowess.[17]

According to David Papitashvili, Soso loved to swim back and forth in the clear, swift waters of the nearby Liakhva and Kura rivers without resting for a breath. "Soso swam so well that no one could equal him" when he was six years old, according to Papitash-vili, and only a certain "vegetable salesman, Mikha Bitsadze," in the prime of life offered him adequate competition. He was profi-cient at a local game similar to "catch," and when childhood games required sides or team play, he always captained his team to vic-tory. He was also a good wrestler.[18]

Thus, as a youngster, Soso developed a strong and wiry physique combined with stamina that was later to stand him in good stead. Photographs of him during this period reveal that he was not as tall as boys of his age. At maturity, he was no more than five feet four inches tall, a bit above average for Georgian men. But during his childhood he compensated for his comparatively short stature by surpassing others in arduous games, competitive sport, and physi-cal exercises. At the age of seven when he fell seriously ill with smallpox, a dreaded disease in Georgia, his excellent health and stamina were important factors in his survival and recuperation. The sickness, however, scarred his face with pockmarks that were discernible all his life.

Young Soso's smallpox must have had a frightful effect on Keke Dzhugashvili. She had already lost three sons and now God was about to take her Joseph, whom she had named after the father of Jesus. She fervently prayed that he might be spared and she prom-ised the Almighty that if Soso lived she would dedicate him to the service of the Church.[19] This was understandable, for she had only her God and her Soso to sustain her. At thirty years of age she was past her prime by Georgian standards. And she had had no hus-band since Vissarion had departed for Tiflis a few years before. As she nursed Soso back to health during a long and tedious convales-cence, Keke, in her provincial piety, envisioned her son as a priest, a bishop, perhaps an archbishop. She probably vowed that his reli-gious education would begin as soon as he recovered.

Although Gori was a small town with fewer than eight thousand inhabitants, at this time it boasted four institutions available to provide some education for its sons and daughters: a municipal school of four grades, a pre-gymnasium for girls, a teachers' seminary, and an elementary theological school. It was to the last institution that Keke's attention turned, and she took the initial steps to have Soso enrolled there. Someone told her—perhaps the parish priest—that each pupil at the school had to be able to converse in the Russian language. To make sure that Soso met this requirement, Keke, according to B. Ivanter, asked her friend Kote Charkviani to teach Soso the Russian alphabet. After several months he was far ahead of Kote's son Peter and ready to enter the middle preparatory class of the Gori theological school.[20] A. M. Tsikhitatrishvili recounts a bizarre story. The Charkviani brothers, students in the Gori theological school, lived in the same part of Gori as Soso. In preparing their lessons they recited so loudly that they were audible throughout the entire quarter of town. Soso learned their recitation and easily memorized their lessons, although at the time the two Charkviani boys were experiencing difficulty at school.[21]

During 1886 and 1887 Soso was conquering smallpox and assaulting the formidable Russian language. Keke meanwhile found time to obtain a stipend for her son at the Gori theological school. Soso's alertness and innate ability, when combined with his mother's dedication to the Church, allowed him three rubles a month. Keke agreed to work for the school and its teachers, apparently as laundress, seamstress and part-time charwoman, for which she was to receive ten rubles a month. These thirteen rubles supported Keke and Soso for several years while Vissarion remained away from home. As far as we know, Vissarion was still alive and working in the Adelkhanov shoe factory in Tiflis. Subtle hints here and there in Soviet literature make it clear that he failed to support his only son and opposed the boy's entering the theological school. Keke, proudly responsible for starting her son on the road to the priesthood, had successfully overcome the objections of her husband.[22]

Soso was three months short of his ninth birthday in September, 1888, when he entered the Gori theological school. Until 1953 a memorial plaque on the façade of the school proclaimed, "Here in the former theological school the great Stalin studied from September 1, 1888, to July, 1894." Thus he spent almost six years there, from the age of eight to the age of fourteen, probably the most formative years of his life.[23] It is regrettable, then, that he failed to record his memories of this period. However, the void has been filled by observations of his schoolmates, some of which are questionable and others contradictory; all are nonetheless in substantial agreement on Soso's salient character and personality traits. These observations solidly but often subtly refute claims of Soviet propaganda that Stalin was mentally a genius and physically a gladiator. He was neither of these, although in the Gori school, as we shall see, he displayed keenness, cleverness, native intelligence, an excellent memory, and tough physical qualities. While it may be difficult to separate facts from fanciful recollections, it is not impossible. Even Soviet propaganda concerning this period of his life fails to darken the truth, and a composite picture of Stalin from ages eight to fourteen emerges in spite of attempts to varnish or distort it.

When he had completely recovered from smallpox, Soso entered the Gori school a skinny but powerful boy. Below average in height, he had copious dark hair and penetrating eyes. Innumerable freckles and pockmarks covered his face. To his schoolmate Elisabedashvili, who in 1939 wrote perhaps not freely, he was a "hero, in all respects first and foremost among his comrades." He recalled that there was not one subject in school that Soso found difficult. "With singular interest and success he learned languages, drawing, science, geography, and music." [24] He always prepared his lessons accurately. Although this is recognizable exaggeration, there is little doubt but that he was a good student. S. P. Goglichidze, the music instructor in the Gori school, remembered that even when young Soso was running a high fever, the boy told his mother that he *must* study; otherwise his grades might suffer.[25]

During the Gori school classes M. Titvinidze sat next to Soso, who helped him with his lessons. He claims that Soso's memory made him the school's outstanding pupil and that he was sufficiently knowledgeable to correct his teachers.[26] Doridemont Gogokhiya became acquainted with Soso in 1890, when courses were in Russian, Georgian being taught only twice weekly. Because Gogokhiya's mother tongue was Mingrelian, his Georgian was heavily accented. Soso "modestly" taught him Georgian and in turn learned the Mingrelian dialect.[27]

Before his fourteenth birthday, Soso had devoured "almost all the books" in the Gori library: the collected works of Ignaty Ninoshvili, Ilya Chavchavadze, Akaky Tsereteli, and the Chavchavadze and Kazbegi classic novels of Georgian mythology. One of Kazbegi's Georgian mountaineer heroes was Koba (The Indomitable), which Soso adopted as his youthful nickname and later his revolutionary first name.[28] Elisabedashvili remembers that even when Soso spent the summer months in the village of Tsroma at the home of Misha Davitashvili, "in the bosom of nature, he spent his time in reading and friendly recreation with comrades." When school was in session, he recalls, Soso and other students patronized a nearby private bookstore whose owner, Arsen Kalandadze, supplied the boys with books that were forbidden by the Gori school authorities. It is said that Soso's admiration for certain authors led him to draw their portraits in remarkable detail, although sketching was not a subject taught during that time, but no sketches or portraits have survived.[29]

According to a classmate, P. Karpanadze, activities quite apart from his studies absorbed his free time. He was involved in seeing that justice prevailed in the Gori theological school. When Kapanadze was ill and unable to take scheduled examinations that his teacher refused to delay, Soso intervened with convincing arguments that the tests had to be postponed. He tutored students who lacked proficiency in their studies, after which they always passed their examinations, and he managed to squeeze the organization and leadership of a chapel choir into his tight schedule, although the authorities frowned on the singing of Georgian national songs.

He was undismayed, and Goglichidze recalls that "one could hear Georgian people's songs" from Soso's choral group resounding from the walls of the Gori school.[30]

Exaggerations abound in these accounts. Soso in all probability was not more learned than his teachers, and while he might have implored an instructor to postpone Karpanadze's examinations, he could not have been a self-appointed monitor of the school's faculty and administration. Some of the chroniclers of his childhood deserve, nonetheless, to be forgiven, for they wrote in the shadow of the great purges of the late nineteen-thirties, when Stalin's paranoia was beginning to manifest itself. A notable example of this sort is provided by Emelyan Yaroslavsky, who later disappeared as an "enemy of the people," in his book *Landmarks in the Life of Stalin,* published in Moscow in 1940. He relates that while Soso was at the Gori school he often conversed with workers and peasants, explaining to them the reasons for their poverty and exploitation by landowners and capitalists. After Soso read Darwin and Marx, he became an atheist and subsequently upbraided G. Glurdzhidze, a boyhood chum:

I began to speak of God and after Joseph heard me out he said: "You know they deceive us, there is no God. . . ."

"How can you say such things, Soso?"

"I'll lend you a book to read; it will show you that the world and all living things are quite different from what you imagined, and all this talk about God is sheer nonsense." [31]

Fortunately, Joseph Iremashvili, a unique witness to Soso's early life, recorded his recollections in 1932 in Berlin, far away from Soviet coercion. Were it not for his reminiscences, the task of separating fact from fiction about Soso's boyhood would be almost impossible. Iremashvili was born in Gori at about the same time as Soso, and they were playmates from the age of four or five. Keke Dzhugashvili called Iremashvili her "other Soso," because he was frequently at No. 10 Cathedral Street and was considered almost a member of the family. The two friends sang in the same church choir, vacationed together, and experienced the usual boyish knockdown fights, which Iremashvili vividly, sometimes pedantically, described. Iremashvili attended the Gori theological school with Stalin and later was a fellow student at the Tiflis Seminary. He became a schoolteacher while Stalin practiced the trade of revolution and, in an odd twist of events, had Stalin's firstborn son, Yasha, as a pupil in Tiflis before the 1917 revolution. The two Sosos, Stalin and Iremashvili, were on amicable terms, at least until they left the Tiflis Seminary. While this might be unimportant, generally speaking, it is altogether possible that Iremashvili was Stalin's only friend in boyhood. Even that may not be proven, for on May 20, 1921 Iremashvili was arrested by the bolshevik secret police operating in the Caucasus under Stalin's guidance. Later Iremashvili's sister, Aneta, personally saw Stalin, pleading for the release of her brother. In one of his unique acts of compassion Stalin did release him from prison, after which he dispatched another schoolmate, Khakhanov to induce Iremashvili to join the bolsheviks. Iremashvili refused. Iremashvili and sixty-one other Georgian prisoners were subsequently deported to Germany on October 11, 1922.

Iremashvili's book *Stalin and the Tragedy of Georgia* (it has never been translated from the German) errs slightly in dates, places, and events. But the author's impressions seem never too far off the mark. His narrative of Soso Dzhugashvili's early life includes analyses of Stalin's character that could not have been fabricated.[32] Even before they entered the Gori theological school, Iremashvili remembered Vissarion, Keke, and Soso at No. 10 Cathedral Street. He claims that the mustachioed and bearded Vissarion, a stocky man, frequently beat his son unmercifully and that Soso, never crying, came to detest him, although he loved his mother. If it is true that Vissarion beat the boy, it tends to explain Stalin's later hatred for anyone whom he related to his father. Moreover, Iremashvili might have confused spankings for youthful pranks with a form of sadism. We cannot be sure, and with the caveat that only mentally ill persons repeatedly and brutally thrash youngsters and that Joseph himself maintained his parents treated him well, we must move on to the life of Soso in the Gori theological school as described by Iremashvili, keeping in mind that his impressions were more than forty years in the past.

Iremashvili remembered Soso Dzhugashvili as a thin and sinewy boy at the time he entered the Gori school. He had an aquiline nose. His face was narrow, elongated and pockmarked. His eyes were dark, bold and vivid, but not the kind to inspire trust. He walked "with an adult stride" on his long, thin legs, with a curious way of swinging his long arms and "bony, thickly veined hands." He was physically stronger than other boys, which enabled him to be intolerant of his schoolmates. Confident that he would win any fist fight, he dared his fellow pupils to disagree with him. He was a typical school bully.

His schoolmates deplored his sulky disposition and disliked his curt manner of speech and, frightened by his physical prowess (he was also the school's champion wrestler), they avoided him. Iremashvili observed that "Soso was different from other children in the Gori school." He sneered at the misfortunes or joys of his schoolmates. He loved nature, but was lacking in compassion for animals or people. He enjoyed scaring other boys. To him friendship meant the submission of others to his domineering will. He loved and respected only one person—Keke, his mother. But he was apparently highly regarded by the teachers of the Gori school because he was an industrious student. His classmate Gogokhiya recalls that when they "finished [at] the Gori school, Joseph outstandingly distinguished himself in the final examinations." This is confirmed by the school administration in its listing of superior students for the academic year 1893-94: Iosif Dzhugashvili graduated at the top of his class and was recommended for transfer to the theological seminary at Tiflis, the capital of Georgia.[33]

Keke was rightfully proud. She had devoted all her efforts toward the education of her son and his qualification as a student of the Tiflis Theological Seminary. In the process Keke had not only rubbed her knuckles to the bone but had also impaired her eyesight. Nonetheless, she was thankful and happy.[34] Her Soso had taken a long step toward eventual priesthood. Her prayers had not been in vain. According to one account, Keke "was such a devout

Christian that she literally prayed her son" into the Tiflis Seminary. The six years that Soso spent in the Gori school were not without misfortune, and that he graduated at all was due to his hardy physical constitution, Keke's singleness of purpose, and a measure of sheer good luck. He suffered at least one, perhaps two, serious injuries about which we know very little. Two brief accounts supply a few details. Elisabedashvili recalls in a short sentence that Soso fell under a carriage and was barely saved from death. He concludes his description of this nearly fatal accident with the remark that "without his strong body we and all humanity would have lost the great Stalin." [35] We do not know when or where the accident occurred, the extent of his injuries, or the period of convalescence. Neither Soso nor his mother mentioned this ghastly and unforgettable experience, and we are left to wonder at the circumstances surrounding it. More than fifty years later Stalin's sister-in-law Anna Allilueva wrote, in her book *Recollections,* about a significant injury Soso had experienced during childhood. She remembered that he had said his left arm had been deformed as a result of an infection followed by blood poisoning. He had been close to death. He survived, but she relates, "The vestiges of that injury remain to the present day." [36] Unfortunately, Allilueva joins Elisabedashvili in giving a curiously indifferent description of what must have been a major crisis in Soso's early life. Whether they presented two versions of the same incident or whether there were two unrelated accidents remains unclear, although we are probably safe in assuming that Soso's fall "under a carriage" irreparably damaged and malformed his left arm. Actually the left arm, shortened some two or three inches by a childhood injury, plays an important and mysterious part in his later pre-1917 life.

Physical affliction was not the only misery Soso suffered during his years in the Gori school. His drunken father, Vissarion, who went away when his son was five years old, unexpectedly reappeared in Gori in 1889 or 1890—the date is not precise. Vissarion's opposition to Soso's theological education had always been a bone of contention between him and his wife, Keke. Goglichidze writes, "The father was of the opinion that the son must follow the profession of his father, but the mother had a completely different point of view." Vissarion had often reproached Keke scornfully. "You want my son to be a priest, a church official, don't you? You'll never live to see it happen! Yes, I'm a cobbler and my son must become a cobbler like me." [37] Many years later Keke explained to a journalist that Soso had been a wonderful student and, understating considerably, she said that "his father, my dead husband Vissarion, considered taking the boy from school in order to teach him the cobbler's trade. I objected as much as I could, even quarrelling with my husband. . . . Some time later I succeeded in putting him in school again." [38]

Keke's statement that she "succeeded in putting him in school again" lends credence to a Soviet account that begins with the declaration "Vissarion never lost the idea that his son was attending school and not learning a trade. So—one fine day Beso, as he was called, arrived in Gori and took Soso to the Adelkhanov shoe factory", located on Erevan Square, in Tiflis. [39] The date of this "fine day" is lost to history; it probably occurred during a recess of the Gori school in 1889. Marya Abramidze wrote in 1939 that "Soso was in the second section [of the Gori school] when Vissarion began to say he would take the child from school and bring him to Tiflis for training in his trade." She continues, "My husband, Egnatashvili, and other comrades of Beso explained at length to him the absurdity of such a decision." Regardless of arguments from his wife and neighbors, it would appear that Vissarion dragged young Soso off to Tiflis and made him spend some time as an apprentice at a shoemaker's lathe in the Adelkhanov factory. [40] It must have been for a short period. Stalin never saw fit to mention the episode, although work in a factory at his tender age would have qualified him as a youthful member of the proletariat. Perhaps he not only hated his father for this episode; he might also have been ashamed of him and suffered embarrassment because of his public drunkenness. Vissarion was probably working only occasionally at the lathe, and in an alcoholic stupor wandering with his son about the town and its environs. This interpretation receives support from Department of Police Report No. 15179, dated August 19, 1909,

which flatly states that Vissarion was a tramp. In part it reads:

> Iosif Vissarionovich Dzhugashvili, a peasant from the village Tidivili [this was a poor translation of Didi-Lilo] of the Tiflis province, 29 years of age, Orthodox; his father, Vissarion Ivanovich, leads the life of a hobo. . . .[41]

On the surface this report suggests that Vissarion was still alive in 1909, although all evidence indicates he died in 1890. The police had apparently drawn together a number of agents' reports on Stalin and failed to cite their respective dates. In other words, Vissarion had been a bum in 1890, not 1909, when the circular was produced by the Ministry of Internal Affairs.[42] In any event, it was Keke who brought Soso back to the Gori school. S. P. Goglichidze writes, without supplying the date, that "after some time the mother went to Tiflis and took her son from the factory." [43] What might have been a disaster in his early schooling turned out to be no more than a minor diversion in his career.

When Soso created his own misfortune in the Gori school, good luck backed up by an alert mind saved him from expulsion. In 1890, according to Iremashvili, the Georgian teachers were replaced by Russians. This enraged Soso, and he incited his youthful Georgian schoolmates to demonstrate against their Russian teachers. Unsurprisingly he was punished, although he achieved high marks in his studies and was considered the "best student," with a "5," the highest attainable mark, for all his courses. The newly appointed Russian teachers apparently were reluctant to expel a student whose marks were so high, and they probably realized that his behavior would improve when he entered the revered Tiflis Theological Seminary. At any rate, young Soso graduated from the Gori school in July, 1894.[44]

Soso was six months short of his fifteenth birthday when he left the Gori theological school with honors. His life to this point had scarcely been easy, although he had enjoyed the affection of a doting mother and the best elementary education that his town of birth could provide. Frequently thrashed by an alcoholic father and punished by Russian schoolteachers, he was a bitter child, knowledgeable beyond his studies and perceptive beyond his years. Having survived illness and accident that marked his body for all time, he was nonetheless a supremely self-confident teen-ager. With a quick mind and a tough body he had no doubt that, after his vacation in the summer of 1894, he would enter the Tiflis Theological Seminary and become a superior student and ultimately a priest.

2 | THE EDUCATION OF A REBEL

Accompanied by his mother, Soso travelled to Tiflis on an exciting and memorable day in late August to register at the seminary. For Keke it meant a dream coming true; for Soso it represented a move from a small town to a metropolis of 150,000 people and the opportunity to partake of big-city life. A plaque on the façade of the former Tiflis Theological Seminary tells us that Soso arrived from Gori in time to register for studies beginning September 1, 1894.

The Great Stalin—leader of the VKP(b)[45] and the proletariat of the world—lived and studied here, in the former theological seminary, from September 1, 1894 to May 29, 1899, leading illegal workers' circles in Tbilisi.[46]

The history of Tiflis Theological Seminary, a gloomy, forbidding place that faced Pushkin Square, had been most unhappy. While its complete records have never been made available for research, many witnesses have testified to the mayhem that had occurred in its dingy four stories. As early as 1873, revolutionary literature had been smuggled in and read by the fiercely nationalistic students, and thereafter officials of the school were beaten and stabbed. In 1885 the student Silvester Dzhibladze (about whom we shall hear more) was sentenced to Siberian exile because he had soundly beaten Chudetsky, the seminary rector, a Russian who had made a slighting remark about Georgia. The following year a fellow student, Lagiashvili, killed Chudetsky. The student body, refusing to attend classes, went on a week-long strike in March, 1890.[47] The year before Soso entered the seminary, Lado Ketskhoveli, who had also attended the Gori school, led another strike. The atmosphere had bred many bitter foes of tsarism and conversely many fanatical Georgian nationalists. Noi Nikolaevich Zhordania originated the Georgian social democratic movement while studying there. Many years before Soso was enrolled, seminary students had forcefully opposed their teachers' dogmatism and had appealed for social equality and personal freedom.[48]

The seminary administration considered Soso's arrival routine. With the elimination of potential troublemakers, it appeared certain that there would be no repetition of the previous assaults and disorders. The authorities noted that "in the autumn of 1894 Iosif Dzhugashvili brilliantly completed the examination for the Tiflis Seminary," and they placed him on a half scholarship during the first part of the 1894-95 scholastic year.[49] The eighteen students in this category received half of their food, clothing, shoes, and school supplies.

However, Soso soon discovered that the Tiflis Theological Seminary was neither a rest home nor a recreation center. As P. Talakvadze, a classmate, bitterly observed, "Our instructors looked on us as animals." [50] The several hundred seminarians, who came from all corners of Georgia, were punished for the slightest deviation from its harsh monastic regime. Discipline came first: the school day started at seven o'clock in the morning with a church service (it sometimes lasted three or four hours) and ended with the strictly enforced five-o'clock curfew. Because Orthodox Church services were conducted with the communicants standing, numbness of feet and legs often resulted. The threat of the dark detention room where students spent hours for even minor misbehavior kept them on edge. Reading newspapers or attending theatres was forbidden. The barely adequate and scarcely nourishing food caused frequent illnesses and a few deaths. Iremashvili, who attended the seminary with Soso, wrote that Germogen, the rector of the seminary, and Inspector Abashidze, both monks, were fearful "jesuitical" inquisitors.[51] Abashidze, whom one student called a degenerate and a fanatic, continually pried open the desks and lockers of the seminarians searching for seditious literature, some of which had been smuggled in from abroad.[52] Grubby monks peered into the students' closets and under their beds. However, students guarded revolutionary books and pamphlets so well that they rarely fell into the hands of the inspectors. According to Vano Ketskhoveli, the brother of Lado, Soso frequently brought literature into the seminary, where he had various secret caches. The monk Dimitry often attempted to entrap him, but such were the wiles of young Dzhugashvili that Dimitry was always outwitted.[53]

The seminary staff intrigued more than it instructed, preferring games of religious bureaucratic rivalry to scholastic and clerical duties. An anonymously written book, *From the Recollections of a Russian Teacher in an Orthodox Georgian Theological Seminary,* published in 1907 in Moscow, surprisingly and candidly discusses personalities and conditions of the seminary during this period.[54] The author, obviously a pious lay instructor, will probably forever remain unidentified. More in sorrow than in anger, he alleged that the seminary authorities were not fools but "despots, capricious egoists, only concerned with their own positions." Until 1900 three hundred students had matriculated, but no more than fifty had completed the prescribed six-year course. In 1901 only eleven students graduated, and in 1905 there were a mere forty students in the institution. It was a sad state of affairs for an institution of higher learning even in nineteenth-century Georgia.

The somber, stifling monotony—not unlike a prison atmosphere —at the seminary contrasted sharply with Soso's life in Gori, where he had resided at home, bullied his schoolmates, and enjoyed freedom to roam the streets and fields. Now he was locked in, a virtual inmate of a monastic penitentiary. Undoubtedly he longed to escape from this grim religious jail that has been so well described by Iremashvili:

> Locked within barrack walls we felt like prisoners, guiltless of any crime, who were forced to spend a long term in jail. A dull and oppressive atmosphere and scarcely any expression of youthful temperament. The reading of Georgian literature and newspapers was forbidden by the Tsarist school inspector. . . . Even the few literary

works that the lay authorities permitted us to read were forbidden by the Church authorities because we were future priests. We could not read Dostoyevsky, Tolstoy, Turgenev and many other authors.[55]

Under circumstances so alien to his volatile, independent, but above all domineering nature, Soso quickly retreated into a world of dreams, memories of Gori, and reading. His eventual disorientation resulted in a pronounced defiance of the seminary regime and everything it represented.

Between 1894 and 1899 Soso not only rebelled against the seminary authorities but he also became alienated from his fellow students. His subsequent paradoxical cooperation with the very seminary officials whom he obviously detested perhaps has a psychological explanation: his shortened left arm, his badly pock-marked face, and his short stature made him the butt of derisive jokes and cruel remarks; and he turned against the seminary because it was a symbol of authority—not because he had read Darwin or Marx. Iremashvili's comments about an earlier period are nonetheless revealing concerning Soso's life in the seminary:

Soso had been constantly and undeservingly punished by his father. The terrible beatings the boy suffered made him hard and heartless just like his father. *People who ruled over others because of their seniority or power reminded Soso of his father. Soon he began to hate everyone who had any authority over him.*[56]

Communist historians have always emphasized the harshness of the seminary regime as the reason for Soso's rebelliousness. And while it must have played a role of some dimension in his attitude toward authority, Iremashvili's analysis is more credible. Although marxist ideas had taken shallow root in Russia more than a decade before Soso entered the seminary, literature on the subject during his early school years was limited to obscure and theoretical writings that by themselves would hardly make a boy resent authority and, according to Soviet accounts, "organize underground marxist circles" at the age of fifteen or sixteen.[57] Orthodox Russian Marxism is generally considered to have been born abroad in 1883 with the formation of the organization "Liberation of Labor," led by Georgy V. Plekhanov, Vera Zasulich, Pavel B. Axelrod, A. N. Potresov and others; but it was not until 1898 that the first congress of the Russian Social Democratic Party, which later split into Bolshevik and Menshevik factions, convened at Minsk.[58]

In 1931 Stalin told Emil Ludwig that he entered the revolutionary movement when he was fifteen, the year he left Gori. The interview included this curious dialogue:

LUDWIG: "Allow me to put a few questions to you concerning your biography. When I went to see Masaryk he told me he was conscious of being a socialist when only six years old. What made you a socialist and when?"

STALIN: "I cannot assert that I was already drawn to socialism at the age of six. Not even at the age of ten or twelve. I joined the revolutionary movement when fifteen years old, when I became connected with underground groups of Russian Marxists then living in Transcaucasia. These groups exerted great influence on me and instilled in me a taste for underground Marxist literature . . . It was a different matter at the Orthodox theological seminary which I was then attending. In protest against the outrageous regime and jesuitical methods prevalent at the seminary, I was ready to become, and actually did become, a revolutionary, a believer in Marxism as a really revolutionary teaching."

LUDWIG: "But do you not admit that the Jesuits have good points?"

STALIN: "Yes, they are systematic and persevering in working to achieve sordid ends. But their principal method is spying, prying, worming their way into people's souls and outraging their feelings. What good can there be in that? For instance, the spying in the hostel. At nine o'clock the bell rings for morning tea, we go to the dining room and when we return to our rooms we find that meantime a search has been made and all our chests have been ransacked. . . . What good can there be in that?"[59]

Stalin mixed truth with fiction in this account, which was intended, of course, for public consumption. He was "in protest" against the seminary regime, and he did join a "group," but he was not a marxist or revolutionary at the age of fifteen. Iremashvili recalls that ten students, including himself and Soso, participated in the first marxist "youth group" in the seminary in 1894. Seid Devdariani, a senior student and real leader, developed a six-year program (apparently to coincide with the six-year seminary course) at the end of which each student would graduate as an accomplished marxist activist.[60] Devdariani prepared a reading list for his would-be revolutionaries that included books on natural science, sociology and marxism. His group met secretly, heard reports submitted by members, and was enlivened by vigorous discussion. Although Iremashvili seemed to stand in awe of his friend Soso, apparently admiring him for his self-control and singleness of purpose, he noted his inability to suffer any criticism, and he observed that Soso deliberately broke up the first closely knit marxist group in the seminary. The opinions and rightful authority of anyone else in the group were apparently repugnant to Soso, who trusted no one, failed to comprehend the real meaning of socialism, was totally negative in his attitude, and was bitingly antagonistic toward those who disagreed with him. Soso then formed another group, which he terrorized by insults and brutality in a repetition of his career in the Gori school. Iremashvili, as if he were speaking of the nineteen-thirties and forties, when Stalin had total power in Soviet Russia, prophetically lamented that, "like parrots they repeated everything said by their little dictator." [61]

Young Soso was not a marxist at the age of fifteen or even seventeen, but simply a rebel already manifesting a furtive opportunism and displaying a personality with a pronounced Napoleonic streak. He had joined a secret circle upon his arrival at the seminary because he wanted to belong, but he reluctantly realized his inability to dominate it. It would appear that the circle's secrecy and conspiracy, more than its marxist coloration, appealed to him, and by the use of force he established his own group of no more than two or three students whom he could bully.

Vano Ketskhoveli, who had also attended the Gori school with Soso, writes that the seminary completely changed his character. Pensive and reserved, he turned away from games, but not from books.[62] Any free corner found him absorbing literature on economics, history, and nature. Since he was unable to dominate as he had at Gori, perhaps he also took to reading as a sort of opiate for his frustrations. He felt the need to know the basis of his worldly origins, but he was searching for something he could not find.[63] Then, and later, when he reached plateaus from which he could not proceed further, it was in his nature to backtrack. During this period persistent application to his studies and an extraordinary memory served him well; he received the highest marks in civil law, history, and literature. The class list of students at the Tiflis Theological Seminary compiled at the end of the 1894-95 scholastic year shows that he was a good student, ranking eighth in his class:

I class, first division.

For promotion to the II class: first section: Aleksander Novikov; Konstantin Feokhari; Mikhail Semenov; Khlampy Skhatov; Ivan Antonenko; Konstantin Tkesheliashvili; Ilya Shubladze; Iosif Dzhugashvili; Konstantin Tsagereli.

The list for the following academic year, 1895-96, reveals that he had moved up to fifth place.[64] (Novikov, who placed first in both the class of 1894 and the class of 1895, disappears after his short-lived seminary fame. With all the Russification going on in Georgia at the time, it is surprising that seven out of the nine students attaining the highest marks in 1895 were Georgian.)

Soso's high rank in the classes of 1894 and 1895 proves that the seminary authorities did not then consider him dangerous, subversive, or iconoclastic. They would not have promoted him with honors unless he had distinguished himself as a budding theologian —or had performed some singular service for them such as denunciation of fellow students. The author of *Recollections of a Russian Teacher* wrote of this widespread practice of unfounded accusation. Intrigues and conspiracy among priests and monks were reflected in student behavior. Very often a seminarian's academic standing depended more on the extent and viciousness of trumped-up charges against his fellow students than on scholarship. The seminary administration, convinced—not without reason—that students were constantly scheming, hatching terroristic plots, enter-taining heretical thoughts, and reading forbidden books, preferred lurid accounts of imagined heathenry from student spies. Informers, for their part, ingratiated themselves with the seminary authorities by fabricating denunciations. The best students often found themselves expelled while the mediocre and less talented seminarians rose to the top of their respective classes.[65] In the seminary Soso contracted the diseases of denunciation and conspiracy, and they forever marked his character as surely as smallpox had forever scarred his face.

The few available records of the Tiflis Theological Seminary reveal that Soso had no overt rebellious or revolutionary tendencies up to the age of eighteen. At least the ubiquitous monks and priests, who would easily have discovered them, were silent about any adverse findings. It was only many years later, when most of Soso's classmates had felt the dread brush of his purges, that the fifteen-year-old was described as having attentively scrutinized the seminary's hierarchical system and explained it to new comrades, and as having gone to meetings of an illegal social-democratic circle. Only then was it disclosed that one of the first books he read in 1894 was Marx's *Das Kapital*. Actually he and some unknown comrades, according to G. Parkanidze, read the book during the 1890's in a handwritten version copied from the first Russian edition published in 1872.[66]

After he became dictator, Soviet biographers alleged that Stalin had also been a youthful poet. N. Nikolaishvili, in an article "Stikhi iunogo Stalina" ("Verses of the Young Stalin"), published in a Tiflis newspaper *Zarya Vostoka* (*Dawn of the East*) on December 21, 1939, the anniversary of Stalin's sixtieth birthday, announced Stalin had written six poems, five of which were published in 1895 and one in 1896.[67] The first five poems appeared from June to December of 1895 in the Tiflis daily newspaper *Iveria* edited by the esteemed Georgian prince, Ilya Chachavadze, in whose murder Stalin was to be strangely implicated years later. The sixth poem was published in July, 1896 in the Tiflis social-democratic newspaper *Kvali* (*The Furrow*).

Nikolaishvili reports that only two of the poems in *Iveria* were given titles—"Lune" ("To the Moon"), and the one dedicated to the celebrated Georgian poet, Prince Rafael Eristavi, "To R. Eristavi." [68] The title of the poem that appeared in *Kvali* was "Starets Nininka" ("Old Man Nininka"). The first five poems were signed "I. Dzh - shvili" and the sixth was signed "Soselo," which is a variation of "Soso."

Nikolaishvili claimed that these poems "were written with great literary taste, in the language of the people," and that the poetry of the young author attracted attention. For in 1901 the "public-spirited Georgian, M. Kelendzheridze, compiling a work on the theory of language, placed the verse signed by Soselo in his book among the best examples of Georgian classical literature." He goes on:

> In 1907 the very same M. Kelendzheridze compiled and edited a "Georgian anthology or collection of the best examples of Georgian literature" (Volume I) in which on page 43 he placed the verse of Iosif Stalin dedicated to R. Eristavi.

Two years after the Nikolaishvili article, M. Kelendzheridze's "Stikhi iunogo Stalina" ("Verses of the Young Stalin") appeared in *Rasskazy o velikom Staline* (*Stories about the Great Stalin*) published in Tiflis in 1941. He confirmed that he had indeed compiled an anthology and a textbook in 1899 and 1907 in Kutais in which he placed the best works of classical Georgian writers to acquaint students with the rules of Georgian literary language. He names the authors: Shota Rustaveli, Ilya Chavchavadze, A. Tsereteli, G. Orbeliani, N. Baratashvili, R. Eristavi, A. Kazbegi—and Stalin. Kelendzheridze explained that at the time he included two of Stalin's poems from *Iveria* and *Kvali* in his anthology he had no idea who had written them. "I must admit," he continues, "that only in very recent years did I discover that the author of these wonderful verses, which I included in both editions of my book concerning Georgian literature, was the great Stalin." Kelendzheridze had been highly pleased, he wrote, to find out that a sixteen-year-old was the author of the poems, but he was sad that all copies of his book had been sold within a few days of publication and that he had not retained even one copy for himself! [69] The six poems that Stalin supposedly wrote appeared in 1895 and 1896, when Stalin was fifteen and sixteen years of age respectively and a student in the Tiflis Theological Seminary. No source friendly or hostile has claimed that Stalin wrote poetry before 1895 or after 1896. Nor did Stalin refer to his verses in his *Collected Works*. In other words, he neither claimed the authorship nor denied it.

The six poems attributed to Stalin are thus quite different from any of his writings after 1896. One finds in these poems of the fifteen or sixteen-year-old author lyrical and romantic references to roses, violets, lilies, larks, nightingales, and the moon. The poet pays tribute to the "learned men of Georgia," hoping that they will "bring joy and happiness" to his "adorable" Georgia. In "To the Moon" he again waxes lyrical:

I shall rip open my shirt
And bare my breast to the moon
And with outstretched hands
Worship her who showers her light on the world.

and in the same poem:

And know that he who fell on the earth like ashes,
Who was long ago enslaved,
He will rise higher than the great mountains
Winged with great hope.[70]

In the poem dedicated to Rafael Davidovich Eristavi there are also highly charged and religious ideas like: ". . . O poet, the Georgians have prepared for you a monument in heaven . . ." [71] Prince Eristavi was seventy-one when Stalin presumably wrote this poem in his honor. Although the Prince must have been moved by this adulatory poem dedicated to him, he never mentioned Stalin and, even though both men were in Tiflis, the two men never met.

With the testimony of two Georgians that Stalin wrote six poems, the possibility may not be discounted that he may just have been the author of these verses. However, it must be remembered that his fellow student, Iremashvili, never mentions Stalin's poetry and it is essential to consider several factors before accepting the alleged authorship. No Soviet or non-Soviet biography of Stalin drew attention to his poetic talent before 1939; these verses were only attributed to him four decades after he supposedly wrote them. While this is not conclusive evidence one way or another, it must be noted that nothing Stalin wrote before 1896 or since resembles these effusions. Although a few letters to Svetlana, his daughter, in the 1920's and 1930's express fatherly affection and tenderness, they are not poetic and, so far as is known, Stalin wrote no other poetry in the remaining sixty years of his life. Kelendzheridze's assertion that he placed the poems of a sixteen-year-old Stalin in an anthology among the works of the titans of Georgian literature, while neglecting to identify him, or even attempting to discover who he was, tests our credulity.

Finally we come to "I. Dzh-shvili" and "Soselo", the two pseudonyms with which the poems were signed. If they both refer to the same author (and we cannot be certain they do), one would have expected him to be proud to retain his family name, "I. Dzh-shvili," on all his poems. Nor may we forget that in Tiflis at this time there were a number of "Soselos" and "Dzh-shvilis" of an age and education to be writing verse. For example, two students at the Tiflis Seminary at about this time were named Dzhaoshvili and Dzhinchvelashvili.[72] A certain Demetriashvili, also a seminarian in Tiflis, later became an Okhrana agent and attended Lenin's school for revolutionaries near Paris.[73]

Ivan Aleksandrovich Dzhavakhishvili is by far the most interesting candidate for authorship of the verses. The "I." and the "Dzh-shvili" of his name are identical with the first signature. Ivan was born in 1876 in Tiflis, after which he attended the University of St. Petersburg, graduating in 1899. Later he was appointed to work in Armenian-Georgian philology. He was one of the organizers of the University of Tiflis, an archeologist, historian, and student of Georgian culture and paleography. Before his death in 1940, Dzhavakhishvili wrote "A Poem About Stalin" published in 1938 in Leningrad. (There is now an "Institute of History named after I. A. Dzhavakhishvili" in Tiflis).[74] In 1885 and 1886 Ivan would have been twenty or twenty-one. There is as much solid evidence (if one excepts the allegations of the two Georgians made after 1939 under the dictatorship) that he wrote the poems as that Stalin did. If Stalin wrote the poems attributed to him, they show not only that he possessed an impressive style never later manifested, but that his character changed radically. And there is impressive documentation that Stalin's post-revolutionary life was so devoid of poetic feeling and artistic appreciation that it plunged Russia into a quarter-century of cultural darkness.[75]

To strengthen the theory of Stalin's superiority, Soviet sources insisted in the nineteen-thirties that Soso the youthful seminarian became an ardent student of the brilliant Russian chemist Mendeleev, whose learned colleagues found his works not easy to understand. Soso was also said to have perused books about the French Revolution of 1848 and about the Paris Commune.[76] It is obvious, as already stated, that Soso during his first three years at the seminary was thirsty for knowledge which the instructors, most of them monks, could scarcely provide, given the repressive regulations of the Church. Books, and more books, took the place of solid teaching. While they supplied him with disconnected bits and pieces of knowledge, his education lacked cohesion. In later years only the religious subjects prescribed by the seminary remained with him. Above all he excelled in liturgy, which always marked his style of speech and writing.

Predictably Soso's insatiable reading ultimately annoyed the seminary authorities:

Dzhugashvili, it appears, has been frequenting the *"Deshevaya Biblioteka"* [Cheap Library]. Today I confiscated from him V. Hugo's *Toilers of the Sea. . . .*[76a]

Thus a priest at the seminary officially reported on Soso during November, 1896. A prolonged sentence in the hated solitary confinement was his punishment. In 1897 he was again caught with forbidden literature and punished by extended imprisonment—we

do not know for how long—in the same cell. These cruel and unusual punishments kindled the fire of his rebellious nature. The boy
who was said to have suffered beatings by a drunken father, who
had reputedly bested men three times his age in swimming through
the swift currents of the Kura River, who had been king of the hill
in the Gori school now found himself caged like a wild beast. He
could not run to his mother, Keke. He had no real friends; no one
to understand his plight. Escape from his father's beatings had
probably always been somewhat possible. But in the seminary isolation cell Soso doubtless decided that society, mankind—call it
what you will—was despicable and rotten. The viewpoints he developed in the punishment cell were certainly major factors in his
life thereafter.

From this point forward he tried, though unsuccessfully at first,
to undertake political activity that did not interfere with his studies.
The 1939 accounts written in honor of his sixtieth birthday claim
that he had resolutely demanded a change in the direction of the
seminary's marxist circle and had suggested that a room be rented
at the foot of Mt. David, not far from Tiflis, for five rubles a
month, where the seminarian marxists could secretly gather once or
twice a week. According to those sources, he carefully selected the
circle's members in order to screen out *agents provocateurs*.[77]

Soso's use of a so-called "conspiratorial apartment" and his fear
of tsarist *agents provocateurs* test our credulity. The years of his
life so far had been confined to provincial Gori and Tiflis, and
nothing in his reading or experience had involved conspiratorial
apartments or provocation. Darwin and Hugo were not noted experts on these subjects. In the seminary conspiracy was limited to
denunciation of students for unorthodoxy. Soso and some of his
acquaintances may have rented a cabin where they temporarily escaped the oppressive seminary regime. And they probably talked
about all sorts of things—as teen-agers do. This did not, however,
constitute a revolutionary marxist circle.

As previously mentioned, Soso had recruited his little group in
opposition to Seid Devdariani's organization. Initially it received
lukewarm approval, but almost immediately Seid and others ob-

served his intrigues and suspected him of treachery. The official Soviet records, indicating that Soso considered Seid's ideas too liberal and unrevolutionary, stated that each student had to be educated as "conscious fighters, revolutionaries, marxists." Significantly, these same accounts admit that Soso as a leader had been challenged—perhaps for the first time in his life—by noting that the rival seminary gangs were feuding.[78] Had the seminary authorities viewed these groups in their true light, as somewhat fraternal, nationalistic groups with marxist overtones, instead of as a dangerous movement, all would probably have been well. However, frightened and suspicious, the seminary monks probably panicked as they had before. They were sufficiently concerned to inform the Tiflis police, who were specialists at nipping subversion in the bud.[79]

It is no wonder that Vano Ketskhoveli feared that police spies had penetrated the groups; he was certain that some seminary students were informers and the seminary administration knew who was involved in the circles. Gogokhiya also had no doubt but that informers had notified Inspector Abashidze about student attitudes and activities, and particularly those of Soso Dzhugashvili.[80] But these fears were premature. No action was taken against the circles by the police or the seminary administration.

In the meantime, Soso allegedly created and edited a handwritten bimonthly student magazine in the Georgian language that was passed from hand to hand in notebook form. During this operation, according to a 1939 Soviet account, he found it necessary to consult various books that he could not afford to buy; his amazing memory came to the fore again as he visited bookshops and memorized the necessary passages. This obvious propaganda contains a kernel of truth. Undoubtedly, Soso was transcribing passages from books he had read and, as a boy would, circulated them among interested seminarians.[81]

Parkadze, a fellow seminarian, claims that in the autumn of 1897, when Lado Ketskhoveli, hiding from the police, arrived illegally in Tiflis, he became Soso's closest friend. They conversed at length about the workers' movement, and about Lenin and Plekhanov. He adds that through Lado and Russian marxists living in Transcaucasia Soso obtained illegal literature, that he skillfully observed conspiratorial rules (*konspiratsiya*), and that only in 1899 did the seminary officials become convinced that he was conducting revolutionary propaganda among seminarians and the workers of Tiflis.

Lado Ketskhoveli, a native of Gori, was four or five years older than Soso. He had led the student strike in the seminary in 1893.[82] Soso apparently admired and coveted his leadership ability. Lado immediately recognized that the eighteen-year-old was consumed with bitterness against all authority and that he could possibly guide his pent-up fury into the channel of social democracy. Although available information reveals they were not the close friends Soviet propaganda makes them out to be, he did provide Soso with illegal marxist literature and introduce him to other Tiflis marxists when, between the hours of three and five in the afternoon, Soso was able to leave the seminary. It was from Lado that he learned for the first time the bare rudiments of conspiracy as practiced in the revolutionary movement.

Thus Stalin took the beginning steps along the revolutionary way not in 1894 when he was fifteen, but in 1897 when he was eighteen. After Lado arrived in Tiflis, Soso's agitation and propaganda activities in the seminary and among workers in the city began to assume a more identifiable form. Correspondingly, during 1898 his academic standing and disciplinary record at the seminary began to deteriorate. Stalin owed Lado a great debt that he never publicly mentioned when he rose to power in Soviet Russia. It must be added that years later Stain apparently did suggest to Avel Enudkidze, a veteran social democrat, that Lado was a greater revolutionary than Lenin.[83]

Sometime during 1898, Soso, probably sponsored by Lado, joined the Tiflis marxist group *Messame-Dasy* (Third Group). It had been founded in 1893 by Noi Zhordania, a former student at the Tiflis Theological Seminary who was later President of the free Republic of Georgia (1918-21).[84] As the first social-democratic organization in Tiflis, *Messame-Dasy* enjoyed legal status, which meant that the police condoned its activities and permitted propagation of its ideas in the press. Zhordania, the first marxist in Georgia, was, curiously, neither a doctrinaire revolutionary nor a conspirator. He steered *Messame-Dasy* along nationalistic and bourgeois lines, although he always remained a social democrat in name.

Both Lavrenty Beria (who was executed after Stalin's death in 1953) and Yaroslavsky (who disappeared in the nineteen-forties) blurred the historical record of the Third Group in their respective books *On the History of Bolshevik Organizations in Transcaucasia* (1937) and *Landmarks in the Life of Stalin* (1940).[85] The first stated that "with his association in *Messame-Dasy* comrade Stalin, by his initiative and under his leadership, conceived and formed the revolutionary-marxist wing of the Georgian social-democrats," while the second asserted that Sasha Tsulukidze, Lado Ketskhoveli, and Stalin, "three young Marxists, united by the great doctrine of Marx, Engels, and Lenin, laid the foundation of a revolutionary Marxist organization in Transcaucasia." This was patent nonsense; Soso's heavy academic schedule in the seminary during 1898 scarcely allowed him time to lead or influence an organization that, at any rate, he had only recently joined. Furthermore, the real founders of Georgian socialism never trusted him, for reasons we will later consider.

A careful analysis of Soviet historians' descriptions of Soso's first revolutionary activities reveals that Soso was cautiously entering the Georgian revolutionary milieu. One inflated example comes from a fellow student in Gori and the seminary, Kapanadze, who recalled:

One morning after tea in 1898 I left the seminary for Pushkin Square when I saw Stalin, surrounded by a group of comrades, in a heated discourse criticizing the views of Zhordania. Here we heard for the first time about Lenin.

The bell sounded and we proceeded to our classes. I approached Iosif, struck by his incisive criticism of Zhordania's views. He informed me that he had read the articles of Tulin [Lenin] which he had liked very much.

"I must see him," he said.

I recalled these words to comrade Stalin at a meeting with him in 1926 and he remembered this episode.[86]

That Stalin failed to mention this episode in public is understandable. Criticism of Noi Zhordania in 1898 would have been met with hoots and jeers, and Soso would not have been so daring as to denigrate the views of the founder of Georgian social democracy.

At the very beginning of 1898, Soso fared well in the seminary.[87] His grades satisfied the authorities and his conduct was tolerable—all of which strongly suggests that he had little time for extracurricular activities. But he still chafed under authority and had become ill-tempered to the point of insufferability. The Napoleonic streak now came to the forefront, and Iremashvili discerned that his ambition for power was becoming all-consuming. Soso apparently was aware of the requirements of power as early as the spring and summer of 1898, for he tried to establish a political base of influence. Cynically he appraised his chances. According to Iremashvili, Soso said that he saw "everywhere and in everything only the negative, the bad side, and had no faith at all in the idealistic motives or attributes of mankind." Soso was now bitterly atheistic.[88]

An old Russian peasant saying has it that "the more quietly one moves, the farther he will get." Soso did not comprehend this wisdom—at least not then. He struck out wildly, probably trying to emulate his hero-image Lado Ketskhoveli. His revolutionary activities were fewer and less intense than later Soviet accounts would have us believe, but he did set off on the long and difficult career of the rebel marxist. Beria writes that Soso began to lead social-democratic workers' circles, whose members' long workdays left only six or eight hours to eat and sleep. The circles (to make matters worse for the unfortunate people) conducted propaganda from the apartments of "progressive toilers"—Mikho Borchoridze, Zakro Chodrishvili, Vano Sturua, S. Dzhibladze, G. Ninua, and others—never meeting twice in the same place.[89] S. Simungulov, who observed Soso's activities during 1898, says that he "conducted broad revolutionary marxist propaganda among progressive workers of Tiflis from the beginning of 1898, organizing and leading *five* illegal circles." [90] This is unbelievable. Although it is apparent that Soso was engaging in revolutionary activities that represented small danger to himself, the two hours permitted him outside the seminary still left little opportunity to emulate Lado or to establish a political base of power. At five o'clock, before the ordinary factory and shop day had ended, the seminary gates slammed shut and he was not an agitator but a prisoner. Thus his revolutionary activities could take place only on weekends and during summer vacations. Shorn of propaganda, these accounts reinforce the conclusion that Soso was attending the meetings of marxists but not leading them, learning from revolutionary propaganda and not spreading it among progressive workers.

Soso seems to have decided in 1898 that the profitable revolutionary work might be accomplished among the workers in the Tiflis railway shops, according to Simungulov. Railroad workers obviously fascinated him, perhaps because railways then were a fantastically modern means of transportation in Georgia. The speedy trains, averaging at the very most twenty-five miles per hour, were at that time the very essence of modernism. He viewed the railways as today's youth views spaceships. Iremashvili recalls:

One evening we secretly made our way out of the Seminary to a small shack owned by a Tiflis railroader on the side of Mount Mtatsmida. Other students who shared our views soon joined us. We met here a social democratic organization of railway workers.[91]

Sergo Alliluev, Stalin's future father-in-law, was a mechanic in a Tiflis railway lathe shop in 1898. According to an unreliable account written under Soviet aegis, Sergo discovered that Soso was anxious to conduct propaganda work in a circle of lathe-shop apprentice mechanics, and later that the workers were impressed with the youthful propagandist who patiently conducted meetings about strikes in understandable and simple language. However, Soso's revolutionary fervor received a setback when he was reproached for criticizing Noi Zhordania.[92] Stalin was never able to forget Zhordania's popularity among his countrymen and in 1921 he forced him to flee Georgia.[93]

According to Soviet historians, Soso played a major role in the 1898 Tiflis railway-shop strike, although he was still a seminarian. Simungulov relates: "The social-democratic shop and depot circles of the progressive workers under the leadership of the Tiflis central party group and comrade Stalin, personally, began preparations for the strike. At eleven o'clock the morning of December 14, 1898, the workers started to leave the shops." Tiflis gendarme officers called on military units to surround the strikers, who "fought heroically." Heroism failed to prevent the arrival of additional military units at three o'clock, and police and cossacks forced the strikers to vacate the railway shops by five o'clock that evening. Although twenty-one persons were already wounded and incarcerated, the strike continued.

During the night of December 14th-15th, the authorities once more descended on the strikers, arresting forty-one persons. It was broken only after eight days and presumably when the workers "demands" were satisfied. The Tiflis Gendarme Administration, in a classified communication to the Department of Police, wrote: "The strikers acted too uniformly, according to a single plan. The strike was led from within by an internal force and was not spontaneous." [94] The police report said nothing about Soso. His participation in the strike was that of a passive observer if, indeed, he had been able to escape the seminary for more than the usual two hours. He witnessed the strike, perhaps he urged a few workers on, but he had no part in planning or leading it.

Georgy Ninua, one of the strikers, remembered that "at the beginning of 1898 our first memorable meeting with the young propagandist—comrade Stalin—occurred at the apartment of Vano Sturua on Elisavetinskaya Street No. 194, where a group of railway workers lived in two small rooms on the first floor." Soso's clarity and simplicity of speech, according to this account, electrified the workers, who found him at his best in answering questions utilizing scientific and artistic literature and his knowledge of the history of the workers' movement in the West. "Comrade Stalin was our teacher, but he often said that he himself learned from the workers." Much later, in an appraisal of the results of the railway strike, Soso tersely summed up its lessons in the single word "Fight!" The significance of this Ninua failed to explain.[95] If Soso made the remark, it was meaningless except perhaps to imply that he looked forward to more bloodshed when the workers next met the overwhelming force of the police and cossacks. However, it is important as the first implication of Soso's preoccupation with bloodshed. Again and again we find him urging the workers on to shed their blood—not his—in pathetically useless clashes with troops and police. And after witnessing a particularly gory event he becomes inexplicably calm, relaxed, almost happy.

Soviet historians claim that at about the same time the workers of the Bozardzhiants tobacco factory illegally gathered at a cemetery on the outskirts of Tiflis, where Soso delivered a speech explaining that workers in the West were fighting as ardently as workers in the Russian Empire.[96] Later he organized a social-democratic circle from "progressive" workers of a tobacco factory, who met at the edge of the city after sundown, observing security precautions, arriving unnoticed in the darkness. New machinery for producing cigarettes—probably one of the earliest examples of automation in Georgia—had presumably upset the workers. The solution, according to the historians: Soso planned and led one more strike on their behalf. This was, of course, impossible. Soso, it must be remembered, was still a seminary student. His conversations with some disaffected workers in certain tobacco enterprises became, under later Soviet conditions of writing history, the planning and execution of strikes.

In the nineteen-thirties, although unwittingly, Stalin and his sycophants made a comedy of the dictator's early life. An eighteen-year-old seminarian could scarcely hop from the leadership of the first socialist organization in Georgia to the position of captain for strikers of railway workers and laborers in a tobacco factory in Tiflis, particularly when he had no more than two free hours each day outside the seminary. As a matter of fact, he was at that time in trouble with the seminary authorities not because he was plotting and leading strikes but because he insisted on reading forbidden books to his fellow seminarians in the dining room.

Actually, except for the transparently inaccurate accounts of his organizing and leading strikes and his creation of marxist circles, little has been written about Soso's life during the first part of 1898. We know that he was placed in solitary confinement at least once during the early part of the year, but his grades were sufficiently good to allow his return to the seminary after the summer recess. How he spent the summer is unknown. He was still in the seminary, still at his studies, but sufficiently subdued in his revolutionary activities to have avoided even the threat of expulsion.

A few months short of his nineteenth birthday in September, 1898, he returned for what was to be his final year of formal education at the seminary. Then his troubles deepened with the teachers and the administration. In mid-December, 1898, the seminary's assistant supervisor reported:

In the course of an inspection of students of the fifth class conducted by members of the board of supervision, Iosif Dzhugashvili tried several times to enter into an argument with them, expressing dissatisfaction with the repeated searches of students and declaring that such searches were never made in other seminaries. He is generally disrespectful and rude toward persons in authority and systematically refuses to bow to one of the masters (S. A. Murakhovsky), as the latter has repeatedly complained to the board of supervision.[97]

This report also included the notation "Reprimanded, confined to the punishment cell for five hours on the orders of the Father Rector—Father Dimitry."

At about the same time P. Talakvadze, a fellow student, remembers another incident that did not ingratiate Soso with the seminary authorities:

Just after dinner we students were seated at Pushkin Square near the seminary. Suddenly someone yelled "Inspector Abashidze is conducting a search of Dzhugashvili!" I rushed to the seminary, went to the locker room, on the lower floor, where we kept our possessions.

Going into the room I noticed that Abashidze had already concluded his search, had broken open comrade Soso's locker, taken from it illegal books and, carrying them under his arms, proceeded to the second floor. Soso was with him.[98]

Gogokhiya writing in a different vein, claims that Abashidze unexpectedly appeared in class one evening when the students were preparing lessons. Having found nothing reprehensible in the lockers, he began to search the students. After a minute inspection he found Iosif in possession of a notebook filled with articles for the handwritten magazine.[99]

Although these accounts are of Soviet origin and written decades after the event, they are eminently credible. From his reading Soso had decided he was an atheist, and not long afterward he had fallen under the influence of the marxists in Tiflis. Or perhaps his admiration for Lado, combined with his reading, had turned him toward marxism. Either way, in late 1898 and early 1899 he obviously could not have cared less about the seminary, his studies, or his future as an Orthodox priest. An anecdote recounted by Elisabedashvili suggests his devil-may-care attitude:

When Father Dimitry, who was then the seminary supervisor [he had hounded Soso for years], entered Stalin's room after a search, Stalin continued reading as if he had not noticed him.

"Don't you see who is standing before you?" the monk demanded. Stalin rose rubbing his eyes. "I don't see anything," he said, "except a black spot before my eyes." [100]

Having become acquainted with Stalinist and Soviet versions of Soso's life in 1898, it is interesting to learn what Noi Zhordania—with whom the reader is now familiar—recalled in 1936 from the relative safety of Paris:

At the end of 1898 I headed up *Kvali* (a Georgian marxist weekly). One day a young man appeared at the editorial offices and presented himself: "I am Dzhugashvili, a student at the Theological Seminary." Having requested that I hear him out, he began with: "I am a faithful reader of your journal and your articles. All of them have made a great impression on me. I have decided to quit the seminary and spend my time amongst the workers. Give me your advice."

His decision pleased me. In the Tiflis social democratic organization there were too few propagandists. But before I gave him any advice I considered it necessary to verify the mental equipment [*bagazh*] of this young man. When I posed several questions about history, sociology, and political economy, I was surprised that he had only a superficial notion concerning all of them. His political knowledge had come from the articles of *Kvali* and Kautsky's Erfurt program. I explained that it would be difficult to function under these conditions. Our workers were curious and wanted knowledge. When they were persuaded that a propagandist was ignorant, they would turn away from him and refuse to listen. I advised Dzhugashvili to remain one more year in the seminary, and to undertake some self-education.

"I'll think about it," he replied and departed.[101]

No educational institution, theological or lay, could allow its regulations to be broken and its student body to be subverted without some sort of recourse to its own form of justice. Consequently Father Dimitry, Stalin's *bête noire,* proposed on May 27, 1899 that the seminary council expel Soso because he was politically unreliable. Yaroslavsky writes:

Officially Comrade Stalin was expelled from the Seminary for failing to pay tuition fees and for "not attending examinations for reasons unknown." But the real reason for his expulsion from the Seminary was because of harbouring views dangerous to tsardom.

We have Comrade Stalin's own comment on this, made many years later. In 1931, against the item "Education?" in a questionnaire submitted to the delegates at the Party Conference of the Stalin District, Moscow he wrote: "Turned out of the theological seminary for propagating Marxism." [102]

The class list of the Tiflis Theological Seminary students for the 1898-99 academic year shows that in the first division of the fifth class:

Iosif Dzhugashvili is dismissed from the Seminary for having missed his examinations for an unexplained reason.[103]

Thus Soso's formal education ended on May 29, 1899. His mother in her old age told H. R. Knickerbocker that Soso was not expelled:

I brought him home on account of his health. When he entered the seminary he was strong as a boy could be. But overwork up to the age of nineteen pulled him down, and the doctors told me that he might develop tuberculosis. So I took him away from school. He did not want to leave. But I took him away. He was my only son.[104]

Iremashvili's explanation for Stalin's expulsion from the seminary seems to confirm Keke's account and emphasizes that the teachers and monks grew increasingly angry because they were unable to catch Koba studying forbidden literature. As his grades plummeted, he became the worst student in the seminary. Captivated by illegal literature, he began to read all night by candlelight. From this curious habit he developed a sickly pallor and a bad cough. At the end of the school year, according to Iremashvili, his poor report card convinced him that it would be pointless to continue his studies. He decided instead to devote himself to the struggle against tsarism. He seemingly considered his knowledge sufficient for agitation among the workers.[105]

His departure from the Tiflis Theological Seminary was against his own wishes, whether it was caused by illness, the propagation of marxism, poor scholarship, failure to take examinations, or the reading of forbidden literature. Even if he simply succumbed to apathy and temporarily impaired his health by night reading, he did not take himself out of school. No source, official or hostile, has suggested that he left voluntarily. Indeed, why should he? In May, 1899, the summer vacation was only a few days away and, having completed five years of the six-year course of instruction, he could envision the coveted diploma with only nine more months of study. He would have been vastly more valuable to the revolutionary cause as a graduate of the seminary, the best educational institution in the area south of Great Russia. And, Zhordania, the foremost marxist in Tiflis, had advised him to stay in the seminary.

Several factors were involved in his departure. As already noted,

Soso's terms of punishment in solitary confinement had embittered him against the seminary and all authority, and this, in turn, had led him to seek an outlet for his rebellion against the establishment —in effect, society. The intrigues and prison-like atmosphere of the seminary no doubt were also important. In 1897, Lado Ketskhoveli introduced him to active revolutionary life and, by his example, showed him that there were other embittered people who were opposed to the existing system. They were social democrats. Soso then saw the light. His studies suffered as he read revolutionary literature and stole away from the seminary to listen to revolutionary activists. He became emboldened to insult the seminary authorities, who in turn disciplined and harassed him, so that he was forced to study and read at night. His health and grades deteriorated. He was unable to go on. Thus there are discernible grains of truth in his mother's account (she took him away because of his health), Iremashvili's (his reading of revolutionary literature by candlelight hurt his health), his own (he was spreading marxist propaganda), and finally Abashidze's (he had failed to take the necessary examinations).

Soso spent four years and nine months at the seminary. That period from 1894 to 1899, extending from a few months before his fifteenth birthday to well after his nineteenth, included years when many influences, ideas, and problems were thrust upon him. He departed from the seminary a person quite different from the provincial boy who had come from Gori. Photographs of him that have survived show his deep-set eyes, his pockmarked face, and his full head of dark hair. He had most assuredly become at least partially educated. He had made much headway with the Russian language, although his accent always reminded listeners that Georgian had been his mother tongue. Since the seminary prepared young men for the priesthood, he had intensively studied the Old and the New Testaments and the formulation and delivery of sermons. The dry, ritualistic rhythm of his later statements and prose revealed a study and discipline in catechism.

No reliable accounts of the seminary's curriculum exist and one can only guess about the extent of his studies. Victor Serge, who wrote much about him, has commented, "The Seminary records do exist and if no one has been able to see them it is not without reason." [105a] The reason that Serge implied requires little explanation. Stalin sequestered the records when the Red Army invaded Georgia in 1921 (upon his orders), so that the true nature of his seminary career and his departure from training for the priesthood would remain unknown. Nevertheless it is possible to approximate from the curriculums of comparable Russian Orthodox theological institutions of the late nineteenth century that the Tiflis institution taught courses in geography, history, natural science, chemistry, mathematics, and Greek. Soso studied at least some of these subjects. He also read literature forbidden by seminary authorities that included books by the Russian masters Chekhov, Gogol, and Tolstoy. He explored Hugo and Balzac, Darwin and Thackeray, Feuerbach and Spinoza, although probably not to the extent that Soviet accounts of his seminary life suggest.

Leaving the seminary a year short of his graduation, he had for all practical purposes completed a five-year course of study at which initially he did uncommonly well. He had learned and absorbed much. He qualified by the standards of the time as a tolerably educated young man, for the Tiflis Theological Seminary was the most important educational institution in the entire Transcaucasian area, regardless of its intriguing personnel and repressive atmosphere. As he left the prison-like seminary, he must have known that his education alone might assure him a good job for the remainder of his years and perhaps a coveted place in a level of society higher than that to which he had been born. He had entered the seminary at fifteen intending to become a priest. He left it with the viewpoint of a rebel and the ambition of a revolutionary.

3 | THE MAKING OF A SECRET AGENT

For almost a year after his departure from the seminary, Stalin's life is largely a mystery. From May 29, 1899 to April 23, 1900, there is a curious hiatus in his own *Collected Works,* and the Barbusse and Beria biographies provide only a few unverifiable anecdotes.[106] Even the customarily prolix former comrades in *The Childhood and Youth of the Leader* are mute about this period. He departed from the seminary almost seven months short of his twentieth birthday and, except for the fact that he began work at the Tiflis Geophysical Observatory, nothing official is known about him until he made an obscure speech on April 23, 1900, about eleven months later.[107] This period of time between his twentieth and twenty-first birthdays has been ignored by the leader and his historians.

What, then, was Soso doing from May till he began working at the observatory in December, 1899? Was he convalescing from the illness and fatigue that he had incurred at the seminary? If so, the most logical place would have been the family home in Gori. However, neither his mother nor he mentioned this. It is unlikely that fellow-students cared for him during a recuperation; only a handful of them held him in any esteem, and their resources were probably limited. The parents of these students might have been asked to take in a convalescent, but evidence is lacking on this. If he recuperated at Gori, perhaps he thereafter had some kind of employment. In fact, one unsubstantiated story claims that during 1899 he tutored children of well-to-do families in the Tiflis area, but it would seem unlikely that the Tiflis families would want their offspring tutored by a student dismissed from the theological seminary. If Keke withdrew him from the seminary because of illness, he would naturally have been unable to tutor anyone during his convalescence.[108]

It is implausible to suppose that after leaving the seminary Soso became a tramp, as his father was later described to be by the tsarist police. Unable to get along with people, alienated from most of them, he needed to control others, and was not one to enjoy the easy camaraderie of hobo life. His schoolmate Iremashvili claimed that "right after he left the seminary" Soso began work at the Tiflis Observatory, where he lived poorly on a barely minimal salary.[109] Other personal accounts and the *Collected Works* reveal that here Iremashvili's memory failed him. Soso began working in the Tiflis Geophysical Observatory on December 28, 1899, when he had just turned twenty.[110]

Surviving photographs of him during this period portray a mature, serious person. Besides his tousled, thick dark hair, he now had the revolutionary affectations of a beard and sideburns, not unlike the beatniks of the nineteen-sixties. His sharply defined features were accented by an aquiline nose, a strong chin, and penetrating eyes. With a respectable haircut he might have been an impressive prospect for employment in one of the Georgian banks. However, his dismissal from the seminary precluded employment in a financial institution or in one of the several growing industries in the area unless he was willing to accept manual labor. Stalin, however, never performed any sort of work with his hands, with the possible exception of a few weeks of forced labor as an apprentice cobbler at his father's insistence. At the beginning of the summer of 1898 he was unemployed, virtually friendless, and with no source of income. His mother could not afford to support him. The few militant social democrats in Tiflis were almost penniless. His age, inexperience, and temperament disqualified him for a leading role in Georgian social democracy, which anyhow was in the competent, conservative hands of Noi Zhordania and Silvester Dzhibladze. Lado Ketskhoveli had inspired him, but he was unable to feed him.

At this juncture a new dimension was added to the picture: the police began to take an interest in him and his activities. Yaroslavsky wrote that "with Comrade Stalin's expulsion [from the theological seminary], the police and gendarmerie began to keep a close watch on him; a dossier was started in which all his movements were recorded." [111] The Russian Department of Police pervaded Soso's life from that time forward; thereafter he encountered the police formally in prison, in exile, and on his various trips in the empire and abroad. Until the Russian revolution of February, 1917, his actions and the Department of Police operations were inextricably enmeshed. Each aspect of his prerevolutionary life can be viewed, therefore, through a Department of Police prism.

Ivan the Terrible had established the Russian police in 1565. Known as the *Oprichniki* and dressed in black, mounted on black horses, with dog's head and broom attached to their saddles, they primarily served to exterminate treason as Ivan chose to define it.[111a] The dog's head was meant to symbolize the sniffing out of treason, the broom sweeping it away. Since that time, Russia has always known some form of secret police. It was not until the Decembrist Revolt, however, that the Russian security forces began to emerge as a professional and significant tsarist institution. The Decembrist Revolt of 1825, although quickly crushed, was a frightening experience to Tsar Nicholas I. Because the revolt took place December 14, 1825, the insurrectionists came to be known as "The Decembrists." They were largely from the Russian upper classes: of the 579 organizers of the revolt more than 460 were regular army personnel. The rebellion lasted only a few days in St. Petersburg, after which 125 Decembrists were brought to trial. Five were hanged, thirty-one were sentenced to penal servitude, and the rest were deported to Siberia.[112] To combat subversion against his rule (and having in mind the infectious germs of sedition imported from Western Europe by some of his military officers and by intellectuals), the tsar formed the Third Section of his own Chancery in 1826. Its first, imposing chief, Count Benkendorf, assembled an intelligence-police-security organization that compared favorably then and later with other European secret services.[113] Indeed, it served as a model for some of them.

Two categories of agents, gendarmes and covert agents, operated from the Third Section. Gendarmes were formal, military persons. The Third Section chief commanded them as he did the tsar's personal military organization. Most of the Third Section officers were cultured, erudite, and from good families, while the numerous clandestine agents were recruited from all walks of society. From the death of Nicholas I to the assassination of Alexander II (1881), two years after Stalin's birth, there were the off-again-on-again variations of Russian secret police. It was in the year 1881 that the Russian Department of Police, otherwise known as the Okhrana, was begun. All tsarist security-intelligence and counterintelligence elements and functions have been generally placed under the controversial umbrella title "Okhrana."

"Okhrana" derives from the Russian *"okhranit,"* meaning to guard, to secure, to preserve. The various tsarist security-intelligence organs were admittedly seeking to preserve tsardom. Their personnel, however, did not collectively refer to themselves as the Okhrana, a term of foggy and inexplicable revolutionary origin from the last decade of the nineteenth century. The Okhrana was, in reality, more complicated than many revolutionaries, historians, or casual observers apprehended. The Ministry of Internal Affairs, one of the various ministries of the tsarist government, had as one of its component parts the Department of Police, which directed counterespionage, counterintelligence, security, and positive intelligence operations. Through its various headquarters, divisions of the Department of Police operated throughout the Empire, in Poland, and in the Grand Duchy of Finland. Provincial, city, and rural gendarme administrations and the railway police were under its jurisdiction. It controlled the important Foreign Agency, as it was commonly called, located in the Imperial Russian Embassy in Paris from about 1882 until 1917. This Paris Okhrana was an extension of the Department of Police, and many of its operations were coordinated by the Special Section of its headquarters. Each revolutionary party in Imperial Russia had branches abroad. Many Russian revolutionary organizations, in fact, operated from foreign soil. Thus the Paris headquarters conducted intelligence-security operations throughout Western Europe, the Balkans, the Near East, and North America, including the United States.

The Okhrana's staff, broadly speaking, consisted of officials, bureaucrats, and agents. The *crème de la crème* were officers of the Separate Corps of Gendarmes, assisted by what would be considered civilian employees today. Surveillance personnel were usually retired noncommissioned officers of the armed forces. Okhrana officers controlled agents of various nationalities and mixed capabilities, who not infrequently became double agents, serving both the Department of Police and a revolutionary group to which their allegiance was questionable. Each domestic Gendarme (Okhrana) Administration had its agents in the local revolutionary organizations.[114] At a given moment in Tiflis, for example, any revolutionary cell included at least one and usually two or more Okhrana agents unknown to each other. If one was exposed, the other would continue to report on the personnel and activities of the revolutionary group.

By the turn of the century, the Okhrana had developed this operational technique, known in police and revolutionary jargon as "provocation" (*provokatsiya* in Russian), to a skillful dimension. It always involved a police agent, an *agent provocateur*. Lenin's organization is a good example. From roughly 1900 to 1917, the tsarist police had Lenin under the most careful surveillance.[115] His residences in and out of the Empire were rarely unknown to the Imperial Police Headquarters. Scores of identifiable Okhrana agents reported on him and his activities. They opened Lenin's and Krupskaya's mail.[116] If it was in secret writing—i.e., in chemical inks, as it was more often than not—the Okhrana readily "raised" it, or developed and made it readable. In short, Lenin made few moves, wrote no letters, sent no propaganda into Russia that the Okhrana was not aware of to some degree. Official Department of Police communications provide numerous similar examples of agent penetration into revolutionary and subversive groups and of detailed, continuous surveillance of revolutionary personalities. Reports from hundreds of agents flowed into the St. Petersburg Department of Police Headquarters to be processed and utilized by the appropriate subdivisions.

From 1900 until the 1917 revolution, the Okhrana (Department of Police)* was a powerful force that by any reckoning exerted great influence on affairs of state and, indeed, international relations. This was partially due to the extreme security it practiced, to the covert nature of its operations, and to its professional "disinformation" (*disinformatsiya*) and dissimulation techniques. In the main, however, the expertise of the Separate Corps of Gendarmes, which directed the Okhrana in Russia and abroad, made it an uncommonly efficient intelligence-security-police service. During Stalin's pre-revolutionary career each town, city, and provincial Gendarme Administration in Russia was directed by a highly trained gendarme officer. In many ways he was like the modern F. B. I. special agent in charge of a given territory. Aware of the subversives in his area of responsibility, he recruited and directed agents into the various revolutionary and anarchist organizations, he forwarded countless reports to St. Petersburg concerning the internal security of his bailiwick, and he considered himself as part of an élite organization in which duty, honor, and country were not idle words. The typical gendarme officer was not predisposed to allow a gang of revolutionaries to take over Russia.

Although the Okhrana operated on various levels throughout the Russian Empire and abroad—recruiting agents, for example, in Georgia or in Paris—its most secret, sensitive, and important agent operations were handled by the Special Section of the Department of Police in St. Petersburg.[117] The chief of the Special Section, usually a colonel, was always an outstanding, experienced official, who reported only to a specified vice-director of the Department of Police. As in all secret security-intelligence organizations, some operations were unknown to other organic parts of the Department of Police, and in several cases the Special Section apparently retained

* Henceforth the gendarmes, the Gendarme Administrations, the Department of Police and the Okhrana will be used interchangeably.

no written record of its agents, referring to them in necessary inter-office reports as "you know who" or "the person we discussed yes-terday," etc. This sort of secrecy makes it difficult to determine when or how the Special Section was established, but it probably grew from a committee or small experimental group within the De-partment of Police during the late eighteen-nineties or the early nineteen-hundreds.[118] Nonetheless by 1910 its status as a quasi-independent organization had been recognized, and it was coordi-nating such diverse operations as the Okhrana Foreign Agency in Paris, penetrations into revolutionary organizations, and espionage activities into foreign diplomatic missions accredited to the Tsar. One Okharana official boasted that he knew about the outcome of the Portsmouth negotiations that settled the Russo-Japanese War before the American Minister in St. Petersburg was informed.[119] The diplomatic mail of the American Legation was being opened and read as early as 1905.

While the Special Section handled numerous operations and agents of critical importance, the workhorses of the Department of Police were the local Gendarme Administration units found in every Russian city of any importance, in every capital of a prov-ince, along all railway lines, and on the Russian frontiers. It bears repeating that officers of the Gendarme Administrations took care of the arrest of subversive elements, conducted interrogations, pre-pared dossiers of revolutionaries with photographs and anthropo-metrical measurements[120] and, most important, recruited and paid agents, double agents, and informers to burrow into local revolu-tionary cells. Agents were rarely identified by their real names in police reports and received their pay in unvouchered funds. The Okhrana had no financial worries. In the Department of Police Headquarters were comprehensive files that, with the exception of certain Special Section operations, included all data on subversive or revolutionary personalities, organizations, and publications. Re-ports and documents were cross-referenced and sent to those Gen-darme Administrations that had reason to know of a particular case. In the absence of electronic communications systems, the Okhrana relied on large quantities of correspondence and an efficient filing system to discharge its far-flung operational responsibilities. Even these techniques, which were well developed for the time, were insufficient for its myriad tasks. What made the Okhrana such a formidable force was its officer corps.

The Separate Corps of Gendarmes was composed of especially selected and trained officers.[121] Each was aware of the Okhrana's guiding principles. Apart from the few scoundrels, opportunists and deadbeats that always infest any élite intelligence-security service, the Okhrana officer, by background and training, was reliable. He knew how his colleagues throughout the Empire and abroad would react to almost any security situation or operational problem. Mutual professionalism and understanding in the Separate Corps of Gendarmes (which, as already noted, directed the Okhrana) was unparalleled to that time.[122] The personnel of the Okhrana inevitably included a few numskulls. Although by historical circumstance it was among the first dedicated anti-communist organizations, some of its officers failed to grasp the fundamentals of marxism and communism—even with elaborate lectures, studies, and charts prepared by the St. Petersburg Headquarters for their edification. However, if some did not comprehend the basics, all saw clearly the subversive threat posed to tsarism by revolutionaries, and they expertly identified the security problem the threat entailed.

While the Okhrana was always duty bound to nip subversion in the bud, particularly in fiercely nationalistic Georgia, it was also anxious to recruit agents whose credentials would enable them to report on revolutionary personalities, organizations, and events, and who were sufficiently dependable to identify and betray the *most important* leaders and agitators in the anti-tsarism milieu. The Department of Police was hardly obsessed with the idea of jailing or exiling every tsarist subject whose skulduggery amounted to no more than the mouthing of marxist propositions or participation in a small marxist discussion group. Such persons were, of course, routinely watched. The local Gendarme Administration often spotted likely recruits in this general category who became highly valuable agents at a later date. Potentially good agents were neither fiery revolutionaries nor wild-eyed nationalists whose idealism kept them from being practical. Rather, they were usually persons whose opportunism meshed with frustrations, despair, lack or shortage of money, shallow character, or who had been caught in a compromising situation that would insure Okhrana control of them. These were the long-range deep-penetration agents, prospects sometimes to become "sleepers," whom the Okhrana found most productive.

Local Okhrana officers had been trained to recognize and then to assess potential agents who could be used in revolutionary subversive organizations and who might graduate to leadership positions on the all-Russian revolutionary level while remaining under police control. The Okhrana had developed this tricky technique to an art by the early nineteen hundreds. Naturally, there were more than a few failures. As professional security-intelligence officers, they realized that no agent operation could be counted a complete success, but they tried to keep the possibility of failure down to a minimum.

The spotting and assessment of a potential agent, and his eventual recruitment, usually required weeks or months. There were no good "instant" agents. In order to obtain specific information on an immediate one-time basis, the Okhrana used what were called "pieceworkers" (*shtuchniki*), but they were usually low-level types motivated by money, and only money. Their "cover" was at best shallow and they generally had no particular affiliation with the revolutionary forces. Regardless of an agent's qualifications for covert Okhrana activity and of the fact that he might be completely controllable, he was useless as a spy if he did not have a plausible and viable cover. The anti-tsarist organizations (the social revolutionaries, the social democrats, the Jewish Workers' Union (the Bund), the anarchists, and others) represented the greatest threat to the monarchy.[123] Any Okhrana agent needed a revolutionary cover to be successful in these organizations. Of course, if the agent's background lent itself to the penetration of a revolutionary organization, so much the better. Once a cover had been laboriously constructed, it required constant attention to be sustained. For this reason it was not unusual for the Okhrana to arrest, imprison, and exile an agent, and thus quiet suspicions that other revolutionaries might have about him. Similarly, the Okhrana facilitated—and, in some cases, arranged for—the escape of its agents from prison or exile in order to improve their image and to make them appear more intrepid and brave in the revolutionary setting—arming them, as it were, with authentic revolutionary and underground credentials.[124]

The Okhrana had a staff of over a hundred officers and specialists in Georgia about the time Soso left the seminary. While it would be pointless to attempt an identification of those gendarme officers engaged in recruitment activities, we know they were searching for agents whom they could control in deep cover. They sought young local Georgian men of about the age of twenty. Teenagers were often reckless and difficult to tame, let alone train, and older men had set habit patterns. Members of the higher social levels were generally to be avoided. However, basic intelligence was highly regarded: stupid workers or peasants had no future in revolutionary organizations. Some education, but not too much, enhanced an agent's potentiality. If he came from impoverished circumstances, the Okhrana was able to assist him financially. And if his future appeared bleak, the Okhrana was able to improve the agent's morale by pointing out vistas of responsible work and important, albeit clandestine positions—providing, of course, he did not stray from the pathway of Okhrana direction or control.

The control factor was crucial in Okhrana operational methodology regarding an agent. This, in turn, required an assessment of his background, character, and personality. Preferably the potential agent would have an opportunistic streak in his character. Carefully monitored, this could lead to the betrayal of revolutionary leaders at an appropriate moment. If he had resented authority from childhood, he would appreciate holding the fate of others in his own hands—in effect, becoming an authority himself. If for some reason he had been an object of derision among his boyhood friends, the Okhrana might serve as a means to retaliate as an agent. If he was moved by nationalistic feelings, the Okhrana officer would find this an advantage, particularly if he was of the same ethnic group, and would patiently explain that revolutionary work could also serve national goals. The recruiting officer would hope to find a potential agent who wanted to improve his position in society. Unscrupulous ambition was a useful agent characteristic. And if he had dabbled in marxism or Western European revolutionary ideas, his cover was thereby improved. A prospective secret agent who had these qualifications—as seen by the police—needed only training in Okhrana tradecraft to begin his career.

Soso admitted some years later that while he was in the seminary he had denounced several of his fellow students to the authorities.[125] He explained that by falsely charging them with subversive activities they would become better revolutionaries, but he failed to add that his malicious and untrue statements alerted the police to spy on innocent persons. The police had previously noticed him, and now, in the summer of 1899, the officers of the Tiflis Gendarme Administration, trained in the St. Petersburg Headquarters of the Department of Police to penetrate subversive and revolutionary organizations with secret agents, had a prime subject for recruitment at hand. Soso's beloved *mamushka,* Keke, was impoverished. The church hierarchy was forever closed to him. He knew no trade or craft. Military service was impossible because of his bad arm. He was inexperienced and untested as a revolutionary. Hating those possessing authority, he nonetheless coveted it for his own purposes. Bitter, lonely, penniless and friendless, frustrated and unemployed, perhaps ill and undernourished, his future appeared dismal. Doubtless the police were not at all displeased at Soso's unfortunate situation. It would serve to facilitate their work.

With this as background we are entitled to consider the possibility that during June or July, 1899, an officer of the Tiflis Gendarme Administration may have made an offer to Soso to serve the police within the Georgian social-democratic movement. Even if initially his affiliation was to be informal, he was to be paid on a modest but regular schedule. Such an obviously appealing proposition would not oblige him to stifle his ardor for marxism or his fervor for the revolution that Lado had inspired. Nor would it be imperative to choose the side of reaction. Soso could have reasonably concluded, in the best tradition of many double agents, that he might well assist the cause of revolution by passing on bits and pieces of information garnered from the police. In the meantime, identification with an organization would dispel his loneliness and frustration, at least temporarily. In 1899 the Tiflis police budget exceeded 100,000 rubles.[126] An agent "belonged" to the police, as if to a family, in which he could feel secure financially and otherwise. A period of six months—until December, 1899—would have been just about right for the new recruit to be trained at this time by one of the Tiflis gendarme officers, who were reputed to be among the best in the empire. Monetary payments as the recruit progressed in his training at Okhrana conspiratorial apartments appeared regularly.[127] He was taught, among other things, the stealthy art of provocation, at which the Imperial police excelled. In short, it was here that one learned the tradecraft of the spy, with the techniques of which the G. P. U. and the N. K. V. D. were later to be invested by Stalin.

Toward the end of an agent's training period, maximum attention was given to the problem of his cover; that is, what ostensible position in society would allow him to reap the greatest intelligence rewards. After all, a secret agent is worthless if he does not have a place where his real work is camouflaged, preferably one in which his prime intelligence targets may be found. The desirable cover employment of a young Georgian agent was in an institution or enterprise where dangerous subversive elements or plots were suspected.

The Tiflis Geophysical Observatory had harbored important Georgian revolutionaries for several years before 1900. Vano Ketskhoveli, who had attended the Gori and Tiflis schools with Soso, had obtained employment there in November, 1899.[128] About Soso he wrote, "At the end of December, 1899, there was a vacancy in the observatory and on the advice of Lado this responsibility was assumed by comrade Stalin. We had to keep awake all night and make observations at stated intervals with the help of intricate instruments. The work demanded great nervous concentration and patience." Other Soviet accounts state that Soso worked as an observer-meteorologist and lived in a small observatory room leading to a courtyard, where "the quietude omnipresent in the voiceless seclusion was highly favorable to the conspiratorial nature of young Stalin's life." Authentic Department of Police reports discount Stalin's work as an observer-meteorologist and flatly describe him as a bookkeeper (*bukhalter*).[129]

Vano Berdzenishvili, who was employed by the observatory in February, 1900, had been expelled from the Tiflis Theological Seminary in the autumn of 1899. He recalls that the person on night duty worked from eight-thirty in the evening until eight in the morning. A sleepless night was followed by a free day. The employees who collated the findings of all the small stations throughout the Caucasus received twenty rubles a month and occupied four rooms in a wing of the observatory that included a beautiful garden:

There were six observers, the so-called hired people, and one civil servant who once a week substituted for each observer. At the time of my affiliation with the observatory Iosif Dzhugashvili, Davitashvili (whom I relieved), and Vano Ketskhoveli, the brother of Lado Ketskhoveli, were already working there.[130]

Stalin's first and only recorded job outside of the Soviet government or the Communist Party was in the Tiflis Geophysical Observatory. A marble tablet that was on its façade until his death read:

The Great Stalin—leader of the V K P(b) and the world proletariat —lived and worked here in the Tbilisi Geophysical Observatory from December 28, 1899 through March 21, 1901, leading illegal social-democratic workers' circles in the Tbilisi.[131]

The observatory was near the Kura River, a place familiar to Soso from his boyhood. The ever-present Iremashvili remembered his quarters as bohemian and dominated by piles of books and brochures.[132] Soso was still reading voraciously. His room in the observatory was rent-free. After the harshness of the seminary and the unhappiness of the previous summer, his life was almost idyllic.

Soso's work in the observatory was not difficult and as a cover for an agent it was almost ideal. He had enough free time to get away from his place of employment for secret meetings. However, if the Tiflis police in the first part of 1899 pressed him to become more militantly revolutionary, the pressure could not easily be ignored. The Okhrana might have been impatient for him to be better known in the social-democratic movement and to undertake definite, although minor, agent assignments. Thus after his working hours and upon the "completion of his scientific observations," a Soviet account reads, he began to visit the workers' quarters where "at the appointed hour the proletariat gathered." [133] Moreover, from the time of Soso's affiliation with the observatory he becomes in Soviet history a "propagandist, agitator, and organizer" for the bolshevik—as opposed to the menshevik—faction of the socialist democrats. A secret Department of Police Special Section report, dated March 3, 1911, maintains that Dzhugashvili had been first a menshevik and only later a bolshevik. [134]

The police may have set up specific clandestine tasks for him to accomplish. According to Berdzenishvili, "Comrade Stalin used to procure illegal pamphlets and the *Iskra,** and let us read them; but where and from whom he got them none of us knew." And a fellow Georgian, G. Lelashvili, wrote: "Mikho Bochoridze told me that at the beginning of 1900 Stalin directed him to find a room in which to organize an underground printing press. A suitable space was found in a house on Lotkinskaya Street." Afterward typesetting in the Russian and Georgian languages was made available. The press could turn out six hundred to seven hundred leaflets every twenty-four hours. [135] Lelashvili recalls that he received materials to be published from Mikho Bochoridze during sidewalk meetings where he sometimes met comrade Stalin who quizzed him about his work,

---

* *Iskra (The Spark)* was the first all-Russian marxist newspaper, established abroad by Lenin, who had taken the title from a celebrated letter of the Decembrists to Pushkin, containing the sentence, "The spark will kindle the flame." *Iskra* first appeared in Germany in December, 1900.

"taught the strictest conspiracy, and stressed the necessity to print as much propaganda about revolutionary marxism as possible." Bochoridze told Lelashvili that the proclamations were Stalin's work, but possibly they were composed in police headquarters. Far fetched as this may seem, it must be remembered that the revolutionary organizations in Tiflis would not have commissioned young Soso to establish a clandestine printing press. He himself had no resources to pay for typesetting and paper or to rent a room. Furthermore, the social-democratic marxist organization in Tiflis, led by Zhordania and Dzhibladze, deplored revolutionary militancy, favoring instead gradualism in achieving their aims. Only the Okhrana wanted to smoke out the revolutionaries from their lairs, and only the Okhrana could easily supply the funds for a secret printing press. The Department of Police had earlier financed a newspaper of the party of the People's Will, the forerunner of the Socialist-Democratic Party, and was to be instrumental in founding the bolshevik newspaper *Pravda* in 1912.[136]

The revolutionaries loved their May Day outings and parades—called *"Mayevki"*—which grew popular toward the end of the nineteenth century. Zealots accompanied by workers would go to some bucolic locale, where they harangued one another, gave rousing speeches, and split dialectical hairs—after, of course, they had sung the "Marseillaise." Georgy Ninua alone among the participants recalled that Soso gave a speech at the illegal *Mayevka* in 1900, in the region of Salt Lake near Tiflis, where some five hundred persons gathered with revolutionary slogans and portraits of Marx and Engels.

"We have grown so strong," Comrade Stalin said, "that next year we will be able to conduct the *Mayevka* not in mountain hollows, but on the main streets of Tiflis."

Stalin's first speech in public was delivered when he was twenty years of age. In it, according to the record, he openly advocated that unarmed workers and revolutionaries risk their lives in a clash with the tsarist gendarmes and cossacks:

Comrade Stalin explained to the workers the great international significance of the May Day holiday and instructed each one to select ten or so comrades in order that during the next year they could lead them on a May Day demonstration in Tiflis. "Our red flag," said Comrade Stalin, "must be in the center of the city, so that tyranny will feel our strength." [137]

The workers, according to this account, answered Soso with a resounding "Hurrah!" Of course, Soso's appeal to take the demonstrations into the Tiflis streets was impractical, to say the least. The Tiflis Gendarme Administration was a force to be reckoned with. Also not to be overlooked were the troops, including cavalry, on call if the police were inadequate in quieting demonstrations. Did Soso want to destroy the Tiflis workers' movement? It would seem so, for there was no more certain way to assure a debacle than to confront the well-armed mounted cossacks with unarmed workers on foot. One interpretation suggests that Soso had been convinced that the revolution would be advanced by this action when actually it only served to identify leading revolutionary workers to the police. Perhaps he was attempting to emulate Lado, when in reality he was a tool in the hands of a Tiflis Okhrana officer.

Undoubtedly the police were also pushing him into the strike movement. And, of course, he was not averse to participation. On the contrary, he visualized the strikes as a major contribution to the revolution, and even when he stood in the background urging a few nondescript workers on, he experienced the exhilarating feeling of being a leader. Concerning this time, Beria wrote, "From May through July, 1900, a wave of strikes in Tiflis enterprises took place. In August of 1900 the workers of the railway shops and depot under the leadership of comrade Stalin, with the active participation of M. I. Kalinin, conducted a massive strike in which up to 4,000 workers took part." [138]

In 1938 an unidentified old worker of the Tiflis main shop wrote, in an article, *The History of Plants and Factories in Tiflis,* that the August strike strengthened the workers' circles, which "grew like mushrooms." Soso the "old worker" claimed, had established close liaison with many workers' circles that esteemed him:

A strike in the railway shops was brewing. We, of course, took part in it. And how happy we were when comrade Stalin directed us in the fight with the strikebreakers!

One strike continued fifteen days. The police and gendarmes were enraged. We quickly convinced them that the working movement in Tiflis had depth and breadth, as they informed the Ministry of Internal Affairs, asking that their corps of spies be strengthened.[139]

These accounts, written many years after the event, contained a particle of accuracy. Soso was not leading strikes, but he was becoming involved in them. The police, no doubt, were intent on improving his credentials as a revolutionary.

An entry in Stalin's *Collected Works* cryptically states, "Summer —J. V. Stalin establishes contact with V. K. Kurnatovsky, a well-known supporter of Lenin's *Iskra,* who had arrived in Tiflis for party work." [140] Lenin's followers were dubbed Iskraites, and Kurnatovsky was one. Essentially an adherent of Lenin's *Iskra* point of view, he cared not one whit about ideology except insofar as it enabled Lenin and his disciples to seize political power. Victor Kurnatovsky's arrival in Tiflis during the summer of 1900, while Stalin was still employed at the observatory, was not overlooked by the Tiflis Gendarme Administration. Beria indicated that it occasioned a "sharp difference (between the majority *Messame-Dasy* and the revolutionary marxist group—A. Tsulukidze, Lado Ketskhoveli and I. Stalin). The question: was it necessary to limit the work of the 'circles' or to be ready to go over to mass agitation, to the open struggle with tyranny?" [141]

Victor Kurnatovsky, a graduate of the Zurich Polytechnical Institute and a chemical engineer, had spent six years in exile because of his activities in the People's Will Party. In the Archangel area he met and became a friend of Lenin's. Having escaped abroad in 1892, he joined Plekhanov's group in 1893. He arrived in Tiflis as a pristine emissary of Lenin's and he "established a strong liaison with Comrade Stalin." The twenty-year-old Koba and the veteran revolutionary Kurnatovsky enjoyed deep friendship from the year 1900, according to Soviet accounts.[142] We are entitled to be skeptical of the report. Kurnatovsky could hardly have considered Koba as an important figure in the Georgian revolutionary movement; he was still a nobody. Thus Beria's statement: "Enormous support, as had already been noted, [was provided] in the propaganda of revolutionary marxism and the creation of a social-democratic organization by comrades Stalin, Tsulukidze, Ketskhoveli, and others." [143]

Soso had much to learn from the toughened revolutionaries whom he supposedly instructed. The insular life in Gori and Tiflis had hardly fitted him to be a teacher of much older, more experienced socialists. However, Georgy Ninua, Stalin's contemporary and a fellow Georgian, followed Beria's lead:

The necessity was growing for broad agitation among the masses, for organization of an open political struggle. Throughout the city illegal mass workers' meetings began in which up to fifty persons participated. Several propagandists were afraid to appear at these mass meetings, fearing arrests, preferring illegal meetings of five or ten persons. But comrade Stalin did not agree with them.[144]

Soso, previously characterized as a secretive, conspiratorial worker, suddenly shifted his revolutionary attitude, disagreeing with those who were—apparently quite properly—fearful of arrest. A question arises: why did he *not* fear arrest? Did his confidence rest on police assurance that he was in no danger? There is no other reasonable explanation.

Interspersed between the entries for 1900 and 1901 in the *Collected Works* is a quotation that shows the difficulty experienced by Stalin's court historians in recapitulating this period of his life:

1898-1900. Under the leadership of J. V. Stalin, V. Z. Ketskhoveli and A. G. Tsulukidze, a central leading group is formed within the Tiflis organization of the R. S. D. R. P.,[145] which passes from propaganda in study circles to mass political agitation. The group organizes the printing of manifestoes and their distribution among the workers, forms underground Social Democratic circles, and leads the strikes and political struggle of the Tiflis proletariat.[146]

From the time of the unbelievable leadership of the strike in

August, 1900, until he quit his observatory job in late March, 1901, we have no official information about Soso's life. Another seven months seems to have passed into oblivion, but in reality this period was full of work that he did for the police. Soso, furthermore, considered his labors equally valuable to the revolution. He had exhorted workers to "rise up" and "make Tiflis bloody," which qualified him as a secret police agent and revolutionary. Barbusse insists that during 1900 Stalin led eight revolutionary circles, conducting discussions with them:

> He would suddenly appear at meetings and would sit down without a word and listen until the time came for him to speak. He was always accompanied by two or three comrades, one of whom would keep watch by the door. He would not speak for long. If he took a train journey, he would take endless trouble to throw people off the track [sic].
>
> He walked into the huge Popov library . . . asked for a book of Belinsky's which he had begun to read attentively, all the time keeping an eye on the maneuvers of one of the assistants, to whom he handed, unseen and unrecognized by anyone, two false passports. They were to secure the escape of two comrades whom the police intended to arrest a little later—a little too late.[147]

This passage indicates that Stalin had emphasized his vaunted conspiratorial talents to Barbusse. Comrades stand guard at clandestine meetings. Stalin eludes "people"—that is, the police during train journeys. He utilizes the Popov library to deliver false passports. (How familiar it sounds! In the days of the N. K. V. D. when Stalin reigned supreme in Soviet Russia, libraries throughout the world were used as convenient "drops" for all sorts of materials and various intelligence operations.) Two or three of the comrades, secret police operatives, were always on hand as guards in clandestine gatherings. However, at the turn of the century false passports were difficult to procure and more difficult to reproduce accurately in order to pass the scrutiny of the Okhrana. But it is ridiculous to credit Stalin with the leadership of eight circles of revolutionaries during this period. Circles of marxists included at least three persons. Even if they had all met in the same place (which would have been most insecure), their leadership would have been time-consuming and his celebrated rules of conspiracy would have been broken. His apparent involvement with secrecy and underground activities contrast curiously with his leadership of strikes. Only within the context of police operations are they understandable.

Soso's first year of work as a secret agent for the Tiflis Okhrana appears to have satisfied his superiors. Presumably he had made contact with Kurnatovsky, and had reported on his activities. He had successfully undertaken modest assignments within the Tiflis social-democratic movement, where he was probably considered strangely unconcerned for his own safety, or that of the workers. By March of 1901 he knew the names and whereabouts of both the militant firebrands and the moderate leaders of the Tiflis social democrats. He had identified persons who were sympathetic to the revolution and some who actively assisted it without becoming directly involved. Most important, he knew the places where revolutionaries secretly met and where comrades in Tiflis "illegally" resided. Using agent information, the Tiflis Okhrana made plans for the most devastating anti-revolutionary operation the capital of Georgia had experienced.

The Tiflis Okhrana arrests and raids made by numerous security officers during the night of March 21-22, 1901, seriously damaged the strongest socialist-democratic movement in the most populous city in the Caucasus. The police arrested scores of prominent intellectuals and leaders, among whom were Kurnatovsky, Skorniakov, Franchesky, Makharadze, Pushkarev, Stepanyan, the Kalandadze brothers, Perets, Prostosterdov, Meshcherin, Dzhibladze, Zhordania, Kalandrashvili, Tsulukidze, and the Komadze brothers. More than fifty prominent worker-organizers were arrested. The dragnet caught one minor police agent, the manual worker Berezniak. Okhrana personnel raided the Sharadze printing press; the newspapers *Novoe Obozrenie* and *Kvali;* the office of the Armenian Welfare Society, the Armenian Workmen's Library, the Krasnova Nurses Home; the merchants Karadzhyan, Karadzhev, Akopyan, Ter-Astvatsatryan, and Lalayan; and the shoe store in the Georgian Nobility building, the Working Class tavern, and the shoeshop called the Social-Democratic Cobbler.[148]

The Okhrana arrested almost everyone of any importance in the socialist-democratic organization on March 21-22, 1901, the night of the long knives in Tiflis—everyone, that is, except Soso, who, curiously, was roaming the streets. He was absent from his quarters in the Tiflis Geophysical Observatory. No record suggests that he was exhorting workers or producing propaganda leaflets that night. That he was simply enjoying the balmy spring air, and in one of his rare to-hell-with-the-revolution moods, is too implausible for serious consideration. While Soso strolled, oblivious to the frantic activity of the Tiflis Gendarme Administration, they raided his quarters in the geophysical observatory.

Berdzenishvili, in a labored and disjointed account in *The Childhood and Youth of the Leader,* almost begs us to accept the Okhrana failure to arrest Soso as a mere coincidence:

Stalin always observed the strictest conspiratorial rules. When he went out into the street he did not go where it was necessary, but to the opposite side, and proceeded by roundabout ways. I suggested that police surveillance of him began not from the Observatory, but from some other place and then later led to our apartment. On March 21, 1901, when the gendarmes conducted a search of our rooms, comrade Stalin was not at home. That day after I finished my duty I went to my room and lay down on the couch without undressing. I was asleep when there was a heavy knock at the door.

"Who's there?" I asked.

They crudely answered, "Open up!"

I repeated my question and I heard them say: "We are from the Gendarme Administration." When I opened the door I saw a pack of police and gendarmes, and in front of them the dejected figure of our doorkeeper.

Bursting into the room they asked who I was, who lived there and began a search of the premises. They searched my room and sealed certain legal books of a marxist nature, drew up a protocol and gave it to me to sign. They found nothing in comrade Stalin's room because he always returned his books after reading them.[149] Illegal brochures we hid among the rocks at the very bank of the Kura river. Stalin was very careful. I was terribly upset after their departure, not knowing how to inform comrade Stalin about the search.

It turned out, as comrade Stalin later told me, that during the search the Observatory was surrounded by police agents in civilian clothes, but it was not difficult to discern that they were detectives.

All this hit comrade Stalin between the eyes when he had returned. Noting the unusual situation he did not come in but walked for a long time along the streets in various directions to kill time and figure out what had happened.

Walking along Mikhailovskaya street comrade Stalin noted that the agents were, as before, surveilling from the Observatory.

He strolled a long time through the city, and, when he approached the building for the second time, he verified there was no one around it. Coming into the room, comrade Stalin asked me what had happened. I answered that we had had some nameless guests.[150]

He ended his account, written in 1938, with the laconic statement, "Comrade Stalin later went over to an illegal situation." This meant that he went underground. Vano Ketskhoveli also writes, "From that time comrade Stalin was completely absorbed in illegal party work." [151]

Beria cites a Department of Police report, No. 1264, dated March 28, 1901:

From January of this year in the city of Tiflis verified to me by the [Gendarme] Administration there has been observed a group of the locals and Russians from the intelligentsia who according to agent reports have founded a social-democratic circle to conduct systematic propaganda among the local workers and to infect them with revolutionary ideas which would prepare a general revolutionary movement of the working class.

According to agent information the following persons are included in the composition of the Tiflis social-democratic circle:

An employee in the Tiflis Physical Observatory, Iosif Dzhugashvili —an intellectual . . . with [connections] among railway workers.

The engineer-chemist Victor Kurnatovsky—intellectual—is [presumably] in the secret circle of railway workers [and] in the circle of type-setters.

That Beria or Stalin, or both, fabricated this report is proved by a clumsy mistake; it was dated March 28th and Kurnatovsky had been arrested a week before.

Poor Kurnatovsky! He was imprisoned for two years in Tiflis and then exiled to Yakutsk in 1903 when he received a sentence of twelve years of penal servitude for participating in a protest movement. After a grisly experience in Siberia (his sentence to be shot was commuted at the last minute, although he was forced to witness the execution of his comrades), he escaped to Japan, then lived in Australia and Paris, where Lenin frequently visited him. He finally became a soft socialist, which meant that he was alienated from Lenin. He was buried in a Paris potter's field after his death in 1912. But what is important to this story is that he was forever removed from the Tiflis revolutionary scene.[152]

The notably efficient Tiflis Okhrana had left Stalin unscathed: he was not in his room at the observatory when it was searched by a "pack" of police officials. He had been clever enough to secrete whatever "illegal" literature he possessed. There were no books in his room because he had hidden them under rocks at the bank of the Kura River. He had eluded the police who had him under surveillance. And yet, according to his official biographers, he had been involved in the formation of workers' groups, the creation of an underground printing press, the writing of revolutionary proclamations and tracts, the organization of May Day demonstrations, and the leadership of strikes in Tiflis. In addition, Yaroslavsky tells us that the Gendarme Administration had started a police file on his activities twenty-two months earlier, when he left the seminary. Thus we see that he amazingly eluded the police dragnet although his activities marked him as one of the important revolutionaries the police were anxious to apprehend in the arrests of March 21-22, 1901.

If the Tiflis police had really wanted to arrest Soso in this massive operation, the observatory would have been staked out in advance, as were the residences of the others arrested. When Soso left the observatory for his stroll, he would have been followed by surveillance agents, and he would have been apprehended at some point during that night in Tiflis. Berdzenishvili remained unmolested when the police raided his living quarters in the observatory. To have arrested him would have pointed the finger of betrayal, of course, directly at Stalin.

One would prefer to believe that Soso escaped the Tiflis Okhrana dragnet by a combination of good fortune and accomplished conspiratorial craftsmanship. To accept this theory, however, one must be convinced that of all the scores of socialist-democratic leaders and workers arrested that night Soso alone decided to absent himself from his quarters, to take a long walk, to evade his "shadows," to avoid the customary meeting places of marxists (which were also raided), to observe that his quarters were being searched, to make himself scarce until the raids and arrests had run their course, to time their conclusion, and only then to return to the observatory. A rational bettor would immediately recognize the long odds on such a series of unlikely coincidences. We are left then with the inescapable conclusion that had Soso not been warned by his superior in the police of the forthcoming arrests and raids, he would have shared a cell with a fellow revolutionary on March 21, 1901. His career until 1917 is marked with analagous episodes that find him recklessly, apparently courageously, flaunting his revolutionary activity in the faces of supposedly astonished Okhrana officers and staffs, only to evade apprehension, detention, or imprisonment at the last minute. And when he was arrested, he managed to escape prison or exile with ease. Stalin was truly the elusive revolutionary.

4 | BLOODSHED AT TIFLIS AND BATUM

Soso never returned to his bookkeeping after the arrests of March 21-22, 1901. He had worked almost fifteen months in the Tiflis Geophysical Observatory, and he was nine months short of his twenty-second birthday, when he quit the job. His co-worker and fellow revolutionary, Vano Berdzenishvili, who was present in the observatory when the Tiflis police raided the rooms he shared with Soso, was unmolested and was merely obliged to sign a "protocol," a document then—and now—used by Russian security forces to attest to what occurs during a search. After Soso learned from Berdzenishvili what had happened, he mysteriously disappeared the next day and was gone for a month.

His activities during the remainder of March and the month of April are officially unknown. No one remembers seeing him during this period. It has been suggested that he was in Gori, and that a few weeks later he returned to Tiflis. If true, this would have been in line with a typical Okhrana tactic that was frequently employed. It involved the movement of an agent from his place of recent usefulness, at the same time providing him with a plausible excuse for his next assignment. Such an operation would have required the easily arranged cooperation of the local Tiflis and Gori gendarme officers. The gendarme officer who planned the Tiflis arrests was a thirty-six-year-old bachelor, Captain Vladimir Aleksandrovich Runich, who had served the Tiflis Police Headquarters since March, 1899, as an adjutant and later as a special assistant to the Chief of the Gendarme Administration. The title of "assistant" usually meant that the officer had been trained in the St. Petersburg Headquarters of The Department of Police and was in charge of secret agent operations. His friend, Captain Aleksei Makarevich Smolensky, had directed police operations in Gori since 1898.[153] Conceivably Runich informed his colleague Smolensky that Soso would be in his home town and was not to be disturbed. Under these circumstances he might well have stayed there safely and, when he returned to Tiflis, circulated the story that he had been in hiding from the police who in fact had provided him with a perfectly logical cover story.

He publicly reappeared in Tiflis for May Day (celebrated on April 22nd), 1901, when more than two thousand worker demonstrators battled tsarist police and troops. In a speech a year earlier, he had apparently advocated this kind of operation. Beria's account of the event not only reveals the senseless character of the action but also shows how Stalin in 1939 wanted his role portrayed:

> The demonstrations began at the Soldatsky bazaar in the region of the former Aleksandrovsky Garden in the center of town. Almost two thousand workers from the plants and factories of Tiflis participated. The demonstrators attacked the police and cossacks. During the strike fourteen workers were wounded and over fifty demonstrators were arrested. Comrade Stalin participated in this demonstration and personally led it.[154]

Other Soviet accounts also state that Soso had planned the demonstration and add that the Okhrana had been alerted by information gathered by *"provocateurs,* traitors, and betrayers among the workers." [155] These statements unwittingly suggest, although they do not prove, that the arrests of socialist-democratic leaders a month earlier had been only Part One of an Okhrana operation aimed at crushing the Tiflis revolutionary movement. If Part Two was to be an audacious provocation of unarmed workers pitted against military units, the Okhrana might have attempted to ensnare anyone daring to show May Day revolutionary leadership.[156] This type of *provokatsiya* (*provocation*) operation, however, required a tested agent, which may serve to explain at least partially Soso's activities from the night of March 21st-22nd until his sudden reappearance on May Day. Beria incorrectly asserted that Stalin led the demonstration. Had he personally marched at the forefront of the workers as a *bona fide* leader, the chances were overwhelming that he would have been hit by rifle fire or injured by a cossack sword, but nothing of this kind was ever reported. Of course it was possible that a charmed life insured his safety, but in that case the Okhrana would have had to apprehend him; neither Stalinist nor Okhrana sources have ventured this claim. Since Soso's role has never been clarified, we can attempt a reconstruction of what might have happened.

The Tiflis Okhrana would have developed the scheme and ordered Stalin to get in touch with leading workmen, making certain that the time and place of the demonstration were known to the Tiflis workers; thus Soso would *appear* to be the planner although he was merely the executor of an Okhrana plot. He probably helped to provoke the demonstration, but rather than lead it he would have stood at the sidelines pressing the hapless workers on— or he would have been elsewhere. The demonstration that began at the Soldatsky Bazar apparently did not end there, and perhaps Soso was forming up other workers' groups in nearby streets. When the mêlée subsided, it was easy to see that the labor movement in Tiflis had been dealt a damaging blow. More than seventy leading workers had been wounded or arrested and thus rendered inactive for months, if not years.[157] By the same token, the Okhrana considered its operation highly successful: it would be a long time before the Tiflis workers would take to the streets again, because most of their leaders were in hospitals or jails. Lenin's newspaper *Iskra,* habitually out of touch with reality, hailed the demonstration as historically important because "this day marks the beginning of an open revolutionary movement in the Caucasus."[158] On the contrary, it had set the revolutionary cause back; the Okhrana had won this round, not the revolution.

Soso emerged from the bloody May Day action unscathed, unmolested, and at liberty. He returned to Gori, where he and Iremashvili met sometime in early May. Obsessed with the demonstration, he appeared able to talk about little else. The subject of the wounded and arrested workers exhilarated him and he seemed to look forward to even more bloodshed the following year. Iremashvili could not understand his attitude until, as he said, "I realized that the blood that had flowed during the demonstration had intoxicated him." [159]

Soso's official whereabouts until November, 1901, are unknown and only Iremashvili, whose memory sometimes went awry as he wrote many years later, recalled:

> Koba was sought by the police as one of the leaders [of the May Day demonstration], but he escaped arrest, the police having unsuccessfully spent weeks looking for him. He fled to his home town of Gori. Unable to stay with his mother because this would be the first place the police would look for him, he hid elsewhere in Gori. Secretly, late at night, he often visited me in my apartment.[160]

Soso deceived the often naïve Iremashvili, for the Okhrana had doubtless ordered him to take an extensive "vacation." Perhaps embarrassing questions were being asked in Tiflis and Soso was suspected of complicity with the Okhrana in their March arrests and of provoking the May Day debacle. To quiet suspicions, Soso, who had survived both operations, went underground.

Vladimir Zakharevich (Lado) Ketskhoveli had escaped the Okhrana dragnet in Tiflis and proceeded to Baku, a city on the Caspian Sea. Perhaps Soso had warned him to leave Tiflis; he was capable at that time of doing favors for the very few people whom he admired. According to Yaroslavsky:

> In 1901, on the initiative of Comrade Stalin and Lado Ketskhoveli, an illegal printing plant was started in Baku, and in September of the same year the first illegal Georgian newspaper, *Brdzola* [*The Struggle*], the organ of the Tiflis revolutionary Social Democrats, began to appear in Tiflis. This was a newspaper of the Leninist *Iskra* trend. It advocated the broad development of agitational work and called upon the workers to take up the struggle against the tsar, the landlords, and the capitalists. It proclaimed the indivisible unity of the ranks of the working class of all Russia in the fight for socialism.[161]

Essentially the same version may be found in Stalin's autobiographical *Collected Works,* where we read that Lado and "his closest colleague," Soso, established the underground printing plant on the instructions of the revolutionary wing of the Tiflis social-democratic organization. This "wing" was admittedly a minority composed of Soso, Lado Ketskhoveli, and Alexander Tsulukidze, who fought against the "oppositionist" majority led by Zhordania.[162] Beria, however, overdraws the report when he writes:

> Ketskhoveli conducted all his varied revolutionary work in Baku under the direction of the Tiflis leadership group of the Russian Socialist-Democratic Workers' Party and comrade Stalin. Lado systematically kept in touch with comrade Stalin by mail, but for direction and advice on the most important questions he came to comrade Stalin either in Tiflis or in Batum.[163]

From this it is clear that Soso had remained in Tiflis: he was not known to be in Batum until the very end of November or the beginning of December. Moreover, even if Lado needed advice from Soso, he would hardly have solicited it through the mails. The Okhrana intercepted the letters of well-known revolutionaries; unsurprisingly, no record of Soso-Lado letters is to be found in Department of Police files.

The Struggle (in the Georgian language) appeared in only four issues, the first in September of 1901 and the last in December of 1902.[164] There can be no doubt that the purchase of printing equipment and newsprint required money and, because the plant was clandestine, probably a large amount. Where did it come from? Since revolutionaries were not notably good credit risks, borrowing from money-lenders or financial institutions was out of the question. The so-called "left-wing social democrats," including Lado and Soso, had no money. Workers' contributions would have been insufficient, and had they been even a minor factor in financing the press, Soviet literature would not have ignored them. However, underwriting revolutionary newspapers was an old Okhrana stratagem. Thus, if Soso was used by the Okhrana to supply Lado with funds, his "correspondence"—perhaps by courier—becomes understandable.

It is interesting that the theme of Soso's first identifiable article in a revolutionary periodical fostered Okhrana objectives. At twenty-two Soso, or Koba (he was then using either name), wrote, or more likely co-authored, "The Russian Social-Democratic Party and Its Immediate Tasks" in *Brdzola*, No. 2-3, in the late autumn of 1901. Parts of the article, which take up some twenty pages in his *Collected Works*, are unmistakably Stalinist while certain passages bear the marks of another author, perhaps Lado or Tsulukidze. Curiously the article denigrates the importance of revolutionary literature—pamphlets, periodicals, and newspapers, one of which he had presumably just helped to establish. He seems to commiserate with all the oppressed peoples in the Russian Empire, he expresses sympathy for persecuted religious sects, and he shows concern for the plight of the peasants, "small-town dwellers," minor government bureaucrats, and "lower- and middle-class bourgeoisie." His major contribution to the article, however, was a predilection for workers' demonstrations against the armed might of the police and cossacks. In his view propaganda was not nearly as effectual as bloodshed. It is "Street demonstrations . . . that quickly draw large masses of people into the movement, acquaint them with our demands," he wrote. "Street demonstrations give rise to street agitation. A man has only to go out into the street during a demonstration to see courageous fighters, to understand what they are fighting for, to hear free voices calling upon everyone to join the struggle, and militant songs denouncing the existing system and exposing our social evils. That is why [the government] threatens with due punishment not only the demonstrators, but also the 'curious onlookers.' "

Utilizing the curious onlooker in street demonstrations to further revolutionary aims reeked of Okhrana operational methodology. From 1900 until the 1917 revolution, it was common practice for an Okhrana *agent provocateur* to incite a workers' demonstration in an apparent attempt to redress injustices or publicly dramatize grievances. Casual bystanders, attracted to a seemingly just cause, would then join the crowd, which eventually would encounter armed cossacks or police detachments. The resulting bloodshed and arrests constituted a powerful depressant to workers' militancy. Soso, writing in 1901, vividly described the vital elements of the operation:

> In the people's curiosity lurks the principal danger threatening the government: today's "curious onlooker" will be tomorrow's demonstrator and rally new groups of "curious onlookers" around himself. And today every large town includes tens of thousands of such "curious onlookers." Russians no longer run into hiding, as they did before, on hearing of disorders taking place somewhere or other ("I'd better get out of the way in case I get into trouble," they used to say); today they flock to the scene of disorders and evince "curiosity": they are eager to know why these disorders are taking place, why so many people offer their backs to the lash of the Cossacks' whip.
>
> In these circumstances, the "curious onlookers" cease to listen indifferently to the swish of the whips and sabers. The "curious onlookers" see that the demonstrators have assembled in the streets to express their wishes and demands, and that the government retaliates by beatings and brutal suppressions. The "curious onlookers" no longer run away on hearing the swish of the whips; on the contrary, they draw nearer, and the whips can no longer distinguish between the "curious onlookers" and the "rioters." Now, conforming to "complete democratic equality," the whips play on the backs of all, irrespective of sex, age, and even class. Thereby, the whip lash is rendering us a great service for it hastens the revolutionisation of the "curious onlookers." . . . Every militant who falls in the struggle, or is torn from our ranks, rouses hundreds of new fighters.[165]

What Iremashvili had discerned a few months previously as Soso's "intoxication with the flow of blood" was now revealed in his own writing and published in a revolutionary journal. But the Okhrana did not necessarily want blood to flow for its own sake: its aim was to repress and discourage anti-tsarist activity. Soso simply added a sadistic dimension to the art of provocation. Again and again he uses the words "whip" and "saber," and he repetitiously intones the "curious onlookers" as their potential victims. He openly expresses the hope that the victims will include innocent elderly women and men, and children too young to have any political consciousness. Apparently, street demonstrations are not to help people but to hurt them, and the bloodier the better.

This attitude was to reappear with dismaying frequency in his later life. What is striking is that it manifested itself so early and that he recorded it. Similarly, although Stalin throughout his life seldom made statements involving his personal feelings, the self-revelation on the few occasions when he did is staggering. His famous words to Kamenev and Dzerzhinsky, in 1923, in which he acknowledged that for him sleep was sweetest after a blood purge, tell us more about his inner nature than all the words written about him. This was his statement to his two colleagues:

To choose the victim, to prepare the blow with care, to slake an implacable vengeance, and then to go to bed . . . there is nothing sweeter in the world.[166]

The official biography asserts that on November 11, 1901 Stalin was "elected a member of the first Committee of the R.S.D.L.P.,* which followed the Leninist-*Iskra* trend," and Yaroslavsky writes, "On November 11, 1901, in Avlabar [a part of Tiflis], the Tiflis Social-Democratic organization held its first conference. It was attended by twenty-five delegates and elected the first Tiflis Committee of the R.S.D.L.P.[167] Comrade Stalin was elected a member of this Committee." An article, "Where the Great Stalin Worked," in the Tiflis newspaper *Dawn of the East* of April 24, 1939, went further:

Along Kropotkin Street there was a little old one-story house. On Sunday, November 11, 1901, delegates of the socialist-democratic workers' circles from various parts of the city gathered here. Iosif Vissarionovich Stalin had created them. In that faraway day in a little house the first Tiflis conference of a socialist-democratic organization met and the first Tiflis Committee of the Russian Socialist-Democratic Workers' Party headed by comrade Stalin was elected.

Finally, Beria produced a spurious document purportedly confirming that "in the autumn of 1901 Dzhugashvili was elected to the Tiflis Committee and participated in two of its sessions." [168] The accuracy of these reports may be judged by the fact that delegates

---

* The initials of the Russian Socialist-Democratic Workers Party (sometimes also R.S.D.R.P).

to the conference unanimously elected Silvester Dzhibladze, not Soso, as chairman of a nine-man central committee.[169] Furthermore, there is no evidence that Soso was even elected a committee member. The majority of the authentic Tiflis social democrats personally disliked him; perhaps they already suspected him of collusion with the police. The March arrests and the May Day uprising were still fresh in their minds. However, when Soso heard the conference was to take place he undoubtedly became a self-appointed delegate. Shortly afterward the Tiflis social-democratic organization expelled him from the party and booted him out of the city. In 1930, the Paris Georgian social-democratic periodical *Brdzolis Khma* (*The Echo of the Struggle*) succinctly described his banishment:

From his earliest days of activity among the workers, he attracted attention *by his intrigues* against the real leader of the social-democratic organization, S. Dzhibladze. He was warned, but took no notice and continued to spread slanders intending to discredit the authorized and recognized representatives of the social-democratic movement, thus attempting to manage the local organization. He was brought before a party court of honor and found guilty of unjustly slandering Dzhibladze and was, by a unanimous vote, excluded from the Tiflis social-democratic organization.[170]

Noi Zhordania later recalled from his exile in Paris a discussion during this period with Dzhibladze:

"That good for nothing [Soso]!" Dzhibladze had exclaimed. We appointed him to conduct propaganda against the government and the capitalists, but as it turned out he was conducting propaganda against us.[171]

The revolutionary credentials of Silvester Dzhibladze were well known; he had contemptuously thrashed a rector of the Tiflis Theological Seminary in 1885, for which he had been summarily exiled to Siberia. As one of the organizers of the social-democratic movement in Georgia, he had been Stalin's "political tutor," according to Iremashvili, when both belonged to the Third Group.[172] It has been suggested that Dzhibladze may have patronized his pupil Koba and wounded his pride. This was incorrect. Dzhibladze, who had been slandered by Koba and arrested during the night of the raids in Tiflis, suspected him of harboring something less than true devotion to the revolutionary cause, an appraisal shared by other members of the Tiflis central party organization.

No better example of Stalin's vengeance may be found than in his later treatment of Dzhibladze. Lenin's government recognized the independence of the Republic of Georgia on May 7, 1920. In spite of this, less than a year later, on February 11, 1921, Stalin ordered the Red Army to invade free Georgia. On May 20, 1921, the first bolshevik secret police, the Cheka, arrested Dzhibladze, together with Iremashvili. Both were subsequently released, but Dzhibladze died soon thereafter from an illness contracted in prison. The puppet bolshevik government of Georgia prohibited public attendance at his funeral. Nevertheless, many hundreds of his followers paid their final respects. As they left the house where the deceased reposed, almost all the leaders of the Georgian Social-Democratic Party, among whom was Iremashvili, were rearrested. He observed that the local prisons were bulging with political prisoners. Thereafter, the bolsheviks made off with Dzhibladze's remains, and the whereabouts of his coffin and his burial place are unknown. Iremashvili grimly concluded, "Thus Stalin expressed his appreciation to his political tutor." [173] Although twenty years had elapsed since the Tiflis Committee had sent Soso packing, he had not forgotten.

S. T. Arkomed, a social-democratic observer of the Tiflis scene, recalls that in the autumn of 1901 (apparently some time before November), at a meeting of party intellectuals that included forty workers' representatives from Tiflis factories and shops, a conflict developed. He and a group of "conscientious workers" deplored the idea of an independent revolutionary workers' movement. Without alluding to Soso by name (although it is unmistakably he), Arkomed describes a young, carelessly energetic, intellectual "unknown" comrade who, opposed by the majority, strongly emphasized conspiracy and ridiculed the inexperience and ineptness

of the Tiflis workers in revolutionary activities. His brazen castiga-
tion of workers whom a few months before he had urged to do
battle with armed cossacks exposes an insolent confidence we will
again encounter. When soon thereafter the "unknown" comrade
arrived in Batum, he acted in character. Tiflis workers learned at
once that he was waging a campaign of "hostile agitation against
the Tiflis organization and its members," which Arkomed partially
explained as being a reflection of selfishness, personal caprice, and
a power complex. This analysis, developed in 1910, qualified as a
portent of things to come after Stalin's rise to power in Soviet
Russia.[174]

By 1940 Yaroslavsky, understandably fearful of being liquidated, had developed the approved version of these events, undoubtedly under Stalin's guidance, when he wrote, "Toward the
end of 1901 the Tiflis Committee decided to send Comrade Stalin
to Batum to form a Social-Democratic organization." The *Collected Works* includes a similar entry, indicating that at the end of
November the Tiflis Committee sent Soso "to Batum to form a
Social-Democratic organization there." The fact of the matter, as
already stated, was that he had been politically expelled from Tiflis.
For one reason or another, he was suspect; he was too much for the
Tiflis social democrats to tolerate. They wanted him out of their
association and out of town. By attempting to seize control of the
Tiflis organization and by criticizing its members and leaders he
had overplayed his hand and possibly committed his first operational error as an Okhrana agent.

Grigory Illarionovich Uratadze,[174a] a respected Georgian social
democrat, who was active in Transcaucasia at that time later recalled:

He [Stalin] had studied at the theological seminary and departed
from the third class in 1899. During this year he started to occupy
himself in workers' circles, but he had not yet entered the organization because in this year the Tiflis organization was comprised only of
the Tiflis committee and they were not accepting "new ones." They
gave him two circles. In these circles from the very first day he began
to intrigue against the main leader—S. Dzhibladze. When this was

disclosed, the organization gave him a corresponding admonition and warning. And when this produced no effect and he continued, the organization brought him before a party court. This was the first party court established by the Georgian social democratic organization to try a comrade in the party. The court was composed of regional representatives. After interrogations, the court unanimously decided to exclude him from the Tiflis organization for slander and improper intriguing. After this sentence they took away from him the circles with which he had occupied himself. Then he moved from Tiflis to Batum. In Batum they knew about the Tiflis decision.[174b]

When Soso left Tiflis in late November, 1901—a month short of his twenty-second birthday—he traveled by rail to Batum, which, though less than two hundred and twenty miles away, was millions of miles from the Gori-Tiflis area culturally and historically. Turks comprised half the population of the city, a burgeoning oil-refining and exporting center of about thirty-five thousand souls. Batum rested on a subtropical and marshy portion of the Black Sea coast, and some twenty-five years before Soso's arrival it had been under Turkish rule. The railroad, which stretched from the sister city of Baku—also oil-producing—on the Caspian Sea, made it an important seaport not only for petroleum products but also for manganese, licorice, silk, and wool. The Georgian monarch, Queen Tamara, had built her castle, Zamok Tamary, in Batum, which Soso remembered from his reading of Georgian legends and history.

Workers' organizations had mushroomed in Batum with the establishment of the Rothschild and Mantashev petroleum works a few years before. Nikolai (Carlo) Semenovich Chkheidze and Isadore Ramishvili, among others, were recognized as the solid marxist and social-democratic leaders in Batum. They realized that the smallness of the town made conspiratorial and revolutionary activity futile. Chkheidze in particular agreed with the gradualism of his Tiflis compatriots Zhordania and Tsereteli. The social-democratic leaders in Batum were systematically attempting to improve the lot of the newly formed proletariat, but interlopers were unnecessary and burdensome.

When Soso arrived in late November or early December, carrying a portable printing press, the local organization was appalled.

Where had he procured it and what were his plans to use it? How had he obtained the money to purchase it? A surviving photograph shows the printing press to be a bulky mechanism that would ordinarily have alerted the railway police who were part of the Tiflis-Batum Okhrana complex.[175] The *Collected Works* assures us that during December, 1901 Soso established contact with "advanced" workers and organized "social-democratic circles at the Rothschild, Mantashev, Sideridis, and other plants." [176] He resided initially on Tbilisi Street, in the apartment of Chkhaidze (not Chkheidze), a worker in the Mantashev plant, where he met with members of Ivlian Shapatava's circle. He annoyed and stirred up the workers by the remark, "Your work is going very slowly; it must proceed more swiftly." [177] A common laborer, Kotrikidze, recalls that Soso made a rousing statement, in which the cadence of the seminary liturgy is apparent, when he met with worker representatives from the Mantashev, Rothschild, and Sideridis plants:

"The Tiflis workers sent me to you, comrades, to talk with you. The Tiflis workers, as you know, have awakened from sleep and are preparing for the struggle with their enemies. The Batum workers still are peacefully asleep. I appeal to you to follow the example of the Tiflis workers." [178]

It is perfectly apparent that the Tiflis workers had not sent Soso to talk with their Batum comrades; and had the Batum workers followed the example set in Tiflis, they would have banished Soso from the town. Later he disguised a secret conference of "representatives of social-democratic study circles" as a New Year's party, held in Silibistro Lomdzhariya's apartment, at which a "leading group headed by Stalin was elected which acted virtually as the Batum Committee of the R.S.D.L.P. of the Leninist-Iskra trend." So the official account goes.[179]

Yaroslavsky, writing in 1939 about the "New Year's party," stressed the "very moving reminiscences of this conference recounted by old workers of Transcaucasia. One of them, Rodion Korkia [a mysterious character], relates that Comrade Stalin ended his speech with the words, 'See, the day is already dawning!

Soon the sun will rise. That sun will shine for us. Believe my words, comrades!' " [180] Again the steady beat of the liturgy he had learned in the seminary is identifiable.

Soviet accounts state that after the New Year's Eve party Soso's activities became more pronounced: during January, 1902, he assembled an "underground printing plant, wrote leaflets, and organized the production and distribution of manifestoes." At about this time, according to these accounts, his work "became known to the police." He scurried back and forth from Lomdzhariya's place to Alaniya's, for his own protection and for the security of his clandestine printing press. As he searched for a suitable apartment in which to turn out revolutionary leaflets, the Mantashev workers' circle directed him to a house in the settlement that was called *Chaoba* (the Swamp) which, unlike central Batum, was apparently not under strict police surveillance. There Soso lived in a *domik* of six rooms that was owned by Niko Natsvalava and Mato Rusidze. The Mantashev circle decided that the unoccupied half of the house would be registered in the name of the Darakhvelidze brothers and that Soso could set up his printing press there. [181] These characters enter and leave our narrative like quicksilver. From the moment he moved to this address, Soviet sources claim, his revolutionary work became even more energetic as additional cadres of workers were formed and the circles assumed revolutionary dimensions.

Almost every night Comrade Soso gathered to himself at the apartment the leaders and activists of underground circles. After the meetings he turned out proclamations on his underground printing press until dawn. [182]

His *modus operandi* re-emerged as he demanded street demonstrations and conversely emphasized the need for conspiracy, with the demonstrators to be the workers, and the conspiratorial activities his own.

With due allowance for the obvious amount of propaganda surrounding the accounts of his activities during his first two months in Batum, it is still apparent that he was stirring up a strong brew of revolution for the workers. It was not to nourish them or, for that matter, to benefit the cause of social democracy in Batum. On the contrary, Soso's agitation ran directly counter to the ideas of Carlo Chkheidze, one of Batum's leaders of social democracy. Carlo, an ex-seminarian like Soso, was not only a spellbinding orator but was also highly regarded for his erudition and honesty. After the February Revolution in 1917, Chkheidze, a chairman of the Petrograd Soviet, greeted Lenin upon his arrival at the Finland Station, but at the same time courageously cautioned him not to be opportunistic.[183] He was a close friend of Silvester Dzhibladze, who headed the Tiflis party committee, and perhaps he had heard from his friend about Stalin's recent suspicious activities in Tiflis that had resulted in his expulsion from the party organization. As a matter of fact, the impeccably honest Arkomed recalled that the Batum social democrats had been quick to inform Tiflis of Soso's disruptive activities.[184] Even Yaroslavsky, writing in 1940, conceded that prior to Stalin's arrival Carlo Chkheidze and other "legal marxists" had been active in Batum.[185] However, he failed to note their importance. We can deduce that Carlo's position was clearly logical and adamant: it was impossible to create a militantly revolutionary organization in Batum without massive arrests and the inevitable unnecessary bloodshed. He had tried unsuccessfully to persuade Soso to leave the city and was aggravated at the disregard of his sincere advice. "However, comrade Stalin knew better than Chkheidze what forces were latent in the working class and what needed to be done," Yaroslavsky tells us.[186] But, most important, angered by Soso's activities, which made no sense in terms of improving the workers' lot, Carlo, like Dzhibladze, viewed him as a reckless conspirator.

Soso chose to ignore Chkheidze and persevered with his activities. The official record states that he organized a strike at the Mantashev plant in early February that ended in a victory for the workers, and that at the end of the month he directed "the activities of the strike committee during a strike at the Rothschild plant."[187] In late February, the Rothschild factory had, in fact, dismissed almost four hundred workers. The ensuing strike that led to clashes with

the police had undoubtedly been exacerbated by Soso's inflamma-
tory propaganda leaflets. The police arrested over thirty workers on
March 7th and, according to his official biography, "Stalin led a
demonstration of strikers on March 8th to the Batum prison where
they demanded the arrestees be released." [188] All three hundred of
these demonstrators were promptly arrested and placed in detention barracks, because the Batum jails, already overcrowded, were
unable to accommodate them. But Koba remained free.

The following day, March 9, 1902, was the date of the celebrated Batum demonstration (*Batumskaya demonstratsiya*). Stalin
later wrote in his official autobiography that he organized and led
this "political demonstration of over six thousand employees from
the various plants of Batum," who demanded that the three hundred workers arrested the day before be immediately released.[189]
The demonstrators, singing the "Marseillaise" and other revolutionary songs, and hoisting red banners, came under fire from
troops protecting the prison barracks. They killed fifteen, wounded
fifty-four, and arrested over five hundred. The old worker I.
Darakhvelidze later recalled that Soso stood in the midst of a sea of
demonstrators, personally directing them. A wounded worker, Kalandadze, was led out of the crowd and afterward taken home by
Soso himself.[190] "That same night," according to the official record, Soso wrote a manifesto concerning the demonstrators who had
been killed or wounded. When the tsarist government later convened a court of inquiry to look into the Batum demonstration,
which had by then become a *cause célèbre* throughout Russia, it
developed testimony that there were two thousand, not six thousand, workers involved. Though no witness mentioned Soso as a
participant, let alone a leader, of the bloody affair he was, nonetheless, a consistent revolutionary cheerleader.[191]

On March 12th, according to the *Collected Works,* he led a
"workers' demonstration which he had organized in connection
with the funeral of the victims of the shooting on March 9." Yaroslavsky's account differs; he writes that Soso merely arranged a
revolutionary funeral for the dead workers. In spite of the recent
carnage, huge numbers of workers attended.[192] A leaflet written by

Soso and widely distributed in Batum and other cities was filled with "revolutionary fire and passion":

> All honor to you who have laid down your lives for the truth! All honor to the breasts that suckled you! All honor to you whose brows are adorned with the crowns of martyrs, and who with pale and faltering lips breathed words of struggle in your hour of death! All honor to your shadows that hover over us and whisper in our ears "Avenge our blood!" [193]

It was not fire and passion that emerged here but liturgical meter and Soso's characteristic obsession with bloodshed.

Soso's role in the Batum demonstration has been variously described. To Trotsky it was "of obscure character." Barbusse saw him as a "target" leading the riot. Yaroslavsky regarded him as a leader in the midst of a "turbulent sea" of workers. Soso's autobiography claimed he "organized and led" the demonstration. The proceedings of the tsarist court of inquiry that investigated the demonstration failed to mention him. A Soviet book, *The Batum Demonstration of 1902,* published and edited by Stalin and Beria in 75,000 copies on the thirty-fifth anniversary of the uprising, lauds Soso for organizing and leading it. Only Boris Souvarine, in his monumental biography of Stalin, approached the crux of the matter as he wrote, "The recent arrest of the principal Party representatives cleared the ground for the time being. Stalin seized the opportunity to incite unarmed workmen to attack the prison, an adventure which cost several of the assailants their lives. The workers of Batum never forgave the useless shedding of workers' blood." [194]

Thirty-five years later the Batum episode in Koba's life was subjected to a curious, almost amusing, analysis in the soviet press that was by this time fully controlled by Stalin. *Izvestia,* the soviet government newspaper, on April 27, 1937, indicated that Soso had organized a strike of Tiflis railway workers in 1902. The April 28th issue of the same paper published a retraction entitled "From the Editorial Board." It read:

The editorial board of *Izvestia* due to an oversight printed in its issue of April 27th the photographic reproduction of a painting by K. Khutsishvili, "Comrade Stalin—the organizer of the Tbilisi railroad workers' strike in 1902." The editorial board recognizes a historical mistake. It is evident from the biography of comrade Stalin that from the end of 1901 until February 1902 he was in freedom in Batum, and he directed the party work there, and that from February 1902 until the end of 1903 he was incarcerated in Batum and Kutais prisons. Therefore comrade Stalin could not have been the organizer of the strike in Tbilisi in 1902. When asked about this comrade Stalin stated, from the point of view of historical truth, it was a complete misunderstanding to represent him as an organizer of the rail workers' strike in Tbilisi in 1902, because at that time he was incarcerated in Batum prison.[195]

He apparently failed to realize that this also made it impossible for him to lead the Batum demonstration in March, 1902.

Obviously there had been a serious disorientation in the Kremlin at that time. How many heads rolled because of this mistake we may never know, but of one thing we may be sure: the party writers did not know the appropriate line concerning his life in Batum, his first arrest, and his activities during this period. Either he was in prison or he was not: no one forgets when he has been behind bars. Thus there must have been a major crisis concerning this period. What did it mean? A revolutionary loyal to the cause would have experienced no difficulty in proving that he had been in prison, or that he had been leading a demonstration. Koba was unable to do either, and the resultant confusion stemmed from an attempt to bring some order and logic into the Batum incident. We are left with the probability that Stalin in 1937 was gripped with a vexing problem from which he tried to extricate himself by a combination of bluster and dissimulation. He asserted he was in prison during 1902 and 1903 and therefore could not have led a strike in Tiflis—although he knew full well he had claimed he was in Batum and leading a strike there. No angle in this episode is free of the suspicion of Okhrana complicity.[196]

Granted Stalin's provocative role in the Batum demonstration, who stood to profit from the scores of dead and wounded and the hundreds of arrests? Not the social democrats, whose leaders Chkheidze and Ramishvili opposed such action. Not the workers, whose legitimate demands might well have been met through peaceful negotiation. As in Tiflis two years earlier, only the Okhrana gained from the Batum insurrection. The instigator and principal agent in both uprisings remained at liberty, unhurt and unperturbed, although the suspicion that he was an Okhrana spy was rapidly forming.

It remained for Zhordania, whose honesty was well known, to analyze this occurrence correctly. In a careful understatement he recalled that:

This young man from his very first steps wanted to be a leader. Because he lacked the necessary comprehension of affairs, he could only act through intrigues. He was not an orator (he spoke boringly as if reciting a lesson learned by rote) and, in order to attract the attention of his listeners, he often used rough language. He also had no talent for writing or publishing. Clearly there remained only the organizational field. . . . Going behind the backs of the local leaders, N. Chkheidze and I. Ramishvili, he based himself in the workers' quarter and began to gather workers around himself. Detesting all the progressive comrades, he accused them of cowardice, lack of ability, and treason to the working class and appealed to the workers for demonstrations on the streets. He created inside the organization *a personal organization* loyal only to himself and which declined any responsibility to the committee. The result of such secret work, as is known, was a demonstration of the workers in front of the prison and their being fired upon. . . . This cannot be called anything except a provocation. Finding him intolerable, the workers started to shun Soso. But he was lucky in being arrested and exiled. This partly retrieved his prestige and saved him from being adjudged an *agent provocateur*.[197]

Koba continued to play the game of an elusive revolutionary. Soviet accounts support this fiction by asserting that after the Batum uprising gendarmes were combing the city for the secret printing press and Soso decided to move it to the home of the Moslem Khashim Smyrba, in the Makhmudia section of Batum.[198] In all probability, Lomdzhariya was suspicious of his police connec-

tions and suggested he would be safer and more productive elsewhere.

Khashim, a deeply religious man whom Soso had met through
the Batum revolutionary organization, is one of the few sentimental
figures in Soso's pre-1917 life. Although he may be fictitious, pic-
tures and paintings show him to be a sort of elderly Caucasian
Hemingway, bearded, with strong facial features and penetrating
eyes. Revolutionary activity did not interest him, but money did.
When Lomdzhariya explained to him that he was seeking a haven
for Soso and the printing press, Khashim reportedly said, "Good."
His son Khemdy and his son-in-law Redzheb fetched the press from
the Darakhvelidzes' house. Soso moved the following day.

Neighboring peasants began to notice women in dark veils (the
Moslem *chadra*) entering the house after old Khashim had departed with his basket of vegetables for the Batum bazaar. The
women were disguised men who worked as typesetters turning out
revolutionary tracts on Soso's printing press. Khashim, meanwhile,
was utilizing his basket of greens to conceal and distribute revolutionary literature in plants and factories, among workers and peasants. One of his tricks was to hide proclamations in fresh cabbage.
A Soviet report reads:

> Khashim's neighbors continued to wonder what was going on at
> the old man's home. People entered under the *chadra;* they departed
> under the *chadra*, while every day Khashim peddled his fruit and
> vegetables.

When the neighbors discovered the activity involved a printing
press and paper, they concluded that the veiled women were helping Khashim counterfeit money. One evening thereafter a delegation of Khashim's neighbors paid Soso a visit. In a friendly Moslem
manner they chatted about unimportant matters, finally coming to
the point: they had little money. Could the counterfeiter help
them? Soso was silent for a long time before he answered: he had
never been a counterfeiter of money. He wanted to help the poor
impoverished peasants, but not with rubles. He was engaged in
printing proclamations to hasten the overthrow of the Tsar, to re-

turn power to the people, who could then improve their lot by their own labor. The Moslems replied through their elder that they understood the Tsar made it impossible to better their lives and added, "And now each of us will be a good helper to you. Until today only Khashim has protected you—for which we are thankful—but now all of us will protect you and your work."

Sometime after they departed, Soso explained to Khashim that if he was arrested Khashim might also go to jail, and perhaps it would be wise to move his illegal printing press.[199] Khashim refused to consider Soso's moving, but he remarked:

"You're a good man, Soso. I'm only sorry you are not a Moslem."
"But what would happen were I to become a Moslem?"
"Then I would get you a wife, a beauty the likes of whom you have never seen. Now, do you want to be a Moslem?"
Comrade Stalin answered with a smile "Good!" and pressed Khashim's hand.

On another occasion Khashim admonished Soso to be of good cheer:

"Don't be afraid. Everything will turn out very well for you. I had a dream, Soso, and do you know what kind of dream? That you freed the entire Caucasus of tsarist soldiers and that then our life became easy, good, and free. This is good, very good, for you, Soso!"

In his old age Khashim fondly recalled this exchange to his son and friends.[200]

The Okhrana arrested Soso for the first time on April 5, 1902, in Batum, some eight months before his twenty-third birthday and about five months after his arrival from Tiflis. We are never more certain about any event in Stalin's pre-revolutionary life. It is useful to summarize the many accounts of the event:

Friday night, April 5, 1902, Kotsia Kandelaki and he visited the home of Darakhvelidze, who had arranged a social gathering. Soso was twenty-two years of age, still slender, with a black beard and mustache. He resembled a "romantic art student" with dark, windblown hair. Someone in the party suddenly realized that the Batum

Okhrana had not only surrounded the house but had also placed informers in the basement. Soso, smoking a "papirosa" and talking with Kandelaki, was unperturbed. He calmly remarked, "It's nothing," and continued smoking. Shortly thereafter the police charged into the room and arrested the Darakhvelidze brothers, Kandelaki, and Soso.[201]

Soso's casual attitude ("It's nothing") seems to indicate that he was expecting the Okhrana to arrest him and was obviously unworried, and it follows that the Okhrana had probably assured him preferential treatment. The provision of police protection—and it was no less than that—in turn would prove that he had been of great service to the Okhrana. By helping to instigate the ill-fated workers' demonstration during March, he had smoked out for the Okhrana the Batum revolutionary workers, most of whom were dead, wounded or in jail. Now, a few weeks later, when the Okhrana decided to round up the leaders still free in Batum, Soso was the finger-man. What other explanation is there for the sudden surrounding of the house where Kandelaki and Soso were visitors? Though the Batum police jailed Soso, he was never tried by a court of law and his prison and exile sentence was not only exceedingly mild but also significantly different from those persons arrested at about the same time.[202] There is also abundant evidence that he was about to be tried by a social-democratic workers' court which would have banished him from the town. Only the arrest by the Okhrana preserved his usefulness as an agent. As Zhordania had put it he was "lucky." [203]

Soso was imprisoned first in Batum and later in Kutais.[203a] After six weeks, on June 17, 1902, the police set up the first known file for him. It included full-face and profile photographs and the following details on the prisoner Dzhugashvili: "Height 2 arshins, 4½ vershoks [about 5 feet 4 inches]. Body medium. Age 23 [he was actually 22]. Second and third toes of the left foot fused. Appearance: ordinary. Hair: dark brown. Beard and mustache: brown. Nose straight and long. Forehead straight and low. Face long, swarthy and pockmarked." The police called him Riaboi, "the Pockmarked One." [204]

The earliest surviving police description of Iosif Vissarionovich

Dzhugashvili was signed by Colonel Sergei Petrovich Shabelsky, who was born on May 24, 1860. After an excellent military education he had entered the élite Separate Corps of Gendarmes in 1898, serving as a staff officer until 1899 in the St. Petersburg Department of Police Headquarters, which included some of the best security-intelligence officers in the force. After a tour of duty with the St. Petersburg police he was posted to Grodnensk as assistant to the Chief of the Gendarme Administration. He was ordered to Batum in March, 1902, just before Soso's first arrest. Shabelsky's fate is unknown.[205] What at first glance appears to be Colonel Shabelsky's standard police record of Stalin's vital statistics and physical characteristics upon careful examination becomes extraordinarily important.

As we have seen, many years later Stalin told his sister-in-law, Anna Allilueva, that he had been rejected for military service when he was in exile in 1916 because of an arm that had been injured in childhood, the effects of which remained forever.[206] Although there are other statements that confirm the shortness of Soso's left arm, it is important to fix in mind Allilueva's emphasis from his own recollections that the arm was injured during childhood. Anna Allilueva's book, published in 1946, was abruptly withdrawn from circulation in 1947. What prompted this decision? As the only account that attempted to explain his shortened left arm, it must have offended the dictator. In 1890 the Frenchman Alphonse Bertillon had devised a system of criminal identification that involved bodily measurements and photographs. By the turn of the century it enjoyed wide use throughout Europe, including Russia. Colonel Shabelsky and his staff had been schooled in the Bertillon anthropometrical system, as his report on Stalin shows: his height, build, and most other distinguishing characteristics were dutifully recorded. However, Stalin's outstanding physical defect, his shortened left arm, was ignored. "Bertillonage," as the method was known, required the "measurement of the length of the arms"; this was accomplished by placing the arrested person, arms horizontally outstretched, flush against a chart divided metrically. The Department of Police considered arm measurements second only to height in Bertillonage. Forms in use by the various Gendarme Administrations at the time of Stalin's first arrest include a section precisely for this calculation. But the Okhrana not only failed to record the shortness of Soso's arm upon his initial arrest, it was ignored on several more subsequent arrests, when it should have been officially noted. If Soso was the great revolutionary he claimed to be, or if he was simply a minor figure in the revolutionary and criminal underworld, the Okhrana would have at some point recognized the infirm left arm. The idea that Stalin's shortened left arm was unnoticed because the police failed to make him undress is doubtful.[207] If his fused toes were noted, his arms certainly could have been. Moreover, the Bertillon system did not require disrobing. Thus there was an unaccountable departure from routine Okhrana procedure, a mistake thereafter never rectified, nor was there a reason given for this omission in Stalin's original police dossier. On the basis of Department of Police operational methodology, Koba's arrest in the early hours of April 5, 1902 went somewhat as follows: he was taken to the Batum prison, placed in a cell and, within a few days, subjected to the usual police interrogation and then Bertillonage.[208] At that point, someone in the Batum Gendarme Administration decided not to include his arm deformity in the official police physical profile. Why? A plausible reason is that it would have alerted future police units in and out of the empire and made it easier than usual to identify and apprehend him. For some reason, the Okhrana did not wish this to happen.

Soso proved he was to be a most unusual prisoner only a short time after his incarceration. On Wednesday, April 21st, visitors' day, he tossed through the bars of his cell two notes that unidentified persons retrieved in the prison outer courtyard. Contradictory accounts about this incident appear in Soviet literature. One version makes the point that the notes were picked up by Koba's friends, so-called "couriers," who passed the information on to the people addressed, Iremashvili and Elisabedashvili. Another says they were retrieved by prison guards and turned over to gendarme Captain Georgy Davidovich Dzhakeli, who concluded from their

contents that "the author was Dzhugashvili." The one to Iremashvili, then a schoolteacher in Gori (over one hundred and sixty-
five miles away), reported that "Soso Dzhugashvili had been arrested and to inform his mother at once. In case a gendarme should
ask her 'When did thy son leave Gori?' she was to say 'All summer
and winter he was here—until March fifteenth [1902].' " [209] The
other note, to be delivered to Elisabedashvili, a teacher and social
democrat in Tiflis, indicated that he should persevere in his revolutionary work regardless of the recent bloody reverses.

Iremashvili remembers that a few days later two strangers appeared at his home requesting that he testify to Soso's presence in
Gori during the bloodshed in Batum. He felt sure that Soso, still a
subject of investigation by the police for his role in the Batum demonstration, needed him to provide an alibi:

Just after May 1, 1902, two men came to my home in Gori late at
night and, by a soft tapping, demanded I let them in. Their frightened
faces proved they had come on a secret mission. "We are workers at
the Mantashev petroleum factory in Batum [and] Koba sent you this
note. The police are searching for the leader of the recent bloody
maevka [in Batum]. If the police come to you, you must say he was
in Gori. He will be depending on your testimony."

Then, "Koba led the demonstration against the police who fired at
the demonstrators, who [in turn] fought back with cobblestones. There
are many dead, and more wounded, on both sides. The Batum jails
are full."

Iremashvili recalls, "I gave the messengers my assurance that I
would do as Koba wished." [210]

Trotsky believes this incident proved the authenticity of Iremashvili's recollections concerning Stalin:

Dzhakeli immediately sent to the chief of the Tiflis gendarme administration to demand a search of Iremashvili's lodgings, to question
Dzhugashvili's mother and also to search and arrest Elisabedashvili
. . . The nature of one of the notes . . . is incontestable proof that
the author of the reminiscences to which we have already referred
more than once was actually on intimate terms with Koba. It is to him,

his childhood friend, that the man under arrest entrusts his instructions to his mother . . . The note dispels the last doubts concerning the credibility of his very valuable reminiscences, which are entirely ignored by Soviet historians.[211]

Koba's notes caused the arrest of Elisabedashvili, whom the Okhrana had failed to apprehend in the dragnets of 1901 and 1902.[212] Perhaps the persons who picked up the notes were also Okhrana messengers.

Since the notes fell into Okhrana hands at about the same time they reached the intended recipients, there is an inescapable conclusion that Soso and the police were in collusion in this operation. If the couriers were police agents, the picture is clear: they were in the courtyard to receive messages that compromised Elisabedashvili and supplied a cover story for Koba at the forthcoming trial concerning the Batum demonstration.

The unique implications inherent in the note-tossing episode have sadly been ignored. Trotsky alone of Stalin's biographers was moved to comment that "one cannot help pausing with amazement at the carelessness with which Koba subjected two of his comrades to danger." He failed to pursue the matter, however, choosing rather to describe it as an act to deceive the gendarmes and explaining that "the deception of gendarmes was a rule in that very serious game which was called revolutionary conspiracy." [213] Predictably, the incident failed to deceive anyone except certain of Stalin's biographers and perhaps some revolutionaries in the Caucasus area; otherwise it was transparent to all. For we know that the notes caused the arrest of Elisabedashvili and police interrogation of Koba's mother and his friend Iremashvili.

After his first arrest Koba spent almost a year and a half in prison, first in Batum until April 19, 1903, and then in Kutais. Because tsarist authorities normally required a year for the investigation of an alleged political offense, his stay at Kutais neatly fitted that time limit. A large part of his twenty-third and twenty-fourth years was behind bars.

In 1937 Lavrenty Beria put together *The 1902 Batum Demonstration* to glorify Stalin. Elisabedashvili, strikingly handsome, with a visage of character and strength, whom Soso had caused to be arrested, wrote an adulatory article for it about his erstwhile comrade. Perhaps it was another of Stalin's cruel jokes that compelled Elisabedashvili to praise the very person who had removed him from the Georgian revolutionary scene. At any rate, Elisabedashvili's essay includes a photograph of secret Cell No. 6 of the Batum prison in which Koba was incarcerated, showing a nondescript door made of wood or iron, not at all of the maximum security type. The usual small sliding window is apparent and a large painted numeral "6" alongside a smaller, scrawled "6" (perhaps put there for the painter?) He related that Soso "in prison did not forget for one minute about work: he issued orders and directions. From the Batum prison he had sent a letter to Tbilisi, in which he had proposed that I go to work in Batum. The letter was intercepted by the gendarmes, and after extended surveillance and searches I was arrested and sent to the Batum prison." [214]

Accompanied by a gendarme guard, Koba was exercising as Elisabedashvili was taken to prison. "When he saw me," [Elisabedashvili continued,] "Stalin rushed to his cell and, passing me, whispered: 'You don't know me . . .' This was a signal that I was to answer all questions of the gendarmes with silence, which I did." He was escorted to Captain Dzhakeli, who had investigated the note-tossing incident. Dzhakeli asked him if he knew Soso, if he had been in Batum, and if he could identify marxists there. "To all these I answered '*nyet*'," Elisabedashvili wrote. Then Dzhakeli wanted to know why the so-called marxists such as Chkheidze and Ramishvili had been so peaceful and yet with the appearance of Dzhugashvili the workers began to strike and were shot down during the recent demonstration. Elisabedashvili failed to record his response to this question.[215]

Elisabedashvili was only ten days in the Batum prison, during which time Soso was in Cell No. 1 (a few pages earlier it was No. 6) with an informer posing as worker, whom Soso exposed and had banished. How we are not told. Elisabedashvili merely comments: "I was a witness to comrade Stalin's freeing himself from this villainous wretch." Soso was directing strikes and protecting the Batum organization of revolutionaries from *agents provoca-teurs*—all from either Cell 6 or 1 in prison, according to Elisabe-dashvili.

During his stay in the Batum and Kutais prisons comrade Stalin not only conducted massive political-educational work among the in-carcerated comrades, but he also continued to lead with unflagging energy all the work of the social-democratic organization of Batum and all Georgia.[216]

Words like "massive" and "unflagging" give away the ghostly edi-torial hand of a Party hack.

An article, "Comrade Stalin in the Batum Prison," written by Varlam Kalandadze, an authentic old Georgian revolutionary, claims that the author met Soso for the first time in an isolated cell, where Soso "wrote letters all day long maintaining communications with the Batum organizations and comrades," in all of which he displayed his outstanding conspiratorial talents.[217] Soviet accounts indicate that he established an orderly routine in his prison life, arising early, exercising, and studying German and economic litera-ture. "He never rested, but he was never fatigued. He loved to share with his comrades his impressions of books he had just read, criticizing their contents and authors." He "organized a prisoners' demonstration in the prison against the Bishop of Georgia. The prison administration increased its repressions. Comrade Stalin continued to lead the Georgian revolutionary movement." [218] No one has explained how this was possible from an isolated cell.

A faded photograph showing indistinct details of the Batum prison has survived. The jail resembles a stockade in the Western United States before the turn of the century. A guard tower over-looks a one-story, sprawling wooden building, unlike the gray stone fortress-like prisons in other parts of Russia. Prisons varied in their architecture and regimes throughout the Empire in those days, but they were more often than not humane, a condition made difficult by provocatory attitudes and actions on the part of political prison-ers. Regardless of what Stalin's sycophants or forced witnesses have to say about him, he appears to have been a docile, if not a model, prisoner in Batum. In fact, he seems to have been almost happy.

Though Stalin had been arrested because of his alleged role in the bloody Batum demonstration, he was not indicted nor was he tried. His case was handled by the police officers of the Batum Okhrana as an administrative matter. Trotsky wondered why. He wrote: "It is surprising that the records of Koba's police examinations pertaining to that first arrest, as well as all the records pertaining to his subsequent arrests, have not yet been published. In April, 1902, Koba attempted to establish his alibi by a ruse for which others were obliged to suffer. It may be supposed that on other occasions as well he relied more on his own cunning than on the standard behavior obligatory for all. Consequently, the entire series of his police depositions present not a 'heroic' record. That is the only possible explanation why the records of Stalin's police examinations are still unpublished." Thus Trotsky led himself into a polemical trap. Through this rationalization there is, of course, another explanation for the police reports not having been published; namely, that the reports would have implicated Soso in the very police apparatus he was supposed to have been fighting.

Soso, in good health, was transferred on April 19, 1903 to the Kutais provincial prison. Following the adjudication of his case at the beginning of November, he was sent back to Batum, from which at the end of November he began the journey to Irkutsk Province in Siberia. To most political figures, a prison term is remembered in great detail and often the subject of memorable literature. It is a time to think and a time to plan future books, among other things. But neither diaries nor essays nor letters dating from the era of the Batum and Kutais prisons exist. Soso chose to ignore this period of his life.

5 | SIBERIAN EXILE AND ESCAPE: A POLICE RUSE

Stalin learned while he was a prisoner at Kutais in the autumn of 1903 that he was to be exiled. Soviet sources have provided a "secret" order from the Main Prison Administration of the Imperial Ministry of Justice dated August 17, 1903, ordering him administratively deported for a state crime to eastern Siberia for three years under open police surveillance.[219] Normally a person indicted and convicted of a "state crime" would have been tried by a court. However, in Koba's case such procedure would have required testimony and witnesses, something the Okhrana would have been reluctant to allow for anyone whose affiliation with them might be exposed. In early November Koba was apparently transferred back to the prison at Batum, before starting the long trek to the small settlement of Novaya Uda near Lake Baikal in Irkutsk province, almost four thousand miles away from Georgia. Earlier that year—in March, 1903—twenty-one persons had been indicted and tried for their parts in the Batum events a year before; neither the indictment nor the trial proceedings mentioned Stalin,[220] and thus he was neither tried nor sentenced by a court of law.

A short but highly significant period of Koba's life began with his exile from Batum in the "autumn of 1903," as most of his Soviet biographers loosely record it. Some sources specifically indicate that he was still in Batum prison until the end of November; the *Life of Stalin, a Symposium* (1930) notes that he was imprisoned in Batum until the very end of 1903 before proceeding to exile;[221] and as late as 1937 Stalin himself in an *Izvestia* article claimed that he had been in prison in Batum until the "end of 1903."[222] When all sources are evaluated, it is obvious that he departed from Batum no earlier than December of 1903, proceeding northward by way of the cities of Novorossiisk, Rostov, Tsaritsyn, and Samara, and thence across the Trans-Siberian railway "by stages" (*po etapu*), as the movement of prisoners was called.[223] This meant that at various points along the exile route to Siberia the "convoy" would halt, sometimes for days or weeks, to await and combine with another group of political exiles moving north and eastward. These stop-overs and the extraordinarily severe Siberian winter of 1903-1904, with the trains averaging less than fifteen miles per hour, slowed the progress of the exile parties considerably.[224] One author who traveled the Trans-Siberian route at the time tells of a young Siberian horseman who challenged "our train" to a race outside Chelyabinsk. "That he won amid the plaudits of us all does not prove so much the swiftness of his horses as the slowness of our train. Fifteen miles an hour was its top speed." [225] At the end of the rail spur-line was the prison village of Aleksandrovsky Tsentral. The exiles still required weeks to reach their final destination from this central point.[226]

Koba could not possibly have arrived at Novaya Uda, his place of exile, before late January, 1904, which at first glance appears to be a bit of trivia. However, some twenty years later, as we hear Stalin addressing a memorial meeting of Kremlin Military Academy cadets a week after Lenin's death, in 1924, it becomes unusually important. In a rather disjointed speech he declared:

I first became acquainted with Lenin in 1903. True, it was not a personal acquaintance; it was made by correspondence. But it left an indelible impression upon me, one which has never left me throughout all my work in the Party. I was an exile in Siberia at the time. My knowledge of Lenin's revolutionary activities since the end of the nineties, and especially after 1901, after the appearance of *Iskra*, had convinced me that in Lenin we had a man of extraordinary caliber. I did not regard him as a mere leader of the Party, but as its actual founder. . . . When I compared him with the other leaders of our Party, it seemed to me that he was head and shoulders above his colleagues, a mountain eagle who knew no fear in the struggle and who led the Party boldly forward along unexplored paths. . . . This impression took such a deep hold on me that I felt impelled to write to a close friend of mine who was living as a political exile abroad, requesting him to give me his opinion. Some time later, when I was already in exile in Siberia—this was at the end of 1903—I received an enthusiastic letter from my friend and a simple but profoundly expressive letter from Lenin to whom, it appeared, my friend had shown my letter. Lenin's note was comparatively short, but it contained a bold and fearless criticism of the practical work of our Party, and a remarkably clear and concise account of the entire plan of work of the Party in the immediate future. . . . This simple and bold letter strengthened my opinion that Lenin was the mountain eagle of our Party. I cannot forgive myself for having, from the habit of an old underground worker, consigned this letter of Lenin's, like many other letters, to the flames. My acquaintance with Lenin dates from that time.[227]

Twice in a few paragraphs Stalin points out that he was in Siberian exile before the end of 1903, leaving no doubt that he considered it important to underscore this date. Yet, under the best of circumstances, two months at a minimum were necessary for prisoner convoys to make the four-thousand-mile journey from Georgia to Irkutsk "by stages." Furthermore, an additional several weeks of travel by sleigh faced him before he arrived at the village of Novaya Uda. Stalin's official biographers all agree that he left Batum in the middle or latter part of November, 1903, which meant that he arrived in exile not in 1903 but in the latter part of January, 1904. How did Stalin's unusually good memory fail him? How was it possible to remember the contents and the time of receipt of Lenin's "note" and not remember the name of the "close friend"? Finally, no record of the exchange of correspondence between the twenty-four-year-old Soso and Lenin, "the mountain eagle," exists in Department of Police files, in Lenin's memorabilia, or in Stalin's *Collected Works.*[228] This is understandable. Lenin, residing in Switzerland, in July and August attended the Second Party Congress, first at Brussels, later at London. Engaged in a bitter internecine party struggle, it is doubtful that he knew Koba's name let alone his whereabouts. Stalin's explanation that he had burned Lenin's letter "from the habit of an old underground worker" is recognizable chicanery: an old underground worker would never have sent the letter in the first instance. In short, Stalin was dissimulating. He did not send Lenin a letter or receive one from him. Nor was he in Siberian exile at the end of 1903. He was elsewhere.

From the time of his "exile" to Siberia until his return to Batum, we know nothing official about him. No old revolutionaries emerge from the grave to hail his courageous and conspiratorial activities, although he was one of sixteen revolutionaries listed in the deportation decree.[229] Among them were Silvester Dzhibladze, who thoroughly distrusted Stalin; Ipolit Franchesky, a veteran Socialist Democrat; and Lenin's old friend, Victor Kurnatovsky. They had been arrested in Tiflis and imprisoned in Tiflis' Metekh prison-fortress and then deported "by stages" on August 4, 1903 for Siberia. But they had first been transferred to Batum prison. Not one of them wrote about Koba. He was supposedly in the Kutais jail. In the autumn of 1903 after more than two months en route, the party of prisoners, which filled several railway cars, arrived in Aleksandrovsky Tsentral, where they remained until the end of November. Kurnatovsky remembers that another two months or more were required to reach his place of exile in the Yakut region. According to one Stalinist account, Koba should have been in Aleksandrovsky Tsentral with Kurnatovsky and the other Georgian exiles.[230] None of them mentioned him in numerous memoirs.[231] Nor is there the usual plethora of adulatory articles about his first deportation to Siberia. Only one *Pravda* article, entitled "In Novaya Uda," appeared on December 25, 1939, to describe the tiny village at the time of his 1903 exile.[232] Two persons remembered that Koba stayed in a "little house" (*domik*) that "unfortunately has not been preserved." It belonged to the peasant-woman Martha Ivanovna Litvintseva. D. P. Litvintsev, a "close relative" of Martha's (incidentally a party member and minor official at that time), recalled that the *"babushka"* Martha loved him very much. Otherwise, Koba reputedly read extensively by candlelight. This is as contrived as a 1940 letter written from Novaya Uda by a few communist "young pioneer" school children praising Soso for escaping the hated gendarmes on January 5, 1904.[233] Both stories, intended to support his own account of exile and escape, are transparently artificial.

One searches for a straightforward record of this period in Soso's life, but, alas, none exists. Official Soviet accounts and Stalin's own autobiographical *Collected Works* maintain that he escaped from Siberia on January 5, 1904—some three weeks before he could possibly have arrived in Novaya Uda.[234] If this is difficult to understand, one is infinitely more confused by the memoirs of seemingly honest revolutionaries who suggest that Soso was back in Georgia not in January, 1904, but in December, 1903. For example, Sergei (Sergo) Yakovlevich Alliluev, his future father-in-law, recalled that he had gone from Baku to Mikho Bochoridze's home in Tiflis to obtain typesettings for an underground printing press. He implies this was "at the end of 1903." [235] Mikho was not at home:

His aunt, Babe, met me. "Mikho will be back right away," I suddenly heard a male voice exclaim. I looked around. From the next room a young man of some twenty-three to twenty-four years of age approached me. The young man, Soso Dzhugashvili, said: "Well, tell me the good news." He had escaped not long before from the village of Novaya Uda in eastern Siberia, where he had been exiled for three years. He had tried to get away a few days after his arrival but he had no warm clothing. With frostbitten face and ears, he turned back. Refusing to abandon his idea, he was able to escape on January 5.

Anna Allilueva essentially repeated her father's story in her book published in 1946. She pointedly adds that her father met Stalin in Tiflis at "the beginning of January 1904." [236] The contradictions in these accounts are apparent. How could Stalin have escaped from Siberia on January 5th and met Sergo at the beginning of the same month? There is an unconfirmed report that he attempted to flee from Siberia on Christmas Eve, 1903 (which would have been January 6, 1904), while his guard was in an alcoholic stupor. Armed with a hunting rifle obtained from a grocer in Novaya Uda, Koba was on his way to the town of Makarovka when he ran into at least a dozen wolves, starved because of the unusual severity of the winter. After being forced back to his exile village by the wolves, he made another attempt to escape some two weeks later on a sledge.[237]

It is not easy to cut through the confusion enveloping Koba's "return" to Transcaucasia from Siberian exile. His *Collected Works* claims he escaped "from his place of exile" on January 5 and arrived in Tiflis during February.[238] On the other hand, Sergo Alliluev's daughter, Anna, distinctly remembered Koba's statement that he had returned to Batum rather than Tiflis.[239] Delbars, a French biographer, has him attempting to escape about January 16, 1904 which, if successful, would have meant Koba could conceivably have reached the Transcaucasus in late February.[240] Yaroslavsky wrote in 1940 that Koba escaped from exile on January 5, 1904 and went "first to Batum and later to Tiflis".[241] Similarly, Beria also claims that he escaped on January 5, 1904 and went "first to Batum and later to Tiflis."[242] Finally, the Department of Police reproduced a report from the Chief of the Tiflis Province Gendarme Administration dated March 14, 1911 asserting that "Dzhugashvili escaped from his place of settlement (in the Balagansk section of Irkutsk province) on January 5, 1904 and was on the wanted-list according to a circular of the Department of Police No. 5500 of May 1, 1904." [243] Perhaps the most important conclusion to be drawn from these differing accounts is that they reflect an uncertainty about what actually happened. That Stalin, Beria and the Department of Police should agree regarding the date of the "escape" arouses suspicion in the face of the other versions.

By the time Sergo's and Anna's recollections saw the light of day in the 1940's, Nadezhda Allilueva, Stalin's second wife, had mysteriously died some years before. Though they wrote under the Stalinist censorship reflected in their narratives, the date of Stalin's reappearance in Georgia must have been fixed in their minds by recalling that it was shortly before or after New Year's Day. It is possible, moreover, that they were attempting to remind history that the Stalin and Beria assertions were untrue. At any rate their recollections not only seem devoid of any reason for falsity but reinforce the idea that Koba was never sent to Siberia in 1903.

Henri Barbusse, Stalin's unofficially commissioned biographer, writes that before Koba escaped, constant overwork and hardship had caused illness among the exiles and Koba had contracted tuberculosis.

He was on open steppes, when suddenly that terrible icy blizzard known as the "purga" or "buran" started to blow. The only means people have of sheltering from it is to lie down and dig themselves into the snow. But Koba kept his course, which was along a frozen river. It took him hours to walk the couple of miles that separated him from the nearest hut. When at last he crossed the threshold, people took him for a ghost: he was nothing but an icicle from head to foot. They thawed him out, and he collapsed and slept for eighteen consecutive hours. As a result of his adventure, his tuberculosis disappeared forever. Siberia is like that: if it does not kill consumptives, it cures them permanently.[244]

This is an unconvincing invention. For a tuberculosis sufferer to walk even two miles in the purga would require six to eight hours, more than sufficient exposure to kill even a healthy young Georgian. It is well known that the purga renders vision extraordinarily difficult, if not impossible, and the people caught in them more often than not go in circles until they die, unless they sensibly try to dig themselves into the snow for the duration of the blizzard.

The three anecdotes, one of doubtful origin, another told to Alliluyeva soon after his "escape," and the last to Barbusse in the nineteen-thirties, are important, representing as they do Stalin's only published recollections of the 1903 "exile," when he was supposedly out of Georgia for the first time. More significantly, these are noteworthy examples of a *legenda* (legend), as the Okhrana called the cover story supplied to its agents. What was Koba to tell about his exile and escape after his "return" to Batum and, later, Tiflis? Anecdotes concerning fellow revolutionaries and the humdrum Siberian winter life, the main features of which were endless conversations with other political exiles, required names of comrades, acquaintances, or friends. And because none of the Georgian revolutionaries exiled with Soso recalled in print having seen or heard of him en route to—or indeed in—Novaya Uda, stories were fabricated to provide color and verisimilitude for the "exile and escape" legend.

Had Koba spent any time in Novaya Uda, had he made the long trip to Siberia, or escaped, traveling back to the Caucasus, some revolutionary exile would have seen him, chatted with him, or assisted him. No one did for the simplest of reasons: he saw Siberia in 1903-1904 only through the eyes of his police mentors and superiors, who supplied him with an additional revolutionary credential, Siberian "exile and escape," before dispatching him on missions that would provide the Okhrana with more and more valuable information first on the insurrectionary and revolutionary milieu in the Caucasus, then in Great Russia, and eventually in Europe. He was not in Siberia but hiding out under Okhrana protection in European Russia or in the Caucasus. We may never know precisely where.

It is demonstrably apparent that, according to the dates of the Soviet record, Stalin could not have arrived in exile in time to escape. But it is nonetheless interesting to see how in later life the dictator presented the "escape" to various biographers and how he would have us believe he managed to overcome the obstacles in returning to the Caucasus. And there were numerous obstacles. First of all, he differed vastly in appearance from the Siberians among whom he presumably would have spent his Novaya Uda exile. A short, swarthy, pockmarked, dark-haired Georgian was in sharp contrast to the majority of taller, fair *Sibiriaki* (Siberians) who had settled the Irkutsk area years before his arrival in Novaya Uda. Lado Ketskhoveli provides an example. He had arrived in Samara some months before and was to report to a "safe house" (a conspiratorial apartment) at four o'clock on a given day. The police discovered the apartment on the night of his arrival, Ketskhoveli, whose whereabouts were unknown, had to be warned, and someone gave his description to several revolutionary underground workers, one of whom found him and delivered the vital message. Later, nervously remembering the incident, Ketskhoveli remarked, "All the Russian cities are such that we Southerners [he referred to people from the Caucasus] are spotted right away." [245]

Not only Soso's physical appearance militated against easy and quick escape. He was in strange surroundings in bitterly low temperatures, many miles from a railroad, knowing neither the customs nor the lay of the land, without friends or acquaintances, when, according to Soviet biographers, he made contacts for transportation back to the Caucasus. He needed money. Moreover, at his deadly peril he had to get past the Gendarmerie Railway Administration points, where travel and identification documents were closely scrutinized, particularly those of political exiles. Police detachments were on the lookout for escaped revolutionaries, about whom all-points bulletins had been circulated. Hundreds of professional security personnel had been trained to apprehend escaped prisoners. If Soso had traveled to the Tiflis-Batum area from Siberia, he would have passed at least twenty-nine Department of Police checkpoints staffed by some five hundred professional security officers and enlisted men. It is not surprising that none of them apprehended him because, of course, he did not encounter them. It is worth while to consider, in this regard, a pro-Soviet account of 1942 undoubtedly inspired by Stalin or his lieutenants:

> In January of 1904 Stalin received, through the usual tortuous avenues, a small package containing money and forged passport, the latter being rendered necessary by the existing laws compelling all citizens to produce their papers even when crossing from one province to another. Within six weeks we find him at the house of a comrade in St. Petersburg using the name Ivanovich gathering information on events which had occurred during his absence and collecting materials for the furtherance of those schemes he had evolved among the tundra of Novaya Uda.
>
> A month later he was back in his old haunts of Tiflis picking up the threads of his former work.[246]

The difficulty of Soso's "escape" is confirmed in this narrative, which is totally incorrect when it touches on Stalin's presence in St. Petersburg and the time necessary for travel. True, all citizens were obliged to produce their vital documents when crossing a provincial border. Koba did need a forged passport and money to escape. However, he could only receive letters "through the usual tortuous avenues" by way of the local gendarmerie, who were not kindly disposed to permit a political prisoner to obtain forged passports through postal channels. However, with no recorded difficulty from the omnipresent tsarist police, with no observable troubles from the elements or from people, Soso made his way back to Batum and Tiflis—the very area where his first arrest occurred, the *locus* of his police dossier—and into the "paws" (as the revolutionaries described them) of a dozen or more professional intelligence-security officers of the Batum Gendarme Administration.

An authentic Special Section circular of the Tsarist Department of Police dated March 31, 1911 (classified *"sovershenno sekretno"* —"top secret") states that on "January 5, 1904, Dzhugashvili escaped from his place of settlement. . . ." [247] This circular, sent to the Paris Chief of the Russian Foreign Intelligence Agency, was signed by Vice-Director of the Department of Police Vissarionov and by the Chief of the Special Section, Colonel Eremin, two of the top five intelligence officers in the tsarist Department of Police at that time. We shall have occasion to meet Director Vissarionov and Colonel Eremin later. For the moment, it should be noted that they had long been involved in double-agent cases; that is, the penetration of revolutionary organizations by the use of *agents provocateurs*. It is also important that the first tsarist Department of Police Special Section circular reporting Stalin's "escape" is dated seven years after the ostensible fact. Soviet sources, almost forty years later, belatedly "confirm" this befuddling event.

What the Department of Police hoped to prove, however, was that Stalin had spent months in Siberian exile and escaped by reason of his conspiratorial talents, thus qualifying him for his next assignment in the revolutionary milieu. Building up Koba's reputation as a revolutionary who could hoodwink and outwit the Okhrana, surrounding him with an aura of heroism—something always desirable for an agent—is discernible in this operation. What the Stalinist court historians many years later desired to prove was that Stalin was a true revolutionary, having been arrested, imprisoned, and exiled to Siberia, from which he had miraculously escaped. A curious wedding of Department of Police and

Stalinist historiography had thus occurred with mutually compatible objectives.

Stalin's own *Collected Works* has him arriving in Tiflis in February after his January 5, 1904 escape, ignoring his previous sojourn in Batum.[248] In *The Life of Stalin, a Symposium* of 1930, we learn that "a month after arriving at his destination [January, 1904] Stalin escaped from exile, returned to Tiflis, and began to work as a member of the Trans-Caucasian organization then known as the Trans-Caucasian Unity Committee."[249] On the other hand, we have shown that Beria, in his *History of the Bolshevik Movement in the Transcaucasus,* wrote that Stalin went first to Batum and later to Tiflis.[250] Trotsky declared that Stalin's return from exile directly to Transcaucasia "cannot help but evoke amazement," adding that Stalin made the formidable trip from Novaya Uda, many miles north of Irkutsk through the Urals, in about a week, although he had earlier explained that the journey to his place of exile required nearly three months.[251] Common sense shows that a trip of about four thousand miles could not be accomplished in less than a week during 1903-1904 conditions. Delbars, a pro-Stalin biographer, wrote this account:

> On the eve of the Day of Kings—12th Night—he escaped once more, but not on foot. The *ouriadnik* [guard] was lying in a drunken sleep when a sledge carrying Koba—now David Nijeredze—set off. On February 1, 1904, Stalin reached Tiflis [and] went to the house of Rosenfeld [Kamenev].[252]

According to Natalia Kirtadze, he went to her home, in Batum, after his so-called escape from Siberia. Was she in charge of a Department of Police "safe house" [*konspirativnaya kvartira*]? We never find her in revolutionary literature again; she vanishes, like poor Alexander Novikov, who excelled at the Tiflis Theological Seminary, and many others in Stalin's life who appear and disappear like comets. Yaroslavsky, writing in 1940, relates:

> In the spring of 1904 Comrade Stalin escaped from his place of exile in Irkutsk and returned to Batum, but was very soon obliged to

leave that city. This is what Natalia Kirtadze says in her reminiscences of Stalin's return from exile:

One night in the early part of 1904, there was a knock at my door: It was already past midnight.

"Who's there?" I called.

"It's me, let me in!"

"Who are you?"

"It's me, Soso."

It seemed so incredible that I would not open the door until he had given the password: Long live a thousand times!

I asked him how he came to be in Batum.

"I escaped," Soso replied.

Soon after, he left for Tiflis, where he wrote to us several times. Comrade Stalin was then directing the activities of the Caucasian Federal Committee.

In the spring of 1904, Soso again returned to Batum. During this stay he conducted several debates with the Mensheviks in the house of Iliko Sharashidze in Bartzkhana.[253]

Shortly after Stalin "returned" to Batum and Tiflis in 1904, he called on another revolutionary, Razden Arsenidze, a member of the city social democratic committee. Arsenidze, about whom we will hear more, remembered that on this occasion Koba was a "young man, lean and bony, his face pallidly brown and cratered with smallpox, with lively and crafty eyes, eager, free and easy, appearing completely self sufficient." [254] About this time Koba also sought out Lev Borisovich Kamenev (Rosenfeld), supposedly for help.

Kamenev was younger than Stalin and only twenty-one at this time. He had graduated in 1901 from the Tiflis gymnasium, where he had been an active socialist. His petition to Bogolepov, the Imperial Minister of Public Instruction, received favorable attention and he was accepted in the Moscow University of Jurisprudence. Continual agitation there plunged him into trouble. He spent time in the Moscow's Butyrka and Taganka prisons. Banished as a sort of exile to Tiflis under police surveillance, he had instructed circles of railroaders and shoemakers until late 1902, when he met Lenin in Paris and became an Iskraite, or Leninist disciple. Also in Paris he became acquainted with Trotsky's sister, Olga, whom he later married. Lenin dispatched Kamenev from Geneva to Tiflis as a bolshevik organizer when the Second Congress of the party ended its business. Then, after being arrested and spending five months in prison in Moscow, Kamenev returned to Tiflis and from there went to London as a delegate to the Third Party Congress. He met Koba for the first time shortly after he "reappeared" in Tiflis. (Soso now preferred to be called Koba.) Koba seemed concerned—and properly so within the terms of his cover story—that he might be picked up by the police. Through Kamenev's good graces, he hid out in the apartment of a worker, Morochkov. A few days later, the Tiflis police arrested Kamenev, removing him to Moscow.

The Stalin-Kamenev relationship was to be a tortuous one. During World War I they were to find themselves together in Siberian exile from which they returned on the same train to Petrograd in 1917. In March 1917 Kamenev and Stalin were to be co-editors (with Muranov) of *Pravda* and in August of that year, when Kamenev was accused of having been an agent of the Okhrana, Stalin, appointed by the Bolshevik central committee to investigate the charge, would fervidly defend Kamenev against the allegations. While almost anything was possible in regard to police-revolutionary interrelationships in the decades preceding 1917, there is no reason to believe Kamenev was affiliated with the Okhrana. Stalin's ardent defense of Kamenev in 1917 probably originated in his feeling that if a similar charge were leveled against him, Kamenev might well rise to his defense. The fate of this person who befriended Koba after his presumable "escape" from Siberia was to be shot by his order in 1936.

"Official information about Koba's activities in 1904 is exceedingly sketchy and unreliable," Trotsky wrote, an assertion confirmed by the paucity of data in Soviet biographies.[255] The *Collected Works* includes ten entries for all of 1904.[256] After citing January 5th as the date for his escape from exile, it claims that he arrived in Tiflis in February to direct the work of the Caucasian Union Committee of the R. S. D. R. P., drafting "the programmatic document entitled 'Credo,' dealing with the disagreements within the Party and with the organizational tasks of the Party." Then we encounter another of those frequent gaps, this one of three months, in his life. The next entry, dated simply "June," has him arriving in Baku, "where, on the instructions of the Caucasian Union Committee," he dissolved the menshevik committee and formed "a new, Bolshevik committee." Dated "Summer," the next item states that he toured "the most important districts of Transcaucasia," debating "with Mensheviks, Federalists, Anarchists and others," and in Kutais he formed "a Bolshevik Imeretia-Mingrelian Committee." On September 1st *Proletarian Struggle,* No. 7, published his article "The Social-Democratic View of the National Question," and during "September-October, in connection with the disagreements within the Party, J. V. Stalin, while in Kutais, wrote letters to the Georgian bolsheviks abroad, expounding Lenin's views on the combination of socialism with the working-class movement." Then he arrived in Baku in November to lead a "campaign for the convocation of the Third Congress of the Party." Finally, in the latter part of December he led "a general strike of the Baku workers."

Even a cursory analysis of the *Collected Works* shows that the official record of Stalin's life in 1904 is dishonest. For example, several witnesses, among them Arsenidze and Yaroslavsky, insist that Stalin reappeared first in Batum, not in Tiflis, after his 1903 "exile." The *Collected Works* ignores this. The first item in the official account for 1904 to the effect that he escaped from exile on January 5, 1904 is, as we have seen, demonstrably false on the basis of testimony from Alliluev and his daughter. This also gives the lie to the second item in the chronology, that he had arrived in Tiflis during February, when actually he was there a month before. Nor can it be proved that Stalin wrote "Credo," the programmatic document "dealing with the disagreements within the Party" during the month of February. As a matter of fact, disagreements in the party in Transcaucasia did not exist in February, 1904. Filip E. Makharadze, the communist historian of the Caucasian revolutionary movement, later wrote that the Georgian social-democratic movement was then solidly unified without substantial intramural squabbles or fusions.[257] Thus, Stalin's "Credo," if he wrote such a document, dealt with fictitious party disagreements. According to the *Collected Works* he arrived in Baku in June on the instructions of the "Caucasian Union Committee." In Baku, he supposedly dissolved the menshevik committee and formed "a new, Bolshevik committee." The Caucasian Union Committee had, amusingly, instructed him to dissolve a nonexistent menshevik organization. Furthermore, the bolsheviks were unable to establish their own factional organization until November, 1904, and not in Baku but in Tiflis. The assertion in the *Collected Works* that he spent the summer of 1904 touring "the most important districts of Transcaucasia," debating "with Mensheviks, Federalists, Anarchists, and others," lacks evidence from any source. His creation of something called the "Bolshevik Imeretia-Mingrelian Committee" during the summer begs for supporting evidence.

The next two items in the *Collected Works* concern Stalin's writings. All we know about him officially from the end of the "Summer" entry until "November," 1904, is that he wrote—in *Proletarian Struggle,* No. 7—an article, "The Social-Democratic View of the National Question," and two letters to unidentified Georgian Bolsheviks abroad, expounding Lenin's views on the combination of socialism with the working-class movement, while he was in Kutais. The article in *Proletarian Struggle* is unsigned, and therefore its authorship is doubtful. The two letters "abroad," crudely edited, are of dubious authenticity. Finally, in November Stalin supposedly arrived in Baku to lead a "campaign for the convocation of the Third Congress of the Party." After the 1903 split in the party at the Second Congress in Brussels, and later in London, which occurred while Stalin was in "prison or exile," Lenin was eager to convene a Third Congress to resolve (naturally, in line with his own ideas) the difficulties that had arisen at London. Only in November, 1904, did the bolsheviks succeed in holding their conference—under the leadership of Kamenev, not Stalin, and in Tiflis, not Baku. Party histories prove that Stalin was not even a delegate to the conference.[258]

Officially, Koba's last act of 1904 was to lead the "general strike of the Baku workers from December 13-31." [259] However, in reality he arrived just as the strike of fifty thousand disaffected workers erupted. The strike, preceding as it did January 9, 1905 ("Bloody Sunday"), in St. Petersburg, caught all of Russia by surprise. And, oddly, the old revolutionary bolsheviks, Stopani and Enukidze, failed to mention Stalin in their memoirs about the Tiflis-Baku events at the end of 1904 and the beginning of 1905. Stopani, a member of the Baku strike committee, lists all the names of mensheviks and bolsheviks who led the Baku strike. And it was a joint venture. Stalin's name was missing. Nor does he appear under one of his numerous aliases. [260]

By 1946—forty-two years later—when Beria and Stalin developed the official version of Koba's life in 1904, it could not be clearer that dishonesty had been utilized to help pad the record. However, not without purpose was a massive deception operation mounted, and not without reason was posterity subjected to a historical farce and the excruciating chore of unscrambling from disparate bits and pieces of information the real life of Stalin during his twenty-fifth year. A torrent of questions, like hailstones, decends on the impartial observer. Where was Koba during 1904? What was he doing? How did he live? Where did he obtain money?

In the light of Stalin's failure to comment about his life in 1904, Trotsky may be forgiven a bit of unkindness as he claims that Koba's marital bliss consumed him and caused a sharp setback in his preoccupation with revolutionary activities. [261] Iremashvili tells us that he married Ekaterina (Keke) Svanidze, who came from the ancestral Dzhugashvili village of Didi-Lilo, sometime in 1903. [262] The wedding might have occurred while Koba was in jail, since marriage in a prison chapel was possible, but nuptial records, which are always prepared by a prison chaplain, have not survived. Some biographers, accepting the official version of Stalin's first arrest, exile, and escape, have faulted Iremashvili's memory, and have claimed the marriage took place in 1904. At any rate, we may be sure that by 1904 he was married and that he and his wife had been joined in holy matrimony by a priest, for Ekaterina was as pious as her mother-in-law (also Ekaterina), who was still living in Gori. Typically, Stalin said nothing in public about the marriage or about his first-born son, Yasha, who came from it.[262a]

We return to Iremashvili, because his recollections of the marriage are all we have. He claims that Koba and Keke were happy:

> It was impossible to discover in his home the equality of sexes that he seemingly favored. It was not in his character, however, to have equal rights with anyone. Because his wife could not measure up to him in intellect, regarding him as a demi-god, his marriage was happy. As a Georgian woman, reared in the almost holy tradition obliging a woman to serve, she tended to her husband with all her heart, spending her nights in fervent prayer while awaiting her Soso, busy at his meetings, praying that he might turn away from ideas displeasing to God and revert instead to a quiet home life of labor and contentment. So restless, this man could only find love in his own impoverished home, where only his wife, child, and mother were free of the scorn he poured out upon everyone else.[263]

Iremashvili, a later menshevik, always a gentle person, felt a certain agony about Stalin's vindictive attitude toward him. By 1906 the two Sosos, Iremashvili and Dzhugashvili, had broken off their earlier relationship, one that had embraced their boyhood and schooling. Iremashvili claimed, not without justification, that Koba's struggle was directed against his former friends. Referring to the overwhelmingly menshevik character of Georgian social-democracy he said:

> He attacked us at every meeting, savagely and unscrupulously discussing matters, trying to sow poison and hatred against us everywhere. That the overwhelming majority of Georgian Marxists remained with us only angered and enraged him.[264]

Keke died in 1907, probably four years after she had wed Stalin. Her demise left her infant son Yasha motherless, and her widower with a broken heart. Iremashvili overlooked Stalin's hatefulness toward him and, in the spirit of their earlier friendship, went to Keke's funeral in the Gori-Tiflis area. It was conducted in the Orthodox Church rites and attended by ornately attired priests. Ire-mashvili found Koba in a state of melancholy dejection:

He was extremely downcast, but he met me in the friendly manner as of old. This hard man's pallid face reflected the heartfelt anguish caused by the death of his faithful companion. At the cemetery gate, Koba firmly pressed my hand, pointed to the coffin and said: "Soso, this creature softened my stony heart. She is dead and with her my last warm feelings for all human beings have died." He placed his right hand over his heart: "It is all so desolate here inside, so unspeakably desolate!"

From the day he buried his wife, he indeed lost the last vestiges of human feeling. His heart filled with the unalterably malicious hatred which his cruel father had begun to engender in him while he was still a child. Ruthless with himself, he became ruthless with all people.[265]

Undoubtedly Iremashvili accurately reported Stalin's behavior on the occasion of Keke's funeral. However, our knowledge of his outspoken malice toward friends, his betrayal of revolutionary comrades, and his biting sarcasm toward everyone who disagreed with him in his youth makes one question Iremashvili's opinion in one respect; that Keke's death marked the *beginning* of Koba's ruthlessness toward "all people." We shall return to this later, but for the moment it is useful to recall Razden Arsenidze's description of Stalin when they first met in 1904, the year with which we are presently concerned, in Batum. His most striking characteristics, Arsenidze found, were crude sarcasm and unrestrained hatred toward people. "More than once," he writes in 1963, "I asked myself the question, what kind of person is this: a revolutionary, whose entire soul is devoted to the affairs of the people, or a dry, heartless, soulless mechanism in the form of a man whose aim is simply to destroy something completely and put something else in its place?" [266]

Iremashvili's sad story about the life and death of Keke Svanidze leaves no doubt that Stalin had a wife, probably pregnant, and a home during 1904. How strange that one finds nothing about them in official or unofficial Soviet literature. The location of the "impoverished" home is unknown, although it was probably near Tiflis and Gori. Stalin was too disliked and distrusted in Batum and too unknown in Baku to have settled in either place. In all likelihood he wanted to be near his mother. His wife shared this feeling, because her relatives were in the same area. Stalin needed money to support his wife and perhaps his mother and to own or rent a house. Yet, he had never been steadily employed and was not employed now.

It is surprising that not one of Stalin's biographers has come to grips with this question: where and how did Stalin obtain the necessary funds for minimal living expenses? The notable theme that runs through the memoirs and literature of revolutionaries of this period is one of continual effort to find and hold a job, to earn money, to provide for a growing family in the face of harassment by the omnipresent Department of Police and its Gendarme Administrations throughout the Empire. True enough, some revolutionaries with a winning way found wealthy patrons. However, Koba was cursed with an acerbic personality that offended nearly everyone. Party funds of the bolsheviks during 1904 were virtually nonexistent. And if the official record is to be believed, Koba wrote only one article, for which he could not have received more than a few rubles. Conceivably his mother was still earning enough to keep herself in food, clothing, and shelter. Now, in 1904, there were soon to be three mouths to feed, three bodies to be clothed and housed. Koba's wife was either with child or nursing Yasha and hardly able to support a family. Perhaps her parents or relatives helped out at a critical period, but this does not explain away the lack of visible income that characterizes his life at that time.

How did he support himself, wife, and child? There are only two possible answers to the question: he was receiving money from a foreign intelligence service or he was getting it from the Russian Department of Police. Indeed, the Japanese had expended a great deal of money in the Caucasus during 1904 for subversive purposes in connection with the Russo-Japanese War,[267] but their money would hardly have gone to a twenty-five-year-old revolutionary who was then unable to influence anyone except possibly a few peasants or random workers. However, the Department of Police had unaudited funds at its disposal for agent payments and it was undoubtedly from this source that Stalin was receiving money during 1904. It was also the Department of Police that revealed, in its customary professional style, a top-secret document that "according to agent information [Soso, or Koba] lived in Tiflis in 1904-1905 and was engaged in revolutionary activities." [268] No details are supplied, and we are permitted to wonder where and when he was engaged in what sort of revolutionary activities. The dossier of any rank-and-file revolutionary under Department of Police surveillance would ordinarily have included details of these "activities."

Then there was the Russo-Japanese war that had begun in early 1904. During the year, many eligible males throughout Russia were conscripted, but nowhere do we find any indication that Koba was called up, or rejected because of his crippled arm. He was at the prime draft age of twenty-five; many of his contemporaries were conscripted for military service, and there are records of some revolutionaries being rejected. In any event, none of the official or unofficial Soviet works makes any reference to the fact that the draft was a matter of primary importance to men of Koba's age. Reading Stalin's biographies, one would never realize that the most serious war in modern Russian history was taking place in this crucial year when Koba was ripe for conscription.

The year 1904 in Stalin's life is satisfactorily explicable only in terms of his police activities. In his own account he entered the year as he left it—unwilling to divulge details about his associations or peregrinations and leaving us with legends of a superhuman walk in a snowstorm and an amazing escape from an undocumented exile that are not credible. As he began the year 1905, the year that was to be only slightly less important than 1917 in the stormy history of Russia, he was probably not fully certain where his future lay. At that time no one could have predicted the events of 1905, let alone those of 1917. From what we have learned of Stalin's character, however, we can be certain of one thing at this juncture: he would stick with the winning side.

6 | A REVOLUTIONARY IGNORES A REVOLUTION

"The question 'What did Koba do in 1905?' remains unanswered," Trotsky wrote, implying that he had done very little, if anything, during the year of the first Russian revolution.[269] Yet Koba's activities during 1905 became clearer and more definable than in previous years. He wrote, he became a bolshevik according to one report,[270] he sired his first-born son, he made a few speeches, he was arrested for the second time, and for the first time he left his native Caucasia to attend the bolshevik conference in Finland, where he met Lenin. Trotsky is right about one thing: Koba failed to make any notable mark on the tumultuous year of 1905 which was, in Lenin's opinion, a rehearsal for the 1917 revolution.[271] When Koba was not ignoring the 1905 revolution in the Caucasus, he seemed to Trotsky to be trying at least to make it accept bolshevik committee leadership.[272] This is doubtful. Stalin never favored committees except when he could control them, and at this point his reputation scarcely would have allowed him to lead a political group. However, if Koba was active in 1905, no evidence of his revolutionary activities has thus far come to light.[273]

The Russian Empire was convoluted in 1905 as it had never been in the history of the Romanov dynasty. It began on December 20, 1904, when Port Arthur surrendered to the Japanese, signalling a serious defeat for the Russian Imperial forces in the war. Although it was not until September 5, 1905 (N.S.) that the Portsmouth Treaty arranged by President Theodore Roosevelt brought an end to the conflict, Port Arthur's capitulation was a clear indication that Russia had suffered a grievous and ignominious defeat. The tsar had lost 400,000 soldiers, dead and wounded, in battle and untold thousands also died from disease and malnutrition in a war that had cost a half billion gold rubles. The Russian Navy was practically non-existent. Although the revolutionary parties were hoping for the defeat of the Russian armed forces, all classes of society were shocked by the appalling corruption and reprehensibly poor leadership exposed by the war.

On the January 7th, 150,000 of St. Petersburg's 175,000 workers, following the example of the labor force at the giant Putilov factory, Russia's largest armament plant, were on strike. The Russian Orthodox priest, Father Georgy Gapon, had a direct but so far unexplained role in these labor disorders. While there is no doubt that Father Gapon had been involved with the Okhrana, the extent of his police status is unclear even today. Some time before 1905 the Okhrana had begun experimenting with what it came to call "police socialism" or *Zubatovshchina*. Zubatov, a former Okhrana official, had developed the idea that the workers, without their knowledge, should be unionized under police auspices. Although Zubatov had earlier left the Department of Police, his theory nonetheless persisted and an "Assembly of Russian Workers" had been organized in St. Petersburg with apparent Okhrana blessing. This "Assembly" and Father Gapon played the role of instigators of a general strike and the events of January 9.

After Father Gapon had requested the tsar to receive him, thousands of workers led by Gapon marched to the Winter Palace on Sunday, January 9, 1905. The procession was not revolutionary. As a matter of fact, the crowd was orderly and the marchers, singing patriotic monarchist songs, carried icons and religious objects. Gapon had decided to present a petition to the tsar which was plainly not anti-monarchist. It pleaded that the tsar call a constituent assembly, it asked for civil rights, it begged for a political amnesty, it appealed for a separation of church and state, it requested an eight-hour working day and recognition of labor's right to organize, and an end to the Russo-Japanese War. Whether these were Okhrana directives, in whole or part, may never be known. It is clear, however, that Father Gapon felt confident that he would be successful in presenting his petition in person and that the demonstration would be without bloodshed. Unfortunately he reasoned incorrectly.

The case of Father Gapon is worth reviewing not only because it shows that the Okhrana had to allow a certain amount of latitude for its collaborators—many of whom had only a loose affiliation with the Department of Police—but reveals that operations sometimes exceeded the limits desired by the police. *"Pop"* (as he is known in the Russian) Gapon had explained to the tsarist Ministry of Interior his plans for the workers' march on January 9. For some reason, probably bureaucratic bungling, neither the seriousness nor the purpose of his petition and march filtered through the various layers of government. In other words, the Okhrana was unable to control events even with the best-laid plans. The uncertainty, even under optimum conditions, of any secret police agent operation will be important to recall later in our narrative.

When around two o'clock on a bitterly cold Sunday afternoon, the main column of marchers reached the Palace Square and were asked to halt, they refused. Temporarily dispersed by a charge of the Horse Grenadier Guards, the marchers quickly reformed and proceeded forward. Tsarist troops then fired. Before the day ended, hundreds were dead and more wounded. With the sobriquet of "Bloody Sunday" never to be forgotten by revolutionaries, January 9th marked the beginning of the 1905 Russian revolution and presaged the overturn of the Romanov monarchy in 1917.[274] Almost as a portent of things to come Nicholas I recorded in his diary:

A grim day! As a result of the desire of the workers to go to the Winter Palace, serious disorders took place in Petersburg. In many parts of the city troops were compelled to fire; many were killed or wounded. God, how sad and grim![275]

Later in 1906 after Father Gapon had met with Lenin, who tried to use him for his own purposes, the social revolutionaries decided that he had been an Okhrana agent and Pincus Rutenberg executed Gapon by hanging him in a house in Finland. Before his death,

Gapon had apparently tried to reinstate himself with the Okhrana. The Okhrana was not totally doctrinaire: it would play an Orthodox priest in one way, a trusted agent in another.

Russia, in truth, never recovered from Bloody Sunday. Within a month a strike movement had spread throughout the length and breadth of the Empire. On February 4th a member of the Socialist Revolutionary Party, Kalyayev, assassinated Grand Duke Sergei, the Governor General of Moscow. Peasants began to react locally against landlords, burning ancestral manors. Tsarist troops, frequently called upon to suppress peasant revolts, did so brutally. The police, particularly the Gendarme Administrations, were not slow in meeting the situation; they knew that to distract attention from strikes and other disorders it would be necessary to mount diversionary operations—pogroms. Thus the gendarmes organized a pogrom of Armenians in Baku from February 19th to 22nd and several pogroms of Jews throughout Western Russia during the year. In the first part of 1905 Russia was aflame from the Arctic to the Black Sea and from Poland to the Pacific Ocean. Included in this conflagration, of course, was the area of Transcaucasia where Koba was living. In Georgia, and particularly in Tiflis, the tsarist authorities were hard put to maintain order. Local peasants' committees had been organized, land was confiscated, officials were replaced, and even organizations of Red Hundreds, a form of armed revolutionary militia, sprang up. For a period of weeks rebels were in almost total control of Guria, Koba's small native province.[275a]

Few of the professional revolutionaries seemed to have anticipated the revolutionary eruption. Thus Lenin was in a state of joy and shock, waiting from one day to the next in Geneva for newspapers and letters from his homeland.[276] The first issue of his new newspaper *Vpered* (*Forward*) had appeared in Geneva on January 4th, and not long thereafter he called for another Social-Democratic Party Congress in which he hoped to bind up the wounds that had been created by the Second Conference. The Third Conference met in London from April 12th to 27th, 1905 (N.S.) Significantly, Koba was not a delegate, although at the time he seems to have finally opted for the bolsheviks and dropped his menshevik status. The mensheviks met in Switzerland at about the same time: the split between the two factions abroad was from that point irreparable.

In all the fire and thunder of 1905, Koba seems almost withdrawn. We find him writing, and certainly the articles and pamphlets from this period are more identifiable as his, but not verbose. He conducts spiteful oral or written harangues against the mensheviks while the cataclysmic events of 1905 pass him by. He spent most of 1905 in Tiflis. However, as Arsenidze wrote, "Soso visited Batum at the beginning of 1905. N. Ramishvili accompanied him. The objective of their visit was a factional discussion [bolshevism *versus* menshevism]. This time Soso was a completely definite, orthodox, devoted Leninist, repeating arguments and ideas of his teacher with the precision of a gramophone." Arsenidze was astounded that Soso had returned to Batum, where he was so well known to the police. His meetings with Soso also puzzled him: there was something strange, abnormal about him. Moreover, "One did not discern an internal fire . . . a soulful warmth in him. He spoke crudely, sharply, and in his crudeness one could feel energy and strength in his words. He frequently used sarcasm, irony, to drive home—as if with a hammer—his sharp crudities." Hardly anyone who knew and wrote about Koba failed to record crudeness as an outstanding personality trait.

Arsenidze vividly recalled that during 1905 Koba was an irrational anti-Semite. He scorned the mensheviks because of the preponderance of Jews among them:

"Lenin," Koba said, "is exasperated that God sent him such comrades as the Mensheviks! Really, what kind of people are these! Martov, Dan, Axelrod—nothing but uncircumcised Jews! And, that old *baba* [this is a deprecatory term in Russian] Vera Zasulich! All right! Go work with them. They won't fight and there is no rejoicing at their feastings. Cowards and shopkeepers. Don't the workers of Georgia know that the Jewish people produce only cowards who are useless in a fight?" [277]

This early anti-Semitism, bitter and deep, remembered so clearly by his contemporary and countryman Arsenidze, was confirmed by

Stalin's removal of most of the old Jewish bolsheviks in the purges of the thirties, his campaign against the Jews as "homeless, pass-portless, cosmopolitans" in the late forties, and the infamous "doctors' plot" just before his death in 1953. On the other hand, Lazar Kaganovich, a Jew, was his faithful colleague in the Politburo. And there seems to be little doubt that he married Rosa Kaganovich, Lazar's sister, sometime in the thirties.[278] Muscovites still claim, moreover, that Beria, Stalin's deputy for the official distortion of history and his secret police chief, was a Jew. Thus it would appear that from 1905 until his death Stalin was a selective anti-Semite, using Jews when it suited his purposes while retaining his basic prejudice against them.

The *Collected Works* claim that at the beginning of February, 1905, on the initiative of Stalin, the Caucasus Social-Democratic Union Committee dissolved the Menshevik Committee in Tiflis, and from it a new Tiflis Bolshevik Committee was then formed.[279] This is simply incorrect, because the bolsheviks were not at the time important enough to organize a new committee. Even when Stalin later in the year went to Finland to the Tammerfors Conference convened by Lenin, he was a bolshevik from an overwhelmingly menshevik social-democratic organization. Nevsky, in his outstanding history of the Russian Communist Party, indicates that in 1905 the mensheviks had about fifteen thousand members, a third of whom were in the Caucasus, contrasted to only a handful of bolsheviks.[280] Batum in 1905 had about a thousand Socialist-Democratic Party members, according to Arsenidze, of which about ten or fifteen were bolsheviks. There were only a few dozen in Tiflis.[281]

Stalin's official autobiography attributes twelve articles, leaflets, and pamphlets to his authorship during 1905. A reading of them leaves one unimpressed.[282] It is remarkable that all were unsigned, and that all were written in the Georgian language. Arsenidze, who read Koba's work in the Georgian language, indicates that his grammar was inferior.[283]

Almost a hundred articles and brochures were reprinted in an official party history of 1905 published in 1926. Stalin was mentioned only once and then only in connection with his attendance, using the name Ivanovich as a pseudonym, as a delegate to the Tammerfors Conference.[284] Filip Makharadze, in his monograph *Notes on the Revolutionary Movement in the Transcaucasus,* the most detailed work concerning the 1905 revolution there (published in 1927 by the Georgian State Press), strongly implied that Koba was insignificant in the Caucasian revolutionary movement.[285] In some four hundred and fifty pages that largely concern 1905, there is not one word about him or his activities. S. Maglakelidze and A. Iovidze, who compiled *The Revolution of 1905-1907 in Georgia—A Collection of Documents,* which was published in Tiflis in 1956 but which was in preparation while Stalin still lived, mentions Koba fewer than ten times in more than eight hundred pages.[286] Most of their references are in his *Collected Works,* and because the compendium is based on the Georgian archives of the Soviet Ministry of Internal Affairs, we are entitled to be highly skeptical of the entries. It is important to note, however, that these sources support the conclusion that Koba was largely inactive and unimportant in the Caucasus revolutionary milieu in 1905.

In the absence of signed articles, documents, or independent confirmatory testimony it is not unfair to doubt that Koba wrote anything at all during 1905. An abundance of literature for this period from various social-democratic authors exists, and its authorship is easily verified by identifiable signatures. For example, there has never been any question of Lenin's or Trotsky's writings, although they were often signed in pseudonym. As a result of Stalin's secretiveness, we are compelled to resort to a stylistic and content analysis of his supposed literary production. Even this approach is subjective, unscientific, and perhaps invalid.

Of all Koba's presumed writing in 1905 his first pamphlet, *Briefly About Disagreements in the Party* (in Georgian), which was published in Tiflis during May, bears the familiar marks of his liturgical prose. It is, however, unsigned and we do not know how many copies were printed. In its forty-two pages he criticizes the mensheviks generally and those in Tiflis particularly. Otherwise he writes an encomium of Lenin and supports his point of view unequivocably. "Our Mensheviks are really too tiresome," Koba maintains. Lengthily citing Lenin, Kautsky, Marx, and Engels to support his hairsplitting and blistering polemics, he concludes that trade unionism is wrong unless it is imbued with social consciousness. Spontaneous workers' organizations led or—better put—controlled by the bolsheviks are good. When the mensheviks cater to the spontaneity of workers' organizations and strikes, they are unmarxian. Perhaps they do not even understand Marx, or perhaps they incorrectly translate him! At any rate, the workers, for their own good, must follow Lenin. Unfortunately, he continues, some of the workers and intelligentsia have been attracted to menshevism. "Yes, it is true, in some towns the workers are on the side of the 'minority' [the mensheviks], but that proves nothing. Workers even follow the revisionists, (the opportunists in Germany) in some towns, but that does not prove that they are not opportunists. One day a crow found a rose, but that did not prove that a crow is a nightingale. It is not for nothing that the saying goes:

"When a crow picks up a rose
'I'm a nightingale,' it crows."

His pamphlet ends: "As is evident, two trends have appeared in our party: the trend of *proletarian firmness* and the trend of *intellectual wavering*. . . . The Tiflis 'Committee' and its *Social-Democrat* are the obedient slaves of this 'minority' [the mensheviks]! True, our pseudo-Marxists often shout that they are opposed to the 'mentality of the intellectual,' and they accuse the 'majority' [the bolsheviks] of 'intellectual wavering'; but this reminds us of the case of the thief who stole some money and began to shout: 'Stop thief!' Moreover, it is well known that the tongue ever turns to the aching tooth." It is noteworthy that he concedes that the mensheviks enjoyed a certain strength in "some towns." [287]

The *Collected Works* places him at a "big meeting in Batum in a debate with the menshevik leaders N. Ramishvili, R. Arsenidze, and others" sometime in April, 1905.[288] Arsenidze does not mention this "big meeting" at Batum, and other sources are notably devoid of any evidence concerning it. We are forced to conclude that it did not take place. However, on June 12th, Koba did deliver a speech at the funeral of A. G. Tsulukidze, where he presumably outlined a program of struggle to be waged by the workers and peasants against the autocracy, supposedly subjecting the tactics of the mensheviks to devastating criticism.[289] Tsulukidze, who had become a bolshevik in 1904, had been a good friend of Arsenidze's. "I considered him," Arsenidze wrote, "one of the oldest esteemed comrades, intelligent, well rounded, capable of becoming one of *the* leaders had not a terrible illness sapped his strength." Alexander Tsulukidze died from tuberculosis contracted in prison.

According to Arsenidze both bolsheviks and mensheviks assembled in full force for the funeral held in Tsulukidze's home town of Khoni (now named Tsulukidze), some twenty-five kilometers from Kutais. Local rural menshevik organizations had encouraged all residents along the route to turn out for the funeral procession, which was met by the entire population of Khoni. Of course, this called for speeches and Arsenidze remembers that bolsheviks and mensheviks, among them Ramishvili and Lordkipanidze, addressed the crowd, but not Koba.

Dr. Kikalishvili, a bolshevik well known to Arsenidze, invited Arsenidze to a discussion group that evening. The large hall he had engaged was full of people. Koba attended. The mood of the listeners was definitely against the bolsheviks, leading one worker to ask if bolsheviks could really be considered social democrats or marxists. Arsenidze answered that "they were in the party and were considered Social Democrats.[290] But Soso was far from satisfied with this. It developed that he had completely different plans for the meeting, which he and his supporters were trying to "implement." Then something unexpected occurred when Koba's small group of supporters hoisted him onto their shoulders and carried him triumphantly out of the hall into the street to show their leader to the people. He apparently failed to impress the public or gain its attention. Angered, Koba later exclaimed, "They carried me out, but where were the people?" Arsenidze adds, "Thus the future all-Russian dictator prepared for his leading role in the revolutionary movement." [291] Koba had attempted for the first time to utilize the death or funeral of a revolutionary comrade to advance his personal political position. He would employ similar tactics when Lenin died in 1924.

In July, 1905, Koba addressed an audience of some two thousand workers in Chiatura in a debate with anarchists, federalists, and social revolutionaries, according to his *Collected Works*.[292] This is unproved and may not have taken place. However, Arsenidze, who was in the area, gave Stalin credit for "conducting very energetic work, travelling around Guria, Imeretia, Chiatura, Baku, Tbilisi, throwing himself back and forth from one place to another. But all of his work was almost exclusively factional . . . trying to stomp the Mensheviks in filth." In other words, he was then uninterested in the success or failure of the revolution engulfing Transcaucasia—indeed, all of Russia. He was consumed with intramural squabbles and not with the overturn of the Russian autocracy, unless it was done under bolshevik auspices. "Everywhere," Arsenidze testifies, "he sought out and recruited partisans, most rarely ten in number, whom he immediately organized in groups or grouplets, providing them with the thunderous name 'Committee.' Such were the Committee of the Kutais Imeretia Group, the one in Chiatura, in Tbilisi and others."

A keen and objective observer of the politics in his native Georgia, Arsenidze wrote in his memoirs, with no apparent recrimination, two years before his death:

This was during that time when the revolutionary movement had developed extraordinarily quickly, embracing the broadest masses of peasants and workers, when, one might say, all of the provinces of Georgia constituted a stormy sea. Soso could play a leading role (it is also doubtful that he played it) at that time only in his little circles. There was not one wide popular or social movement, not one of the strikes that was conducted under his leadership or even one in which he participated. Koba only busied himself with that which would bring thunder and lightning down on the heads of mensheviks.[293]

Hurling thunder and lightning down upon the heads of Georgian mensheviks was perfectly understandable in terms of Department of Police objectives. The mensheviks were the most important revolutionary force in Transcaucasia. Okhrana operational methodology in such circumstances was to encourage a splintering of the strongest revolutionary organization that would be in turn weakened and less influential. Whether unwittingly or not, Koba and his bolsheviks were therefore assisting the forces of reaction.

At the end of November, again according to his officially edited *Collected Works,* he directed the proceedings of the Fourth Bolshevik Conference of the Caucasian Union of the Social-Democratic Party. This is palpably false. Neither his position nor that of the Bolsheviks in Tiflis at that time would have permitted it. Arsenidze tells a different story:

> Koba, as is known, was a great advocate of the strength of armament. He preferred the weapon of criticism to the criticism of the weapon. But, when in 1905 the December uprising erupted, when in Tbilisi and throughout all Georgia the revolution raged, engaging really all the people, Koba (perhaps not by his own will) did nothing. In any case Koba was not in Tbilisi. As a member of the Tbilisi Strike Committee, which held in its hands all power, I can testify that the Bolsheviks entered the Committee, but not Koba.[294]

Arsenidze failed to explain why Koba "perhaps not by his own will" did nothing during the 1905 revolution in the Caucasus. His scanty writings and speeches permits one to wonder what force importuned him to remain an inactive revolutionary? Hardly the bolsheviks or the mensheviks. Most other revolutionaries in Russia were on the barricades. For example, a small Soviet book, *Twelve Biographies,* published in 1924, concerns Bukharin, Dzerzhinsky, Zinoviev, Kalinin, Kamenev, Kuibyshev, Rykov, Smirnov, Stalin, Tomsky, Trotsky, and Frunze.[295] With the exception of two or three of these twelve men, who were either abroad or in prison, they all actively participated in the 1905 revolution. Stalin did not. He was apparently content to inveigh against the mensheviks and attend his wife and son—about whom, of course, he said not a word.

Trotsky observes that "in the writings of Koba for the year 1905, sparse in both form and content, we find nothing at all about the Soviets." [296] The Soviets—that is, the committees of workers and deputies that had sprung up spontaneously through Russia —were representative of the 1905 forces of the revolution. These Koba condemned. The spontaneity with which they had been formed, the clear lack of prior organization, made them suspect to him. For analagous reasons the Soviets worried the Okhrana.

As we know, Koba had been living near Tiflis, with his wife, Keke, who was probably with child or had just given birth. We know, too, that his financial responsibilities could not have been met by the money he earned from his meager articles and pamphlets—if, indeed, he was paid for them. We know also that he travelled to Baku and Batum, as well as to other places in the Caucasus during the year, though he had no visible means of support. And we know that in all likelihood the funds he received from the Department of Police financed his frequent trips in the Caucasus as well as supporting him and his wife. His work for the police involved reporting on revolutionary developments in Transcaucasia, denouncing revolutionary personalities, who were later arrested and exiled, and frequent harassing of the mensheviks, then the most significant revolutionary organization in Georgia. As we have seen, these tasks performed at the direction of his police superiors in no way cut across the lines of his ambitions. The more revolutionary leaders who were removed from the Transcaucasian scene, the more important Stalin became.

Stalin's denunciation of Stepan Georgievich Shaumyan to the Tiflis Gendarme Administration in 1905 is a notable case in point. Shaumyan, then twenty-seven years of age, a year older than Stalin, had been born in Tiflis of Armenian parents and attended secondary school in his home town, after which he had gone to Latvia. He was expelled from the Riga Polytechnicum in 1900 after having become active in the workers' movement and having developed a deep interest in marxism. He was deported in 1900 from the Baltic provinces back to his native Tiflis, where he joined the Social-Democratic Party in 1901. From that time on, he became a close associate and pupil of Lenin. At the Sixth Party Congress in 1917 he was elected a member of the Party Central Committee. He was made chairman of the Council of People's Commissars in Baku in April, 1918. A few months later the British armed forces then occupying Baku executed Shaumyan as one of the twenty-five so-called "Baku Commissars." [297]

When N. Vakar, correspondent for the Russian émigré paper *Latest News,* interviewed Noi Zhordania in Paris in December, 1936,[298] the latter spoke at length about Stalin and his activities during the early nineteen-hundreds. He recalled that Koba had at that time deliberately spread "dirty gossip" about Shaumyan, "a person who was straight, warm and sincere. . . . Koba, on the contrary, was always quiet, sullen, never raising his voice, never reacting at once to an offense, but not forgetting, waiting for the appropriate moment in order to get back. . . . At the climax of this fight, the police arrested Shaumyan. The suspicion arose that Stalin had denounced him. Some time later I personally met with Shaumyan and asked him about this. He answered 'I am certain that Stalin denounced me to the police, there is proof. I had a conspiratorial apartment where I sometimes spent the night. No one except Koba knew the address. When they arrested me first of all they asked about the apartment . . . What could I tell them?' " Zhordania added, "This is how Koba's closest comrades in the Bolshevik faction thought of him." Even if Zhordania and Shaumyan were not of unquestionable honesty, this episode would fit neatly into the Stalin habit pattern that was identifiable from his days in the Tiflis Theological Seminary. Shaumyan, a popular personality in the revolutionary milieu would be removed by a denunciation to the police. Koba might thus advance one more rung on the ladder of his ambition, at the same time satisfying for the moment his Department of Police superiors.

Sometime in 1905, probably in the autumn of the year, Stalin was presumably arrested by the Okhrana, a fact never noted in any of his official or unofficial biographies. A memorandum from the Special Section of the Department of Police marked "top secret," dated March 31, 1911, signed by Vice-Director Vissarionov, and countersigned by Colonel Eremin, Chief of the Special Section, includes the statement "He [Stalin] was arrested in 1905 and escaped from prison." [299] Oddly enough, this does not appear in any of the other Department of Police documents about Stalin. We will return to this, but for the moment it is noteworthy that no date, place, or reason is provided for his arrest. This is unlike the Department of Police and particularly uncharacteristic of Vissarionov and Eremin.

But the document, which was sent from the St. Petersburg Headquarters to its Paris Foreign Agency, otherwise confirms Stalin's ostensible arrests, exiles, and escapes until 1911. Stalin's access to this document while he was preparing and editing his autobiographical *Collected Works* raises another question: inasmuch as arrests and escapes from prison were *pour le mérite,* why was this not included in his official works? Why was it not mentioned in some of the literature after he became dictator of Soviet Russia? Quite obviously, Stalin wanted to forget about this "arrest and escape from prison." It is one more puzzle, clues to which may be found within Department of Police operational methodology. The reason for the "arrest and escape" in his dossier and, conversely, Stalin's failure to acknowledge it, or even allow it to be noted in his officially edited works, doubtless had to do with the building of his legend. For it was characteristic of a police agent to be continually at work on his cover story—or legend. Sometimes this became a matter of habit, persisting when there was no further need for cover stories, and thus creating fictional dates, places, and events that served only to cast suspicion when the facts would have stood alone. Of course the "escape from prison" was fictitious, but it served to enhance his cover story. This so-called "arrest and escape" perhaps occurred sometime before Koba began his journey to the bolshevik conference at Tammerfors, which met from December 12th to 17th.[300] There he met Lenin for the first time.

Lenin had returned from Geneva to St. Petersburg on November 8, 1905.[301] Perhaps because he recognized the preponderance of mensheviks and their influence in the 1905 upheaval and entertained ideas of joining forces with them, or because he was spurred by a menshevik all-Russian conference that had met in St. Petersburg in November, he decided to convene his own Bolshevik Congress. In any event, it was to be expected that he would want his own conference. The day after his arrival, the Bolshevik Central Committee hurriedly met. On November 10th the newspaper *Novaya Zhizn* (*New Life*) carried instructions alerting all local organizations to elect delegates for the Fourth Congress of the Russian Socialist-Democratic Workers Party, which would meet on December 10th in St. Petersburg.[302] The first issue of the *Tiflis Caucasian Workers Leaflet*, the legally sanctioned organ of the Caucasian Union of the Social Democrats, reprinted the directives ten days later.[303]

As late as 1964, a Soviet account claimed that the Second Conference of the Caucasian Union of the Russian Socialist-Democratic Workers Party met in Tiflis from November 26th to 30th and elected three delegates to the Fourth Party Congress: Koba from Tiflis, P. V. Montin from Baku, and G. P. Teliya representing the Imeretia-Mingrelian Committee.[304] Neither documents nor witnesses have survived to confirm this election, but we know the Caucasian Union was dominated by persons who did not favor most of the bolsheviks and who detested Koba. Soviet sources claim that the Baku delegate, Peter Montin, was shot and killed by tsarist troops in his home town on December 6th.[305] He had apparently decided that it would be impossible to attend Lenin's congress in view of strikes enveloping the railways. G. P. Teliya did attend the meeting as a delegate. He succumbed a few years later, and Stalin's eulogy at that time suggested that Teliya might also have had an Okhrana affiliation.[306] Of the three delegates only Koba survived after 1907.

At the end of 1905 there were about three thousand mensheviks in the Tiflis area contrasted with a few hundred followers of Lenin.[307] How many of these were illiterate peasants or workers recruited by Koba through appeals to nationalism or selfish economic interests may never be known. Only the mensheviks in the Caucasus, and particularly in Georgia, could be considered a political movement in any sense of the word. Even menshevism was embryonic, although it spoke perhaps for unknown members of the peasantry, workers, and intelligentsia. The Caucasian Socialist-Democratic Workers Party was thus overwhelmingly menshevik in its personnel and organization through 1905. True enough, it included bolsheviks but the party histories reveal that the two factions remained unified, although definite splits elsewhere had resulted from Lenin's idea that the mensheviks had excluded themselves from the party. This concept had not yet filtered down to the Caucasus—at least, not by the time Lenin decided to convene the Fourth Congress. The mensheviks—led by Zhordania, among others—had the Caucasian socialist movement firmly in their hands. Bolshevik leaders were conveniently absent, dead, in jail, or in exile. Kurnatovsky, Franchesky, and Dzhibladze, to mention only three, were in Siberian exile; Ketskhoveli had been shot in prison; Tsulukidze was dead from tuberculosis. Thus, in November and December of 1905, the Leninists in the Caucasus were woefully short of well-known or distinguished leaders, as well as membership. On the other hand, the mensheviks were comparatively well off in both categories.

What Lenin and the Central Committee had scheduled as the Fourth Party Congress was modified by the railway strike and became a party *conference,* not in St. Petersburg on December 10th, but in Tammerfors, Finland, on December 12th.[308] After his return to Russia, Lenin had found himself continually surrounded by Okhrana surveillance agents in St. Petersburg, and during his one trip to Moscow. Krupskaya reported, "Vladimir Ilich took a trip to Moscow. I went to see him as soon as he returned. I was struck by the number of spies lurking round every corner. We had to get out as soon as possible." [309] This influenced him to select the conference city in Finland which still enjoyed a measure of autonomy and where the police were not quite so numerous nor efficient.

Koba, using the alias of Ivanovich, and Teliya had to set out for St. Petersburg no later than December 1st to arrive in time for the conference. Both were on time for the initial session at Tammerfors (Tampere), some three hundred miles northwest of St. Petersburg and more than twenty-nine hundred miles from Tiflis.

Koba was selected—by some obscure means—as a delegate after November 20th. He then needed a passport, which was not easy to come by. A political ex-prisoner who lived in Georgia, he would be obliged to apply for it in the same area of Georgia where he had twice been arrested and where his dossier was well known to many professional police officers. A false passport in the name of Ivanovich required time and money. At any rate, he and Teliya did represent the entire Transcaucasian area at the Tammerfors Conference. A party history for the year 1905, published in Moscow during 1926, notes Ivanovich as a delegate, although it does not identify the name as Stalin's alias.[310] Yaroslavsky, himself a delegate, recalls Stalin and Teliya as being present.[311]

Although there is no evidence that they travelled together on their way to Tammerfors, Koba and Teliya had to go through nineteen police checkpoints, including over six hundred professionally trained staff personnel. For the first time he crossed a quasi-national frontier. Although we have no record of his experience en route to Tammerfors, we do have a photograph that shows the Department of Police checking trains at the Finnish-Russian border. Gendarmes swarm over the engine and tender, the passenger and baggage cars, in a thoroughly detailed inspection. Some revolutionaries evaded interrogation by jumping off before each inspection point and walking to the next station, where they would again board one of the trains that ran unpredictably every other day or so. This practice greatly lengthened travel time and was not a likely tactic for Koba, who seemingly proceeded swiftly, always on schedule, from one end of Russia to the other. As far as the record shows, he was never questioned, never stopped by the police, on any of his trips. "Luck" was apparently with him.

Other revolutionaries were travelling in Russia during this period and their difficulties may not be overlooked. Some of the delegates to the Tammerfors Conference were unable to attend because of the railway strike. Of those that attended—as far as may be determined—Koba was the only "escapee" from exile: he was the sole delegate sought by the Department of Police as a fugitive. While the possible inefficiency of the Okhrana might account for his easy travel, one wonders why Koba, alone among the many revolutionaries, was so unmolested by the police.

Under ordinary circumstances, Koba's attendance at the Tammerfors Conference would be plausible only if scores of coincidences occurred and only if complete order emerged from the extreme disorder in Russia during 1905. Had he received the information about the Tammerfors Conference in time to have been appointed or elected a delegate, had he already obtained a passport in the name of Ivanovich, had he had sufficient funds for his trip, had he miraculously not been stopped by the railway strike or the uprising in Moscow and elsewhere—had all these conditions existed, he could conceivably have made it to Tammerfors on time. His *Collected Works* claims he attended the conference from the first day, December 12th, and saw it through to its termination on December 17th.[312]

As in so many other matters concerning Stalin, one sees that some truth reposes in the account of the Tammerfors episode: he was at the conference. But his getting there may not be ascribed to mere chance. Setting aside for the moment the well-known fact that he was a revolutionary nobody in the Caucasus, he simply could not have been at those places at the times he claims, obtained the documents for travel, made the six-thousand-mile round trip, and at the same time supported a family without extraordinary financial and operational assistance. Once more, only the Department of Police, with its resources, was in a position to provide him such extensive help. It alone could supply funds for the journey, immediately procure a false passport, and make transit through nineteen checkpoints in 1905 an easy matter. Thus Stalin and the "worker" Teliya doubtless journeyed to Tammerfors with the help of the Department of Police. The *gruppochki* (grouplets), as Arsenidze described Stalin's little committees, had presumably decided that he was their representative, and the police were elated to send him off to the conference, its objectives fusing neatly and profitably with Stalin's personal ambitions.

Stalin at that time wrote nothing about his first trip outside Georgia, and spoke only about his meeting Lenin many years later.[313] Moreover, the surviving accounts of his contemporaries reveal that he failed to impress the other forty delegates. Krupskaya, who was generally dependable in remembering those persons whom Lenin found noteworthy, does not include Ivanovich-Stalin in her Tammerfors narrative.[314] Yaroslavsky, writing in 1939 and 1940 under Stalinist duress, gave a major role in the conference to the future dictator, while Gorev simply noted that he had been a delegate.[315]

Koba's real function in the conference proceedings may never be known, for something happened to the minutes and records. Krupskaya's short passage is worth repeating:

> The Tammerfors Conference was held in the middle of December. What a pity the minutes of this conference have been lost! The enthusiasm that reigned there! The revolution was in full swing, and the enthusiasm was tremendous. Every comrade was ready for the fight. In the intervals we learned to shoot. One evening we attended a Finnish mass torchlight meeting, and the solemnity of it fully harmonized with the temper of the delegates. I doubt whether anyone who was at that conference could ever forget it. Lozovsky, Baransky, Yaroslavsky and many others were there. I remember these comrades because of the interest which their "local reports" aroused.
>
> The Tammerfors Conference, which was attended only by Bolsheviks, passed a resolution calling for the immediate preparation and organization of an armed uprising.
>
> The uprising in Moscow was developing apace, and so the conference had to be cut short. . . .[316]

Apparently, Koba did not make a "local report" on the revolutionary events in the Caucasus. Strange: Koba and Teliya had travelled farther than any of the other delegates to Finland, and Lenin most certainly would have wanted to learn what had happened in Baku, Batum, and Tiflis, to say nothing of the peasant uprising in Guria that had seized power from the tsarist authorities. During most of the conference, Koba probably remained reserved and silent, observing the more sophisticated party leaders. His crudeness and his style of speech would have shown him up as a kind of Caucasian country-bumpkin revolutionary, something he wanted to avoid, although unsupported Soviet accounts allude to his participating in debates with Lenin.[317]

Stalin was perhaps surprised to learn that Lenin's conference agenda had as its first item a proposed synthetic reunification of mensheviks and bolsheviks. The delegate Lozovsky submitted a resolution calling for the immediate merging of local organizations. It was adopted. Stalin had spent months in castigating mensheviks in the Caucasus. Now he would be obliged to cease his attacks and, worse, to amalgamate with them, as it were, upon his return to Georgia. According to what we know, Stalin was also disturbed at Lenin's attitude toward elections to the state Duma, the Russian parliament. He favored a boycott, but he found Lenin surprisingly for participation in the elections and against the boycott.[318] Before the conference ended Lenin changed his mind and declared for the boycott.

Emelyan Yaroslavsky, head of the Communist League for the Militant Godless—an organization established in the nineteen-twenties to propagandize against religion—provided in a 1939 *Pravda* article more details about Tammerfors than any other delegate.[319] He recalls that Tammerfors in 1905 was a mighty workers' center, having a strong social-democratic organization with a leftist orientation. The Finnish comrades instructed the bolsheviks on how to evade the registration of their passports: when the hotel clerk asked for his passport, the bolshevik was to reply that it had already been given to the Tammerfors chief of police. The ruse worked. "The Tammerfors Conference met in the People's Home of Finnish Workers where at this time the staff of the Tammerfors' Red Guard was quartered," he wrote. The delegates learned how to fire Mausers, Brownings, and Manchesters (he meant Winchesters). In the conference meetings Yaroslavsky noted that Stalin opposed Lenin's idea of participating in the Duma elections. The year following the *Pravda* article, 1940, Yaroslavsky wrote *Landmarks in the Life of Stalin,* which omitted the mildly colorful details of the Tammerfors Conference.[320] The later account was marked by its brevity:

As we know, the Tammerfors Bolshevik Conference was held not long prior to the outbreak of the uprising. It was my great fortune to be present at this Conference, which was attended by Lenin and

Stalin and to work with Comrade Stalin on the commission for drawing up the political resolution. It is to be regretted that not even a
pamphlet has yet been written about this Conference. Many of the
documents relating to it have been actually been lost, and our histories
should make it their business to reconstruct the picture of this Conference.

Who was in charge of the records? Krupskaya was at that time
head of the Secretariat of the Party faction, but she inferentially
clears herself of blame for their loss.[321] In all probability the records, or minutes, and a complete list of delegates were apprehended
on the person of a delegate attempting to cross the Finnish-Russian
frontier after the conference ended, or they were purloined by the
Okhrana. At any rate, there is no information to date about their
disappearance.

The list of forty-one delegates, still undisclosed, included at least
one identifiable Department of Police agent.[322] It would be most
unusual if there were more. From the few available recollections of
the conference, a partial list may be reconstructed: Lenin and
Krupskaya, Yaroslavsky, Baransky, P. N. Mostovenko, Arnold
Lozovsky (the future head of the Profintern), the Red International
of Labor Unions formed in Moscow in July of 1921, Nevsky,
Borodin [Michael Markovich Gruzenberg] (the famous advisor to
Chiang Kai-shek in the twenties), V. A. Radus-Zenkovich, P. F.
Kudelli, L. M. Knipovich, P. N. Krasin, Kamenev, and, of course,
Ivanovich-Stalin and his worker comrade from the Caucasus, G. P.
Teliya. Twenty-six delegates to the conference remain unknown.[322a]

Stalin reviewed the Tammerfors gathering in six paragraphs
many years later, remembering that Lenin had made two speeches
at the conference:

The two speeches Lenin delivered at this Conference were remarkable: one was on the political situation and the other on the agrarian
question. Unfortunately, they have not been preserved. They were
inspired, and they roused the whole Conference to a pitch of stormy
enthusiasm. The extraordinary power of conviction, the simplicity and
clarity of argument, the brief and easily understandable sentences, the

absence of affection, of dizzying gestures and theatrical phrases aiming for effect—all this made Lenin's speech a favorable contrast to the speech of the usual "parliamentary" orator.

But what captivated me at the time was not these features of Lenin's speeches. I was captivated by that irresistible force of logic in them which, although somewhat terse, thoroughly overpowered his audience, gradually electrified it, and then, as the saying goes, captivated it completely. I remember that many of the delegates said: "The logic of Lenin's speeches is like a mighty tentacle which seizes you on all sides as in a vice and from whose grip you are powerless to tear yourself away: You must either surrender or make up your mind to utter defeat."

I think that this characteristic of Lenin's speeches was the strongest feature of his art as an orator.

Proudly Stalin related:

I first met Lenin in December 1905 at the Bolshevik Conference in Tammerfors. I was hoping to see the mountain eagle of our Party, the great man, great not only politically, but, if you will, physically, because in my imagination I pictured Lenin as a giant, stately and imposing. What, then, was my disappointment to see a most ordinary looking man, below average height, in no way, literally in no way, distinguishable from ordinary mortals. . . .

It is accepted as the usual thing for a "great man" to come late to meetings so that the assembly may await his appearance with bated breath; and then, just before the great man enters, the warning goes up: "Hush! . . . Silence! . . . He's coming." This rite did not seem to me superfluous, because it creates an impression, inspires respect. What, then, was my disappointment to learn that Lenin had arrived at the Conference before the delegates, had settled himself somewhere in a corner and was unassumingly carrying on a conversation, a most ordinary conversation with the most ordinary delegates at the Conference. I will not conceal from you that at that time this seemed to me to be rather a violation of certain essential rules.

Only later did I realize that this simplicity and modesty, this striving to remain unobserved, or, at least, not to make himself conspicuous and not to emphasize his high position—that this feature was one of Lenin's strongest points as the new leader of the new masses, of the simple and ordinary masses, of the very "rank and file" of humanity.[323]

The brief reports of his first encounter with Lenin are puzzling. He had been shocked at Lenin's position on the Duma elections, and he claims he debated him on the tactical decision to make common cause with the mensheviks. He was initially disappointed in the bolshevik leader, "a most ordinary looking man," and "only later" realized Lenin's outstanding qualities. One is tempted to conclude that as a result of the debate (in which Lenin undoubtedly bested him), the sharp reversal of Lenin's attitude toward the mensheviks, and the general disregard from the conference delegates, Koba-Ivanovich was not at all happy at the conference. Tammerfors may have marked the beginning of Stalin's hatred of Lenin, which reached its culmination in 1924.

Now in late December, 1905, the train that threaded its way through the interminable frozen Finnish lakes and snow took him back to St. Petersburg. He was confident, we can be sure, that he would cross the frontier with no difficulty, as he had done before.

7 | THE AVLABAR AFFAIR

The Tammerfors Conference makes a small chapter in bolshevik history. The forty-one delegates, meeting from December 12 to 17, debated whether to boycott the forthcoming Duma elections; but numbering at best a few thousand in Russia at that time, they would have exercised little influence on the elections, boycott or not. Also, their resolution calling for "the immediate preparation and organization of an armed uprising" was redundant, inasmuch as the workers of Moscow had already risen in armed rebellion. (After troops unmercifully crushed the revolt, the Okhrana official, Rachkovsky, was awarded seventy-five thousand rubles by the government,[324] indicating this may have been another instance of Okhrana provocation.) The delegates were now anxious to leave the bitterly cold Tammerfors, where they had been relatively cut off from the swiftly moving events in Russia. Their departure was duly reported by the Okhrana agent at the Conference, whose notebooks containing details of his surveillance of Lenin during this period have survived.[325] Singly or in pairs, the delegates entrained in the latter half of December for St. Petersburg, where they arrived in a day or two without experiencing any recorded difficulty.

Koba spent several days in St. Petersburg, a magnificent city, quite different from the cities of his native Caucasus. One can well imagine his fascination with the capital and the tempo of its life during this first visit. He called at the faction Headquarters, the party's newspaper offices, and had an opportunity to meet a few party leaders. Trotsky aptly remarked that this trip was a milestone in Koba's career, something he must have contemplated as he began his return to Tiflis on Russian Christmas Eve, January 6, 1906.[326]

In his ten-day journey by train en route to the Caucasus, Koba experienced no difficulty, although this was a period when the gendarmerie and Department of Police reaction to the events of 1905 should have made winter travel less than easy for an ostensibly twice-arrested and escaped Georgian revolutionary. Within a month he had travelled almost six thousand miles in a country ravaged by uprisings, through cities under siege, and via railways on strike. The movement of travellers through Moscow and St. Petersburg was subject to strict security regulations during this period.[327]

Koba was purposefully vague when he indicated in his *Collected Works* that he arrived in Tiflis from Tammerfors sometime in January, 1906. At the earliest he was back in his home-town haunts by January 21, 1906, unavoidable delays adding probably five days to his journey. When he returned to Tiflis, the mensheviks retained complete control of the Georgian party organization and operations. At about this time a "secret" Caucasian bolshevik factional organization had been formed outside the context of the St. Petersburg Martov-Lenin conversations to which Koba had apparently been privy. Little was known about that curious outfit, which had been devised by Lenin to keep control of a small bolshevik conspiratorial group in the Caucasian fortress of menshevism. The "secret" bolshevik unit in Tiflis included Koba, although most of the other members remain unknown. Alipi (Kote) Tsintsadze, another member, throws light on the activities of the bolshevik organization in early 1906:

An era of reaction ensued at the outset of 1906 after the defeat of the [1905] revolution. Arsenius Dzhordzhashvili, a comrade, was supposed to kill General Griaznov who was both a horrid reactionary and the person responsible for the suppression of the Georgian revolutionary movement. The terrorist act was delayed. Stalin sent for me and stated: "If within the following week Dzhordzhashvili does not murder Griaznov, the job is yours, for which you must organize selected terrorists." Dzhordzhashvili accomplished his mission, however.[328]

Koba's part in planning the assassination of General Griaznov suggests that in early 1906 when he returned to Tiflis, he was directing

terrorist acts. He was also doing a bit of writing. His unsigned article "Two Skirmishes," in the Georgian language, appeared January
7, 1906, in a pamphlet under the auspices of the Caucasian Union
Committee of the Georgian Social Democratic Party. Written before Tammerfors, it is unmistakably a Koba commentary on
Bloody Sunday. Typically, his analysis repetitiously hammered
home the theme that Bloody Sunday failed because organization
within a unified party (needless to say, with bolshevik direction)
was lacking. Arms were necessary, but organization, and more organization, was the quintessence of revolutionary success and eventual victory.[329]

On March 8th, his next article, "The State Duma and the Tactics
of Social Democracy," was published in the Georgian language
newspaper *The Dawn*. For the first time, he displayed a clear confidence in an idea he supposedly had personally developed and ar-
ticulated in opposition to Lenin; namely, that the bolsheviks must
boycott the elections for the Duma, which he denigrated as a
"mongrel parliament."

> Boycott tactics—this is the direction in which the development of
> revolution is now going. This is the direction in which Social-Democ-
> racy, too, should go.[330]

Also for the first time, he signed this article "I. Besoshvili," com-
prising the initial of his first name Iosif and the nickname "Beso"
(another diminutive meaning Little Joe) with the Georgian equivalent of "Mac" to make his last name "the family of Little Joe."

Using the same signature, he wrote a series of four articles titled
"Concerning the Agrarian Question," published in the Tiflis journal
Elva (*Lightning*), during the latter part of March. He emphasized
that only peasant ownership of land could solve the agricultural
problem in Russia. And he was perhaps the first bolshevik to insist
that

> transfer of the land to the peasants and the division of these lands
> will sap the foundations of the survival of serfdom, prepare the ground
> for the development of capitalist farming, give a great impetus to the

revolutionary upsurge, and precisely for these reasons these measures are acceptable to the Social-Democratic Party.

Thus to abolish the remnants of serfdom it is necessary to confiscate all the lands of the landlords, and then the peasants must take this land as their property and divide it up among themselves in conformity with their interests.[331]

Toward the end of March, more than two months after his return to Tiflis, he was "elected" a delegate to the Stockholm "Unity" Congress, where Lenin and others hoped to bring into agreement the mensheviks and the bolsheviks. Souvarine, Stalin's biographer, indignantly asks:

Stalin, under the name of Ivanovich, represented the provinces of Tiflis at the Congress. By what subterfuge had he secured election in a district practically entirely in Menshevik hands? In reality, he represented only the handful of local Bolsheviks, too weak in every respect to stand up against the traditions of Georgian socialism, but clever enough to constitute an obscure spirit of conciliation.[332]

After his return from Finland, Stalin's two months in Tiflis had been marked not by political activity but by his possible involvement in a murder, in writing some revolutionary literature, and in one of the most controversial episodes of his career: the police raid on the Avlabar secret printing press in Tiflis.

In 1903 the overwhelmingly menshevik Caucasian Union Committee commissioned Mikho Bochoridze, a former railway employee, to set up an illegal printing plant. Mikho had had some previous experience in this type of operation. When David Rostomashvili, also a former railway employee and Mikho's closest friend, made some land available to the Caucasian Union Committee, work began on the most elaborate installation of its kind in the Caucasus, if not in all Russia.[333] By November of 1903, Mikho and several other reliable social democrats had completed the construction of a two-room single-story brick building with a tiled roof and a basement that also consisted of two rooms. It was located on the outskirts of Tiflis in the suburb of Avlabar. Across the nearby railway tracks was the Petropavlovsk cemetery not far, the record tells us, from a "new barracks for contagious diseases." Neither the exterior appearance of the house nor the carriage shed behind it was unusual in any way. However, the shed had been built over a well, the wall of which was bricked and its top covered with wooden lattice and a wire net. Wooden rungs and steps were arranged down the side of the well almost to the very water level, forty-nine feet below the surface. At that point an entrance led to a large room equipped with a fresh-air ventilator. Here the illegal printing press was located.[334] The construction of such a clandestine enterprise in 1903 represented a highly professional accomplishment on the part of the Georgian social democrats and they were justifiably proud of it.

"Avlabar," as it came to be known, functioned without interruption from the end of 1903 until March of 1906. Stalin was to imply almost until his death that he had escaped from Siberian exile at the beginning of 1904 and, together with M. G. Tskhakaya, "led the Caucasian Union Committee of the R.S.D.R.P.," and thus he had been in charge of the Avlabar underground installation. Some of his sycophants even claimed that he had organized the operation —an obvious falsehood, because during 1903 he was in Batum and Kutais prisons. One source writing in 1937 went so far as to insist that the Avlabar printing plant had been created on the specific order of Koba while he was still in prison.[335] All of this was patently fraudulent, for he had absolutely nothing to do with the construction or operation of the illegal Avlabar printing press. Even in the period 1904 to 1906, Koba Dzhugashvili had a shady reputation in Tiflis social-democratic circles and no one would have trusted him with the direction of such a sensitive operation.[336]

The Avlabar typesetters and printers, gnome-like in their deep underground room with its presses and its Armenian, Georgian, and Russian type, were industrious. In less than a month—from November 20th to December 16, 1904—they turned out more than thirty thousand copies of various publications. From January to November of 1905, the clandestine printers produced over 275,-000 copies of illegal newspapers, brochures, and leaflets on a "Boston" type-press. (It must be remembered that small proclamations or announcements half the size of a piece of stationery constituted the majority of Avlabar's production.) Well-refined distribution channels and outlets were in the hands of a special group including a man called Kamo, about whom we shall hear more. But Avlabar was more than an illegal printing-press. According to the record, it served as a secret workshop for the preparation of "passports and other documents for party underground workers." Conceivably, Koba might have obtained his illegal passports in 1905 and 1906 from Avlabar, but in light of the fact that the mensheviks detested and distrusted him, this seems unlikely. As a storage place for sensitive records of the Union Committee, lists of "conspiratorial addresses" throughout the Caucasus were secured at Avlabar.[337]

The Tiflis Gendarme Administration, noting the ever-increasing amount of illegal literature appearing in the area, conducted numerous "sweeps" of all parts of Tiflis and its environs during 1904 and 1905 in attempts to locate the press. However, regardless of the concern of the Department of Police in St. Petersburg and the Tiflis Gendarme Administration (evidenced by plentiful correspondence), Avlabar remained secure and unknown to the police for more than two years. Its difficulties began in early 1906, several weeks after Koba had returned from the Tammerfors Conference to Tiflis.

As a result of decisions at the Tammerfors Conference and the Lenin-Martov discussions in St. Petersburg—to which, as already noted, Koba had apparently been privy—a loose partnership of mensheviks and bolsheviks had been arranged. The Georgian social-democratic organization, as will be recalled, was largely menshevik, although in January and February of 1906 "unifying conferences" of the R.S.D.R.P. were convened in Tiflis and Baku and other cities of Transcaucasia. These, in turn, elected "unified" committees that included the few bolsheviks, who, nonetheless, secretly continued as a nucleus opposed to the other social democrats. In February, 1906, a Tiflis unified committee was established and the Caucasian Union dissolved. Thereafter, Avlabar was directed by the Tiflis unified committee.[338]

Although Koba was to claim much later that some of his own

articles and leaflets were printed at Avlabar, his first knowledge of
the operational intricacies of the installation and its precise location came after the dreary and complex meetings of unifying conferences and unified committees in the latter part of February or
the first part of March. Only then did the mensheviks reluctantly
reveal the information to the likes of Stalin. Two or three weeks
later the Tiflis Okhrana received its first definite information about
Avlabar from one of its agents who has never been identified.[339] In
the meantime, probably during the early days of March, the printing press at Avlabar ceased operation. Upon the order of the Central Committee of the R.S.D.R.P., which was largely menshevik,
the operators of the Avlabar press had departed for St. Petersburg
to work at the presses of the Central Committee there. A more
sinister operation replaced the production of leaflets and newspapers at Avlabar. What were euphemistically called "military-
technical" groups of the Tiflis unified committee of the R.S.D.R.P.
commenced training in the two rooms above the underground
printing press "preparing instructors for the leadership of armed
revolutionary worker uprisings . . . [and] in one of the rooms
there was a laboratory for making bombs and explosives." In other
words, Avlabar had been converted into a school for terrorism and
under the auspices not of the bolsheviks but of a menshevik-
dominated "unified" Tiflis committee.[340]

The Tiflis Okhrana could well have moved against Avlabar and
crushed it at the end of March when agent information identified
the location of the operation. Instead Avlabar was placed under
intensive "special surveillance" from the first of April, in order to
identify persons connected with the operation. Only two weeks
later, on April 15th, "early in the morning was the house surrounded by gendarmes, police, and rifle detachments. A search was
begun . . . [and] the illegal printing press was discovered."
Later in the day a general Okhrana dragnet enveloped Tiflis. David
Rostomashvili, the titular owner of the Avlabar property, was arrested. The Okhrana descended on the offices of *Elva* [*Lightning*],
the legal newspaper of the unified social democrats, and arrested
twenty-four persons, among whom were Bochoridze, who had done

so much in the construction of Avlabar, and Makharadze, a prominent party member. The latest Soviet account of the raid on Avlabar notes that "in connection with the printing press M. Tskakaya
and N. Aladzhalova were also arrested," adding that "at the moment of the downfall of the Avlabar illegal printing press I. V.
Stalin and S. G. Shaumyan were in Stockholm as delegates to the
IV 'unification' congress of the RSDRP." [341] It might have been
added that at the very end of March, when Koba had departed
from Tiflis en route to Stockholm, the Tiflis Okhrana had begun its
round-the-clock physical surveillance of Avlabar and it had delayed its raid on the installation until April 15th. Stalin had arrived
in Stockholm six days earlier, on April 9th.

Soviet accounts complain that the so-called "bourgeoisie-
national" press in Tiflis carried extensive front-page accounts
about Avlabar's downfall. Indeed it was a story that could scarcely
be ignored. At one point the Avlabar affair had been sufficiently
important for a report from Durnovo, the Minister of the Interior,
to Premier Witte.[342] An account in the St. Petersburg newspaper
Novoye Vremia (*New Times*), of April 19, 1906, is worth summa-
rizing:

On April 15 in the courtyard of an uninhabited house in Avlabar
belonging to D. Rostomashvili near the Municipal Hospital for Contagious Diseases a seventy-foot-deep well which could be descended
by rope and pulley was discovered. A tunnel led to another well at a
depth of fifty feet where a ladder of about thirty-five feet provided
access to a vault underneath the house. The vault contained a completely equipped illegal printing plant with twenty cases of Russian,
Georgian, and Armenian type, a hand press, various acids and para-
phernalia for the manufacture of bombs, a great deal of illegal literature, various governmental seals, and infernal machines. Acetylene
lamps illuminated the plant which had an electrical signalling system.
Bombs, casings and similar materials were found in a shed in the
courtyard of the house. At a meeting in the editorial offices of the
newspaper *Elva* twenty-four persons were arrested, and charged with
implication in the affair. A great quantity of subversive literature and
more than twenty blank passport forms were found in the *Elva* offices
which were sealed. Electric wires proceeding in several directions have
caused other excavations to be made. Five carts were needed to re-

move the equipment found in Avlabar. Three persons arrested in connection with the printing plant sang the *Marseillaise* on the way to prison.

On April 17th, two days after the raid, the Chief of the Tiflis Gendarme Administration telegraphically reported the events of April 15th to the St. Petersburg Headquarters of the Department of Police. Numerous detailed Okhrana reports about Avlabar have emanated from Soviet sources and must be cautiously viewed. However, one account appears somewhat accurate and, at any rate, it is too droll to be overlooked. It states that on April 15, 1906, Captain Yulipets[343] of the Separate Corps of Gendarmes conducted a search in the home of the mechanic David Rostomashvili in the settlement of Novo-Troitsk, situated between Tiflis and the small town of Navtlug. On one window was a "For Rent" sign. There were no residents, but it was apparent that the house had recently been inhabited, for a samovar, cold water, and a lamp were discovered in one room together with a teapot with tea, "three pieces of sugar, two glasses, and a spoon." Coal, potatoes, pepper, butter, green onions, and water were discovered in the two basement rooms. This was not unusual and thus far the little house appeared no different from many others. However, the Captain found four copper bomb casings in the nearby shed. Naturally this led him to a closer inspection of the premises, and his attention was attracted to a well in the shed. He decided to perform a simple test: he threw burning paper down the well. It came to rest toward the bottom and burned out against the side of the well, thus providing fairly conclusive evidence that a source of air impelled it to that position and indicating an entrance from the well. Finally it was established that not far above the water level an entrance led from the well to an area underneath the house and to a room twenty-four feet in length, fifteen feet in width, and about nine feet in height. A ventilating system brought fresh air to the underground area.

In the cave the gendarmes found dynamite, bomb casings, bickford fuses, and various types of acids and materials for the manufacture of bombs. Cases of ammunition and several revolvers were stacked in the room. Two benzine lamps on a table illuminated an

Augsburg typesetting machine, No. 1346, with about eighteen hundred pounds of type. Among proclamations, brochures, and handwritten items were "two passport books, five clean passport blanks and seven passports. . . ." That the Okhrana seized only two passport books for travel abroad of the fourteen official documents testifies to the difficulty of obtaining false papers for foreign travel. Stamps necessary for passports were discovered, plus a number of seals of social-democratic organizations in the Caucasus. The hundreds of incendiary revolutionary proclamations included pamphlets and brochures that called for an armed uprising and an overthrow of the monarchy. Copies of *Iskra* and articles by Lenin, Plekhanov, Martov, Vera Zasulich "and others" were found. One document that dealt with revolutionary subjects particularly arrested the attention of the Okhrana. It called for an uprising of troops and declared, "Don't listen to your officers, better yet—kill them." [344]

On the same date—April 15, 1906—a search was conducted also on the premises of the editoral offices of the Tiflis Georgian newspaper *Elva*. Here, among other things, there were seized 25 passports and 7 passport blanks. . . . During the raids on the editorial offices of *Elva* 24 persons found there were arrested.

In the prosecution of this case two female witnesses—Khistinia Medvedeva and Lukeriia Degaeva—who lived near the home [Avlabar] of David Rostomashvili and observed persons visiting it provided formal testimony.

These witnesses were among those arrested at the editorial offices of *Elva* and identified several visitors at the Rostomashvili home. [345]

Expert opinion, according to this report, established the fact that seals in the *Elva* offices were the same as those seized at Avlabar and that copies of stamps and passports and blanks were one and the same at *Elva* and Avlabar. Thus there was a connection between the two operations. [346]

The police raid on Avlabar and *Elva* on April 15, 1906, was followed by the arrests of many social-democratic activists in Tiflis. And, of course, Koba in Stockholm was untouched. However, the official Okhrana reports of this incident—of which there are several—bear evidence of heavy editing. Because many of them reposed so long in Stalin's personal domain of Georgia, this is not surprising. Yet one account of the raid on Avlabar, and the events leading up to it, is unmistakably accurate although it is on a completely different subject.

In November of 1909—three years after Avlabar—the Department of Police decided to improve the surveillance techniques of its detectives or surveillance agents [*filery*]. To that end a special commission headed by Major General Aleksander V. Gerasimov, who held the imposing title of Chief of the Division for Guarding the General Security and Order in St. Petersburg, was appointed to study the problem. It invited testimony from officers of the Separate Corps of Gendarmes and others, who could cite examples that might lead to corrections of errors in surveillance and provide suggestions for an improvement in methods of observing revolutionaries. Colonel Nikolai A. Zasypkin, who had been on duty in Tiflis at the time of the Avlabar raid, provided testimony:

About April of 1905 [he related] I received agent data about the location of a central printing plant of the Caucasian social-democratic union that generally served the entire Transcaucasian area. It included a laboratory for making explosive charges. Because of the agent information concerning the extraordinary conspiratorial nature of the printing plant's underground premises and entrance and, moreover, because the agent himself had not seen the premises or entrances . . . it was desirable to find out the connection between the organization and the leaders of this technical enterprise. Earlier there had been agent information about the aforementioned leaders and the locality in which the printing plant had to be found; the leaders were placed under surveillance, but to observe the whereabouts [of the printing plant] in such an unfavorable area had been unsuccessful. Upon receiving the above mentioned agent data about the house that was located completely outside the city and opposite a cemetery, the most experienced surveillance agents were directed to establish observation. Regardless of the situation [of the house] that was in a relatively uninhabited and empty area outside the city, by pulling together all the surveillance agents it was established who was living at the house, their connection with an organization and the leaders of the operation —after which it was decided to carry out liquidation. But one unexpected meaningless occurrence . . . involving one of the surveillance agents took place: he unexpectedly ran into one of the persons under observation. . . . He did not know how to take conspiratorial measures and, proceeding several steps further, he turned around and noted the subject under surveillance was intently staring at him. That very same night, on April 15, the printing press and laboratory, actually a semi-fantastic conspiracy, with grandiose materials, bombs, infernal machines and documents were seized, while the very same day, thanks to the very same surveillance, an entire social-democratic collective with documents establishing the connection between the said printing plant and the laboratory was seized at a meeting, but none of the residents at the said printing plant could be apprehended. A day or so later the surveillance agent who had been identified by his subject was killed on the street by revolutionaries.[347]

It is clear from this passage that bureaucratic intelligence officers of today do not enjoy a monopoly of gobbledygook in their speeches or reports. Gendarme Colonel Zasypkin was attempting to tell a story that revealed the following significant points: An agent of the Tiflis Okhrana, who was also a social democrat, had learned about the general location of Avlabar and the persons who were the "leaders" of the operation. In order to determine the precise location of the printing plant, Zasypkin had these persons shadowed, but the leaders were able to throw off their shadows before they reached the installation or the shadows found it impossible to avoid recognition in the open area around the Avlabar printing plant. In any event, the Okhrana had been frustrated in its surveillance for many months. Though the agent had reported the precise location and all the details, he had not unfortunately seen "the premises or entrances." One of the social democrats who frequented the Avlabar premises, after spotting his Okhrana shadow accidentally encountered him in Tiflis. The Okhrana agent was not sufficiently trained to remain casual and revealed his identity to the revolutionary; he was murdered on a Tiflis street a day or so after the happenings of April 15, 1906.

There are several noteworthy facets of Colonel Zasypkin's account not the least of which is that it was published in 1917, and before the bolshevik seizure of power in Russia. Thus it had not been censored by Stalin or any of his cronies. Furthermore the Colonel, testifying in 1909 about a raid he knew had occurred in 1906, began his narrative by incorrectly stating that he had received agent information "about April of *1905*." We are entitled to regard a mistake of this sort as an attempt to provide an additional measure of cover to the agent who had betrayed the Avlabar operation. Since the agent knew the general location of Avlabar and its leaders before he learned its exact location and operational details leaves no doubt that he had been affiliated with the Okhrana long before 1906, that he was a bolshevik, and that he was in a position to know only the broad outlines of the Avlabar operation until after the "unification" of bolsheviks and mensheviks in late February or early March of 1906. Had the agent been a menshevik, the Okhrana doubtlessly would have known long before about the location of Avlabar. During the weeks between that date and the end of March the agent had been able to supply the Okhrana with information denied them for more than two years.

It is not to be overlooked that in all the official Okhrana reports about Avlabar, Stalin is mentioned only as author of a few articles turned out by its presses. However, Trotsky would later claim, along with several Georgians who had emigrated to Western Europe, that Stalin had been arrested and released in connection with the raid on Avlabar.[348] It was usually suggested that Stalin had informed the police about Avlabar in return for an Okhrana promise that he would be allowed to attend the forthcoming Stockholm Congress. If the Okhrana had arrested Koba in 1906, it was before April 1 or after June 1 and, as we have seen, he must have departed Tiflis at the latest by March 31st in order to reach Stockholm in time for the Congress. An arrest in connection with Avlabar could only have been in February or March, and was necessary as an extension of Koba's "cover" status within the Okhrana. Of one thing we may be sure, Koba was not arrested with the other revolutionaries on April 15, 1906. He was already in Stockholm.

There remain the perplexing statement made by Trotsky and the puzzling and jumbled account of Koba's arrest in either 1905 or 1906 by Arzenidze, who was incarcerated in Tiflis in April 1906. The latter wrote:

I well remember one 1906 meeting in the "Kharpukhi" section of Tiflis in which several responsible comrades including some in an illegal status (comrades Ramishvili, Dzhaparidze, a member of the 2nd State Duma) and others participated. That day I had been chairman of the meeting. The bolsheviks turned out in an insignificant minority. Koba was sullen, quite defiant, crude, evidently trying to disrupt the meeting. I found myself obliged to exchange sharp remarks with him. To my observation that he was behaving indecently, he jauntily answered that he had not yet let down his trousers and that there had been nothing indecent in his behavior. I remarked that he was conducting himself like someone without his pants on and like a "wanderer without drawers." This was a popular expression meaning "a woman of the streets." I thought this remark would arouse his indignation. Nothing at all happened: he merely grinned spitefully from the left side of his mouth and remained in place. After several minutes he got up and left the meeting. Immediately after his departure we heard the agreed-upon whistle warning us that the police were coming. We had to scatter without concluding the meeting, but there were no police anywhere on the street, only our bewildered patrols guarding the meeting. They had been unable to point out who had whistled and who had personally seen the police detachments. It was clear to everyone that this had been Koba's prank.[349]

In the paragraph following this account Arsenidze apparently is concerned with a different episode as he continues:

I will finish my story about the arrest of Soso by Zasypkin who proposed that he become an agent of the *okhranki* [Okhrana]. This event, *i.e.*, the arrest of Stalin actually took place and I can categorically verify that Soso was released from the gendarme administration but did not appear in Metekh fortress.[350]

Arsenidze was "sitting" (as political prisoners then and now describe their incarcerations) in Metekh prison in Tiflis. Had Koba appeared in prison, Arsenidze insists he would have been greeted, as were all prisoners, with applause. However, no one saw him arrive. Unfortunately Arsenidze sometimes confused dates and in this instance we are unable to determine when Koba's arrest occurred, although it must have been in Tiflis and in 1905 or 1906.

Trotsky's assertion (made twenty-five years before Arsenidze's account) that Koba had been arrested in connection with Avlabar now assumes greater significance. So does Arsenidze's reference to Captain Zasypkin, whose agent provided the information leading to the Avlabar raid and who later in 1909 described it in an uncensored version. Not to be overlooked in this regard is the Okhrana report stating that Koba was arrested in 1905 and escaped—a bit of information curiously missing from all Stalin's official or unofficial biographies.

There are several interesting ingredients in this mélange. First of all is the near certainty that Koba was arrested in 1905 or 1906 by Okhrana officer Zasypkin. Although an arrest just before Avlabar conceivably would have enhanced Koba's revolutionary image, it would have been out of character for the Okhrana to make an arrest for this purpose without broadcasting it. As a matter of fact Koba, himself, could have been expected to advertise such an event. That neither he nor the Okhrana mention the arrest is reasonably good evidence that it took place before the Avlabar raid, and was a camouflage for a briefing with Koba. While it would have been risky to talk with Koba in a Tiflis Okhrana "safe house," to "arrest" him provided a plausible reason for receiving his knowledge recently gained about Avlabar. This may explain the cryptic Okhrana entry in Stalin's dossier that he was arrested and escaped from prison in 1905. While this might have been a typographical error, there is a possibility that the Okhrana was playing it safe and substituting 1905 for 1906. Zasypkin's account of the 1905 Avlabar raid is somewhat more understandable within the context of this interpretation.

Over twenty months passed before the persons arrested in connection with Avlabar and *Elva* were tried by a Tiflis court of law on December 24, 1907.[351] They had remained incarcerated during the intervening months but one of those convicted was released from prison in less than two months, by her own admission.[352] She was Nina Nikitchna Aladzhalova, a bolshevik and self-styled music teacher who had maintained a "safe house" for democratic circles. Koba had frequented her apartment at No. 63 Avchalskaya Street in Tiflis for conspiratorial purposes.

Nina Aladzhalova was two or three years younger than Koba. She had joined the social democrats in 1902—although one account reads "communist party of the Soviet Union"—and had then worked as a "propagandist" in the Tiflis social-democratic organization. From January of 1905 she had been a member of the Caucasus Union Committee as "technical" secretary. It is interesting that the official Soviet account claims she was an important party member in the Caucasus from 1917 to 1919, that the Georgian menshevik government arrested her twice during the period 1919-21, that after the establishment of Soviet authority in Georgia she occupied increasingly important party positions, and that, unlike most of the Georgian bolsheviks then associated with Stalin, she survived his purges. As of 1954 Nina, almost seventy-three years of age, was retired and still living in Georgia on a pension. She outlived Stalin.[353]

Her own piquant account, "Little Pages from Recollections," of the Avlabar operation, which was published in Tiflis in 1954, is told in less than four pages.[354] "During the summer of 1904," she relates, "I was residing at Avchalskaya Street, No. 63 [now Sovietskaya 55, she adds], and occupying one room in a courtyard to the right side of a gate. The door of my room went out to a balcony." At that time she was employed as a technical secretary of the Caucasus Union Committee and her "room became a conspiratorial apartment of the committee," in which sensitive materials were kept. These included the protocols of the Second Party Congress written on "thin cigarette paper," materials from the Avlabar press, party documents, and conspiratorial addresses. She noted that the bolsheviks at that time were training instructors in military affairs, in "partisan street fighting," and in the preparation of explosives. To this end a specialist engineer had been "recruited" who was instructing bolsheviks and mensheviks in Tiflis. Unfortunately during an instruction period an unexpected explosion had filled the apartment with smoke and had worried the neighbors. The instructions thereafter took place at Avlabar, to which Nina moved. One day Mikho noted one of Zasypkin's surveillance agents reading a newspaper near the Avlabar premises. This was enough; they departed for Tiflis. A day passed, and then at dawn she was awakened by a strong rap on the door of her Tiflis apartment. "Open the door, it's a telegram. . . ." Then, instantly, dozens of irate gendarmes, according to Nina, charged into her apartment and conducted a search of the premises that lasted three hours. She proudly relates that although everything was examined, they found nothing of a compromising character. But she was arrested there and then and incarcerated in the formidable Metekh prison-fortress that rested on a rock pile high above the city of Tiflis. But, she adds, "after a month and one-half I was free."

Out of the dozens of arrests made in connection with Avlabar and *Elva* only two persons were relatively unhurt: Stalin because he was in Stockholm and Nina Aladzhalova whose "safe house" Stalin had frequented. This pattern of police raids when Stalin is conveniently somewhere else is already familiar to the reader and it will recur. Also there is almost always a person in a "safe house" or in Stalin's quarters who somehow survived Stalin's purges unscathed. Many outlived him. But there were always arrests, always his absence, and always a plausible explanation for his absence.

8 | STOCKHOLM AND LONDON

The Fourth Stockholm Congress of the social democratic party was held in April, 1906. The minutes of the menshevik-dominated Congress prove that Koba was on hand for the first session on April 10th.[355] Because at least ten days were required for his journey to Stockholm, he left Tiflis at the latest on March 31st, just after an unidentified agent had provided the Okhrana with information leading to the raid on Avlabar.

Koba needed documents for his trip to Stockholm. Since 1903 imperial laws had been explicit about local residence permits, passports, and foreign travel, all of which were interrelated.[356] His residence permit, which recorded Koba's arrests and exiles, served as a basic identification and travel document (persons under police supervision or surveillance could obtain a residence permit only from the police). It included information about crimes, sentences, and the notation, "The bearer is forbidden to live in national capitals or their provinces, near military forts, and all other cities are off limits." To go abroad a citizen was also required to submit a written petition to the provincial governor or to a mayor and obtain a document certifying that there were no legal obstacles to foreign travel. With police approval, a booktype "passport for foreign travel" was issued with two detachable coupons—one removable at the time of departure, and the other at the time of return, by the Governor General or the Provincial Police Chief in Tiflis. Each passport included a photograph, the bearer's name and profession, the name of the issuer, and date and place of issue, all in Russian, French, and German. Presumably Koba was photographed in a studio in Tiflis before he embarked on his several trips abroad

(Okhrana standard operational procedure preferred an informant at such passport photographic studios), but it was also possible, on the other hand, that Koba obtained from private bolshevik sources his necessary passport photographs. Koba may have purchased a false passport from one of the foreign consulates in Tiflis, or might have stolen one; if he had procured it in the "spirit of the revolution," we may be sure this fact would have been perpetuated as a bit of Soviet lore, but there is nothing about it in official or unofficial literature.

The government fee of fifteen rubles for each passport was slightly less than the monthly wages of an average worker at that time. There was also the crucial problem of obtaining rubles for rail and steamship tickets and food, details always ignored in Soviet accounts of Koba's travels. Although he could not have known how long he would be away from Tiflis (as it turned out, he was gone almost two months), he needed a minimum of a hundred and fifty rubles, based on rail and ship fares then current, a sum ten times the average monthly wages of a factory worker. Moreover, we must also remember that Koba had been unemployed for five years and was leaving at home a wife and baby whose welfare was apparently of some importance to him. It is doubtful whether by this time bolshevik brigandage in Georgia could have raked in sufficient funds to finance his trip to Stockholm. The so-called "expropriations" of banks, the major robberies, that were to net money for the bolshevik coffers, had not yet reached large proportions. They were to become a matter of serious deliberation at Stockholm. At any rate, Koba, without any apparent financial means, started out in late March on a sixty-two-hundred mile journey.

He was the one bolshevik in a delegation of eleven from Tiflis,[357] the other ten being mensheviks whose organization would not have contributed a kopek to transport Koba anywhere. Stepan Georgievich Shaumyan also attended the Congress as a delegate from Erevan.

The Tiflis Okhrana, closely observing the departure of the social democrats for Stockholm, failed to cite Koba in police reports. Reacting to the events of 1905, tsarist authorities by this time had imposed tight security measures throughout the empire. Travellers were frequently asked to show their documents and otherwise identify themselves. Koba experienced no difficulty as he proceeded to Stockholm through the same corps of security troops and officers he had twice encountered just a short time before. His route took him by rail through Moscow to St. Petersburg and thence to the Finnish port of Abo, from which the United Steamship Company, Ltd., of Copenhagen, carried most of the delegates to Stockholm.[358] For the third time in four months he crossed the Finnish-Russian frontier uneventfully, evaded nineteen gendarme rail checkpoints, and hoodwinked the security officials as he set sail from Finland.

One delegate, Stanislav G. Strumilo-Petrashevich, who may have been Koba's fellow passenger—but does not mention him—recalled an amusing incident. Between Finland and Sweden the ship struck a rock off one of the innumerable islands in the Gulf of Bothnia, and the sailors feared the vessel would sink. As the delegates, unperturbed when the ship began to take on a dangerous amount of water, continued to debate the agrarian question even when they were transferred to another ship, a sailor remarked, "Those Russian revolutionaries are certainly curious people!" [359]

Sixty-six mensheviks and forty-five bolsheviks with voting rights, as well as forty-odd observers from Polish, Lithuanian, Latvian, and the Jewish parties, attended the Fourth Stockholm Congress of the Russian Social-Democratic Party.[360] Dubbed the "Unity" Congress, it had a curious genesis. Elena Stasova, Secretary of the St. Petersburg Social-Democratic Committee, had approached the Swedish socialists Bergegren and Holmström, asking them to make arrangements for the Congress, and with their agreement it convened in Stockholm from April 10th to 25th at the Folkets Hus, where the delegates were served tea, milk, and sandwiches during intermissions from their factional wrangling. Hjalmar Branting, later the Swedish Prime Minister—in 1920, 1921-23, and 1924-25—greeted the delegates in the name of Swedish socialism. There was no public announcement in Sweden concerning the Congress until weeks after it ended, when Branting described it in a newspaper article.[361]

If the Swedish public at large was ignorant of the Congress, the authorities were not. The Russian delegates were obliged to register with the notably efficient Stockholm police, who closely scrutinized their passports. One revolutionary protested that they "even measured fingers." [362] Stockholm police records dispute those biographers who have claimed that Koba was in Stockholm as Ivanovich, for he is listed as Ivan Ivanovich Vissarionovich, a journalist, in their files.[363] If Koba attended the Tammerfors Conference as Ivanovich in December, 1905, how was it possible for him to appear at the Stockholm Congress four months later with a passport as Vissarionovich? Had the Okhrana not only supplied him with funds, but a new passport also? [363a]

The 1906 Stockholm Congress debated many problems, but two of them were fundamental: the distribution of land under socialist conditions and the financing of the revolution.[364] Both were sticky questions and implied, of course, truth and consequences. To be truthful might well jeopardize the cause of social democracy in Russia. Knowing nothing about Marx and caring less, the Russian peasant yearned with ever-increasing impatience for his own arable plot of ground. Yet the consequence of a policy that would allow millions of Russian peasants to own land in perpetuity was a frightening idea to the social democrats. The conventional marxist position regarding land seemed to be that come the revolution, the peasant would have moved to the city and be a member of the urban proletariat, and if he remained in the village, he would be a sort of indentured employee of the state working on state property. But the Russian *muzhik* would reject out of hand any political party or person mouthing this nonsensical idea. Nonetheless, after much thought, Lenin favored nationalizing the land; the mensheviks preferred that it be turned over to municipalities. Although the latter policy was adopted by the Congress, it remained for Koba to cut through the dialectical underbrush and, in opposition to Lenin, advance an essentially simple, pragmatic solution he had earlier advocated in one of his articles. The *muzhik's* grievances may not be turned to our advantage, he pointed out, by splitting Marxist-Engelian hairs. The peasant craves a farm of his own, even in his dreams. So why not give the peasant his own piece of property? Or, rather, let him seize what he wants from the landlord.[365] Although he did not articulate it at Stockholm, there was probably the thought in the back of Koba's shrewd mind that *after* the revolution there would be sufficient time to find a lasting solution to the agricultural problem. Ironically, it was Lenin's proposal that Stalin adopted after he became dictator. Under the guise of "collectivization," he nationalized the land with the result that millions of peasants perished from starvation and many were deported to Siberia. Later Stalin complained that the resistance of the "damned" peasants made collectivization a difficult task.

Of much more importance than finding a solution to the agrarian question was the troublesome problem of raising money to finance the revolution. Lenin in particular was acutely aware of the need for funds, without which newspapers remained unpublished, delegates were unable to attend conferences, militant organizers became inactive, and propaganda tracts were not distributed among the Russian workers. The truth of the matter was that he could envision a situation in which the bolsheviks might be impecunious. While the mensheviks generally favored traditional methods of finance, such as voluntary contributions in the established European tradition of social democracy, Lenin knew that they would hardly keep him and his faction in pocket money. Armed robbery and extortion—in short, "expropriations," which passed into the international argot as the "exes"—seemed to be the only answer to his problem. Of course, he could not openly advocate terrorism and robberies; the consequence would have been outraged protest. The mensheviks at Stockholm were vehemently opposed to expropriations, and the Congress adopted their resolution that opposed robbery, stealing of private property, the expropriation of private bank deposits, protection money, and the destruction of public buildings, property, and railways. While in ostensible disapproval of what he called "apache deviation," Lenin condoned "confiscation of State monies" and, in practice, favored any operation that would bring in funds for *his* revolutionary cause without harming it.[366]

There is no indication that Koba participated in discussions concerning the "exes," although he later did take part in their gory proceedings. What is interesting is that the twenty-six-year-old Stalin, finding himself in a menshevik-dominated Congress, was sufficiently confident to oppose the bolshevik leader Lenin and his ideas in cocksure speeches. Years later he untruthfully attempted to prove that he had always been Lenin's ally. Actually, Koba's respect was declining for Lenin, whose influence seemed to be slipping. Furthermore, the period of reaction had set in. To anyone with any political sense, it was clear that the 1905 revolution, with all its hopes and dreams, had been crushed, and that tsarism would not be effectively challenged for many years, if ever. The idea of a few thousand revolutionaries (at most fourteen thousand bolsheviks and twenty thousand mensheviks were represented at Stockholm[367]) besting the overwhelming might of the Tsar, and particularly his Department of Police, was a distant fantasy.

Stalin publicly mentioned the Stockholm conference only once after his rise to power in Soviet Russia. At a meeting of Kremlin military cadets on January 28, 1924 he recalled:

I met Lenin the second time in 1906, at the Stockholm Congress of our Party. It is well known that at this Congress the Bolsheviks were in the minority, they were defeated. This was the first time I saw Lenin in the role of vanquished. He did not in the least look like those leaders who snivel and become despondent after defeat. On the contrary, defeat transformed Lenin into a coil of energy, inspiring his adherents with courage for fresh battle and for future victory. I said that Lenin was defeated. But what sort of a defeat was it? You should have seen Lenin's opponents, the victors of Stockholm-Plekhanov, Axelrod, Martov and the others; they did not in the least look like real victors because, in his ruthless criticism of Menshevism, Lenin left them, so to speak, without a rag to their name. I remember the Bolshevik delegates gathering together in a small crowd, gazing at Lenin and asking him for advice. In the conversation of some of the delegates one detected a note of weariness and despondency. I remember Lenin, in reply to this kind of talk, sharply saying through his clenched teeth: 'No snivelling, comrades, we shall certainly win, because we are right.' Hatred for snivelling intellectuals, confidence in one's own strength, confidence in victory—this is what Lenin talked to us about at that time. One felt that the defeat of the Bolsheviks was a temporary one, that the Bolsheviks must be victorious in the near future.

"No snivelling over defeat." This is the peculiar feature in the activities of Lenin that helped him to rally around himself an army that was faithful to the last and had confidence in its strength.[368]

Among the delegates at Stockholm were several Okhrana agents, one of whom reported in detail the adopted resolutions, the positions taken by the various factions, and the general attitudes of the delegates. Okhrana agent reports were in St. Petersburg Headquarters before the official hectographed minutes of the Congress that ended April 25, 1906, reached the delegates.[369] The Congress had a semi-comic postlude: although the Chief of Police, Lars Stendahl, had permitted the meetings to be held in Stockholm, provided they were conducted in a civilized and orderly manner, he now discovered that there were insufficient funds for the transportation of some of the delegates back to Russia; he thereupon loaned Hinke Bergegren the necessary money to remove the social democrats from Swedish territory. Whether or not this money was repaid is unknown, but Chief Stendahl obviously took a dim view of Russian revolutionaries remaining in Stockholm.[370]

Koba had little opportunity to see much of the Swedish capital. The sessions of the Congress had literally gone on day and night. He departed from Stockholm no earlier than April 29th, on one of the ships of the United Steamship Company, Ltd., from Stockholm to Abo. Then he proceeded to Helsinki and St. Petersburg, on through Moscow, and back to Tiflis by rail. In over twelve thousand miles, using two false passports, he had evaded hundreds of trained security officials without any recorded difficulty, a truly amazing feat. Moreover, without visible financial resources he had advanced from an inconspicuous revolutionary to a delegate at an important Congress. And he had again engaged the leader of the bolshevik faction of the Social-Democratic Party in debate.

In his *Collected Works* Koba hints that he was back in Tiflis be-

fore June 20, 1906, when he states that No. 1 of *Akhali Tskhovreba*
(*New Life*) under his direction appeared on that date.[371] If he departed from Stockholm on or about April 29th, he would not have
arrived in Tiflis until May 9th. The record suggests that he was
involved in some other activity between early May and the first part
of June. He may have tarried in St. Petersburg for conferences or
he may have been delayed by a revolutionary task in line with his
police cover. Perhaps he returned straightway from Stockholm to
Tiflis and his activities, including "exes" in his home town, have
not been divulged.

Until the end of 1906 there is little information about him except in the autobiographical *Collected Works*. In June and July he
wrote for the newspaper *Akhali,* which he "directed." He claims
that from June to November he also directed the organizational
work of the first trade unions in Tiflis among printers, shop assistants, and others. From June until December he composed a total of
six articles and one pamphlet, among which was a banal report on
the Stockholm Congress. For the first time, he began to use the
signature "Koba," then simply "K." and later "Ko." All his articles
published in Tiflis perodicals were in the Georgian language.[372]

Six articles and one pamphlet, when combined with his desultory
organizing of workers, do not appear sufficient to occupy a period
of almost seven months of his life. A clue to Koba's unreported
activities came from Kote Tsintsadze, who reported:

> After the Congress it became clear that we Bolsheviks could not
> continue to work in one organization with the Mensheviks. I decided
> to create a purely Bolshevik unit for expropriating state funds. Our
> advanced comrades and particularly Koba-Stalin approved my sugges-
> tion. In the middle of November 1906, the expropriators club was
> organized and at the railway junction of Chiatura we attacked a post-
> office railway car and took twenty-one thousand rubles of which fif-
> teen thousand were sent to the Bolshevik faction and the rest to our
> own group to provide for a series of later expropriations.[373]

Stalin would have us believe that during this period he was con-
tinuing to write in Tiflis; otherwise there is no information about

his real activities. According to his *Collected Works,* on February 10th he wrote a preface for the Georgian edition of Kautsky's pamphlet "The Driving Forces and Prospects of the Russian Revolution" and signed it "Koba." From January 1, 1907, until the approximate date of his departure for the Fifth Congress of the Socialist-Democratic Party in London, he wrote a total of five articles, three of them unsigned, one signed "Koba," another signed simply "Ko," and all in Georgian. In the last, unpublished article he sentimentally eulogized G. P. Teliya, his co-delegate to the Tammerfors Conference, who died sometime in March; Koba probably was fond of Teliya, an ex-domestic servant in Tiflis who had been converted to bolshevism from menshevism.

Because there is no solid information concerning his activities for approximately nine months, from about July 1, 1906, until April 1, 1907, it again becomes necessary to attempt a reconstruction of this period of his life.[374] It is not easy. We are certain that he was not gainfully employed and yet that he was able to live near Tiflis, where he was well known by the Okhrana. Probably two months of this period were occupied with his wife's fatal illness (there is no reliable information concerning the reason for her death), the funeral and interment, and the placement of Yasha, his son, in someone's home. There is speculation that Koba's mother agreed to rear the child. Seven months remain in oblivion.

We know that the police had a hand in the scores of terroristic acts that occurred in the Caucasus during this period. Undoubtedly, too, Stalin was involved in the "exes." In the *Collected Works,* however, he ignores the robberies and states that on March 28th and 30th the newspaper *Dro* published the "decision of the worker Bolsheviks in Tiflis to elect J. V. Stalin as a delegate" to the Fifth Congress of the Social-Democratic Party in London.[375] We shall have occasion to return to this matter, but for the moment it is sufficient to note that its minutes prove he was not an "elected" delegate to the Congress, since Lenin proposed him as a consultative delegate after the London conference had opened.

The Social Democrats had initially intended to convene the Fifth Congress in Copenhagen. On May 1, 1907 (N.S.), the Paris Foreign Agency of the Department of Police reported to Prince I. A. Kudashev, then Russian Envoy Extraordinary and Minister Plenipotentiary to Denmark:

> Next week, in Copenhagen, a meeting of Russian revolutionaries is to be held. It is a sort of a congress which is expected to be attended by some 300-400 people. The necessary measures are underway to insure that I get detailed information about the proceedings of the meeting; it is possible that for the surveillance of the participants specially desig-nated people will be sent from Russia, and that I might personally go to Copenhagen (the latter has not yet been decided). Therefore, to aid our cause, I suppose it would be the best if the participants of the Con-gress are given complete freedom to live in Copenhagen so that they do not suspect that the Mission and the local police are well informed. Otherwise they will immediately select Norway or Sweden as the place for their meeting, where observation of them will be more difficult. I informed the Chief of the Copenhagen secret police about it and asked him to explain the situation to Mr. Petersen, Director of the Danish Police Dept. Hoping that you share my aforementioned opinion, I re-main etc., etc. . . .[375a]

A week later the Foreign Agency, somewhat frantically, informed the Director of the Department of Police:

> As soon as I received information about the intention of the soc.-dem. to organize a new congress, I clearly realized the inconvenience of al-lowing this congress to be held abroad because of the freedom they en-joy there, but since I also was convinced that it will be impossible to pre-vent it I applied *all my efforts* to have it take place in Copenhagen. Not mentioning the complete cooperation of the Danish police forces, of which I was certain, I *assured* the presence of the Agency at this con-gress and *undertook all measures* to have the official meetings and the private life and the apartments of the main participants under the con-trol and observation of the Foreign Agency.
> I reported the foregoing on April 17 in Report No. 145.
> As soon as I received your order by cable, dated April 22, indicating the congress could not be held in Copenhagen, I immediately informed the Chief of the Copenhagen Police. Today I received a telegram that the delegates to the congress are leaving for London, where this congress may possibly be held.
> Because of special residence conditions in London it will be impos-

sible to count on the cooperation of the local police forces, and the Agency would be hardly able, fearing a failure, to take an active part in the congress.

I have the honor to report that I have undertaken all measures pursuant to Order No. 1101, dated January 24, 1907, and that, in connection with it, I issued 1000 francs to the agent for his traveling expenses connected with the organization of this congress. Today I sent him another 500 francs following his request for additional funds for travel to London, although there is no guaranty that he will be able to take part in the congress.[375b]

Most of the Russian delegates gathered first in Helsinki, then at Hange, where they boarded the Finnish ship "Astrea" bound for Denmark. Lenin left Finland about April 21st, perhaps on the same ship. Two or three days later, having arrived in Copenhagen, he fired off a telegram to Nissen, Chairman of the Norwegian Social-Democratic Party, who in turn requested the permission of the Norwegian Foreign Office to hold the Congress in Oslo. It was flatly turned down. At this point, London was chosen as the meeting site. In the meantime, the Danish police, deciding that the social democrats were unwelcome, banished them to Malmö, Sweden, a short distance across the straits from Copenhagen, but they found the Swedish authorities less than enthusiastic, so back to Copenhagen. After a wait of some days, the delegates sailed from Esbjerg, Denmark, on the S.S. "J. C. le Cour" for Harwich, at which town they entrained for London.[376]

Meanwhile, Lenin made an unexpected trip from Copenhagen to Berlin, where he spent several days.[377] According to his account, he went sightseeing and met with Maxim Gorky, Kautsky, and Rosa Luxemburg, but that probably did not take up all his time. Krupskaya does not mention this detour, nor is there any reason provided in communist literature for a meeting in Berlin with persons he was to see a few days later in London. Nor was he sightseeing. As for Maxim Gorky, he was later to remember in some detail that he met Lenin for the first time in London in 1907.[378] Gorky, already a famous Russian writer, possessed the keen memory of an experienced journalist. Thus his recollection must be accepted and

Lenin's *Collected Works* must remain suspect insofar as the purpose of Lenin's trip to Berlin is concerned; "sightseeing" and meetings were apparently a camouflage for his real activities there. At any rate, Lenin arrived in London for the Fifth Congress on April 29, 1907.

Koba left Tiflis for London no later than April 2nd. Other Caucasian social democrats—Zhordania, Tsereteli, Dzhibladze, and Shaumyan—left at about the same time. None of them mentioned him as a member of the Caucasian delegation, and because the Georgians did not like him, he probably travelled alone past the same checkpoints and security officials that he had negotiated without difficulty before. If all went well and no one questioned or detained him during the rail trip to St. Petersburg and thence to Helsinki across the carefully guarded Russian-Finnish frontier, he would have arrived in Helsinki about April 13, 1907. From Helsinki he proceeded by rail to the port of Hange, from which he embarked for Copenhagen. He arrived there at the earliest on April 15th. With the erratic comings and goings of the delegates upon their arrival in Copenhagen, it probably required two more weeks for him to reach London in time for the opening of the London Congress on April 30th. But he made it, and he was documented once more as Ivanovich.[379] Within fifteen months on three trips abroad Koba had now utilized three different passports. At both Tammerfors and London his travel documents had been in the name of Ivanovich, but this did not necessarily mean he was carrying the passport at London he had used at Tammerfors. Border guards inevitably stamped pages of his passport that would be scrutinized first upon his return to Russia and later in the Caucasus. Because Koba was presumably "wanted" by the Department of Police, it was risky business for a Georgian "escapee" to utilize the same passport on two trips abroad. Koba never experienced difficulty with border police in regard to his passports. Captain Valdemar Christiansen, captain of the "J. C. le Cour" that carried Stalin and other delegates to London, was fond of relating in later years that he had talked with a passenger "named Stalin" en route to England;[380] this claim tends to disintegrate when we realize that

Koba did not utilize the pseudonym Stalin until years later—but he was on the ship.

London press accounts of 1907 reveal that the delegates arrived in two parties by boat from Denmark to Harwich. On May 10th the *Daily Express* named Mr. Sevieff as one of the Russian police watching the socialist delegates and reported that it was mainly on "his representations that Norway, Sweden, and Denmark refused to shelter these revolutionaries," and on May 11th the paper quoted a conference spokesman who said, "the meetings will be all held in secret." The delegates managed to cause a question to be raised in the House of Commons: Mr. Hart Davies asked Mr. Herbert Gladstone whether it was true that the Russian police were shadowing "the Russian socialists." [381]

The socialist newspaper *Justice* was quite excited about the meeting of the "Fifth Conference of the Social-Democrat Labour Party of Russia." In stating that there were numerous delegates from Georgia, they failed to mention Stalin under any of his aliases as being in attendance.[382] One story stressed Okhrana surveillance of the meetings and noted the rigid conspiratorial measures at the Congress. When the Okhrana, working with Scotland Yard, attempted to photograph the delegates, an English-speaking Russian exclaimed, "Do you realize that the reproduction of portraits of delegates may mean death? Most of us have to cross the frontier again." [383] As if in support of this view, Reuters reported from St. Petersburg that "should the Socialist delegates who have gone to London attempt to return to Russia they shall be stopped at the frontier or else arrested, on the ground that they left Russia without passports." [384] This may have referred to those revolutionaries like Trotsky and Martov who had been living in European exile. On May 10th the *Daily Mirror,* under the headline, "MOCK DUMA IN LONDON," reported: "Among the 180 delegates of the Russian Social-Democratic Labor Party who arrived at Liverpool Street last night were eight women, burning with zeal for the great cause. Very few in the crowd had any luggage worth talking about, and many came in their blue working blouses. It was a picturesque crowd, but this did not appeal to the business-like dozen of detectives who came to see them. The revolutionaries all trooped off to Fullbourne Street, Whitechapel, and there they took up their quarters in various lodging houses in the district. The detectives went down with them just to see that all was made comfortable." The next day the paper reported: "The women are said to be conspicuous for their unflinching courage and nerve. . . . Revolver practice enters into their daily exercise. They drill themselves constantly in front of mirrors, by which they become adepts (sic) in aiming and pulling the trigger." [385]

Some delegates to the Congress doubled as Russian Department of Police agents. Dr. Jacob Abramovich Zhitomirsky, the Okhrana's topnotch intelligence operative in Western Europe, whom Lenin considered a great revolutionary and a friend, was a delegate. Zhitomirsky, described as "dandified, dapper, and perfumed" had a party cover name *Otsov,* "the paternal one." [386] Indeed he had been paternal in his concern with social democratic party activities since the Okhrana had recruited him, as a medical student, in Berlin during 1902 (the same year Koba had been involved in the Baku demonstrations in faraway Caucasia). *Otsov* had been in charge of bolshevik propaganda distribution in Russia and had known scores of secret addresses there about which he had consistently informed the Okhrana. He had betrayed many bolsheviks to the police. As a measure of his importance he received a monthly salary of two thousand French francs from the Okhrana. The last information concerning "Andre", Zhitomirsky's police cover name, was that he had volunteered during World War I and was serving on the western front with the French army. Afterwards he disappears. Zhitomirsky's deep and valuable penetration into the Social-Democratic Party apparatus probably made the Okhrana think twice before asking him to report on the Congress.

One other agent turned in a report that was in excess of a hundred pages. In a letter of transmission (classified "top secret") to the Director of the Department of Police in St. Petersburg, the Paris Foreign Agency identified the agent only as a member of the Social-Democratic Party who had performed "quite serious services" on behalf of the Okhrana, for which it was recommended that he receive a special award of fifteen hundred rubles, nearly ten thousand dollars by today's reckoning.[387] The agent deserved the award, for the report he produced of the London Congress included a list of delegates, their pseudonyms, short biographies of many, a list of resolutions, and an account of debates with participants by name. Koba-Ivanovich was strangely ignored by all police reportage concerning the Congress.

Three hundred and two voting delegates were certified at the Congress, each delegate representing five hundred party members. There were ninety bolsheviks and eighty-five mensheviks. This was not a matter of popular votes, for Lenin and his adherents had obtained travel funds even for dubious delegates, some of whom also brought their wives. The mensheviks, as already mentioned, relied on regular contribution from party members and were thus hamstrung for funds. The bolsheviks' more exotic means of finance was adequate, to say the least.

"We could not find a single Bolshevik in Gori, Stalin's and my native town," Iremashvili wrote about this period.[388] Even in Tiflis Koba was unable to accumulate the five hundred votes that would make him a full-fledged delegate at London. The eighteen thousand party members in the Caucasus at that time were largely menshevik.[389] Koba-Ivanovich was, therefore, an interloper at London— or, specifically, a "deliberative delegate" without voting rights. Trotsky, who was present at the London Congress, wrote, "When it was Lenin's turn to preside at the Congress, he proposed adoption without discussion of a resolution by the mandate commission which recommended the granting of deliberative participation to four delegates, including Ivanovich." The menshevik Martov ("what a splendid comrade," Lenin once said of him) thundered, "I should like to know who is being granted an advisory voice. Who are these people, where do they come from, and so forth?" Lenin answered, *"I really don't know,* but the Congress may rely on the unanimous opinion of the mandate commission."[390] Even when Koba had attained a consultative vote, the minutes of the Congress and the Okhrana agent reports agree, he spoke not one official word at the Congress, even though each national delegation caucused and selected a speaker to comment on a specific subject.[391]

Trotsky's later question about London resembled Souvarine's about Stockholm:

> In view of all this, why did Koba come at all to London? He could not raise his arm as a voting delegate. He proved unnecessary as a speaker. He obviously played no role whatever at the closed sessions of the Bolshevik faction. It is inconceivable that he should have to come out of mere curiosity—to listen and to look around. He must have had other tasks. Just what were they? [392]

The London Congress, which ended on May 19, 1907, failed to settle the differences between bolsheviks and mensheviks. Upon his return to the Caucasus in early June, Koba recorded his impressions in two articles titled "The London Congress of the Russian Social-Democratic Workers Party (Notes of a Delegate)," signed "Koba Ivanovich," in the newspaper Baku *Proletarian,* No. 1 & 2. He apologetically explained that their "completion was prevented by intensified police shadowing of J. V. Stalin in the latter half of 1907 and his subsequent arrest." [393] This was a thin alibi: his next arrest was nine months away, an event that he could scarcely have foreseen. And, at any rate, neither it nor police surveillance made interim writing impossible.

His unfinished articles, as usual, castigated the mensheviks. While it is not within the scope of this narrative to analyze the debates at London as seen through the eyes of Dzhugashvili, it must be noted that his impressions included one more crude anti-Semitic passage, plus an incorrect account of a resolution condemning expropriations—robbery, extortion, and terrorism—that the mensheviks insisted the Congress adopt.

Koba wrote in his account of the London Congress that Jews constituted the majority of the menshevik group (not counting the Bundists). "The overwhelming majority of the Bolshevik group were Russians, then came Jews," and, "of the Bundists [Jewish], only eight to ten delegates supported the Bolsheviks and then not always." He told an anecdote of incredible but revealing bad taste:

In this connection one of the Bolsheviks (I think it was Comrade Alexinsky) observed in jest that the Mensheviks constituted a Jewish group while the Bolsheviks constitute a true-Russian group, and, therefore, it would not be a bad idea for us Bolsheviks to organize a pogrom in the Party.[394]

His impression of the London Congress was that "in general, predominance, and rather considerable predominance, was on the side of the Bolsheviks":

Thus, the congress was a Bolshevik congress, although not sharply Bolshevik. Of the Menshevik resolutions only the one on guerilla actions was carried, and that by a sheer accident; on that point the Bolsheviks did not accept battle, or rather, they did not wish to fight the issue to a conclusion, purely out of the desire to "give the Menshevik comrades at least one opportunity to rejoice." [395]

After 1917 Stalin mentioned the London Congress only once and in two paragraphs. It was at the Kremlin memorial evening in January of 1924 with which we are now familiar. He said:

At the next Congress, in 1907, in London, the Bolsheviks were the victors. I then saw Lenin for the first time in the role of victor. Usually, victory turns the heads of some leaders, makes them proud and boastful. Most frequently, in such cases, they begin to celebrate their victory and rest on their laurels. But Lenin was not in the least like such leaders. On the contrary, it was precisely after victory that he became particularly vigilant, on the alert. I remember Lenin at that time earnestly impressing upon the delegates: "The first thing is, not to be carried away by victory; the second thing is, consolidate the victory; the third thing is, crush your opponent, because he is only defeated, but far from being crushed yet." He heaped withering scorn on those delegates who frivolously declared that "from now on the Mensheviks are finished." It was not difficult for him to prove that the Mensheviks still had roots in the labour movement, that they had to be fought skillfully, and that overestimation of one's own strength, and particularly underestimation of the strength of the enemy, was to be avoided.

"No boasting of victory"—this is the peculiar trait in Lenin's character and helped him soberly to weigh up the forces of the enemy and to insure the Party against possible surprises.[396]

Soviet literature has not described how Koba returned to the
Caucasus or when he arrived there. It is reasonably certain that he
came back to Baku, rather than to Tiflis, from which he had departed. Sergo Ordzhonikidze claims that he arrived in "Baku from
London" in mid-June. However, Tovstukha, writing in 1927,
places Stalin in Tiflis after the London Congress.[397] In the *Collected Works* it states that during the first half of June, after his
return from London, he went to Baku and Tiflis and a series of
regions in western Georgia, probably explained by the necessity to
pass through Tiflis en route to Baku. On the occasion of Stalin's
fiftieth birthday, *Komsomolskaya Pravda* reported: "Having returned from the London party conference, to which he was sent as
a delegate by the Bolshevik section of the Tiflis organization, Stalin
left Tiflis and based himself in Baku, where he conducted work in
the Baku organization around the slogans of the London party conference."

As we have seen, Koba at twenty-seven was unique among revolutionaries of his age if for no other reason than the number of
miles he had travelled and the number of gendarmes he had
evaded. By mid-1907 he had made two long trips, to Finland and
Stockholm, the first round-trip journey being six thousand miles
and the second sixty-two hundred miles; and a round trip of nine
thousand miles was required to go from the Caucasus to London.
From a reading of the official accounts we learn that he had travelled almost twenty-three thousand miles largely through territory
admittedly hostile to revolutionaries. Nor had he experienced any
official trouble from the police since 1905, although, again according to the records, he had been arrested twice, exiled once, and
escaped twice. The Okhrana all-points bulletin disseminated for his
apprehension in 1905 was not very old. Nonetheless he was to remain free for another nine months.

By 1907 Koba had been involved in revolutionary activities for
about eight years. He was now to embark on even more serious
operations eventually culminating in his being included in Lenin's
narrow bolshevik council. However, a review of those eight years
—roughly one-half of his pre-1917 career—raises questions about

his loyalty to the revolution as against the Okhrana. Among the indications that he was a genuine revolutionary, with no police affiliation, is the refusal of such titans as Lenin and Trotsky to suggest he had worked for the Okhrana. Even Iremashvili and Elisabedashvili, Koba's friends from childhood, never alluded to his possible Okhrana connections, although Iremashvili in particular noted Koba's distasteful personality and untrustworthy character. As we have seen, the Okhrana had arrested Koba in 1902 and 1905 or 1906, and he had been imprisoned in Batum and Kutais jails. Furthermore the idea that he was a genuine revolutionary is supported by his writing and speeches; though vastly exaggerated in Soviet literature, they nonetheless advanced anti-tsarist points of view. Moreover, in the Caucasus he had organized a few small bolshevik cells, albeit ineffectual, clearly opposed to the tsarist government. Finally, though Koba's severest critics considered him appallingly crude and headstrong with a cruel streak, even a sadistic one, capable of treachery and murder, yet few besides an important minority believed that he had been an Okhrana agent.

The darker side of Koba's life until 1907 includes puzzles that seem impossible to solve except in the light of a connection with the Okhrana. He had personally boasted that, as a teenager, he had denounced to the authorities his fellow-students in the Tiflis Theological Seminary in order to make them good revolutionaries. From the time he had left the Seminary in 1899, we find frequent unexplained and suspicious periods of many months in his life about which nothing is known. After he left his first and only job in the Tiflis Geophysical Observatory in 1901, he had no visible income. Because the social democrats had suspected him of complicity in the Okhrana arrests in 1901 and of provocation in the Tiflis May Day riots, he had been expelled from that city. The next year he had a hand in provoking the senseless Batum riots, after which an arrest had saved him from a party court of honor. His 1902 arrest had been followed by an "exile" that had all the earmarks of an Okhrana operation. During these eight years the great majority of the Caucasian social democrats had come to dislike and distrust him, and he was suspected of being affiliated with the Okhrana by several outstandingly honest social democrats like Zhordania, Dzhib-ladze and Shaumyan. To any objective observer of 1907, the facility Koba enjoyed in the past eight years in travel outside Russia had been nothing less than fabulous.

9 | THE EREVAN SQUARE ROBBERY

Koba's presence in London, not as a delegate, is as puzzling as the fact that his name is found on only four of the nine hundred and fifty-one pages of the stenographic record of the Congress. He is first mentioned during the eighth session, chaired by the menshevik Dan, when the "mandate commission," headed by a bolshevik, recommended that the four candidates be given a deliberative vote but not a delegate's full rights; and, as we know, it was not until the fourteenth session, when Lenin was chairman for the first time, that the matter was put to a vote.[398] Naturally Martov and Zhordania both protested Lenin's obvious attempt to ram through a consultative status for his Caucasian bolshevik, and it was at this point that Martov exclaimed, "Who are these people [meaning Koba-Ivanovich, among others], where do they come from . . . ?"

When Koba received the title of consultative, or deliberative, delegate, he owed it to Lenin.[399] Since Lenin was unaccustomed to acts of philanthropy in the political arena, his sponsorship of an obscure Georgian could not have been without purpose and must have been connected with Koba's furtherance of Lenin's personal objectives, or with some idea that appealed to him. It is not credible as a desire on Lenin's part simply to carve a political foothold in the Caucasian redoubt of mensheviks; Koba, who was generally distrusted and who represented only a handful of people, would scarcely form a bolshevik political nucleus in Russia's southern tier. Lenin's support must have been in recognition of his usefulness in an area separate from bolshevik propaganda and agitation or political organization among workers.

This perplexing action may be explained by Lenin's two visits to

Berlin during 1907, which official Soviet works and other biographies of both Lenin and Stalin have glossed over, misinterpreted, or ignored. As we know, Lenin had arrived in Copenhagen about April 2, 1907, expecting the Fifth Party Congress to be held there.[400] The King of Denmark, however, cancelled the meeting in deference to his nephew Tsar Nicholas of Russia. After Lenin knew the Congress was to be convened in London at the end of April, he made the unexpected trip to Berlin that has already been disclosed. His *Collected Works* states that he spent four days (April 24th to 28th) sightseeing there and having conversations with Maxim Gorky, Karl Kautsky, and Rosa Luxemburg.[401] Then he proceeded to London. At the end of the Congress, Lenin returned to Finland and less than three months later participated in the International Socialist Congress that met from August 5th to 11th in Stuttgart.[402] He went back to Finland at the end of the summer, and began his final exile to Western Europe in December.

His wife, Krupskaya, writes that, at the end of the year, "Ilyich and I proceeded to Geneva *via* Berlin. Searches and arrests had been made among the Russians in Berlin on the eve of our arrival. We were met by Avramov, a member of the Berlin group, who therefore advised us not to go to any of the homes of our comrades. He led us about from café to café all day long. We spent the evening with Rosa Luxemburg." Lenin's *Collected Works* supplies a few more details but omits the fact that they were both suffering from a severe stomach ailment contracted in a Berlin café.[403] On December 15th he had written a Swedish social democrat requesting an address to which he could send "correspondence" from Russia to Geneva and vice versa. Lenin added that he would be arriving in Berlin on December 21, 1907. Actually he and Krupskaya reached Berlin December 22nd; Lenin had been thoroughly shaken when he nearly drowned while he was walking on weak ice in the Gulf of Bothnia. He met with the social democrats I. P. Ladyzhnikov, P. B. Avramov (Abramov), and "others." [404] Then he and Krupskaya left for Geneva on December 25th. Ten years passed before they returned to Russia.

But where was Koba during this period? We know that he saw

the London Congress through to its end, and that he had first gone to Copenhagen in the belief that it would be held there, leaving several days of free time in which to make a trip to Berlin. At the conclusion of the London Congress on May 19th, he apparently made his way back to Tiflis after a delay of some weeks. According to his official chronology, he was busy during the summer and autumn in Baku.[405] However, at "the end of November he arrived in Tiflis from Baku on Party business." During the next two or three months, his whereabouts are unknown. This period, one of the more vexatious ones, commands our attention. The Tiflis social democrats had earlier expelled him in no uncertain terms, so he scarcely had party business to conduct there. However, if he stopped briefly on his way to meet Lenin in Germany, the Aesopian language (his having proceeded through Tiflis en route to Europe) of his official autobiography makes sense.

All of this would be a rather pointless recitation were it not for Stalin's later insistence that during 1907 he and Lenin engaged in serious discussions in Germany not once but twice. In the early nineteen-thirties he told his semi-official biographer, Henri Barbusse, that on two occasions during 1907 he conferred with Lenin in Berlin.[406] When Emil Ludwig interviewed him on the eve of World War II, Stalin claimed he visited Lenin in Germany in 1907, 1908, and 1912.[407] Neither account suggests how they made contact or how Koba traveled to Germany. At the Teheran Conference in 1943, Stalin unexpectedly related to Churchill and Roosevelt that during 1907 he had accompanied two hundred German communists to an international conference in Leipzig.[408] He had neglected to tell Ludwig or Barbusse about this. What an obscure Georgian revolutionary without a working knowledge of German would be doing in Leipzig with two hundred native communists is difficult to imagine, unless it had something to do with his meeting Lenin. Stalin was, naturally, capable of deliberately lying to Churchill, Roosevelt, Ludwig, and Barbusse over a period of ten years if it served some purpose. As we have seen, twisting the facts and falsifying the record was second-nature to him. In the matter of the German trips, however, one vainly tries to explain the fabrications. It would have been much simpler and more plausible to maintain that he had visited Lenin in Finland, where Lenin spent most of 1907. Thus his insistence that he met Lenin twice in Germany during 1907 (or early 1908) must not be taken lightly.

It is easy to forget that when these meetings occurred Lenin was almost ten years senior to the twenty-seven-year-old Koba, who had not yet published an article in the Russian language. Koba's grasp of revolutionary theory was vastly inferior to Lenin's. Trotsky, in his critical biography of Stalin, while conceding that the Koba-Lenin meetings took place, appropriately adds, "If Lenin journeyed especially to the capital of Germany, then in any event it was not for the sake of theoretical conversations." [409] He adds that the conference "almost undoubtedly was devoted to the impending expropriations, the means of forwarding the money, and the like. Why did these negotiations take place in Berlin and not in London? It is quite likely that Lenin might have deemed it careless to meet with Ivanovich in London, where he was in full sight of the other delegates and of numerous Tsarist and other spies attracted by the Congress. It is also possible that a third person who had nothing to do with the Congress, was supposed to participate in the conference."

Trotsky's argument appears invalid because, although the London Congress was penetrated by "Tsarist and other spies," it was Lenin who suggested in open assembly to the other delegates[410] that Stalin-Ivanovich be given a consultative status at London. His statement also seems to indicate he had knowledge about the meeting which he did not care to divulge in detail. He is right, of course, in saying that Koba could have contributed nothing of a political, ideological, or theoretical nature that Lenin would have found even remotely interesting. The one subject that above all could have made it worth Lenin's time to confer with Koba before and after the London Congress was money for the bolsheviks.

As we know, Lenin had relentlessly sought funds to finance newspapers and journals, to pay transportation costs of delegates to conferences, to purchase documents, to underwrite agitation and propaganda, and also to sustain him and his entourage in exile. He had tried orthodox methods to obtain funds, but he finally realized that only unorthodox means would be successful. He was painfully aware that money in large amounts was essential to the seizure of power in Russia. At one time or another before 1917, Lenin obtained money from the following sources—a bolshevik who seduced a young lady and then made off with her inheritance; a purveyor of contraceptives; at least three foreign intelligence services —the Japanese, Austrian and the German. Soviet historians have naturally been reluctant to write about Lenin's finances and his connections with foreign intelligence services. However, by the time of the Tammerfors Conference at the end of 1905, he and his bolsheviks were in dire financial straits.[411] It was shortly afterward that Lenin expanded his "secret" bolshevik organization, which presumably was to train armed revolutionary cadres. This was a thinly veiled strategem, for they quickly became instruments for terrorism, principally in Central Russia and the Caucasus area. Lenin's lieutenant for "technical" affairs—as terrorism was euphemistically called—was a talented engineer, Leonid Borisovich Krassin ("Nikitich"), who operated from both St. Petersburg and the relative safety of Finland. His so-called "laboratory" was a center for hatching bolshevik robberies and manufacturing bombs and infernal machines. The Okhrana, aware but oddly tolerant of his nefarious activities, almost seemed to be indulging him. Though he was arrested several times, he was usually quickly released and, in 1907, was even issued a passport to reside abroad. Such favored treatment, when combined with a dearth of material about Krassin in police files after 1908, creates a nagging but unprovable suspicion that he was affiliated with the Okhrana.[412] There is general agreement, nonetheless, that the Okhrana had a hand in some of the numerous expropriations planned by Krassin (and Lenin) from 1905 on. There were over two hundred in the first part of 1906.[413]

Nevertheless, the bolsheviks at both the Stockholm Congress and the London Congress were, for all practical purposes, broke. On both occasions loans provided the funds for the comrades to return to Russia.[414] The menshevik resolutions condemning the expropriations, therefore, particularly galled Lenin, who not only condoned them but also feebly attempted to justify them in theory. He did not intend to refrain from pursuing the main source of his faction's income because of the killing of bystanders or because of ethical or moral considerations. He remained unperturbed at the menshevik protest that armed banditry was damaging the public idea of social democracy. At the London Congress he and thirty-four other bolsheviks voted against a strong resolution condemning and barring expropriations and providing that persons guilty of organizing or participating in armed robberies, extortion, murders— terrorism—should be expelled from the party. It had little noticeable impact on Lenin for at the moment the Congress was overwhelmingly carrying the resolution, he was contemplating the most grandiose robbery of them all. It is my belief that Koba had outlined it a few days before in Berlin. Lenin was confident that the bolshevik coffers would be replenished for months, if not years, by the holdup on Erevan Square in Tiflis already scheduled for June 12th, just a few weeks away.

The Erevan Square robbery has received only minor attention in Lenin's *Collected Works*. It has been ignored in Stalin's *Collected Works,* and for good reason.[415] The ugly operation involved the killing and maiming of innocent people. Lenin never publicly mentioned the event, and when Emil Ludwig interviewed Stalin in the nineteen-thirties, he refused to discuss it. Ludwig writes:

Since this story has been suppressed in Stalin's official biography, though it is definitely established that he had the directing hand in the robbery, I asked him about it, expecting that he would deny it in so many words, but that I would be able to get the truth from the expression on his face.

"In Europe," I said to him, "you are described either as a bloody Czar or as a Georgian bandit. . . ."

Stalin began to laugh in that heavy way of his, blinked several times and stood up, for the first time in our three-hour interview. He walked over, with his somewhat dragging footsteps, to the writing desk, and brought me a pamphlet of some thirty pages, his biography in Russian; but, of course, there was nothing in it about my question:

"You will find all the necessary information here," he said—laughing slyly to himself because he had "put one over" on me. The ques-

tion of the bank robbery was the only one he would not answer—
except to the extent that he answered it by passing it over.

His manner of evasion gave me a new insight into his character.
He could have denied it; he could have confessed it; or he could simply have described the whole thing as a legend. But he acted instead
like a perfect Asiatic. . . .[416]

By the same token, official Soviet works have failed to take note of
the Lenin-Stalin meetings in Berlin during 1907. To do so would
automatically raise the embarrassing question of the Erevan operation, which turned out to be a horrendous mess.

It was probably at a meeting with Lenin in Berlin between April
24th and 28th that Koba described a bold but idiotic venture to
refurbish the bolshevik exchequer. Lenin's strange blind spot regarding police operations, combined with his shortage of funds,
clouded his better judgment and led him to approve, perhaps en-
thusiastically (as his political patronage of Koba at London suggests), an ill-advised plan. The Erevan Square expropriation, Koba
explained, would net at least three hundred thousand rubles—or
more than a million dollars in terms of present value. Lenin would
have been ecstatic at hearing this before he happily rushed off to
London.

At about half past ten on the morning of June 12, 1907, Erevan
Square in Tiflis was teeming with people. A correspondent of the
French news service on the spot reported that at least ten bombs
exploded, one after the other, with such force that they shattered
windows, caved in doors, and tumbled chimneys. Interspersed with
the detonation of bombs were audible revolver shots. The Paris
newspaper *Le Petit Temps* called it a catastrophe and added that
"the square was covered with debris and many were killed and
wounded." [417] Although it could have been planned by the
Okhrana and organized by Koba, the operation was executed by
his Armenian subordinate and cohort, Semyen Arshakovich Ter-
Petrosyan, whose revolutionary nickname was "Kamo."

Kamo, who was not exceptionally brilliant, was outstandingly
courageous and in fact was perhaps the bravest and most dedicated
bolshevik of them all. Few other figures in pre-revolutionary lore

can hold a candle to him in sheer fortitude and stolid devotion to the Leninist cause. He was born in Gori, Stalin's home town, of middle-class parents. He was three years younger than Koba and there is some evidence that they were boyhood acquaintances. Apparently he was expelled from a "religious school" in Gori and thereafter decided to become an army officer. Kamo's parents, recognizing that he had no particular academic qualifications, are said to have engaged Koba as his tutor for the pending examinations. At any rate, he seems to have been strongly devoted to Stalin who, it is said, converted him to marxism.[418] At the time of the Erevan Square expropriation, Kamo could look back on a dangerous and adventurous career in the service of bolshevism. He had organized a number of robberies, he had been arrested twice for carrying illegal literature but escaped both times, once by jumping over a prison wall, the second time by impersonating someone else so well that the police were mistakenly convinced they had arrested the wrong person. According to the Okhrana, he was a bomb maker, an organizer of underground printing presses, and a terrorist par excellence.[419] His penchant for disguise and impersonation served him well. When he visited Lenin in Finland during 1907, he went as a first-class passenger on the Tiflis-St. Petersburg train; he was a certain Prince Dadiani in the uniform of a cossack officer. Lenin, who was temporarily residing in Kuokkala, was publishing and distributing his newspaper *Proletary* (*Proletariat*), assisted by Mr. and Mrs. Komisarov, both Okhrana agents.[420] Krupskaya describes Kamo's arrival:

Kamo came to the canteen in full Caucasian dress carrying a ball-shaped object. . . . Everyone stopped eating and stared at the striking visitor. "He has brought a bomb," most of them probably thought. But it was not a bomb. It was a watermelon. Kamo had brought the watermelon and some candied nuts as a treat for Ilich and me. "My aunt sent them," he explained in his bashful way. A daredevil fighter of indomitable will and courage, Kamo was a man of the highest character, a rather naïve and affectionate comrade. He was passionately devoted to Ilich, Krassin, and Bogdanov. He used to visit us at Kuokkala where he made friends with my mother and used to tell her all about his aunt and sisters. Kamo travelled frequently between Finland and St. Petersburg and always took arms back with him. Mother used to help him strap the revolvers on his back with affectionate care.[421]

Kamo, disguised as an army captain, displayed his "indomitable will and courage" during the Erevan Square robbery. For some hours before the bombs burst in the area, he had been sauntering about the plaza on the lookout for a cossack detachment guarding a shipment of over three hundred thousand rubles in bank notes and certain other securities that were to be transferred from the post office to the Imperial Bank of Tiflis. One story has it that he had been warning persons to vacate the square. If so, he had been unsuccessful, for on-the-spot observers reported that the square was full of people.[422] Shortly after ten o'clock two bank clerks signed for the mail sack that contained the bank notes and securities and, in a carriage escorted by a cossack detachment, approached Erevan Square by way of Sololakskaya Street. From that moment the operation's incredible machinery functioned like clockwork. What happened is best described by Mrs. Ter-Petrosyan in a book about her husband, Kamo:

At Pushkin Square, from which the post office was visible, Patsiya Goldava signalled Stepko Kitskirvelli that they are starting out!

Stepko immediately communicated with Annette S—, who in turn, passed on the message to the activists who were waiting in the Tilipuchuri Restaurant. Bachua K— strolled around Erevan Square unfolding a newspaper. This was the signal for preparing the attack awaited by comrades posted at various points. [She mentions ten more persons who had been briefed and played a role in the robbery.]

Surrounded by horsemen the carriages drove rapidly through clouds of dust. The Cossacks in front were already turning into S— Street. At that moment Daniko stepped forward and all the conspirators hurled their bombs with all their strength.

Two explosions, and then another two. Two policemen and a Cossack lay on the pavement. The horse charged through the escort. But the carriage with the money was not destroyed and the horse sped it toward the bazaar. . . .

Bachua alone kept his head at this decisive moment. He dashed forward, cut off the horses, and caught the carriage at the end of the

Square. . . . With no thought for his own safety he hurled another bomb between the horses' legs. The explosion threw him to the ground. . . . Chibriashvili came up just in time to drag the bags of money from the carriage and in the direction of V— Street.

When Kamo came out of G— Street into Erevan Square in accordance with the plan, he thought the attempt had failed. . . . Rising in his saddle, firing his revolver, shouting and swearing like a real captain, he urged his horse toward V— Street where he encountered Daniko. He took the bag to Bochoridze's house and later to the private office of the Director of the Tiflis Observatory.

Several persons had been killed and more than fifty seriously wounded. But there was more to the Erevan Square affair than Mrs. Ter-Petrosyan's account had revealed.[423] For example, one source has written that the money had been safely hidden away in the mattress of the curator of a museum which he probably mistook for the Tiflis Observatory. But, he adds that, "Many years later this man told me that he never dreamed he was sleeping on a fortune. Three weeks after the raid Koba collected the notes and sent them by an underground route to Krassin. Koba's complicity was unsuspected, indeed his presence was unknown. He continued to sit around the riverside taverns drinking freely, often with the police." [424]

Trotsky, writing in 1938, states: "In Party circles, Koba's personal participation in the Tiflis apropriation had long ago been regarded as indubitable . . . In 1932 I still had no doubt about Stalin's leading role in the armed attack on Erevan Square and referred to it incidentally in one of my articles. However, a closer study of the circumstances of those days compels me to revise my view of the traditional version . . . Koba was not in direct contact with the members of the detachments, did not instruct them, consequently was not the organizer of the act in the real sense of the word, let alone a direct participant." He continues:

The Congress in London came to an end on April twenty-seventh. The expropriation in Tiflis occurred on June twelfth, a month and a half later. Stalin had too little time left between his return from abroad and the day of the expropriation to supervise the preparation of such a complicated enterprise. It is more likely that the fighters had been selected and had been drawn together in the course of several preceding reckless adventures. Possibly they marked time pending the Congress's decision. Some of them might have had doubts as to how Lenin would look upon expropriations. The fighters were waiting for the signal. Stalin might have brought them that signal. But did his participation go beyond that?

Trotsky reasons that Lenin knew all about the Tiflis expropriation "As far as he [Lenin] was concerned, the problem consisted this time of a simple attempt to assure financial means to the Party at the expense of the enemy, for the impending period of uncertainty. Lenin could not resist the temptation, took advantage of a favorable opportunity, of a happy 'exception.' In that sense, one might say outright that the idea of the Tiflis expropriation contained in it a goodly element of adventurism which, as a rule, was foreign to Lenin's politics. The case with Stalin was different. Broad historical considerations had little value in his eyes. The resolution of the London Congress was only an irksome scrap of paper, to be nullified by means of a crude trick." [425]

Here Trotsky's prejudice got the best of him. If Lenin knew all about the Tiflis "ex," from what source did the information come? And, if he took advantage of it, who told him about it? Furthermore, if Stalin had too little time between the conclusion of the London Congress and June 12th, when the Tiflis robbery occurred, it must have been organized elsewhere before the London Congress —that is, Koba could have described it to Lenin in Berlin in April. The Tiflis expropriation was not a "crude trick," but a most serious undertaking. As David Shub wrote, "Kamo was the field commander of those operations; Stalin represented Lenin's supreme headquarters." [426]

An operation of this dimension was not easy to organize. For example, it is not inappropriate to wonder who informed Kamo and his conspirators that a shipment of over three hundred thousand rubles, railroad stocks, treasury bonds, and other debentures would arrive at Tiflis from St. Petersburg on June 12th. To many persons who have written about the event, it is sufficient that some worker in the know tipped off Kamo or his superior, Koba. The money, stocks, and bonds, which today would amount to a million dollars, were shipped from St. Petersburg. The authorities had been plagued with robberies and they did not broadcast in advance the transfer of large amounts of money, yet the Imperial Bank in Tiflis had to know the approximate date it would receive the shipment. And although it is possible that the bolsheviks had an informer somewhere along the line who could predict with certainty that the money and securities would arrive in Tiflis on a given date, it would seem that several days—if not weeks—would be necessary to arrange such a precise operation, in which at least sixty-three persons participated.[427] That person has never been identified.

It would be seemingly plausible to conclude that the disguised Kamo, the sixty-three conspirators, the unknown informer, and the bomb throwers were all part of an operation that, although not laudable, was a success of sorts. Had the bolsheviks benefited in any way, in the slightest degree, from the Erevan Square robbery and killing, it might have been recorded as a plus for Lenin and Koba. However, the fact is that it was a total failure: it provided not one kopek for the bolsheviks, and it plunged Lenin's political fortunes to an all-time low (from which he was barely able to recover), and this strongly suggests that the plan had a sinister origin. Trotsky correctly maintains that "the Tiflis booty brought no good," but fails to note how much the Okhrana gained from the Tiflis robbery, which outraged world opinion with its senseless slaughter of innocent bystanders. Within a few months "Erevan" was a famous case in much of the Western press. The reputation of Lenin and his faction was damaged in Russia itself, and it seemed to many at the time that the bolsheviks were finished. In an understatement Trotsky commented, "The consequences of this tragic adventure, which rounded out an entire phase of Party life, were rather serious." [428]

Kamo's loot, seven hundred and fifty five-hundred ruble notes, bore the serial numbers from AM62900 to AM63650. For all practical purposes they were "marked" and bolshevik attempts to exchange them in Europe failed completely. A side effect was the arrest of Litvinov (Wallach), the future Soviet Foreign Minister, Kamo and others by the European police services that were alerted by the Russian Department of Police to be on the watch for persons attempting to cash the stolen bank notes. Olga Ravich, Zinoviev's future wife, and Semashko, later to be People's Commissar of Public Health, were arrested in Stockholm and Geneva respectively. According to Krupskaya, "The average Swiss was scared to death. All they talked about was the Russian expropriators. They talked about it with horror at the boarding house where Ilich and I took our meals." [429] In addition to the five-hundred ruble notes, Kamo had stolen unnegotiable securities. The bolsheviks gained nothing from the robbery and, conversely, the financial loss to tsarist financial institutions was minimal. An official Okhrana report later asserted: "All the money except for a small amount for the Caucasian organization of the Bolsheviks was transferred to the Bolsheviks, and particularly into the hands of the well known Krassin and Lenin (Ulyanov). The Mensheviks did not receive one *kopek* of this money and on the basis of the resolution of the Social Democratic London Congress demanded that the persons involved in the expropriation be excluded from the Party." [430]

What became of Kamo? The Berlin police arrested him in 1908 with an Austrian passport in the name of Mirsky, but, according to an Okhrana report, they were unable to determine his real name.[431] Dr. Jacob Zhitomirsky, Lenin's great friend in charge of the distribution of bolshevik literature in Russia—and, as already noted, an Okhrana agent—had denounced him to the German police. As a prisoner in Berlin's Alt Moabit jail, Kamo the "naïve comrade"— as Krupskaya had called him—and "Caucasian brigand"—as Lenin dubbed him—displayed extraordinary fortitude, not knowing, of course, that he had been betrayed by Lenin's police-agent associate. He summoned all his powers as an impersonator and feigned madness for almost four years, during which he underwent horrible torture, tried to commit suicide, and attempted to starve himself. He finally returned to the Caucasus, where he was incarcerated once more in the Tiflis Metekh prison. Condemned to death, he was saved in a general amnesty of prisoners on the three-hundredth anniversary of the Romanov dynasty. In 1926 he met an ignoble fate in Tiflis when, on his bicycle, he was run down and killed by an official Soviet car.[432]

After the Erevan Square operation the Okhrana reported that Kamo spent "all July and August with Lenin in his *dacha* in Finland," where Lenin, Krassin, and Kamo had developed a plan to obtain about fifteen million rubles by way of another "expropriation." The details of the plan—except for the bombs, the necessary firearms and ammunition, and the infernal machines—were to be kept not only from the mensheviks but also from the bolsheviks.[433] This secrecy is extremely important: it meant that, in all probability, the Department of Police was launching another operation to discredit the bolsheviks even further. There is some information that this involved a robbery of the Mendellsohn Bank in Berlin.[434] Interestingly enough Captain Runich, who had planned the May Day demonstration in 1901, was still on duty in Tiflis Okhrana Headquarters at the time of the Erevan Square robbery.[435]

What was Koba doing when the bombs were exploding and the shots were being fired that morning in Tiflis? As in the bloody Tiflis May Day demonstration he had instigated six years earlier at the Soldatsky bazaar (not far from Erevan Square), he was in the city but on the sidelines and not directly involved in the action. Stalin skirted the subject in his talks with Ludwig and Barbusse, and Soviet literature was notably shy, during his lifetime, about his role in the episode, sometimes hinting that he secretly guided the operation. On the other hand, Shaumyan's son, in a biography of Kamo, insists that Stalin had nothing to do with it, and Kamo's widow does not allude to Koba in connection with the robbery. Of even greater significance, the detailed report of the Department of Police concerning Kamo in dealing with the Tiflis expropriation failed to mention Koba.[436] The inescapable conclusion is, therefore, that he did not directly participate in the bloody Tiflis affair, and that his services on behalf of the Okhrana were something other than fighting.[436a]

The Erevan Square robbery seriously affected Koba's revolutionary career. Three investigating commissions began work almost immediately on the Erevan affair; one under the auspices of the social democratic party was headed by Chicherin, the future Soviet Commissar for Foreign Affairs; another was conducted by the International Socialist Bureau;[437] and, according to Arsenidze, the Transcaucasian social democratics established a third special commission, headed by Silvester Dzhibladze, which concluded that the participants and organizers, headed by Koba, were to be expelled from the party. Earlier in 1901 Stalin had simply been told to leave Tiflis. It will be remembered that the London Congress had adopted a resolution explicitly forbidding terrorism. Arsenidze adds:

> From that moment Koba never appeared again on the Georgian horizon. I accidentally read in the memoirs of the Bolshevik Kiasashvili that Koba came to Tiflis for two days in 1909, but that only his very close friends saw him. During these two days his own trusted guards watched his conspiratorial apartment day and night and not only because of the police. The Georgian organization was always closed thereafter to Koba.[438]

More than ten years later, Stalin's expulsion from the Tiflis party organization in 1907 was disinterred to haunt him. L. Martov (Yuly Osipovich Tsederbaum) was briefly allowed to publish an oppositional menshevik newspaper, *Vpered* (*Forward*), in Moscow during 1918. On March 18th this newspaper carried an article by Martov devoted to the military situation in the Caucasus; he casually mentioned the expulsion of Stalin from the party for his role in the Tiflis expropriation in these words:

> That the Caucasian Bolsheviks attached themselves to all sorts of daring enterprises of an expropriatory nature should be well known to that same Citizen Stalin, who was expelled in his time from the Party organization for having had something to do with expropriation.[439]

Stalin, then a principal member of the new bolshevik government as Commissar of Nationalities, flew into a rage and had Martov indicted for "criminal libel of a Soviet official and slander of the

Soviet Government." Citing Stalin's expulsion from the Caucasian
party organization was scarcely a slander of the Soviet government.
Stalin's subsequent insistence that Martov be tried by a trio of bolshevik judges, rather than by a jury of his peers, revealed his apprehension at having the reasons for his expulsion from the party
come to light. Then Martov asked for affidavits from Georgian bolsheviks who had looked into Stalin's participation in the attempted
murder of a certain Zharinov for exposing his covert role in the Tiflis
affair; to this, Stalin attempted evasive action by citing poor communications with the Transcaucasian area. Nonetheless, the bolshevik court postponed its proceedings and appointed Boris
Ivanovich Nicolaevsky, a menshevik, to collect statements from
Dzhibladze, Ramishvili, and other Georgians who had specialized
knowledge of the Erevan Square robbery. Nicolaevsky fulfilled his
mission, obtaining the necessary affidavits, but when he returned to
Moscow, he found that all records of the first court session had
disappeared. This version reconstructed by Bertram Wolfe from
"interviews with Rafael Abramovich, Boris Nicolaevsky, and Sam-
uel Levitas, all of whom were present in the courtroom" is undoubtedly as accurate as the memoirs of those three old revolutionaries could have preserved it.[440] However, the Petrograd
newspaper, *Dawn of Russia,* carried an article on April 17, 1918
that said:

> Yesterday, the case of the Commissar for Nationalities, Stalin-
> Dzhugashvili vs. L. Martov (Tsederbaum) was scheduled for the sec-
> ond time. Initially, this case was postponed a week ago at the request
> of the defense to call the witness Zhordania, Ramishvili and others,
> who were supposed to prove that Dzhugashvili-Stalin had been ex-
> cluded from the s.-d. party because of his participation in an expro-
> priation. The mention of this fact in the newspaper *Vpered* (*Forward*)
> was the reason for a suit for slander against Martov, the author of the
> article. The witnesses, Mirov, Ezhov, Gukovsky and others, who had
> arrived from the Caucasus where the revolutionary activity of Stalin
> took place, appeared before the tribunal. Defending L. Martov were
> Abramovich and Pleskov. The public prosecutor, Sosnovsky, assisted
> Dzhugashvili's private attorney for the prosecution. After a long dis-
> cussion the court decided the following: "The Tribunal does not

recognize the case presented by Stalin as falling within paragraph 1 of the Tribunal decree (*i.e.* crimes committed on duty, provoking an uprising, speculation and sabotage), therefore cannot try the case, and thus has decided to dismiss Stalin's complaint.[441]

During the first session of the trial Stalin swore, "Never in my life was I placed on trial before my party or expelled. This is a vicious libel . . . One has no right to come out with accusations like Martov's except with documents in one's hands. It is dishonest to throw mud on the basis of mere rumors . . ."[442]

Technically Stalin was perhaps correct in asserting that he had never been expelled from *his* party, for in 1901, 1902, and 1907 he had merely been told to leave the local party organization or a city. However, his failure to question the reliability of the witnesses Martov proposed to call and his silence regarding the charges against him are no less important than his refusal to be tried by a jury of his peers. If Stalin had nothing to hide, he would have welcomed a jury trial to clear his name. Perhaps Stalin was apprehensive that a trial would reveal other important facts about his double life in the Caucasus.

And what about Martov? Would he have dared ask for expert testimony from Zhordania, Ramishvili, and Dzhibladze—all of unquestionable honesty—had he not known the general thrust of their collective evidence? While Martov escaped with a reproval for "damaging the reputation" of a member of the Soviet government, Lenin, referring to the fact that Martov was a menshevik, later told Gorky, "I am sorry, deeply sorry, that Martov is not with us. What a splendid comrade he was, what an absolutely sincere man."

Perhaps there was more to the Tiflis party court of honor that sat in judgment on Stalin in 1907 than even Arsenidze, who was inclined to naiveté, and Martov, who was courageous but uninformed, knew. Because the records of the court were conveniently "lost," even as early as 1918, we must look at other reasons for which Stalin's Tiflis party comrades found him suspicious. His dismissal from the party was not based solely on his participation in the Tiflis expropriation or, for that matter, on his attempt to murder Zharinov, who probably had knowledge of its Okhrana implications. Although these matters involved killing, the Georgian bolsheviks were not averse to the drawing of blood, provided it was not accompanied by some sort of betrayal. Furthermore, Stalin could easily have responded to charges that he had participated in the Tiflis "ex" with a resounding "Yes," and claimed he had been working on behalf of Lenin and the party in that unhappy enterprise. But he was obviously afraid of a full exposure of his activities in Tiflis.

About two months after the Erevan Square disaster, Prince Ilya Chavchavadze, one of the most beloved Georgians of his day, was shot down near Mtskheta. A former Okhrana officer confessed to this brutal crime during World War II, but as Iremashvili insisted, "Koba was behind it; he was the man indirectly responsible for the murder." [443] These two versions are not incompatible; the Prince had bitterly criticized both bolshevik and Department of Police extremism and it is possible that Koba and the Okhrana were both involved.

The Tiflis robbery, the attempt to murder Zharinov, and the cold-blooded assassination of Prince Chavchavadze, like the Erevan Square incident, were not the only reasons for expelling Stalin from the Social-Democratic Party ranks in 1907. The party court of honor was headed by Dzhibladze, who had long suspected Stalin of treacherous collusion with the Okhrana. The "lost" records of the party court would doubtless have revealed that Stalin had a connection with the Department of Police; it was for this reason that in 1918 Stalin was so incensed at Martov's claim that the Tiflis organization had expelled him. Had Nicolaevsky located the minutes of the meetings convened in the matter of Stalin, he would have found that they pointed an unmistakable finger at Stalin's double dealing. By brazenly destroying evidence and distorting the record, Stalin had once more avoided the exposure of his work for the Okhrana.

However, he was unable to use such savage tactics when in 1907 he was forced to leave Tiflis for the same reasons that he had been obliged to leave Batum in 1902: the social democrats suspected him of treachery to the revolutionary cause, betrayal of party members to the police, and senseless terrorism. In the back of many minds was the unanswered question: was he affiliated with the Okhrana?

Because Batum and Tiflis were now closed to him, he needed a new locale in which to operate. The most logical place was Baku.

10 | THE BLACK CITY

Baku's population of two hundred thousand was a caldron of Tartars, Armenians, Persians, and Russians. Situated on a peninsula in the Caspian Sea, and fifty-six feet below sea level, it derived its name from the Persian *"badkube,"* meaning "squall." For almost a thousand years it had been Persian; it had become Russian about a century before Koba's arrival. The "Black City" supplied all of Russia with petroleum products. Oil bubbled through holes in the mud flats around the Caspian, and sometimes was unintentionally ignited. Baku was the site of the Nobel, Rothschild, and other oil refineries. Without oil there would have been no Baku proletariat and little reason for Koba to go there.

From the time of Koba's arrival, in mid-summer of 1907, we are confronted with another vague and mysterious period in his life. The *Collected Works* would have us believe that in August he organized the bolshevik newspaper *Gudok (The Whistle)*, supposedly an organ for the oil workers' union, that he was elected a member of a committee to reconvene a city party conference, that he directed a campaign during September and October for the Third State Duma elections, and that on September 29th he delivered a speech at the grave of Khanlar Safarallyev, a bolshevik worker killed by "hired agents of the capitalists." His one article during the period was "Boycott the Conference!" published in *Gudok*. On October 25th "he was elected a member of the Baku committee of the R.S.D.R.P." At the end of November he arrived in Tiflis "on party business." There is only a single entry in his *Collected Works* for the period between November, 1907 and January, 1908: "J. V. Stalin directs the campaign for the participation of the Baku workers in a conference with the oil owners on the condition that the rights of the workers are guaranteed." This vague wording suggests Stalin had something to do with the negotiation with the management of the oil refineries.[444] At any rate, it purports to describe the sum total of his activities in Baku during 1907. Obviously he was busy at something else and one wonders why he fails to mention it. Indeed, if it were not for the independent testimony of Enukidze and Sergo Ordzhonikidze, who wrote before Stalin could effectively muzzle them, we would be entitled to doubt that he was in Baku during the second half of 1907. But they saw him there and witnessed his bitterly divisive tactics. Sergo recalled that Koba favored a proposed strike of oil workers at the Balakhan refinery during the summer of 1907, in opposition to the bolsheviks and the mensheviks.[445]

After the gory happening at Erevan Square and after having been thrown out of the Tiflis party, Koba might have been a bit subdued. But not at all. Although he was a minor figure among the prominent Baku Social-Democratic Party members, which included Stepan Shaumyan, Prokofy Dzhaparidze, and Avel Enukidze, Koba at once showed his real character. Shaumyan, perhaps the most important party member in Baku, was a special target of Koba's malice and treachery. In many ways, Koba's campaign to discredit and undermine Shaumyan was simply a repetition of his earlier operations to destroy Chekheidze in Batum and Dzhibladze in Tiflis. It will be remembered that Shaumyan had suspected Koba of having denounced him to the Okhrana in Tiflis in 1905. Once more the party rank and file suspected Koba—this time of betraying Shaumyan to the Baku Gendarme Administration. Souvarine writes:

> Between the two there began a long struggle, pushed to such length that the Baku workmen even suspected Dzhugashvili of having denounced Shaumyan to the police, and wanted to bring him up before a Party tribunal. He [Stalin] was saved by arrest and exile in Siberia.[446]

That Koba "was saved by arrest and exile" from a party tribunal about to look into the matter of this second denunciation of Shau-myan to the police could not have been mere coincidence.

In the first three months of 1908, before Koba was arrested, he wrote five short articles in Baku, according to his *Collected Works*. All were in the Georgian language and only one had a signature, "K. Kato." Beyond these insignificant polemics, his official chro-nology has him organizing "a series of big strikes" in January and February, and forming within the Baku Social-Democratic Com-mittee a "Self-Defense Staff" in connection with the growing fre-quency of assaults by the Black Hundreds.[447] The Black Hundreds (founded in 1905) were armed reactionary groups, often sup-ported or organized by the government, which fomented pogroms and other depredations against revolutionaries and Jews. These claims on behalf of Koba were patently fraudulent. Any organizing done at Baku during this time was by the well-known revolution-aries Shaumyan, Dzhaparidze, Spandaryan, and Enukidze, as the pre-Stalinist-dictatorship record plainly shows.

Department of Police reports, happily, correspond with Soviet accounts that Iosif Vissarionovich Dzhugashvili was arrested on March 25, 1908, in Baku, where he had been living under the doc-umented alias of Kaios Vissarionov Nizheradze.[448] We do not know the name of the gendarme officer who made the arrest or where in Baku it occurred. By Soviet accounts, his second arrest was six years after his first. Department of Police records, however, prove that it was his third, the previous one having been in 1905-6, two or three years before. It is strange that no one was arrested at the same time as Koba, when usually the Okhrana rounded up as many revolutionaries as possible at one time. Koba was sent to the Bailov prison.

Tsarist prisons, never pleasant, had the dubious distinction of being preferable to Stalinist prisons—at least in the opinion of in-mates who experienced both. Bailov, where Koba went after his March 25th arrest, was no exception; an unimposing two-story building, it was located on a promontory on the Caspian Sea a mile or so from the center of Baku, in the ancient remains of the town of

Baila. It was designed to accommodate four hundred people, but in 1908 it bulged at its iron and wooden seams with fourteen hundred political prisoners and common criminals. The regime at Bailov was mild, the food palatable, and—since it was an "open" prison —its inmates roamed the corridors and yards most of the day.[449]

I. Vatsek, chairman of the Bailov Social-Democratic Committee, lived on a hill opposite the Bailov prison, which was visible from the upper story of his house. The second floor of the prison held the political prisoners, including Koba, who had told Vatsek that when a handkerchief was waved from his cell window, it would indicate a request for a meeting. Vatsek's wife usually sat sewing at the window. One day when the handkerchief fluttered, she rushed to the inner prison courtyard where prisoners normally met their visitors. Koba led her off to one side and engaged her in conversation until a bell signalled the end of the visitation period. One of the comrades (never identified) escaped as a departing visitor while Stalin kept Mrs. Vatsek talking. According to Vatsek, the "workers who heard about this story exclaimed, 'Good for Koba, he certainly cooked up something clever!' " Whether this Soviet yarn is true or apocryphal, it nonetheless typifies the prison regime's reputation for slackness.[450]

In the volumes of literature about Stalin, he seems to come alive only in the biography by Iremashvili, in a moderately long article by the former menshevik Arsenidze and, perhaps most of all, in two short articles titled "Stalin in Prison," written by the ex-social revolutionary Semyen Vereshchak. Vereshchak was an expatriate when in 1928 he contributed his knowledge of Stalin to the émigré newspaper *Dni (The Days)* in Paris. The few thousand words by Vereshchak constitute the most conclusive analysis available of Koba's pre-revolutionary character and personality.

Who was Semyen Vereshchak? As a social revolutionary, he had politically opposed both bolsheviks and mensheviks in his native Caucasus. One author has written, "Vereshchak had a faultless moral reputation in various revolutionary circles; the Bolsheviks themselves gave indisputable proof of it by reproducing his recollections, in their own fashion, in *Pravda,* the official party organ." [451] Bolshevik editing later distorted the text of his objective and psychological incisive articles. As a young revolutionary, Vereshchak was imprisoned in 1908 and spent more than three years in the Bailov prison. He was present when Koba entered prison in March, 1908, and was still there when he went off to exile and when he was rearrested in Baku in March, 1910. Stalin and Vereshchak next met as fellow-exiles in Narym, Siberia, in 1912. Then, after the revolution of February, 1917, Vereshchak, representing the Tiflis Soviet, talked with Stalin at the First Congress of the Soviets in Petrograd. His impressions, written with the benefit of an obviously good memory, spanned ten years. [452]

Political prisoners in the Bailov prison had their own organization, from which common criminals were excluded. Social revolutionaries, mensheviks, and bolsheviks were equally represented on a sort of "credentials commission," headed by a chairman as a part of the "commune." Vereshchak, the social-revolutionary member of the commission for two years, recalled that Koba arrived in prison wearing a blue satin-like smock with no belt. Bareheaded, he had a *bashlik*—a hood—over his shoulders. He walked slowly, like a cat. Slender, with a pointed pockmarked face, he had a sharp nose and small eyes that peered out from his narrow forehead. He spoke very little and apparently had no use for friends or associates. Vereshchak wrote:

> When a new prisoner unknown to the reception commission appeared in the Bolshevik room, a member of the commission had the right to question the chairman about the newly arrived person. When I asked who this comrade was, they secretly told me: "That is Koba." Because the name meant nothing to me, and his outward appearance definitely did not impress me, I asked for a factional guarantee. [453] My persistence annoyed the Bolsheviks, whose chief, in providing the guarantee and information about Koba, noted that I was attempting to square accounts with the Bolsheviks for something that had happened before I was imprisoned. He produced proof of an incident in which sailors had beaten up a propagandist sent by Koba into my area. But, before prison I did not know him.

Without further ado Koba entered the prison system, where Vereshchak closely observed him during a period of just over six months in "communal rooms, in an open prison," and also learned about him from fellow-prisoners with whom he had been acquainted outside the prison walls. His own observations and the experiences of others enabled Vereshchak to develop a keen analysis of Stalin's character and personality, which at the age of twenty-nine, were definitely shaped.

In Vereshchak's view, Koba was naturally a man of little or no culture. Confirming the judgment of Iremashvili and Arsenidze, he noted that Stalin was coarse and crude. Fifteen years later, on his deathbed, Lenin was to use the same word, *grubyi* (crude), to describe Stalin.[454] Vereshchak recognized that Koba was a complete cynic. "Stalin was always the underground type," Vereshchak wrote, "[and] in the underground, like so many revolutionaries, he developed a particular psychology, a mistrust, a suspiciousness not only toward those around him, but to himself, in which reason and slyness, truth and falsehood were interwoven." He was always the conspirator, never becoming directly involved in an act that might rebound to his personal disadvantage. He was a wire-puller, a revolutionary puppeteer, and Vereshchak also noted "his remarkable lack of principle and his practical cunning." Cautious and dry in speech, generally uncommunicative, he admired the "doer," the person who had accomplished something—even though it was a bloody crime. His memory was machine-like. But it was Koba's steel nerves and penchant for treachery that set him off from other prisoners and revolutionaries.

The Bailov political prisoners, to relieve boredom and avoid what today's slang calls "going stir-crazy," played a game of coarse needling, insulting allegations, and contrived accusations, aimed at making the subject react with incriminating admissions about his past life. In prison jargon the game was called "harassing the bladder." Vereshchak admits that the prisoners were unable to make Koba lose his equilibrium in this unpleasant game; he remained imperturbable to every insult.

On Easter Sunday, 1908, when the prisoners apparently had been misbehaving, they were punished by having to run a gauntlet of rifle butts belonging to soldiers of the First Company of the Saliansky Regiment, brought into the prison courtyard for that purpose. Many soldiers and officers of the Russian Army deplored this type of punishment, but there were no doubt always a sadist or two. According to Vereshchak, Koba proceeded calmly, book in hand, through the double line of soldiers while all the others ran; later Koba used his slop-bucket to beat on the door of his cell, despite the threat of the guards' bayonets.[455] Koba's coolness impressed everyone, and even Trotsky was moved to comment, "That self-contained man [Stalin], true, on rare occasions was capable of blinding rage." [456]

Koba's steel nerves and apparently unfeeling nature were also observed by Vereshchak during the infrequent but ghastly nocturnal hangings. The prisoners who were to be executed had slept and eaten the same day with their comrades. Wide awake, Vereshchak and others became tense and nervous at the screams and outcries of the condemned being forced to the gallows. However, "Koba slept soundly, or quietly studied Esperanto [he had decided it was to be the future language of the Communist International], while the entire prison nervously, almost audibly, anticipated the next execution," Vereshchak wrote.

Probably never has Koba's treachery been more clearly documented than it was in the Bailov prison. It was here Vereshchak learned that Koba had denounced his fellow-students years before in the Tiflis Seminary. Vereshchak recalled another betrayal, which limned the Baku political situation:

Beginning with 1908, Bolshevik activity in Baku was practically at an end. No signs of life came from the Baku Committee. So, when a leaflet of the Baku Committee appeared in 1908 it attracted general attention, interesting most of all the Mensheviks who had recently lost their regional underground printing press and had their leaders arrested. The Mensheviks controlled the printers' union. The Bolsheviks could not utilize a private printing press while ignoring the Social Revolutionaries or Mensheviks. The organization of any underground printing press for any party entailed great complications and many difficulties. An examination of the typesetting of this particular proclamation, however, disclosed that it had been done on the printing press of the Baku Chief of Police. The simultaneous appearance of

Koba back in Baku convinced everyone of the identity of the organization and author of the leaflet.

Vereshchak remarks that Stalin was, oddly, never tried by a tsarist court of justice, and adds, "The Mensheviks feared the Bolsheviks more than the police."

Two incidents in Bailov prison provide examples of Koba's underhandedness and his instinct for murder. Vereshchak remembered the arrival of a young Georgian who was nearly beaten to death by other political prisoners. Because of a rumor floating about that the Georgian was an *agent provocateur,* all the authentic revolutionaries wanted to assist in pummelling the despicable man. Finally, the guards carried his bruised body, dripping blood, along the corridors to the prison infirmary. "When everything quieted down," Vereshchak recalled, "we began to ask each other, friend to friend, just who was he? Who knew that he was an agent, a *provocateur?* If he was a police agent, then why hadn't they done him in? No one understood it. Only much later did it become clear that Koba had started the rumor."

The story of Mitka the Greek, a former bolshevik, is even more heinous. Mitka, on the prison stairway, used his knife to kill a young worker from the Balakhan region who had arrived that day in Bailov. The revolutionary reception commission had not even begun to verify his credentials. According to Vereshchak, "Mitka himself did not know whom he had killed. In his own words he had stabbed an informer [*shpik*]. Among political prisoners such acts could not be undertaken on personal initiative." The murder, quite naturally, interested everyone in the prison's political sector. Mitka finally disclosed that Koba had told him the young worker was a *provocateur* and had to be liquidated. This, however, was never substantiated. Had Koba recognized the young worker as a police colleague capable of identifying him? If so, it was of critical importance to seal his lips forever. Had Koba been able to prove him to be a police agent, and had he no worries about his own status, it would have been in the best revolutionary tradition to have the matter adjudicated by the prisoners' commission.[457] But Stalin always shied away from impartial tribunals.

Vereshchak noted that Koba, contrary to the best judgment of senior prisoners, often egged people on to engage in absurd and useless demonstrations against the prison administration. He did not seem to fear that he would be punished. He was indifferent to the unwritten but absolute rule that forbade political prisoners to associate with common criminals. In Bailov prison, "Koba was always seen in the company of cutthroats, political blackmailers, robbers, and gun slingers." He particularly enjoyed a good relationship with the Sakvarelidze brothers, notorious forgers of five-hundred-ruble notes.

As already noted, Koba's personal appearance, his rudeness, his lack of humor, and his dryness made him a poor speaker. But nevertheless, he enjoyed prison debates, in which, as far as he was concerned, a quotation from Marx was a clinching end to any argument. Vereshchak writes that the agrarian question then engendered heated discussions sometimes leading to fist fights. He tells this story about Ordzhonikidze, who was imprisoned in Bailov from November 4, 1907 to March 27, 1908:

> I shall never forget one agrarian discussion of Koba's, when his comrade Sergo Ordzhonikidze, defending his position, struck the Social Revolutionary Ilya Kartsevadze in the face. The other Social Revolutionaries proceeded to thrash Ordzhonikidze unmercifully.[458]

After less than two hundred days behind bars, Koba was deported from the Bailov prison to Vologda Province, under open police surveillance, on September 29, 1908.[459] He had received a two-year term of exile. His *Collected Works* claims that he arrived at Vologda prison in January, 1909. However on January 27th the authorities decided that his place of exile was to be Solvychegodsk, after which he fell ill with relapsing fever and was taken to the hospital at Vyatka. Relapsing fever—caused by vermin, not uncommon among prisoners—delayed his arrival at Solvychegodsk until February 27th. Travel time "by stages" for prisoners from

Baku to Solvychegodsk in 1908 was almost a hundred and forty days. Because of Koba's hospitalization at Vyatka, he reached his town of exile on February 27, 1909, a hundred and fifty-two days after he had departed.[460]

Solvychegodsk, located in Northern European Russia near the Sukhona River, approximately thirteen miles from Kotlas, was later one of Stalin's central N.K.V.D. concentration camps. The province capital, Vologda, was about three hundred and fifty miles southwest. Solvychegodsk, a seven-hundred-year-old fur-trading settlement, had some two thousand residents. Its climate was not as severe as that of the far reaches of eastern Siberia and its relative proximity to the principal Russian cities made it desirable from the political exile's point of view. Koba lived as an exile in Solvychegodsk from the end of February to the last of June, 1909. Little can be said about this part of his twenty-ninth year simply because it represents another void in his life. An official police report described him as coarse, insolent and disrespectful to his superiors during this period.[460a] His obvious contempt for the local country gendarmes apparently stemmed from the knowledge that he would soon escape. So he did, carrying a passport in the name of Oganess Vartanovich Totomyants, an Armenian resident of Tiflis.[461] The story of the issuance of this passport is of unusual interest.

In 1935 Lavrenty P. Beria, Stalin's future police chief, began the vast campaign of rewriting the record of Stalin's pre-revolutionary life in the Caucasus. This formidable enterprise was undertaken on Stalin's direct order. Recent Soviet works—for example, one by N. K. Sarkisov—tend to confirm this. Sarkisov, writing in 1965 from Baku, states that Beria and Bagirov, another bolshevik who had once eulogized Stalin, were "enemies of the people" and falsified history under the influence of Stalin's cult of personality; i.e., upon Stalin's explicit orders. Only once does he mention Stalin in his book, and then to damn him:

> The harmful influence of Stalin's cult of the personality led to serious mistakes and perversions in the illumination of the revolutionary movement in Azerbaidzhan in general and of the workers' movement in Baku during the years of the first Russian revolution—in particular.

The enemies of the people, Beria and Bagirov, in their insignificant books corrupted and falsified historical reality connected with the origin and system of the bolshevik organization in Transcaucasia and Azerbaidzhan, represented the development of the revolutionary movement in the region in a distorted light, etc. They attempted to belittle the significance and role of the Baku proletariat—one of the progressive detachments of the Russian workers' movement in the revolution of 1905-1907 and they ignored the services of the outstanding activists of the Baku bolshevik organization: S. Shaumyan, G. Ordzhonikidze, N. Narimanov, M. Azizbekov, P. Dzhaparidze, P. Montin, M. B. Kasumov and many others. In this manner was Stalin's personality glorified.[462]

Beria's task of falsification was not an easy one. Police records and other documents had to be altered or sometimes forged. Any suspicion of Stalin's connection with the Okhrana had to be covered up and his pre-eminence in Caucasian revolutionary matters had to be established. In something like a preview of George Orwell's *1984,* Beria disclosed the results of his rewriting of history in a "lecture delivered at a meeting of active workers of the Tiflis party organization July 21-22, 1935." Later the lecture became a book, published in nine Russian editions, the last one in 1952, entitled *On the History of the Bolshevik Organization in Transcaucasia.*[463] Anyone who tries to distort twentieth-century history finds his job full of enormous possibilities for contradictions and mistakes that, in turn, tend to be counter-productive, revealing the truth the distortion seeks to suppress. One of the passages in Beria's lecture is an outstanding example of the pitfalls that must be avoided in an exercise of deception. He wrote:

> During his work in Baku, Comrade Stalin was arrested and sentenced to exile many times. The tsarist secret police dogged him tenaciously. One of Comrade Stalin's arrests took place in March 1908. Of the numerous police records of Comrade Stalin's activity, I will cite a few passages from the documents of the Gendarmerie Department.
>
> FIRST
>
> In compliance with the request from the Department of Police of September 30, ult., No. 136706, the Caucasian District Secret Police Department reports that according to the information of the

chief of the Baku Secret Police Department "Soso," who escaped from Siberia and is known in the organization as "Koba," has been identified as Oganess Vartanov Totomyants, a resident of the city of Tiflis in whose name he has a passport, No. 982, issued by the Tiflis superintendent of police on May 12 of this year and valid for one year. . . .

Of the people named, "Totomyants"-"Koba" (also reported to be known as "Molochny") is at the head of the Baku organization of the R.S.D.L.P.; two others are members of Bibi-Eibat district of the same organization. They are under constant secret surveillance, and in some cases open surveillance and all will come under the measures being taken to break up the organizations.[464]

SECOND

Dzhugashvili is a member of the Baku Committee of the R.S.D.-L.P., known in the organization under the alias of "Koba". . . . In view of his stubborn participation, despite all administrative penalties, in the activity of the revolutionary parties in which *he has always occupied an extremely prominent position,* and in view of his escape on two occasions from the locality of his exile, as a result of which he has not undergone a single one of the administrative penalties imposed upon him, I would suggest recourse to a stricter measure of punishment—exile to the most remote districts of Siberia for *five* years.[465]

Apparently Beria had overlooked the implications of the statement in the gendarme report, which he had probably studied at length before editing, that Soso had escaped from Siberia as Oganess Vartanov Totomyants, a resident of the city of Tiflis in whose name he held passport No. 982, issued by the Tiflis superintendent of police on May 12, 1909. By all accounts Koba escaped from Solvychegodsk on June 24th. This meant the passport must have been in Koba's hands by that day at the latest. How did he obtain it? If it had been sent through the mail from Tiflis to Solvychegodsk, the gendarmes in all probability would have intercepted it. A special courier from the Tiflis social democrats might have made the long trip to Solvychegodsk. This is doubtful, because Koba's reputation was not good in Tiflis and another revolutionary would scarcely hazard such a trip with all its inherent risks merely to insure the escape from exile of Koba, a relatively unimportant

man. It is hardly possible that the Tiflis police had issued a passport to Totomyants on May 12th, arrested him immediately thereafter, failed to retrieve the passport, and whisked him off in record
speed to Solvychegodsk, where Koba purchased it. Whatever happened, Stalin's escape from exile in Solvychegodsk on June 24,
1909, using a passport issued some weeks before on May 12th by
the Tiflis Okhrana, inevitably leads one to Okhrana connivance in
the matter and points to the suspicion that the Okhrana wanted
Koba back in the Transcaucasus for operational reasons. This interpretation is fortified by the fact that Koba's destination after his
escape was precisely the Baku-Tiflis area. If so, it is not unlikely
that reporting on party activities and personalities in the Caucasus
was involved. Perhaps the Okhrana agent network within the Baku
party organization had been exposed or had collapsed for any
number of reasons and a trustworthy agent-replacement had become imperative. If the Okhrana placed a passport in Koba's
hands, it did so with forethought and a predetermined task he
would perform.

Eluding the gendarme guards, Koba slipped away to Kotlas, thirteen miles distant from Solvychegodsk, on June 24th.[466] From
there he travelled by rail to Vyatka, Vologda, and St. Petersburg,
almost a thousand miles from his village of exile. If he was able to
meet all train schedules, he probably arrived in St. Petersburg on
July 1st. Unfortunately, the official chronology is as vague about
his escape as it is indefinite concerning the length of his stay in St.
Petersburg. Sergo Alliluev maintains he had received a letter from
Koba some months earlier requesting his address, which he sent
him. Nonetheless, upon his arrival Koba was unable to locate Alliluev, and quite by accident Alliluev saw him strolling around the
city. As far as we know, Alliluev was not a liar, and his story of
this accidental encounter rings true. He provides the additional information that Koba lived for a few days with a certain Savchenko,
a Guards regimental quartermaster who sympathized with the revolutionaries.[467] During these few days, Koba presumably saw some
of the bolshevik deputies to the Third Duma, although no one has
recalled the gist of these conversations.[468] The deputies could hardly

have learned anything important from Koba—recently returned from the dreary settlement of Solvychegodsk—and certainly he profited little from conversations that might place his freedom in jeopardy. He discovered, if these conversations took place, that the bolsheviks were in a membership and financial crisis.

When Stalin entered St. Petersburg (perhaps for the tenth time, undoubtedly for the sixth[469]), he was matching wits with more than twenty-five hundred professional intelligence personnel guarding the railroads into the capital. He faced the best of the tsarist police in the city where the Department of Police Headquarters, headed by Major General Klykov,[470] had already received a telegraphic report from Vologda concerning his escape. Well over a hundred and fifty professional intelligence operatives who had read the bulletin for his arrest issued years earlier had been alerted—if standard operating procedure was followed. With a host of informants and plainclothesmen and with furtive penetrations into various revolutionary organizations, it is inconceivable that he would have gone long unnoticed by the Okhrana, even had he evaded the railway gendarmes in the Nikolaevsky Station.

There is no reliable way of estimating the number of *filery* ("shadows" or "tails") who augmented the official security personnel in St. Petersburg. *Filery* were surveillance agents and detectives who acted on information collected by the police headquarters. A *filer*, often a retired noncommissioned army officer and an expert at physical surveillance and disguise, was customarily "on the bricks" (following a subject of surveillance along the street) as their American security counterparts would put it today. What complicated any revolutionary's stay in St. Petersburg during this period was the *filer* school. Hundreds of "shadows" were sent out on training exercises in St. Petersburg in much the same fashion that C.I.A. trainees are assigned to metropolitan Washington. In St. Petersburg, however, there was a certain urgency because of the legion of revolutionary agents infesting the capital. Unlike their contemporary counterparts, the *filery* had plenty of live targets. Thus, when a telegram from Vologda to St. Petersburg announced the escape of a "wanted" revolutionary, the *filery,* following the scent, began surveillance of the subject.[471]

Stalin experienced not the slightest difficulty with the police prior to setting out for Moscow in the first week of July.[472] Before he arrived in Moscow, he went through at least four detailed checkpoints: St. Petersburg, Bologoye, Tver, and the environs of Moscow. On his journey back to the Caucasus in the summer, he was faced with the knowledge that professional security officers were looking for him at nine points along his Moscow-Baku escape route. Nowhere do we read that he outwitted the gendarmes. He lived a charmed life, extraordinarily different from that of other revolutionaries. According to the official chronicle, Koba arrived at Baku in mid-July.[473] He seemed almost eager to rush back into the Caucasus, where he was especially well known to the Okhrana. Common sense and his boasted conspiratorial talents should have warned him away from Baku, where he had been arrested fifteen months previously.

Koba should have been apprehensive for his safety had he been an ordinary revolutionary. However, this return to Baku is striking when we remember that he had returned to Batum in 1904 after his arrest there in 1902. He had now established a unique pattern in which he did not attempt to evade the Okhrana, but rather placed himself voluntarily in those areas where he was particularly well known to the police, thus almost inviting arrest. From the time of his arrival in Baku in mid-July until the end of 1909, there is no reliable information about Koba.[474] The official chronology states that he immediately became active directing "the work of restoring and consolidating the Bolshevik organizations in Baku and Transcaucasia." [475] This is easily recognized as a Stalinist falsification, because reliable sources point out that this period in Transcaucasia was marked by a precipitate drop in the party fortunes. As late as 1912, when Ordzhonikidze was in Baku, he found workers and party organizations practically nonexistent.[476] Koba claims that he wrote three articles for the Baku party newspaper during this period of over five months. Additionally, his official chronology includes a long article in two parts, "Letters from the Caucasus," in November and December, although they appeared later, in February and May of 1910. He signed only three of the five pieces: the first "K. Ko." and the "Letters from the Caucasus," "K. S." and "K. Stefin." [477] Five such unimaginative and commonplace articles hardly consumed five months of his time. To fill the gap, his official biographers and his *Collected Works* have him organizing workers' party conferences and a secret printing press and evading the police. Beria, in particular, emphasizes Koba's difficulties with the Okhrana. Thus on August 2nd he led the Baku Committee of the Social Democratic Party in adopting a resolution that concerned the editorial board of *Proletary*, supporting "the stand taken by the majority of the editorial board represented by Comrade Lenin." Six weeks later he left Baku for Tiflis, where he organized and directed the struggle of the Tiflis bolshevik organization against the menshevik liquidators. The liquidators, sometimes called "revisionists," advocated less revolutionary activity in order to attract the Russian bourgeoisie and liberals. Lenin was adamantly opposed to this tactic: the term "liquidators" came from proposals to liquidate the illegal party groups, the expropriators, and the terrorists. At the end of September Stalin supposedly re-established the underground printing plant of the Baku committee, and from October 19th to the beginning of November he was in Tiflis preparing for the convocation of the Tiflis City Party Conference and for the publication of the bolshevik newspaper *Tiflissky Proletary*.[478]

M. D. Bagirov, (who, as already noted, has since been labelled by Soviet authors as an "enemy of the people"), writing in 1946, pointed to an interesting bit of narrative concerning Stalin. He maintained that in a secret report to the Tiflis provincial gendarme administration the Chief of the Baku Okhrana, Captain Martynov, reported October 19, 1909:

"Koba" has departed for Tiflis to participate in the conference at which he has full power from the Baku organization to act in its behalf. A decision concerning the question of the situation in general in Baku with the Tiflis technique and publication of the organ called *"Kavkazsky Proletariat."* In view of the fact that they want to publish it in three languages (Russian, Armenian, and Tatar), an increase in the technical means is required for a corresponding equipment and large size of the newspaper, the addition of Armenian and Tatar type-setting; the insufficiency of means of the Baku organization . . . and others, connected with the publication of the paper, are questions that will be subjects of the conference, after which "Koba" must return to Baku and at once be involved in the technical matter. Please telegraph about his departure from Tiflis and the train number. (Partarkhiv TsKP(b) Az., d. 8, L. 49.) [479]

We cannot be sure that this report is authentic, but it bears all the marks of one Okhrana officer notifying another of the travel arrangements of an Okhrana agent. Although Koba had an interesting record of arrests and escapes from prison and exile, Captain Martynov asks not that Koba be arrested in Tiflis (which would have been operationally and professionally correct) but rather requests information about his estimated time of arrival in Baku, almost as if he wanted to be on hand to greet him upon his return. It is important to remember that Captain Martynov's request was directed to the Tiflis Okhrana officer, Lieutenant Colonel Eremin, the future chief of the highly secret Special Section in the Department of Police Headquarters, about whom we shall be concerned later on.

The official record for the latter half of 1909 is also transparently fabricated. We know from Arsenidze that Stalin, having been expelled from the Tiflis social-democratic organization, never returned, except for a day or two, and that he organized no one in Tiflis during the one or two episodic forays he made into that menshevik stronghold. His re-establishment of the Baku underground printing-press was also a lie. As Vereshchak pointed out long before Stalin's *Collected Works* was published, the Baku typesetters were mensheviks and totally unresponsive to bolshevik entreaties that they reinstitute a printing-press.

We do not know where or how Koba lived in Baku during 1909. Approximately the same Okhrana staff as that of the time of his 1908 arrest was present. Major General Kozintsov had been transferred. However, Lieutenant Podolsky, the official interpreter-translator Ali Razbekov, Captain Martynov, Captain Zaitsev, and a staff of twenty-two were well acquainted with his dossier and were able to recognize him on sight. While it is amazing that he remained at liberty until March, 1910, it is possible, of course, that the local Baku Gendarme Administration had received instructions not to molest him for the time being. This is underscored by passages from Bagirov's book. He notes that Stalin was arrested March, 1910, and after several months of incarceration in the Baku prison he was sent to Solvychegodsk. "A characteristic report of the chief of the Baku Okhrannoe Otdelenie" concerns Stalin's arrest:

[The person] mentioned in the summaries of external surveillance . . . under the cover name "Molochnyi," [is] known in the organization under the cover name "Koba," a member of the BK RSDRP, a most active party worker [who] occupies a leading party role . . . [and] was detained on my order by external surveillance agents the 23rd of this March.

The complete impossibility of further surveillance of him made "Molochnyi's" arrest urgently necessary, because all the surveillance agents have become known to him and even those newly appointed arriving from Tiflis immediately become known by which "Molochnyi," succeeding each time in throwing off surveillance, even pointed them out to comrades meeting with him, by which, of course, he has already evidently damaged the operation. (*Bakinsky rabochy*, No. 174, 30 July 1933, p. 3.)[480]

The reader will recognize that the Baku Okhrana is apologizing to the Tiflis Okhrana (Colonel Eremin) for the arrest of Eremin's agent. It could be paraphrased as follows: "Don't you understand that your agent Stalin ['Molochnyi'] had become insufferable? It was all right when he merely eluded the surveillance agents I assigned to cover him as a matter of course. But then he engaged in identifying to his cronies the surveillance agents assigned to other revolutionaries. Stalin was beginning to jeopardize the entire plan of surveillance in Baku and I had no other recourse than to lock him up. Because you and I are fellow officers in the Separate Corps of Gendarmes, I am sure you will understand."

For 1910 there are only three entries in his personally edited *Collected Works* before his March 23rd arrest. The entry "Beginning with 1910, Stalin is a representative of the Central Committee of the Party" opens the year. Then, on January 5th, "The newspaper *Tiflissky Proletary,* [was] founded with the direct participation of J. V. Stalin." On January 22nd the Baku Committee adopted his resolution to convene a general party conference, to transfer the practical center for directing the activities of the party to Russia, and to publish an all-Russian leading newspaper.[481] The final entry records his arrest in Baku on March 23rd.

Captain Martynov, who had extensive police experience in Moscow and elsewhere, arrested Koba, documented as Zakhar Grigorian Melikiants, on March 23, 1910.[482] Precisely how and where he was arrested has never been made clear, but police records and Soviet accounts agree on the date, which was two years after his last arrest. However, the Soviet version has it as his third arrest: Department of Police documents prove it was his fourth.[483] Koba was transferred to the Bailov prison in Baku on March 26, 1910, where he again met Vereshchak.

Almost six months pass before there is any official or unofficial information regarding Koba-Dzhugashvili. In September the Viceroy of the Caucasus issued an order forbidding Koba to live in the Caucasus for five years. On September 23rd he was removed under escort from Bailov to Solvychegodsk, where he arrived on October 29th. Meantime, after Stalin's arrest a member of the Baku Gendarme Administration, Captain Fedor Ivanovich Galimbatovsky, suggested that "in view of the persistent participation of Dzhugashvili in revolutionary activity and his two escapes . . . the highest measure of punishment [should be] invoked." [484] This meant exile to remote Siberia for five years.

But a strange thing happened to Stalin while he was incarcerated in Bailov prison during 1910: the Ministry of Internal Affairs in St. Petersburg rejected Captain Galimbatovsky's recommendation, and decided instead that the revolutionary Dzhugashvili should be sent back to Solvychegodsk merely to serve his unexpired term. There was to be no additional penalty for his three escapes from prison and exile.

From his arrival in Solvychegodsk in October until the end of

1910, little is known of Koba's real activities, although, not unexpectedly, the official record casts him in the role of an organizer of meetings at which exiles read papers and discussed current political questions. Koba, as we know, lacked talent at organizing unless he worked behind the scenes with coercive authority. In all likelihood, therefore, he was not engaging in organizational activities. However, before the new year he made an unusual and cryptic move in writing Lenin.

The final days of the Paris winter of 1910-11 found Lenin gloomily recalling the past and viewing the future with little hope. His fortunes and those of the bolsheviks were at a low point. He needed as much political support as he could muster. Far away in Solvychegodsk, meanwhile, Koba was composing a letter for his attention. On New Year's Eve, 1910, Stalin posted a letter signed "K. S." to a Mr. Veltman (Avenue de Gobelen [Gobelins] 52, Paris), a prominent social democrat and journalist who could be depended on to give the letter to "Comrade Semyen," for whom the letter was intended, and who, in turn, would show it to Lenin. "Comrade Semyen" was Isaak Izrailevich Shvarts, a bolshevik long active in the Urals and the Caucasus, where he had met Koba. He was in Paris at this time apparently assisting Lenin in arranging for the Prague Conference. Quite predictably, the Department of Police Special Section intercepted and copied it on January 7th and dispatched it to the Okhrana Foreign Agency in Paris on January 10th. Koba would have expected this to happen.

As far as may be determined, this is the first Stalin letter intercepted by the Okhrana, his first personal letter that appears in print, and his only letter written from prison or exile before 1911.[485] Thus it is worth quoting:

COMRADE SEMYEN!
Yesterday I received your letter from the comrades. First of all, hearty greetings to Lenin, Kamenev[486] and the others. Next about your letter and, in general about the "damned questions." [487]
In my opinion, the line of the bloc (Lenin-Plekhanov) is the only correct one: 1) this line, and it alone, answers to the real interests of

the work in Russia, which demand that all real Party elements should rally together; 2) this line, and it alone, will expedite the process of emancipation of the legal organizations from the yoke of the Liquidators, by digging a gulf between the Menshevik workers and the Liquidators, and dispersing and disposing of the latter. A fight for influence in the legal organizations is the burning question of the day, a necessary stage on the road towards the regeneration of the Party; and a bloc is the only means by which these organizations can be cleansed of the garbage of Liquidationism.

The plan for a bloc reveals the hand of Lenin—he is a shrewd fellow, and knows where the crayfish hide in the winter. . . . The more unitedly the Bolsheviks act, the more organized they are in their action, the greater will be the chances of taming. We must, therefore, tirelessly hammer away on all anvils. I shall say nothing about the *Veperedists*,* because they are now of less interest than the Liquidators and the Plekhanovites. If they do wake up one of these days— all to the good, of course; but if not—well, never mind, let them stew in their own juice.

That is what I think about things abroad.

But that is not all, nor even the most important. The most important thing is to organize the work in Russia. The history of our Party shows that disagreements are ironed out not in debates, but mainly in the course of the work, in the course of applying principles. Hence, the task of the day is to organize work in Russia around a strictly defined principle. The Liquidators at once realized what was in the wind (their sense of smell is highly developed) and have begun to penetrate . . . the legal workers' organizations, and it appears that they already have their underground centre in Russia, which is directing, etc., the work. We, however, are still only preparing!, still in the stage of rehearsals. In my opinion, our immediate task, the one that brooks no delay, is to organize a central group (in Russia), to coordinate the illegal, semi-legal and legal work at first in the main centres (St. Petersburg, Moscow, the Urals, the South). Call it what you like—the "Russian section of the Central Committee" or auxiliary group of the Central Committee—it makes no difference, but such a group is as essential as air, as bread. At the present time lack of in-

---

* The Veperedists (pronounced "Veperyodists") were dissident bolsheviks whom Lenin, in 1909, decided had excluded themselves from his position. They took their name from the newspaper *Vpered* (*Forward*), the first bolshevik paper set up by Lenin and Bogdanov in 1904. See Wolfe (p. 510) for a more detailed account of this group.

formation, loneliness and isolation reign among the Party workers in the localities and they are all becoming discouraged. . . .

Now about myself. I have another six months to go here. When the term expires I shall be entirely at your service. If the need for Party workers is really acute, I could get away at once. . . .

There is a decent crowd here in exile, and it would be a very good thing if they could be supplied with the illegal periodicals. Send us *Sotsial-Demokrat* No. 17 and onwards. . . . We have not received *Rabochaya Gazeta*, neither No. 1 or No. 2, nor have we received *Golos Sotsial Demokrata*. I suppose we shall receive *Zvezda*. Send to the following addresses: 1) Solvychegodsk, Vologda Gubernia, for Ivan Isaakovich Bogomolov; 2) Solvychegodsk, Vologda Gubernia, for Petr Mikhailovich Serafimov. The address for correspondence with me is: Solvychegodsk, Vologda Gubernia, the house of Grigorov, for Nikolai Alexandrovich Voznesensky.

With comradely greetings,
K. S.

Don't send by registered mail. Write about how things are going on your side, I beg of you.

Koba apparently had received a letter from someone in Paris who had provided him with Veltman's address. This was his excuse for the long discourse on party and revolutionary matters, but it does not explain why he felt so sure about his ability to escape at any moment he was needed by the Central Committee. Only stupidity or the knowledge that he would receive Okhrana assistance in his escape emboldened him to be certain. And Koba was not noted for a lack of native intelligence. Moreover, one detects the outline of an Okhrana operation in Koba's emphasis that a bolshevik "center group" be established in Russia for the coordination of all party activities. Not that such a center would not be advisable and desirable for the bolsheviks, but it turned out that within a short time a center was established and its eventual chief was the Okhrana agent, Roman Malinovsky.

By the time Koba wrote his "Comrade Semyen" letter on New Year's Eve, 1910, he could point to an extraordinary record of travel, party meetings, border crossing, arrests, exiles and escapes. And he was supremely confident he could go anywhere at will, and even travel to Paris.

11 | LENIN REDISCOVERS DZHUGASHVILI

On December 9, 1910 Koba celebrated his thirty-first birthday among two thousand free residents and four hundred and fifty exiles living in the village of Solvychegodsk. He was occupying a room at the Grigorov home, the government allowance of twelve rubles a month being sufficient for board and lodging. A month later he moved to a comfortable dwelling owned by the widow Maria Prokopevna Kuzakova. She later recalled that although Koba read greatly, it was his constant writing, night and day, that had most impressed her. From six months of this incessant work, only two letters in several pages have survived. What was he writing? Maria's recollection of Koba and his activity during the long Northern night remains thought-provoking.[488]

Three weeks after writing Lenin in Paris, by way of "Comrade Semyen," he defied all rules of conspiracy by sending a letter, on January 24, 1911, to the Moscow bolshevik organization. Conspiracy was not a laughing matter, as Badaev, a bolshevik delegate to the Duma, commented: "Every violation of the system of conspiracy was in itself a ground for suspicion and made us wonder whether a police scheme was being hatched." [489] Koba's letter, addressed to "The Teacher Bobrovskaya, for VI. S. Bobrovsky, Kaluzhskaya Gates, Medvednikovskaya Hospital, Moscow," went as follows:

The Caucasian Soso is writing to you. You remember in 1904 in Tiflis and Baku. First of all my cordial greetings to Olga, to you, to Germanov, (I. M. Golubev, with whom I am spending my days in exile, told me about all of you.) Germanov knows me as K . . . b . . . a (he'll understand). I am finishing here in July of this year. Ilich and

Co. are calling me to one of two centers, without waiting for the end
of the term (a legal person has more possibilities) . . . but if there
is a great need (I await their answer), then, of course, I'll fly the
coop. . . . We are stifling here without anything to do. I am literally
choking.

We have heard, of course, about the "tempest in the teapot" abroad.
The blocs of Lenin-Plekhanov on the one hand, and those of Trotsky-
Martov-Bogdanov on the other. The workers' attitude toward the first
bloc is, as far as I know, favorable. But in general the workers are
beginning to look contemptuously on "abroad" saying:

"Let them crawl on the wall to their hearts' desire, but the way we
feel about it, he who has the interests of the movement at heart should
keep busy; as for the rest it will take care of itself."

This, I think, is for the best.

[signed] IOSIF

My address: Solvychegodsk, Vologda Province, political exile, Iosif
Dzhugashvili.[490]

On December 23, 1925, the Tiflis communist newspaper *Zarya
Vostoka* (*Dawn of the East*) not astutely published the letter,
which it had obtained from Georgian Okhrana files. History may
take some solace in the fact that Stalin was not then in a position of
total power in Soviet Russia. Nonetheless, after he became dictator
the fate of the persons responsible for exhuming the letter is easily
imaginable. Because it has never appeared again in Soviet literature, the surmise that it was an attempt to expose Koba's double-
dealing may not be discounted. The publication in 1925 of Koba's
letter to the Moscow bolsheviks might well have been a form of
retaliation, because two years earlier Stalin had released documents
denigrating Lenin while the latter was gravely ill.[491]

It is noteworthy that all of Koba's intercepted letters were processed, rerouted, and generally handled by the Special Section of
Department of Police Headquarters in St. Petersburg. Although
this was not an unusual practice in the case of very important revolutionaries, it was a bit extraordinary in the case of a relatively
insignificant party member such as Koba. The Special Section, it
must be remembered, was the *sanctum sanctorum* of the Okhrana
that developed and managed agent penetration operations into rev-

olutionary organizations. When Koba's two letters were intercepted and read by the Special Section and quickly forwarded from St. Petersburg to the Paris Foreign Agency, the Special Section had a new chief, Colonel Eremin, who had formerly been in Tiflis at the time of Koba's previous arrest in 1908. No less important is the fact that the Special Section marked its correspondence on Stalin with the highest security classification *sovershenno sekretno* ("completely secret," or "top secret") with one or two exceptions. This security classification was not surprising when used in connection with someone important, but often even in highly significant matters the classification was lower, that is, *sekretno* ("secret") or *lichno* ("personal"). When the Department of Police intercepted this letter, several days after it was mailed, the Tiflis Okhrana Chief, Colonel Ivan Iosifovich Pastriulin, was ordered by his St. Petersburg superiors to determine whether or not "Iosif" was Dzhugashvili. It was some weeks before he perused his files, developed agent information, and replied on March 14th, in a professional top-secret report to the élite Special Section of the Department of Police Headquarters:

I have the honor to inform your Excellency that the author of the "Solvychegodsk" letter, "Iosif," to the teacher Bobrovskaya, for VI. S. Bobrovsky, at the Kaluzhskaya Gates, Medvednikovskaya Hospital . . . is the peasant from the Tiflis Province, Iosif Vissarionov Dzhugashvili.

Colonel Pastriulin's report revealed that he had checked out all possible leads about the persons Koba had named in his letter. Everyone mentioned by Koba received detailed attention in the document, a copy of which was sent to the Chief of the Okhrana in Moscow and to the Chief of the Vologda Provincial Gendarme Administration.[492]

Two weeks later Captain Plotto, of the Vologda Gendarme Administration, replied in another top-secret report to the Special Section, with copies to the Moscow and Tiflis Okhrana:

In order to prevent his proposed escape from exile by the aforementioned Dzhugashvili before the completion of his term under surveillance . . . [I will] increase observation of him. . . . [The person mentioned in his] letter I. M. Golubev, a social democrat and a peasant from Tver Province is living in Solvychegodsk, having been sent administratively from Moscow under open surveillance.[493]

Koba's letters represent his only known writing during 1911, despite Maria Kuzakova's statement that he wrote a great deal. He had no articles published during the year, although exile was conducive to revolutionary theorizing and, in general, putting pen to paper.

Stalin's official chronology covers the six-month period before June 1911 with only one entry, remarkable in light of his "Iosif" letter to Moscow (which, of course, is not cited):

> March–June—The police make repeated searches in Stalin's lodgings (at the house of M. P. Kuzakova) in Solvychegodsk.

The local police had been alerted by Koba's remarks in his two intercepted letters that he could escape at any time. However, the *Collected Works* omits the fact, included in the police report, that he had lived in the house of a certain Grigorov before his residence with Mrs. Kuzakova.[494]

Koba knew, as a political exile and conspirator, that his letters would be intercepted by the ubiquitous Okhrana censors. In retrospect it almost appears that by his letter to the Moscow bolsheviks he intended to cause their arrest or to have them placed under surveillance. At any rate, Koba had committed a fantastic violation of conspiratorial security. Furthermore, this letter was clearly and strongly anti-Leninist in tone and context. Trotsky, attributing the letter to sheer boastfulness, fails to recognize that Koba's audience was the Department of Police. What did Koba hope to gain from these letters? The one intended for Lenin's eyes was quite apparently a bid for acceptance in the bolshevik hierarchy, as if Koba were trying to convince Lenin that, in setting up a Russian center, he would enormously help the bolshevik cause. In this he was to succeed because, among other reasons, Lenin—whose fortunes at this moment were at a low ebb—was prepared to welcome any support from Russia, even from someone in exile. At this time the "reaction," as the revolutionaries described it, had most certainly set in. It meant renewed Department of Police measures to penetrate and control the revolutionary organizations at home and in Western Europe, and it connoted a decline of party membership accompanied by increased monetary problems.

The incredible ineptness of the "Iosif" letter, however, tempts one to conclude that it involved a Department of Police operation. Yet it is difficult to discern what purpose the Okhrana might have had in encouraging Koba to send it to Moscow. Perhaps Koba did not want to escape. Perhaps Mrs. Kuzakova, with whom he had been living, figures in his decision to make sure the police would prevent his "flying the coop." In his thirty-second year he was undoubtedly devoting much thought to his future: was it better to cast his lot irrevocably with the Department of Police, or to become a committed bolshevik? He needed time to make a realistic judgment, to contemplate his chances for advancement in the party, to weigh the party's chances to await a response from Lenin, and to become "legal" at the expiration of his exile term. After all, as he had put it in his letter, "a legal person has more possibilities."

Lenin, in Paris, somehow heard about the "Iosif" letter to the Moscow bolsheviks, according to a Soviet account published in Moscow in 1963. He was not at all pleased. From November 1910 to July 1911 Sergo Ordzhonikidze was in Paris, involved with Lenin's operations there. The two often enjoyed long walks together and once, after the theater, Lenin asked:

"What do you think of the proposition that has just come from Russia?"

Sergo blushed. "Vladimir Ilich, you are asking. You are not sure?!"

Lenin took Sergo's arm. For the first time instead of the usual salutation "tovarishch" he cordially remarked: "Dear friend! It is too late to convince me. Today at a meeting of those members of the Central Committee living abroad, I finally obtained agreement to send a representative to Russia. You go. Semyen and Zakhar will go with you. Set up a Russian organizational commission. Begin at once to prepare for a party conference. It will end forever the remains of the formal unification with the mensheviks, regenerating our revolutionary bolshevik party. I underscore 'regenerate', because bolshevism has existed as a trend of political thought and as a political party from 1903!"

Later when they were again strolling along the Paris boulevards Lenin asked, "Are you, Sergo, acquainted with the expression 'a tempest in a teapot abroad'?" Ordzhonikidze had also apparently heard about the letter, but he attempted to disguise his own feelings about the matter. He wondered who had informed Lenin.

"How do you like that?" Lenin continued. " 'A tempest in a teapot abroad.' What nonsense!"
"Vladimir Ilich, please. Koba is our comrade!"
"I knew that very well," Ilich readily conceded. "I have the very best recollections of Stalin. I commended his 'Note of a Delegate' about the London Congress of the party and particularly his 'Letters from the Caucasus.' But until the revolution has been victorious we have no right to place personal sympathies or any kind of good recollections in its way . . . You people from the Caucasus hold very dear your *camaraderie.* . . ."
Lenin again scowled: "You say that 'Koba is our comrade.' But do you close your eyes to his inconsistency? Nihilistic little jokes about 'a tempest in a teapot' betray the immaturity of Koba as a marxist." [495]

This period in Koba's life was one of disappointment. After the Tiflis expropriation at Erevan Square, he may have felt that the Department of Police had dealt with him too harshly. A jail sentence and exile he recognized as unavoidable under the circumstances, but perhaps he considered his "punishment" somewhat excessive and his reward for past services to the Okhrana insufficient. He undoubtedly wanted to further his career in Social-Democratic Party ranks. But how was this to be accomplished? Certainly not by being stuck off in the Godforsaken village of Solvychegodsk! Nor could advancement as an agent in the Department of Police come about outside a Russian revolutionary organization. It would seem that a deterioration in his relationship with the Okhrana for some unknown reason had, in turn, deepened his inability to improve his party figure—and a good party figure was something that in this vicious circle was essential if he was to become more important with the Special Section of the Department of Police. Many years after Koba's soul-searching, General Kurlov, a former Director of the Department of Police and Commander of the Separate Corps of Gendarmes, would ponder the question: how far should the Okhrana go in advancing an agent in his own revolutionary party?[496] The secret police-intelligence agent who feels abandoned by his parent organization and unable to communicate with his superiors sinks into a dismal pit of frustration and melancholia. Moreover, Koba was unwilling, for solidly logical reasons, to approach the Solvychegodsk police with his problem. The village gendarmes would have been unable to comprehend the sophistication of Special Section intelligence operations. He may have decided to kill two birds with one stone by showing the Department of Police he was still capable of operational work, at the same time striving for greater party responsibility and position. Letters to Lenin and to the Moscow comrades were the only feasible means to accomplish this dual objective from faraway Solvychegodsk.

Koba was still in control of his choices. In the letter to "Comrade Semyen," intended for Lenin, he made a fawning, thinly veiled suggestion that he could assist him and the bolsheviks in Russia. A few weeks later, in the "Iosif" missive to the Moscow comrades, his attitude toward Lenin was deprecating as he compared him and émigrés abroad with miserable insects that "crawl on the walls." But in both letters he advanced the idea, unique until that time, of establishing a bolshevik "center" in Russia, hinting that he would be a good choice to head it. He had cunningly analyzed Department of Police tactics: Lenin and his bolsheviks were to remain strong and separate from the mensheviks, but not *too* strong.

From January 1st to June 1, 1911, we know nothing officially about him except that the local gendarmes repeatedly checked his room in Maria's house. She complained bitterly in a 1940 account that the local gendarmes prevented the exiles from leaving Solvychegodsk to pick mushrooms or berries and that Koba was forbidden to receive letters or telegrams.[497] The Department of Police had not forgotten Koba or his letters; Colonel Shtoltsenburg, Chief of the Provincial Gendarme Administration in Vologda, sent a top-secret report to the Special Section of the Department of Police on May 18, 1911:

> I can report to your Excellency that the author of the document signed "K. S." is Iosif Vissarionov Dzhugashvili under open police surveillance in Solvychegodsk. . . . The said Dzhugashvili from December 29, 1910 through January 10 of this year lived in Solvychegodsk in the house of Grigorov and at present lives in the house of [Mrs.] Kuzakova. He will be in exile only six months (until June 27 of this year).
>
> According to recently received agent information, Dzhugashvili and other exiles are attempting to organize a social-democratic group in Solvychegodsk ([see] my report of May 17, No. 2161) which group I will liquidate at the appropriate time. Surveillance of Dzhugashvili has been increased.[498]

This report, referring to the New Year's Eve letter to Lenin, augured no good for Koba. The Vologda gendarmes placed him under even more severe surveillance, instituting a mail cover on other revolutionaries he had mentioned, and decided that at the appropriate moment his little ineffectual social-democratic circle would, as the police put it, be "liquidated"—a term Stalin was to use frequently after he became dictator of Soviet Russia. Unsurprisingly in his *Collected Works* he notes that from June 23rd to 26th he was "kept under close arrest for three days for organizing a meeting of exiled Social Democrats." [499]

We also find the letter to Lenin from Solvychegodsk on New Year's Eve of 1910 appearing in the *Collected Works* as an entry of July, 1911. How else to explain "July—J. V. Stalin writes a letter to the editorial board of the *Workers Newspaper,* directed by Lenin, informing it of his intentions to work in St. Petersburg or in Moscow." No record of this letter exists. It was probably placed in the official chronology at this point to fill an embarrassing gap. As we have seen, Koba wrote no article during 1911 and the "Iosif" letter could not be included in a book for the party faithful. This is another of Stalin's distortions of history.[500]

Neither Lenin in Paris nor the Moscow bolsheviks appeared to be pleased by Koba's "Comrade Semyen" and "Iosif" letters. Almost six months passed without a response of any kind. Apparently his services were not in strikingly great demand. The Department of Police Special Section, after opening and reading his letters (as he had correctly foreseen), also appeared uninterested in summoning him for further work. Koba gloomily noted, moreover, that the St. Petersburg authorities had failed to stop local gendarme harassment. His quarters were being regularly searched, he was under strict surveillance, and he had been arrested and detained for several days because of his participation in a sorry meeting of exiled social democrats. These were disturbing omens.

On June 27, 1911, according to the *Collected Works* he was released from police surveillance because of the expiration of his term of exile. Prohibited from residing in the Caucasus, in large cities, and in industrial centers, he chose Vologda, on the way to St. Petersburg, as his place of residence. On June 6, 1911, he departed with a police travel certificate and arrived in Vologda July 16th.[501] The local gendarmes were amazingly kind to Koba—who, after all, had twice escaped from exile and had recently been placed under "close arrest"—when they permitted him to live in the province capital, which was vastly more comfortable than Solvychegodsk. According to his official account, however, he remained under police surveillance for the next two months. The Vologda Gendarme Administration, made up of twenty-three officers and men, was still commanded by Colonel Shtoltensburg and Captain Plotto, who had written the top-secret reports with which the reader is familiar. But they were unable to prevent Koba, the still-elusive revolutionary, from slipping away to St. Petersburg, even though a Soviet account claims that the Vologda detective Ilchukov witnessed his departure on Train No. 3 at 3:45 P.M. September 6th.[502]

As usual, there is a striking and convenient meshing of railway schedules, identification procedures, lack of difficulties with the gendarmes, and a general aura of good luck surrounding his three-hundred and seventy-mile railway journey in early September from

Vologda to St. Petersburg. Just over two months after he had received permission to live in Vologda, he arrived safely in St. Petersburg, where he registered under the name of Petr Aleksandrovich Chizhikov, whose documents he had acquired in exile. They were stolen, purchased, or supplied by the Okhrana.

From the recollections of Sergo Alliluev, and Sergo's daughter Anna, it is easy to reconstruct his brief sojourn, September 7th to 9th, in St. Petersburg. Koba arrived late in the evening at the Nikolaevsky Station. He decided to stroll through the city, hoping to meet comrades on the street, reasoning correctly that "this was less dangerous than to look for them at their addresses." In this unpromising endeavor he was incredibly successful. While walking around the city for the second or third time, he spotted Silvester Iaseevich "Sila" Todriya, a professional typesetter whom he had known in Baku, on the Nevsky Prospekt, St. Petersburg's main street.[503] He followed and whispered a greeting to him. Sila explained the situation was very dangerous because of the murder of Prime Minister Stolypin, who had been assassinated in Kiev on September 5 by Dmitry Bogrov, a social revolutionary and an Okhrana agent. The police were demanding that everyone identify himself and show his passport. Koba thereupon suggested that they "look for a furnished room somewhere, not far away." They found one in the Hotel Rossiya, at No. 3 Goncharnaya Street, where the doorkeeper looked a long time at Koba and examined the passport he carried in the name of Chizhikov, an employee of a Vologda fruit store.[504] The next day Anna Allilueva answered the doorbell to find Sila Todriya, an old family friend, with someone apparently unknown to her. The very thin and pallid stranger wore a black coat and a soft hat. It was Koba. He soon calmly proceeded to read the newspapers and magazines in the room. When Sergo Alliluev came home, he "grasped Soso's hand for a long time and said something to him and Sila." Then all three went to a window that opened on Saratov Street. "Well, do you see?" Sergo asked. "They don't fool me. I saw them at once as I was coming up to the house." There were two "tails" in the courtyard below. But Soso was unperturbed. "Let's wait and see what happens," he said.[504a]

Trotsky has a different version of this event:

Alliluev tells how one day early in September, on his way home, he noticed spies at the gate of his house, and, going upstairs to his flat he found Stalin and another Georgian bolshevik there. When Alliluev told him about the "tail" he left downstairs, Stalin retorted not too court-eously: "What the devil is the matter with you? . . . Some comrades are turning into scared Philistines and yokels!" [505]

Indeed, the comrades should have been scared. Alliluev was not new to the revolutionary-conspiratorial game: he knew quite well that it was utterly fatuous for Stalin to lead a "tail" to his apartment. As an old conspirator, furthermore, he must have wondered about his future son-in-law. As it turned out, the Philistines and yokels were able to say, "I told you so."

On September 9th, two days after he had arrived in St. Petersburg, Koba was arrested—for the fourth time by Soviet accounts, and for the fifth according to Department of Police records.[506] He later insisted that during this forty-eight hours he had established contact with the St. Petersburg party organization. If so, it was only because he stumbled onto Alliluev and Todriya. No one else remembers having seen him. The gendarmes unceremoniously seized him in his hotel room in the Hotel Rossiya and removed him to the St. Petersburg Preliminary Detention Prison, where he spent three months.[507] Unfortunately, there is not a word in friendly or hostile literature about this interval in Koba's life. He ignored it and we may surmise that it was not terribly unpleasant or of great significance. Otherwise it would have been noted.

The Department of Police once more punished Koba lightly; on December 14, 1911, he was deported to Vologda, the pleasant twelfth-century town where he had chosen to live several months before. He began a three-year exile term under police surveillance on Christmas Day, 1911.[508] As a result of his five arrests the Department of Police could reasonably have been expected to deport him to the far reaches of eastern Siberia, where he would truly be buried. But instead, by a curious combination of circumstances and an incredible stroke of good luck, his formal political career was in January, 1912, about to begin.

In mid-1911 Lenin decided to convene a new Social-Democratic Congress. He wrote the Czech social-democrat leader Anton Nemec on November 1, 1911, about the possibility of holding it in Prague, but he cautioned him that most of the delegates would be without passports and unable to identify themselves, so it had to be a secret gathering.[509] He held preparatory meetings in Paris during June and December. Although Stalin's *Collected Works* claims that on June 1, 1911, at a conference of the Central Committee held in Paris, he was appointed in his absence as an alternate member of the Organizing Committee for convening a party conference, the official record fails to mention him.[510]

Lenin desperately wanted to mold a personal power élite of militant revolutionaries unswervingly loyal to him, even if it was unrepresentative of the revolutionary forces in Russia. From Paris he sent a letter to those Social-Democratic Party groups in Russia that he felt sure would unstintingly follow his leadership, asking that they send delegates to Prague, the capital of Bohemia in Austro-Hungary. There is some evidence that the Austrian police-intelligence services played a part in his designating Prague as the Congress site.[511] The *concertmeister* of the Prague Conference was not the notoriously inefficient Austro-Hungarian intelligence service or Lenin, but the Russian Department of Police, which Soviet historians conveniently ignore when it serves their purposes. Even today, with a partial denigration of Stalin and presumably a more methodological approach to party history, Soviet literature tends to take evasive action when the Sixth Party Conference is involved. Through agents and mail intercepts, the Department of Police had learned almost at once of Lenin's decision to convene a Congress in Prague during January, 1912.[512] As Koba had shrewdly concluded, Okhrana policy at that time was to prevent at all costs the unification of mensheviks and bolsheviks—or, put another way, to make certain that the two factions were moved irrevocably apart. Lenin was thus unwittingly committed to strategy favored by the Okhrana.[513] Above all else, he wanted a party under his personal control and separate from other revolutionary organizations. The Paris preparatory conferences that Lenin had convened to facilitate

As restored (view from inside enclosure).

ouse in Gori where Stalin was born,
it originally appeared.

terior of magnificent enclosure around the re-
ored house, erected during Stalin's lifetime.

Stalin (*center top*) in Gori
school around 1888.

At the seminary around
1894.

Stalin's mother
in later years.

Stalin in 1900.

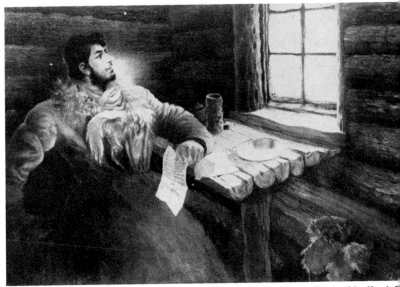

Transfiguration: Stalin in 1903 receiving Lenin's letter in exile, as idealized
the Soviet painter, M. Mariasch.

Stalin's first wife, Ekaterina Svanidze, in
1905.

Stalin in 1906

Stalin's police record, 1910. (Note shortness of left arm here and in photo below.)

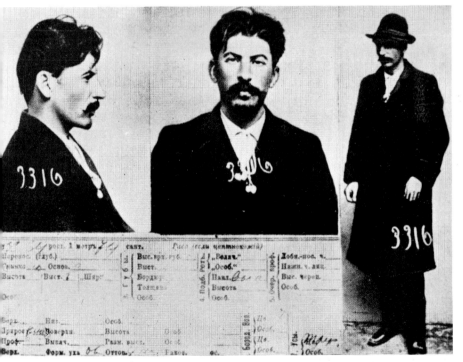

Stalin's police record, 1913.

Gendarmes inspecting train at Finnish border around 1905.

St. Petersburg gendarmes frisking a suspect, 1912.

Drawing in Tiflis newspaper in 1906: police searching a streetcar.

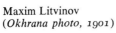
Maxim Litvinov
(*Okhrana photo, 1901*)

Noi (Naum) V. Ramishvili
(*Okhrana photo, 1904*)

S. Spandaryan

G. I. Petrovsky, 1897

Alesha Dzhaparidze, 1905

Noi N. Zhordania

Avel S. Enukidze

Georgy Teliya, 1905

Jacob M. Sverdlov, 1915
(in Turukhansk exile
with Stalin)

Olga Allilueva in 1904
with children, Pavel, Fedor,
Nadezhda (Stalin's future wife),
and Anna.

Nadezhda Allilueva,
Stalin's second wife,
in St. Petersburg at age 15.

M. G. Tskaya (Barsov)

G. K. (Sergo) Ordzhonikidze, 1904

G. I. Elisabedashvili

M. I. Kalinin, 1900

Alexander Tsulukidze

V. Z. (Lado) Ketskhoveli

V. K. Kurnatovsky

Ipolit Franchesky

Silvester Todriya

Roman V. Malinovsky

Leon Trotsky as a student of 19,
at the time of his first arrest.

Grigory E. Zinoviev
(*Okhrana photo*)

Kamo (*Berlin police photo*)

Silvester Dzhibladze
(*Tiflis Okhrana photo, 1909*)

Leonid Krasin, 1903

Stepan Shaumyan, 1904

Alexandra Kolontai,
at age 65.

CZAR'S DETECTIVES IN LONDON.

RUSSIAN SOCIALISTS "SHADOWED."

MORE ARRIVALS.

A sturdy, resolute-looking man stood at the corner of Fulborne-street, Whitechapel, yesterday.

He was obviously a foreigner, and, equally obviously, a person of some importance. Apparently unconcerned, he none the less was taking a lively interest in an unpretentious building half way down the thoroughfare and on the opposite side, and carefully scrutinised all who passed in and out.

This tireless watcher was M. Sevieff, one of Russia's secret police, and his duty is to keep watch on the Russian Socialists who have crossed the ocean to hold a conference in London. It was mainly on his representations that Norway, Sweden, and Denmark refused shelter to these revolutionaries. He and his assistants are following every member of the band, many of whom visit, and are welcomed at, the Socialist club in Fulborne-street.

The revolutionaries themselves are well aware of the harassing vigilance with which they are "shadowed." They manifest extreme distrust of strangers, almost of each other.

"We will neither be photographed nor interviewed," said one of them, speaking through an interpreter to an "Express" representative yesterday. "It would not be safe."

LEADING SPIRIT.

The leading spirit of the conference will be a M. Pekinoff. But it is extremely doubtful whether or not he will come much to the front in debate.

He is a quiet, reserved, dignified man of middle age, and is the living force behind the struggles of the peasantry and the middle classes with the autocracy.

"M. Pekinoff plans," said one delegate. "He it is who tries to reconcile the conflicting factions, and to give a lead to our discussions."

The delegates are as varied in type as they are in aim. A few have faith in the Duma as the ultimate salvation of the unhappy country from which they have come. Others would destroy the existing Government at one fell swoop, and set up in its stead the rule of the people absolute.

Among the delegates are students, farmers, mechanics, and labourers. They are staying with friends of the "cause" in the East End. Prominent English Socialists have met them and bidden them welcome.

A second batch of Russians arrived at Parkeston Quay yesterday afternoon, and came on to London to take part in the conference. There were 180 of them, and eight of that number were women. They had little luggage.

Daily Express account of Russian delegates in London in 1907.

Stalin around 1912.

Stalin (*center top*) with group in exile, 1913.

Group photo with Stalin (*top left*) in exile.

Stalin's house
in Kureika,
1913-1916.

Sergei Y. Alliluev, Stalin's
father-in-law, in 1941.

Stalin's room in 1917
at the Alliluevs',
St. Petersburg.

V. I. Lenin in 1917,
before he shaved off his beard.

Stalin as a Commissar.

On the eve of Lenin's death.

President Truman and Premier Stalin at Potsdam in 1945. Note shortness of Stalin's left arm.

the Prague Congress were matched by the Department of Police. Colonel Martynov, Chief of the Moscow Gendarme Administration, had his agent Kukushkin organize a conference of the city's normally bolshevik trade unions. Actually this was not a difficult task, for Colonel Martynov's penetration into the Moscow bolshevik organization was sufficient to control it. Under these circumstances it was a foregone conclusion that the Moscow bolshevik delegate would be an Okhrana agent, Roman Vatslavovich Malinovsky.[514]

Malinovsky was thirty-four years of age, with seemingly impeccable credentials as a workingman and trade-union organizer. He had first been a tailor (his Okhrana cover name was *Portnoi*—the Tailor) and later a metalworker. As a menshevik, he had helped organize the St. Petersburg metalworkers' union in 1907. Later he had become a bolshevik and been "exiled" from St. Petersburg by the Department of Police to Moscow, as part of an operation to quiet suspicions about his police affiliation. His criminal record, unknown to his trade union and the bolsheviks, included burglary and a charge of rape. After a prison sentence extending from 1899 to 1902, the Okhrana had recruited him as an agent. At the time of his pre-arranged "election" as a delegate to the Prague Conference, he was an experienced intelligence operative, a fact that Lenin indignantly refused to recognize. Romanov, the bolshevik delegate from Tula was also a police agent. Another Okhrana *agent provocateur*, Brendinsky had been chased off by Krupskaya.[515]

Malinovsky was also a talented leader, gifted with the art of earthy oratory that appealed to ordinary workers. Although he was a heavy drinker, he held his liquor well unless he was intent on getting drunk. He was the only Pole and Roman Catholic among the bolsheviks at Prague. Like Lenin, he was a redhead.[516] By insinuating Malinovsky into the bolshevik faction, the Okhrana had attained a high level of extremely important operational penetration. Among the means used to attain the Okhrana objective of deepening the split in the social-democratic party was the establishment of a legal bolshevik newspaper in which Lenin's polemics against the mensheviks, the Okhrana hoped, would drive the two factions farther apart and weaken the entire party. Malinovsky was a capable and intelligent politician, a bit conceited, who appeared with great and spirited optimism at all workers' club and union meetings. In order to safeguard him, the police frequently arrested him together with others present at an illegal meeting; after a few days he would be released, the others sentenced to long prison terms or exile. At other times, the Okhrana would release all those arrested and then rearrest all but Malinovsky in the course of a few weeks.[517]

Cecilia Bobrovskaya (she and her husband, had been Lenin's protégés) noted Malinovsky's charm. She also recalled that toward the end of 1911, when she was a university student, she found it impossible to study with spies all around her. Her brother, also a bolshevik, had arrived from abroad in 1912. Lenin had entrusted him with organizing the Moscow delegation for the Prague Conference. Anxious to help her brother, Bobrovskaya arranged a meeting, after great difficulty, with Malinovsky at the Bacteriological Institute. Malinovsky was very intelligent and possessed a good command of the language, but she said his strong temperament made him "perhaps a little too self-confident," but he was "a commanding person in all respects." However, her brother, who had supplied Malinovsky with secret addresses and meeting places on the frontier, was arrested two days later in Moscow en route to Prague. The Okhrana also placed her house under surveillance.[518]

Even Krupskaya, writing about Paris in 1911 and 1912, tried to analyze the prevalence of police spies:

> The Tsarist government had the experience of the 1905 revolution behind it. . . . It now had the whole workers' organizations enmeshed in its network of spies who used to hang around the street corners and whom it was impossible to evade. There were now the Malinovskys, the Romanovs, the Brendinskys, and the Chernomazovs, who held high Party posts. The business of spying and making arrests was no longer done haphazardly. It was carefully planned.[519]

Krupskaya, like Lenin, was sometimes incredibly naïve about Okhrana operational methodology.[519a] Long before 1911—and not because of the 1905 revolution—the Department of Police had been highly successful in penetrating revolutionary organizations and in manipulating them. Before Prague, Malinovsky had not met Lenin and had no knowledge of Koba, although ironically he was to have a great impact on the political fortunes of both in different ways and degrees. Lenin found him a wonderful bolshevik who had been converted from menshevism. Here was an authentic worker, a trade-union organizer from Moscow itself, and a personable, dynamic leader. Some months after Prague, Lenin was to write that Malinovsky was "our outstanding worker-*leader*" (Lenin's emphasis).[520] Indeed he was. His personality traits made him equally effective with both the organization trying to uphold the Tsar and the one attempting to cause the Tsar's collapse. Soviet historians have always been understandably shy of the Lenin-Malinovsky relationship.

In this regard it is interesting to note how an honest Russian journalist, Vladimir Burtsev, described his conversations with Beletsky, a Director of the Department of Police, with whom he shared a cell after being arrested by the bolsheviks at the end of 1917. Beletsky informed Burtsev that "Lenin and Malinovsky (the best Department of Police agent around Lenin) could carry out only what the Police deemed necessary for its purpose." [521] Beletsky was executed in November of 1918.

Lenin, in a domineering mood, refused to tolerate dissension at Prague. Representing hardly anyone, the fifteen delegates did little more in the twelve days of the Conference, from January 5th to 27th, than establish the original Bolshevik Central Committee: Lenin, Zinoviev, Malinovsky, Shvartzman, Goloshchekin, Ordzhonikidze, and Spandaryan.[522] There were four alternate members elected—Bubnov, Kalinin, Smirnov, and Elena Stasova. Nor was anything really accomplished in the way of theory or resolutions, except one that empowered Lenin to add members at his discretion to the Party Central Committee by the curious mechanism of "co-optation." Koba, still in Vologda, came into the Central Committee by this route—not elected but "co-opted." It was at Prague that Lenin and his bolsheviks came into their own as an "independent organization." [523]

No satisfactory explanation has been advanced for Lenin's immediate use of his co-optation right. He waited only until the end of the Prague Conference and then increased the Central Committee membership to nine, naming Koba and a St. Petersburg metalworker, Belostotsky, who had caught his fancy during a visit to Lenin's Longjumeau school outside Paris.[524] Koba was a strange choice for, unlike Belostotsky, he was in exile where he would presumably remain some time. Perhaps Lenin felt he needed one more Caucasian eventually to do battle for him in menshevik Georgia, although Ordzhonikidze and Spandaryan were already Central Committee members. The haunting thought that Malinovsky might have persuaded Lenin into co-opting Stalin must not be discarded out of hand. As a matter of fact, David Shub, a member of the Russian Social-Democratic Party from 1903, flatly asserted in 1948 that Lenin had placed Stalin in the first Bolshevik Central Committee on Malinovsky's suggestion.[525] This interpretation has always been questionable if for no other reason than that Lenin held the power of co-optation in his own hands, where his personally chosen conferees at Prague had deposited it. Other sources have suggested that Ordzhonikidze had persuaded Lenin to co-opt for Stalin after Prague. There is no evidence to support this theory and we are, at any rate, forced to accept the fact that Lenin was the only person empowered by the Prague Conference to co-opt, and that in all probability he chose Stalin after having discussed it with Malinovsky, the most important bolshevik in Russia at that time. If this assumption is valid, Malinovsky would have gone along with Lenin's selection. Although the Okhrana would never have revealed one principal agent to another, the desired end would be achieved because the natural course of events might have propelled Stalin, with Malinovsky's approval, into the Central Committee. Perhaps Ordzhonikidze mentioned the name of the "wonderful [*chudesnyi*] Georgian," as Lenin later called him; or perhaps Lenin was attracted by Koba's idea of a Russian bolshevik center. It is most likely, of course, that Lenin was repaying Koba for his audacious though unsuccessful attempt to replenish the party coffers by the Tiflis 1907 expropriation. Moreover, the plain fact of the matter was that

Lenin was also impressed with "doers." He and Koba, in this regard and at this time, were of one mind.

Twenty-five years after the 1912 Prague Conference Stalin wrote that it "had the greatest significance in the history of our party." [526] More than that, he might have said that it had been the most significant event in his life, the beginning of his formal political career. He lied in later years when he claimed that he had been "elected a member of the Central Committee of the Bolshevik Party" at the Prague Conference. The record clearly shows that Lenin co-opted for him at Prague. He was never elected by *free* voters, in public or party, to any office on any occasion. Stalin's *Collected Works* states that the Prague Conference set up the Russian Bureau of the Central Committee to direct revolutionary activities in Russia and that he was placed in charge of the center.[527] This is false if for no other reason than Koba's residence in exile. How could he direct revolutionary activities from his Siberian residence in Vologda? Nonetheless on February 24, 1912, Ordzhonikidze wrote Lenin that he had personally got in touch with Koba in his Vologda exile and informed him that he was a member of the Central Committee.[528] Why Ordzhonikidze made a miserable journey of almost four hundred miles north of St. Petersburg in the dead of a severe winter to give Koba this information has never been clarified. Ordzhonikidze reported to Lenin, "I have seen Ivanovich and have a definite understanding with him. He is most pleased with the turn of events and is splendidly impressed." [529] Dzhugashvili, now an important party personage, accordingly escaped from Vologda on February 29, 1912, after he learned of his good fortune.[530] Lenin's fateful rediscovery of Dzhugashvili would have an unforeseen impact on both their lives, on the bolshevik faction, on Russia, and on mankind.

Koba hurried back to St. Petersburg to begin work as a Central Committee member, and Malinovsky returned from Prague with the information that Lenin wanted Malinovsky to be a candidate for the forthcoming Duma elections.[531] The Department of Police could not have been more delighted. It took immediate steps to assure Malinovsky's election.[532] Meantime, Koba, who was to be at liberty for less than two months before his next arrest, made his way to the Caucasus, according to the official chronology.[533] During the first part of March, he was in Tiflis and Baku organizing the work of "the Transcaucasian Bolsheviks in carrying out the decisions of the Prague Conference." Before he departed for St. Petersburg, he supposedly wrote a leaflet of five pages ("For the Party!") that was "widely distributed in Russia." There is no precise date or place of publication of this leaflet and we are forced to conclude he invented it after his rise to power. He would have us believe that while moving about in the Caucasus, where he had been forbidden to reside, he also wrote during the first half of March "Circular Letter No. 1 of the Central Committee" to the party organizations, announcing the formation of the Central Committee; that on March 29th he conducted a conference of bolshevik districts in Baku which endorsed the Prague decisions; and that on March 30th he wrote a report on the conference in Baku for the newspaper *Sotsial-Democrat*. The absence of the two last-mentioned pieces from his *Collected Works* would seem to be sufficient evidence that they never appeared in print.[534]

According to the official chronology, he departed from Baku for St. Petersburg on April 1, 1912. Because he needed a minimum of twelve days for travel, if (as they usually did) all railway schedules meshed, if the police did not delay him, and if he did not tarry en route, eighteen days was the maximum he could have spent in Tiflis and Baku organizing unknown workers, explaining Prague Conference resolutions and writing unrecorded leaflets and articles. Vologda was twenty-nine hundred miles from Baku. Did Koba really return to the Caucasus—forbidden to him by an official edict—after his escape from Vologda, back into the hands of the Baku and Tiflis police who knew him by sight? Why would he chance apprehension at the Okhrana railway checkpoints staffed by many of the same gendarmes he had encountered so many times before? As a member of the Bolshevik Central Committee, why would he risk imprisonment and exile? There is no doubt, however, that Koba had returned to Baku after his "escape" from Vologda, for we have independent testimony from Boris Ivanovich Nicolaevsky confirming this episode.

Nicolaevsky, born in 1887, the son of a Russian Orthodox priest in Ufa province had been involved in social democratic activities from 1904. Except for the first year, he was a menshevik from the beginning to the end of his career. By 1917 the Okhrana had arrested him eight times and exiled him thrice to Siberia or Northern European Russia. After the revolution he served as a director of the History Department of the Archives of the Revolution in Moscow. He spent a year in prison during bolshevik rule in 1921. Then he was exiled, went to Germany, and eventually made his way in 1942 to the United States where he died in 1966.[534a] Nicolaevsky's revolutionary career was not unusual but his unexcelled contribution to the history of the Russian revolution stemmed from his compulsiveness as an archivist, an exceptional memory, and a keen analytical mind. In the autumn of 1910 the Okhrana had arrested Nicolaevsky in Samara and exiled him for three years to the White Sea area of northern European Russia. In early 1911 he escaped to the city of Archangelsk, travelled by train through St. Petersburg, Moscow, the Ukraine and on to Baku where he found employment with a local newspaper. He had learned erroneously, as it turned out, that police control in Baku was weak, for which reason he had proceeded there. Soon he became a member of the Baku social democratic committee which, before his arrival, had apparently been controlled by the bolsheviks although they were in the minority. Nicolaevsky's arrival in Baku marked his first visit to the Caucasus and he recalled many years later that initially he had not been bothered by the local Okhrana.

Upon Nicolaevsky's arrival Avel Safronovich Enukidze and he had a long conversation in a Baku café. Enukidze had joined the revolutionary movement in the Caucasus in the 1890's, became the secretary of the all-Russian Central Executive Committee of the Soviets after 1917, was later made a member of the central committee of the Party, and finally was condemned as an "enemy of the people" and was liquidated in Stalin's purges in the 1930's. Enukidze, an honorable man, tried to steer young Nicolaevsky along the proper path. He talked with him as father to son, explaining to Nicolaevsky, in the Caucasus for the first time, that people from the Caucasus were different from "you Russians." He said they would do anything for friends, but "we don't fool around with enemies. We are a very vengeful people!" Enukidze then asked, "Do you know Koba?" Nicolaevsky at this time had never heard of him. "Well," Enukidze warned, "don't forget that name, and be very wary of him."

After the bolshevik conference held in Prague during January 1912 the social democrats in Baku held a conference of their own which was apparently attended by about twenty-five delegates, most of whom were bolsheviks—according to Mgeladze, a reporter of this period.[535] Little is known about this conference except that it did take place and followed the arrest of a number of Baku bolsheviks in late 1911. At the Baku conference the social democratic committee discovered that one of the "old" bolsheviks, who had not been arrested in the autumn of 1911, had a two-year-old party seal on his party credentials. However, because the Okhrana had found out about this particular party seal, the social democrats had changed its circular shape to an oval. Thus the "old" bolshevik delegate who arrived with the outmoded seal could be an Okhrana agent; the matter had to be investigated.

Meanwhile Stalin, impressively titled as a member of the newly formed bolshevik central committee, arrived in Baku. The social democrats had empowered Nicolaevsky to talk with him about the "old" bolshevik delegate, in spite of the fact that the Baku party organization was united in its determination not to have any dealings with Stalin. Nicolaevsky, a sort of neutral referee, was only to ask Stalin for an explanation of the seal. Nicolaevsky and Koba met twice in Baku at the home of Sosnovsky, a journalist and future editor of *Pravda* who perished in the Stalinist purges of 1937. At the first meeting Koba arrived early and sat in the shade so his face would be invisible to Nicolaevsky.

Just prior to this meeting, the Baku mensheviks had received a disturbing letter from a former member who had been carrying out

Stalin's orders. The writer said he had refused to execute one order of Stalin's, although we can only speculate what it involved. He also accused Stalin of wanting to get money from the oil-well owners under false pretenses; for this reason, he said, Stalin wanted to kill him. In fact, the writer revealed that he had almost been murdered by other members of Stalin's group who had left him seriously wounded, thinking he was dead, at a cemetery where peasants had "rescued him." The writer not only accused Stalin of wanting to kill him, but also of working for the Okhrana. The reason behind his letter was that the writer wanted to be "rehabilitated" in the party. Thus Nicolaevsky discloses two warnings about Koba's possible Okhrana connections that he had received before their first meeting.

When they met, Stalin began to explain the significance of Prague and the "Bolshevik party organization." Nicolaevsky told Stalin he was interested only in the Baku bolshevik representative who had attended the local conference with the false seal. Koba replied that he had been in exile when this particular conference took place and it would be necessary to investigate the matter. He was vague. Nicolaevsky then made it clearly evident that he suspected Koba of collusion with the Okhrana. He admitted that this was surely imprudent, incurring Stalin's hostility at this early date.

At a second meeting Koba told Nicolaevsky a complicated story about two unions of oil workers, "one of which had issued the 'seal', *etc* . . ." But Nicolaevsky persisted and told Stalin to his face that he knew all about the changed seal and that the Okhrana had been involved in the operation. Koba remained vague, promising to investigate the matter, but stating that he did not want to meet a third time.

According to Nicolaevsky, it was discovered after the revolution that Stalin had empowered an *agent provocateur,* a certain Sipan, the head of a trade union and a friend of Stalin, to issue the false seal. Sipan wanted his own man at the Baku conference of social democrats. After Nicolaevsky's second meeting with Koba, he noticed that the Okhrana was shadowing him; a month later, Nicolaevsky was arrested. Nicolaevsky thought that Stalin had probably revealed their first meeting to Sipan, the Okhrana agent, who had then betrayed him.[535a] What Nicolaevsky strangely failed to realize was the nature of the Stalin-Sipan relationship. The Okhrana had probably replaced Stalin with Sipan, when Stalin had been arrested and exiled. Sipan had been then left in charge of certain Baku bolshevik activities in Stalin's absence. Thus Stalin's protestations that he knew nothing of the "round" seal were essentially correct. But the implications went much deeper. Stalin's evasive action *vis à vis* Nicolaevsky's obvious suspicion, revealed that Stalin did not want to pursue the simple matter of the "seal," for to do so would open a Pandora's box of Okhrana operations. Therefore, Stalin understandably decided not to meet with Nicolaevsky the third time.

Nicolaevsky next saw Koba in Vologda, in a special jail for transient exiles, as he was proceeding from Baku to the White Sea Coast and Koba, who had been arrested in July of 1912, was en route to Siberia. Nicolaevsky recalled that they were then comrades in arms and chatted, even though they were not overly friendly. When Koba noticed that Nicolaevsky had a kettle, he remarked that unfortuntely he lacked one and would have no tea or hot water on his trip to Siberia—because he was journeying without comrades. Koba noted also that Nicolaevsky was in a group with others who owned kettles. So Nicolaevsky gave Koba his own.[536]

However unimportant the gift of the kettle may appear, it reveals Nicolaevsky's basic goodness as it points up Koba's character. After Nicolaevsky and Koba met in Baku, the Okhrana had begun its surveillance that resulted in Nicolaevsky's arrest, and although Nicolaevsky had received two warnings that Stalin was possibly connected with the Okhrana, he did not learn his lesson. Nor did he learn it later, even in the years of Stalin's terror when he murdered Enukidze and Sosnovsky in whose home they had met. Stalin, a great poseur, was able to play two convincing roles simultaneously. Even a chief of state, President Truman, would one day describe Stalin as a "prisoner of the Politburo" while Stalin held that body and Russia in a bloody grip.[537] Stalin was an accomplished actor.

In 1924, before Stalin had become the undisputed censor of all Soviet literature about his pre-revolutionary life, a fellow Georgian bolshevik Ilya Vardin (Mgeladze) wrote that at the beginning of May, 1912, the Baku bolsheviks were practically put out of business. The Okhrana arrested Shaumyan, Enukidze, Chernomazov— Vardin parenthetically wonders, "Was he already a *provocateur?*" —and "many other outstanding Bolsheviks, workers, and intellectuals." [538] (M. E. Chernomazov, an Okhrana agent who committed suicide in 1917, was among the first official editors of *Pravda*.) Stalin, according to Vardin's account, had visited Baku but departed just before the Okhrana "purge." Rampant suspicions spread about the person who had betrayed the bolsheviks. Vardin had not been arrested and he also was suspected of being a *provocateur*. [539] Thus we discover that Koba was back in Baku and shortly after he departed an Okhrana dragnet arrested many of his comrades.

Once more unscathed, Koba left Baku on April 1st for St. Petersburg and at the beginning of April, his record states, met Ordzhonikidze in Moscow. During April, after his "secret" return to St. Petersburg, he wrote an unsigned leaflet ("Long Live the First of May!"), according to his *Collected Works,* which also says that he sent to Tiflis "a copy of the resolution adopted by a group of Moscow Party workers welcoming the decisions of the Prague Conference and the newly formed Central Committee." In addition, at the beginning of April he wrote Clara Zetkin requesting that she transfer the party funds held by her to the Central Committee for the purpose of conducting the Fourth State Duma election campaign. [540] Clara had what remained of the five-hundred-ruble notes Kamo had stolen in Tiflis, and although Krassin had attempted to alter their serial numbers they were still of doubtful negotiability. [541] But Lenin in 1912 badly needed money. Why would Zetkin respond to a letter from a Georgian whom she scarcely knew, if at all, unless Lenin approved? There is no record of the letter; Stalin's official chronology includes only a reference to it. [542]

After Koba's arrival in St. Petersburg, on April 12, 1912, he conveys the impression of feverish revolutionary work. During the ten days remaining before his next arrest, he claims that he edited the bolshevik workers' newspaper *Zvezda* (*The Star*), which published seven of his articles signed "K.S.-n," "K. Salin," "K. Solin," or simply "K.S." His articles lacked party or literary significance. He was later to claim that he made arrangements with "members of the Social-Democratic group in the Third State Duma, N. G. Poletayev and I. P. Pokrovsky, as well as with the bolshevik journalists M. S. Olminsky and N. N. Baturin," for the publication of the newspaper *Pravda* (*The Truth*) and for the drafting of its program, and together with them "made up the first number of *Pravda* on April 22, 1912." [543] He avers that his unsigned article, "Our Aims," appeared in its first issue. Stalin's role in the founding of *Pravda* was clearly negligible; he had little, if anything, to do with it. Neither by temperament nor talent was he a journalist, a writer, or an editor. Furthermore, ten days were totally insufficient for Koba to have organized a newspaper. Thus his statement on *Pravda's* tenth anniversary in 1922 contains only a small bit of truth:

> It was one evening in the middle of April, 1912, at the house of Comrade Poletayev, when two Duma members (Pokrovsky and Poletayev), two writers (Olminsky and Baturin) and I, a member of the Central Committee (being illegal I was hiding in the house of Poletayev who had parliamentary immunity), came to an agreement about the *Pravda* platform and made up its first issue. [544]

Koba undoubtedly attended the meeting under sufferance of the four bolsheviks noted in his paragraph. Poletayev was an experienced journalist and had edited *Zvezda* since 1910. Olminsky was also a veteran bolshevik, the former editor of *Vpered* (*Forward*) and *Proletary*. A brief bibliographical guide to *Pravda* published in 1962 by the Moscow Institute of Marxism-Leninism mentions Stalin only once, as one of thirty-eight members of the editorial board or active collaborators from 1912 to 1914. [545] This is sufficient to show that his role in the founding of *Pravda* was much less than he would have us believe.

As we know, the bolsheviks at this point lacked the necessary funds to start a newspaper, rent offices, hire typesetters, or buy the necessary supply of newsprint. Various theories have been advanced to explain how *Pravda* obtained the money to begin publication. The unsavory fact of the matter is that bolshevik funds in Russia were in the main controlled by Malinovsky, the Department of Police agent. He, not Koba, was Lenin's lieutenant in Russia. It was Malinovsky who registered the paper and named M. E. Chernomazov, also an Okhrana agent, as its editor. Moreover, because Malinovsky was soon to become the "treasurer" of *Pravda,* there is every reason to believe that the Department of Police had decided the bolsheviks needed their own newspaper to compete with the menshevik daily *Luch* (*The Light*). Bolsheviks and mensheviks had to be kept at sword's point. Thus the Okhrana initially financed *Pravda,* as it had previously financed *Nachalo* (*The Beginning*), the first legal marxist organ in Russia.[546]

Meanwhile, at the end of March, a letter from Lenin complained, "There is no word from Ivanovich [Koba's party pseudonym at the time]. Is he all right? Where and how is he?."[547] Koba, free and able to communicate with Lenin, had apparently not seen fit to do so in writing since he was co-opted into the Central Committee. We are confronted with one more puzzle. If Koba in exile was sufficiently bold to write Lenin in Paris, it is strange he failed to state his appreciation to Lenin on this important occasion.

The official chronology and Department of Police records confirm he was arrested in St. Petersburg on April 22, 1912, the day the first issue of *Pravda* was made up.[548] He spent eight weeks more in the dreary St. Petersburg Preliminary Detention Prison, about which nothing is known. On July 2nd he was deported under escort to Narym territory under open police surveillance for three years. Sixteen days were necessary for him to reach Tomsk, where, on July 18th, "accompanied by a prison warden he departed on the steamer *Kolpashevets* for his place of exile in Narym."[549] He travelled over three hundred miles on the Ob River before he reached his exile point in Siberia, arriving there at the earliest on July 22nd. He was more than twenty-six hundred miles from St. Petersburg.

Koba wrote nothing about this period in his life, but fortunately other exiles did. Vereshchak who, as we know, had served time with him in the Baku Bailov prison, and Jacob Sverdlov, who later became his roommate, were also in Narym. Vereshchak reports that he found Koba in good spirits and that his arrival coincided with a series of attempted escapes. Sverdlov was the first to try, but the gendarmes seized him near Tomsk. "Then Lashevich escaped and finally Stalin, almost openly through Tomsk Province." [550] Narym at that time was a settlement of some hundred and fifty homes and a little over a thousand inhabitants. Years later, in the euphoria that surrounded Stalin's fiftieth birthday, *Pravda* carried an article, "In Narym," concerning his exile there. The author reported that Koba read a great deal, as might be expected, during his six weeks in Narym; that it was difficult to escape; but that Koba managed to elude his guards on Saturday, September 1, 1912, which the local gendarme official, Titkov, reported the following day.[551] This article says nothing about his social-revolutionary friend Surin who, according to Souvarine, was a Department of Police agent.[552] Souvarine writes, "In a Shanghai paper the singer Karganov, a former Social Revolutionary, published some Siberian reminiscences in which Stalin appeared as defending a common thief, as an anti-Semite, and as a friend of the local commissar of police. For the last connection he is said to have been brought before an exiles' tribunal."

If Koba required twenty days for his journey from St. Petersburg to Narym, it is impossible to accept the statement in the *Collected Works* that he escaped on September 1st and arrived in St. Petersburg on September 12th, after only eleven days of travel unless he had some unrecorded assistance or was uncommonly lucky.[553] And, as usual, there is no indication how he obtained documents and money to run away once more. Nonetheless, he made the twenty-six-hundred-mile trip back to St. Petersburg through all the Okhrana railway checkpoints and arrived at the earliest about September 21, 1912.

Anna Allilueva remembers that Koba and Sverdlov arrived in St. Petersburg in the autumn of 1912. Koba always proceeded to the Alliluev household after his many escapes—not because of revolutionary reasons, but rather because he was already fond of Nadezhda, Anna's younger sister, whom he later married. Mama Olga Allilueva obviously saw him as a future son-in-law. She arranged a bed for him in a corner room of their apartment, although he was unable to spend much time there. He was obliged to move from place to place in order to evade the Okhrana. Often Mama went out with Koba to throw the Okhrana detectives off his trail.[554] According to Anna, he frequently talked about how he and Sverdlov had lived in exile. They had been most interested in the infrequent delivery of mail—which they considered "holidays." Koba "loved to slip away" the several kilometers to pick up their mail. Apparently Sverdlov was the housekeeper, firing the stove and cleaning up their modest room in Narym. (Later Sverdlov protested that Koba was untidy and disorganized in his personal habits.)[555]

Stalin's *Collected Works* claims that during September and October he directed the "Fourth State Duma campaign" and organized "the struggle against the Menshevik Liquidators." He would also have us believe that throughout the autumn he was in charge of bolshevik election activities in St. Petersburg and was editing and writing articles for *Pravda*.[556] But it is quite apparent that he would be unable to organize an election campaign, for his personality would have meant ruin for the candidates he supported. Nor did he edit *Pravda* during this period—although, to Lenin's dismay, he overplayed his hand, insisting he was an accomplished "editor." To be as near as possible to St. Petersburg and *Pravda*, Lenin was in Cracow. At one point he commanded Koba in no uncertain terms to publish "my article in a prominent place and in large type."[557] Clearly, Koba, interfering with Lenin's articles and his plans, was also upsetting, willingly or not, the carefully laid program of the Department of Police; their agent Malinovsky was, in turn, displeased. And not only because his police superiors were disturbed.

Koba had an unfailing trait of alienating almost everyone with whom he was associated. It had something to do with his crudity of speech, his clever grin, his "yellow" eyes (Trotsky's adjective), and his general demeanor. Malinovsky, on the other hand, was a gregarious, personable politician—and an accomplished police spy. He was the top bolshevik in the *Pravda* operation, and he was not inappropriately aware of his position. In sum, Malinovsky apparently came to detest Koba, whose tactics against Lenin were beginning to disrupt Okhrana strategy in maintaining a sharp division between mensheviks and bolsheviks. Stalin claims in his *Collected Works* that toward the end of October he paid a short visit to Moscow and established contact with the "newly elected workingmen Bolshevik deputies of the Fourth State Duma" and that he returned to St. Petersburg on October 29th.[558] If this is true, Stalin was paying a visit to Malinovsky, who was the foremost "workingman Bolshevik" deputy from Moscow. Of course, as already noted, Koba did not know that Malinovsky was working for the Department of Police, nor was Malinovsky aware of Stalin's connection. But at the time Stalin's *Collected Works* were published Malinovsky's work for the Okhrana was widely known.

The official chronology maintains that Stalin "secretly" arrived in Cracow to visit Lenin sometime "before November 10" in 1912, and that he participated in a Party Central Committee meeting during the "first half of November." [559] The Central Committee meeting was held on either November 12th or 13th, according to Lenin. Stalin remained in Cracow until the end of November, if we accept his account.[560]

It appears almost certain that Stalin attended the Central Committee meeting, having just escaped from his Narym exile. To get to Cracow, he needed a passport, which was legally unobtainable, of course, from the authorities in St. Petersburg. However, Lenin was so intent on removing Stalin from the capital that he sent special instructions to Valentina (Vera) Lobova, the wife of an Okhrana agent and the unofficial secretary of the bolshevik Duma faction, to get in touch with Alexander Shotman, nicknamed "the bolshevik Foreign Minister of Foreign Affairs" because of his ability to obtain illegal passports. He was living in Helsinki at the time. In his memoirs, published in 1935, Shotman proudly relates:

Beginning with 1911 we succeeded in repairing our foreign connections and we began receiving illegal literature on time and accurately. We were also successful in recommending the dispatch to foreign countries of comrades arriving from Russia. If the escapee [from Russia] was in a great hurry and was not frightened by a certain amount of risk, we provided him with a Finnish passport for foreign travel, conducted him to Abo by steamship, actually under weak police control, and everything went off well! If the comrade was in danger of being exiled, we would supply him with a Finnish foreign passport and send him to the north through Tornio—that is over the Gulf of Bothnia—where in Harapanda he travelled on foot across the Swedish frontier without danger. Not one of our escapees was detained.

A border crossing by this means required only three days. A foreign passport issued to a Finnish citizen for five years cost five Finmarks, or 1 ruble 85 kopeks. We obtained a great number of these passports for persons of any age or gender.

We succeeded in getting across the borders several major party workers among whom was even Iosif Vissarionovich Stalin.

During my trips to Piter [St. Petersburg] or abroad my duty as "minister of foreign affairs," as my brothers named me, was fulfilled by Ivan Rakhia, now deceased.[561]

Understandably, Shotman felt a certain amount of self-esteem because of his ability to outwit the Finnish authorities; after all, Finland was a grand duchy of Russia. Doubtless the pride he took in his work made him recall that when "Inessa Armand arrived in Helsingfors in order to cross the border illegally, I was then in Helsingfors and the crossing was arranged by I. Rakhia, who immediately made two mistakes. . . ." (Inessa Armand was Lenin's great and good lady friend. Shotman obviously recognized this.) Shotman explains that Rakhia provided her with the passport of a delegate to the Finnish parliament and then sent her by steamship to Helsinki rather than to Abo, where the authorities verified documents of those going abroad. He describes how Finnish ship captains verified passports. The captain addressed Inessa in Finnish and Swedish, of which she knew not a word. Then he spoke English, in which she was fluent. The captain realized that she was not a delegate of the Finnish parliament, but he also recognized the pretense and he did not report her to the police. "This is explained by the fact that the Finnish bourgeoisie and, yes, almost all the intelligentsia, in those years conducted an active struggle against the tsarist tyranny for the security of that autonomy which Finland had enjoyed from the reign of Alexander I," Shotman declared. His account continues:

I don't remember precisely, but it seems to me it was at the end of the summer in 1912 when Comrade Stalin arrived in Petersburg in the company of the now deceased Comrade Valentina Lobova (she died of tuberculosis in 1924).

V. Lobova came to my apartment and explained that a responsible comrade had to get across the border. It was Stalin about whom she spoke. He had to be dispatched "with maximum speed and absolute security," as she described it. She added, "This is a directive from Lenin." I explained to her that under such circumstances I could not send him off. If this was to be with "absolute security." On the contrary. They decided that I, myself, should talk with Stalin. He was staying in a hotel as a Persian citizen and had a good Persian passport in his pocket. Here I first became acquainted with Comrade Stalin, although I had heard a great deal about him, as one of the bedrock bolsheviks, who most of all detested the mensheviks, particularly the Caucasian ones.

Comrade Stalin had made his way abroad from Siberia from which he had escaped, having been sent there without a trial.

I explained to him the system of crossing the border, telling him exactly what I had told V. Lobova.

Having weighed both variants, he decided to cross by way of Abo, regardless of a certain risk.

Considering Lenin's special concern for him and the Central Committee instructions transmitted to Comrade Lobova, I arranged his trip with a maximum guarantee of security.

With the agreement of Comrade Stalin, I ordered Comrade Ivan Rakhia to make the arrangements who received from me the strictest instructions to do all possible and impossible in order that Comrade Stalin cross securely. Knowing the supreme fidelity of I. Rakhia to the revolution, I felt sure that he would do everything to make his crossing safe.

Approaching the steamship from the train there was a control booth where two policeman verified documents, and particularly passports. Comrade Stalin handed over his Finnish foreign passport, although he himself did not at all resemble a Finn. This upset me somewhat, but I quieted myself with the thought that other comrades also poorly resembling Finns, had securely travelled this route. . . . Happily, everything went off without a hitch.[562]

Apparently Stalin took a steamer from Abo to a port on the German or Polish coast, from which he proceeded to Cracow. This is curious. It is also noteworthy that Stalin, in possession of a good

Persian passport (for some reason perhaps unusable) according to Shotman, made an inexplicable trip to Helsinki for a new Finnish one. Stalin's swarthy features were most unlike a fair blue-eyed Finn—as Shotman noted. None of this appears in Stalin's autobiographical *Collected Works* nor does it merit a word in the many biographies about him. Once again it may be safely assumed that Stalin did not want it to be generally known. It would have been damaging to him and to his particularization of the history of these times.

Shotman's recollection that Stalin and Lobova came to Helsinki at the summer's end strongly suggests that he appeared in Helsinki right after he had returned to St. Petersburg from the Narym exile. The break between summer and winter is sharp in Helsinki. Usually the Finns enjoy few, if any, autumn days. Thus Stalin's first move must have been to obtain a passport for travel abroad. Winter was shortly to set in.

However, Koba told Anna Allilueva that he proceeded to Cracow "without a foreign passport." He laughingly related how he frightened two passengers in his train compartment who throughout the trip, read loudly from a "reactionary" paper. Koba finally inquired why they were reading nonsense. "There are better newspapers," he told them and the passengers left the compartment. Anna says that a Polish cobbler took him across the border, because Poles, like Georgians, were a minority group oppressed by the Russians. The Pole noticed his shoemaker's tools. "So you are a Georgian. . . . You have Gendarmes just as in Poland . . . ?" "Yes, just like Poland, but not one school of our own language." Koba wondered if he could trust him to guide him across the frontier. He tried to pay him. The Pole said, "No—we are sons of oppressed nations and should help one another. . . ."[562a] This unctuous literature is important only because it is notably false. As we have seen, Koba had obtained a passport before proceeding to Cracow and had no need of the Polish cobbler's help.[563]

In December, 1912, Koba began his last sojourn abroad until World War II, thirty years later. He was about to help produce a political tract and enjoy the sights, sounds, and smells of Vienna, and be rid of his vexing status with the Department of Police for at least two months. Within the year, Lenin had discovered a great *"leader,"* Malinovsky, and rediscovered Koba, both under measured control of the Okhrana, both politically ambitious. Lenin, who always valued conspiratorial activities, seems to have been incredibly inefficient when it came to counter-intelligence matters involving his bolsheviks. Malinovsky almost caused his political downfall; and Stalin, with his help, became a more powerful ruler of Russia than any tsar.

12 | THE CRACOW-VIENNA EPISODE

Upon his return from exile, Koba again thrust himself into the *Pravda* operation, although his *Collected Works* claims that he was directing the "activities of the Social Democratic Group in the Fourth State Duma." [564] Malinovsky was the undisputed leader of the bolshevik delegation. Chkheidze, who had clashed with Koba over a decade before, led the mensheviks, who numbered seven. Koba continued his bungling interference in *Pravda,* and this was emphasized by an angry letter from Lenin to St. Petersburg. Later he wrote from Cracow, "Those are not men but pitiful dishrags and they are ruining the cause." [565] Lenin usually reserved this sort of language for the mensheviks, the "liquidators," or other real or imagined political enemies. The "dishrags" here, however, were the *Pravda* staff, which included Koba. Lenin summoned "the pitiful dishrags," the Central Committee members, and the bolshevik delegates to Cracow for another meeting, which was held from December 26th to January 1, 1913. Actually Lenin had written Stalin on November 23rd concerning a meeting at Cracow when the Duma would be in recess. Koba had returned to St. Petersburg only a week or so before. His *Collected Works* maintains that during the first half of December Krupskaya, on Lenin's instructions, wrote Stalin urging him to come to Cracow for a meeting of the Central Committee and the bolshevik deputies in the Duma,[566] but as Krupskaya later recalled, "Ilich (Lenin) was worried about *Pravda,* so was Stalin. They discussed ways of putting things right." Koba, in other words, went to Cracow to answer for his anti-Leninist tactics in *Pravda*. Essentially, it had been Koba's call for unity of the social democrats that infuriated Lenin and, incidentally, the Okhrana.

As early as April, when *Pravda* had first appeared, Koba had written that the newspaper stood "for unity in the proletarian class struggle, for unity at all costs. Just as we must be uncompromising toward our enemies, so must we yield to one another." This was heady and heretical. Lenin had taken note of it and by the end of November his dissatisfaction with Koba reached a climax. In a letter dated December 1st, Lenin ordered, "Get rid of Vasiliev as soon as possible, otherwise he cannot be saved; he has already done the most important work but he is needed." [567] Vasiliev was one of Koba's party cover names. While it is apparent that Lenin considered Stalin a spoiler of the *Pravda* operation, a non-Russian was needed for an important task Lenin already envisaged on the nationality problem. Stalin could "not be saved" for this task unless his thoughts and energies were removed from *Pravda* and redirected into the other channels. At the same time, Lenin was obviously trying to soften the blow by saying that Stalin had "already done the most important work"—perhaps his suggesting the creation of a Russian bureau for the coordination of party activities within the empire.

Koba had returned to St. Petersburg from Cracow toward the end of November;[568] after the Party Central Committee meeting—and it may be surmised that Lenin made his decision to "get rid of him" after talking with the other Central Committee members of Cracow in mid-November. Throughout December Lenin communicated with the *Pravda* editorial staff and contributed several articles for the newspaper itself. On December 7th he wrote Stalin and Malinovsky protesting a declaration adopted by the social-democratic Duma faction that included a demand for cultural autonomy of the nationalities.[569] In a letter to Maxim Gorky on December 26th he told him, among other things, that the bolshevik Duma delegates and party workers had arrived in Cracow.[570]

The Special Section of the Department of Police reported that Lenin, Zinoviev, Krupskaya, Malinovsky, Petrovsky, Badaev, Mrs. Lobova, Medvedev, Troyanovsky, Mrs. Troyanovsky, and

Koba (Iosif Dzhugashvili) attended the Cracow Conference.[571] Malinovsky was the first to arrive. Krupskaya recalls that "at first I did not like his eyes, his free and easy manner, which was so obviously put on. The impression wore off the very first time we talked business with him. . . . [He] gave one the impression of being a very intelligent and influential worker." Lenin was so pleased after his talks with Malinovsky, Badaev, and Petrovsky (the latter two bolshevik Duma delegates arrived next after Malinovsky) that on January 1, 1913, he wrote Gorky, "Malinovsky, Petrovsky and Badaev send you their warm regards and best wishes. . . . Cracow headquarters have proved useful. Our moving to Cracow has proved a paying proposition (from the point of view of the cause)." He was in an ebullient mood.[572]

According to a typical entry in his official biographical record, Koba departed from St. Petersburg for Cracow "secretly" at the "end of December." [573] Only by utilizing the St. Petersburg-Warsaw-Cracow train could he expect to arrive in time for the conference if he left St. Petersburg then. The circuitous route through Finland and Germany and thence to Cracow would have made him miss the conference altogether. The "express" train normally required almost thirty hours for the trip, not counting the unavoidable delays at border points and the change of trains at Warsaw. Thus the traveller who arrived in two days considered himself lucky, and Koba needed to depart from St. Petersburg no later than December 23rd. In the dead of winter it was hardly possible to make a seven hundred-mile train trip secretly, and we may justifiably conclude that Koba was once again emphasizing his artistry at conspiracy while falsifying the record. Nonetheless, Stalin did arrive in Cracow for the formal beginning of the "February" Conference on December 26, 1912.[574] For reasons of conspiracy, the Soviet record explains, the January Cracow Conference was called the "February" Conference, a designation that failed to deceive the Okhrana. The six bolshevik Duma deputies in attendance were away from St. Petersburg during January, and not February. At any rate, the Department of Police had all of them under the strictest surveillance.[575] Frontier guard detachments checked and re-

corded their crossings and passport data. Moreover, at least two of
the conferees at Cracow were Department of Police agents. As
happened at the Tammerfors Conference, all the Cracow Conference records were inexplicably lost.[576]

However, we know that Lenin headed the "February" Conference. There is some inconclusive evidence that Aleksei I. Lobov,
an Okhrana agent from about 1910, was present and under orders
to report on Malinovsky, although, of course, neither knew of the
other's police affiliation.[577] Lobov had denounced many of his social-democratic comrades to Colonel Martynov's Okhrana in Moscow, his home town, and later was to betray secret letter drops to
the Okhrana. As we have seen, his wife, Valentina N. Lobova, had
a perhaps unusual and so far unexplained relationship with Koba.
In the autumn of 1912[578] she and Koba had travelled from St.
Petersburg to Helsinki to obtain a false passport from Shotman.
Koba, again accompanied by Valentina Lobova, used the Finnish
passport procured by Shotman for his trip to the Cracow Conference.[579] Even though Koba did not remotely resemble a Finn,
Shotman's earlier expressed fears were not realized. Upon arriving
at Cracow, Koba had crossed at least five frontiers as a Finn without any reported difficulty from the police when he arrived in Cracow with Valentina. She enjoyed the dubious distinction as Koba's
only reported female travelling companion before 1917.

Upon their arrival in Cracow, they had journeyed almost two
thousand miles together. As we shall shortly learn, Koba would
refer to her in one of his few letters written before the revolution.
The sparse evidence available suggests a love affair between the
two that began in 1912 and continued until Koba's final arrest in
1913. Characteristically Stalin never mentioned her after his rise to
power. Although Valentina was probably aware of her husband's
work for the Okhrana, she was arrested and exiled to Siberia in
September of 1913.[580] There was a tragic sequel to this episode. In
1939, when Stalin ordered Shotman liquidated, his wife wrote to
Mikhail Kalinin, then the nominal President of the Soviet Union
and, hoping to save her husband, requested an interview with Stalin. "I am certain," she said, "that Stalin will see me. He surely

remembers me from Finland, when I helped to organize his trip abroad in 1912." [581] A. V. Shotman, born in 1880, could point to a notable and varied revolutionary career. During 1890-1900 he organized and led social-democratic circles in St. Petersburg, where he became an agent of Lenin's newspaper, *Iskra*. In 1903 he attended the Second Social-Democratic Congress as a delegate from the St. Petersburg organization. In 1905, as a member of the Helsinki social-democratic committee, he had been a liaison officer between the St. Petersburg organization and the Party Central Committee abroad. In 1917, when Lenin was in hiding, Shotman had the very responsible position of establishing communications between him and the Central Committee. [582] He had acted, in reality, as a sort of security officer for Lenin. Stalin refused to see Mrs. Shotman or to mitigate her husband's sentence; he was executed by Stalin's firing squads. [583]

The official chronology states that Koba and Lenin proposed measures at Cracow for improving the work of the editorial board of *Pravda*. [584] Koba made no proposals, for it was not in his nature to be a journalistic innovator and he knew Lenin was thoroughly enraged with the way *Pravda* had been run. Both Koba and the Department of Police, for completely different reasons, wanted to maintain a sharp cleavage between bolsheviks and mensheviks. The Vice-Director of the Department of Police, Beletsky, was to testify later that Okhrana policy during this period was to "divide and rule" the social democrats. [585] As a matter of fact, records show that the Okhrana specifically ordered Malinovsky to deepen the split.

Koba claimed that at the beginning of January he wrote a leaflet called "To All the Working Men and Working Women of Russia!" It was unsigned. Then on January 12, 1913, while he was in Cracow or en route to Vienna, his article "The Elections in St. Petersburg (A Letter from St. Petersburg)" appeared in the *Social-Democrat* signed "K. Stalin." [586]

Dzhugashvili had finally become Stalin.

There is abundant evidence that he had long been thinking about his pseudonym, which revolutionaries selected with the same care that contemporary performing artists choose stage names. Bronstein ironically became Trotsky, the name of one of his prison wardens. Rosenfeld, Trotsky's brother-in-law, became Kamenev, "man of stone." Skriabin, Stalin's ever-faithful Molotov, took his pseudonym from the Russian word for "hammer." Tsederbaum became the menshevik Martov. Soso had used various signatures for his articles: "Salin," "K. Solin," "K. S.," "K. S-n," "Koba—K.," "Koba Ivanovich," "Ko.," "K. Kato," and "K. Stefin." The letters "K" and "S" predominated as the initials he preferred. While it is quite clear that "Koba" was always his choice as a first name (those of his revolutionary acquaintances who were unafraid always used "Koba" in addressing him after he became dictator), it is equally apparent that he had been searching for the appropriate last name. He found the answer in his *real* name. In the ancient language of Georgia, still used by its mountaineers, the word *"dzhuga"* meant "iron." The suffix *"vili"* was the equivalent of "Mac" or "O' " and indicated "the son of." Thus, a literal translation of Dzhugashvili was "son of iron." It was not difficult to go from "son of iron" to the Russian word for steel, *"stal,"* and thus become the "man of steel," Stalin. Henceforth he adopted his given name and patronymic, Iosif (Joseph) Vissarionovich (Son of Vissarion), but he never again used Dzhugashvili as his surname.

The *Social-Democrat* of January 12, 1913, carried a second Stalin article, "On the Road to Nationalism (A Letter from the Caucasus)." Evidently he had been exploring the nationality problem even before his initial conversations with Lenin, who had also had it on his mind in recent weeks. The five pages of "On the Road to Nationalism" were primarily polemic and reproving those Caucasians who were in favor of "national-cultural autonomy"; it also displayed the author's essential grasp of the nationality problem and the Leninist approach toward it.[587] One wonders if Lenin had edited or rewritten it? The article was, in a sense, a prologue to "Marxism and the National Question," [588] which he investigated in January during the trip to Vienna, his last venture abroad until the 1943 Teheran Conference thirty years later.

From about January 1st to 8th Lenin edited the minutes of the Cracow Conference and conferred with the bolshevik Duma delegates concerning their various electoral districts and campaigns. On January 12th he wrote Podvoisky in St. Petersburg and complained about the absence of news concerning his (Lenin's) plans for reorganizing *Pravda,* criticized the newspaper's editorial board, and demanded that some sort of accounting be established for its finances. Then "after January 12th," as his *Collected Works* dates it, he sent to Paris an "announcement" and the resolutions of the Cracow Conference for publication in a separate brochure that appeared in the first part of February.[589]

In a deliberately vague statement, Stalin claims that he arrived in Vienna from Cracow during "the latter half of January." [590] He adds, in the same entry of his *Collected Works,* that in Vienna he arranged for the printing in Paris of the "announcement" written by Lenin concerning the Cracow Conference and of the resolutions adopted by the meeting.[591] Stalin had never been in Paris and had little more than an acquaintance with the names of party members there; it is probably with "conspiracy for the sake of conspiracy" in mind that Lenin ordered Stalin to mail the materials from Vienna. Thus posting the manuscript was embellished by Stalin into arranging for its publication. By inserting this fabrication in his *Collected Works* Stalin was obviously attempting to display how important he was to Lenin.

Lenin dispatched Stalin to Vienna because he wanted him away from St. Petersburg while Jacob Sverdlov, his personal emissary, straightened out the *Pravda* mess.[592] A second reason for Stalin's trip to Vienna centered, as already mentioned, on the question of nationalities, the two hundred ethnic groups within the Russian Empire. What role they were to have in a revolutionary government after the downfall of the tsarist government was no less important than the development of a theory the bolsheviks could use, among other things, for propaganda aimed at the national minorities.[592a] There are indications, too, that political warfare experts in the Austro-Hungarian intelligence service had suggested that an approach to the nationalities might serve to further weaken Russian internal security—also one of Lenin's goals.[593] While Lenin became an unwitting ally of the Okhrana in removing Stalin from St.

Petersburg, he unknowingly had another intelligence service on his side when he sent Stalin to Vienna for work on the nationalities question.

The entire structure of Lenin's bolshevik party was threatening to collapse because of a failure to solve the nationality problem. Essentially the matter revolved dangerously around the question: was Lenin to have a single bolshevik party embracing the many nationalities in the empire? If so, how were the national groups, such as the Polish social democrats and the Jewish social democratic Bund, to remain as allies in the revolutionary struggle? If Poles, Jews, Georgians and others decided for national autonomy, what would this do to Lenin's bolshevik organization? Lenin could visualize, in other words, a situation in which the nationalities' group deserted him because no viable theory had been developed by his faction to keep them united.[593a] Desperately needing such a theory, he chose Stalin, the Georgian and non-Russian, as a logical choice to work out and lend his name to a theoretical solution that might at least serve temporarily.

Lenin had undoubtedly outlined the article he hoped Stalin would produce after his research in Vienna. He also advised him to get in touch with the Austrian social democrats Bauer, Springer, or Renner, who were supposedly experts on the problem that had long bedevilled the polygot Austro-Hungarian Empire.[594] Krupskaya writes that Lenin and Stalin had long talks at Cracow on the nationalities question. "[Lenin] was glad to have met a man who was seriously interested in that question and well informed on it." She continues, about Stalin's return to Cracow after his sojourn in Vienna:

> Previously Stalin had spent two months in Vienna, where he had studied the national question. He had become closely acquainted with other comrades there, notably Bukharin and the Troyanovskys.[595]

Krupskaya erred in writing Stalin had been two months in Vienna. We will learn that he had spent only two or three weeks in that city. In a letter to Malinovsky about this period Stalin would deprecate his work on the nationality question which he would call "rubbish."

However, Lenin must have recognized that Stalin's most important qualification for the chore was his birth in Georgia, one of the smaller nations in the Russian Empire. Stalin did not possess the erudition, the research skill, or the knowledge of German that would enable him to perform meaningful work on the complicated subject. Perhaps either Bauer, Springer or Renner had some knowledge of a Slavic language.[595a] Although Stalin claims to have written one, possibly two, previous short pieces that dealt in part with the problem of nationalities in the Russian Empire, it is difficult to be sure the articles were from his pen. One was apparently a manuscript suspiciously included in Stalin's *Collected Works*.[596] Nevertheless in Lenin's view it was essential to have Stalin out of St. Petersburg.

Fortunately, Alexander Antonovich Troyanovsky (later to be Stalin's first Ambassador to Washington) and Nikolai Bukharin were living in Vienna at that time. It was apparently to Troyanovsky, whom Trotsky unfairly labelled "insignificant and unstable," [597] and his wife, Elena Rozmirovich, that Stalin turned for assistance in his project on the nationalities question. When he arrived in Vienna, he moved into the Troyanovsky residence at Schönbrunner Schlosstrasse No. 30, 7. The house still stands. In 1949, during the Allied quadripartite occupation of the city, a marble plaque with a bronze insert of Stalin's profile was placed on the façade of the building, apparently upon the initiation of Soviet authorities. There it remains, with a German inscription: "J. V. Stalin resided in this house during January, 1913. He wrote his important work *Marxism and the National Question* here." [598] And that represents the total available information about his stay with the Troyanovskys. It may be safely assumed, however, that Lenin had requested the Troyanovskys to provide lodging for Stalin. Heretofore our only knowledge of this sojourn in Vienna was Trotsky's recollection of his first, brief encounter there and his remark about Stalin's "evil yellow eyes." Trotsky was disinclined to help Koba, not because they were enemies at the time but because he took a dim view of any follower of Lenin, whom he had described shortly before as "the master squabbler, the professional exploiter of the backwardness of the Russian workers' movement." Leninism, he had written, flourished only on the "dung heap of sectionalism." On his part Stalin never mentioned his first meeting with Trotsky. Almost deliberately, it would seem, Soviet accounts of Stalin's life have de-emphasized the Vienna episode.

Stalin had been in Vienna less than a week when he wrote a letter to Malinovsky in St. Petersburg that, as far as may be determined, is published for the first time here. Its implications are as fascinating as its text is meaningful. He addressed the letter, dated January 20, 1913 (it actually carried the Western calendar date of February 2nd), to Roman Vatslavovich Malinovsky, Peski, Mytinskaya 25, Apt. 10, St. Petersburg. Stalin's ungrammatical Russian style is easily recognizable:

> Greetings, friend. I am still sitting in Vienna and . . . I am writing all sorts of rubbish. We shall see each other. Please answer the following questions:
> 1. How are things with "Pravda." 2. How are things with you in the faction. 3. How is the group. 4. How are A., Sh. and Bi. . . . 5. How is Aleksei.
> Ilich doesn't know anything about all of this and he worries. If you have no time, let B. write without delay. Tell Vetrov not to publish the "Nation. question" but to send it here. Address: Vienna, Schönbrunner Schlosstrasse, No. 30, G. Troyanovsky. If possible send the article this very day. The letter from B-na to Vienna received. Galina sends regards to her and you. Galina says that she gave Ilich the letter you left behind with her for delivery, but Ilich evidently forgot to give it back. I will shortly be with Ilich and I will try to take it from him and send it to you. Greetings to Stefania and the kids.
> Yours
> Vas . . .[599]

Quite predictably the Special Section of the Department of Police in St. Petersburg intercepted Stalin's letter three days later. And two weeks afterward a typed copy reached the Foreign Agency of the Department of Police in the Russian Embassy in Paris, with a cover letter classified "top secret." As so often happens with official papers of the *ancien régime,* the document ends with the signature of an officer of the Special Section that is illegible; it begins with a "K" and trails off into artistic flourishes. Nonetheless it is an official letter, No. 94182 of January 25, 1913. In footnotes, the Special Section identified "Ilich" as Lenin, (Ulyanov), and "Vetrov" as the cover name of Savelev, a collaborator on *Pravda.* Surprisingly nothing was said about the other persons Stalin mentioned in the letter, nor did the Okhrana indicate that "Vas . . ." meant "Vasilii," Stalin's well-known party cover name at the time, or that he was the author. It was unnecessary to identify Malinovsky, who at the time was the foremost Okhrana agent and also a bolshevik delegate in the Fourth Duma.

Stalin addressed Malinovsky throughout in the familiar *"ty,"* which a Russian reserves for those with whom he is close or friendly. The chuminess of his remarks raises anew the possibility that because of a friendship between them the Okhrana agent Malinovsky suggested to Lenin at the Prague Conference in 1912 that Stalin should be co-opted into the first Bolshevik Central Committee. For this letter is conclusive evidence that Stalin considered Malinovsky at least an amicable acquaintance if not a real friend, although in all probability Malinovsky came to dislike the abrasiveness of Stalin like everyone else.

The fact that Stalin posted the letter to Malinovsky is astonishing. On at least two previous occasions his letters had placed fellow bolsheviks in extreme jeopardy. By this time, as we know, Stalin's sense of conspiracy was highly refined, and he knew full well that a letter—particularly to a Duma delegate and from abroad—would be intercepted, opened, and read with careful attention by the Okhrana. Evidently this did not bother him. Substituting an initial or first and last letter for the names of those persons he mentioned in his letter was a transparent disguise for their identities and did not fool the Okhrana. When he asked "How are A., Sh. and Bi . . . ," the Okhrana knew that "A" was the cover name for Andrei, or Jacob Sverdlov, then an important personage in the *Pravda* operation, and that "Sh." was the bolshevik Duma deputy Shagov. "B.," "Bi . . . ," and "B-na" referred to Vera Lobova, who had accompanied Stalin from St. Petersburg to Helsinki and Cracow. When Stalin, in the same letter, asked "How is Aleksei," he was inquiring about her husband, Lobov, another Okhrana agent. "Stefania and the kids" to whom Stalin sent his regards were Mrs. Malinovsky and their two children. The Okhrana knew that "Galina," who sent her regards to Vera Lobova (B-na) and to Malinovsky, was the party cover name of Elena Rozmirovich, Troyanovsky's wife.[600]

Were the greetings of Elena ill timed? Within a few weeks someone would denounce her to the Okhrana and she would be imprisoned when she returned to Kiev. The Okhrana found secret documents on her person. For some unexplained reason Troyanovsky and Bukharin, according to one version, had concluded that Malinovsky was responsible for her arrest. From Vienna or Cracow her husband posted a registered letter to Elena's father in Kiev. Troyanovsky knew, as did any intelligent revolutionary, that the Okhrana would intercept and read his letter. He wrote that a man playing a double role had caused his wife's incarceration and he threatened a scandal of earth-shaking political dimensions if she was not released. The Vice-Director of the Department of Police, S. P. Beletsky, who was personally in charge of Malinovsky from the Okhrana side at this time, was perturbed. He realized that from an operational point of view Malinovsky had to be apprised of the situation. Later on (before he was shot by the bolsheviks), Beletsky testified that Malinovsky was frantic, almost hysterical, after reading Troyanovsky's letter. The Okhrana, upset by the justifiable nervousness of its principal bolshevik spy, released Elena Rozmirovich a month later.[601] Alexander Troyanovsky had apparently proved himself a good detective. Or had he?

That Mrs. Troyanovsky—"Galina" in the Stalin letter—tendered her regards to Malinovsky's wife and two children suggests a mutually friendly relationship between the two families. As if this were not sufficiently puzzling, one wonders why the Okhrana would risk the exposure of its foremost bolshevik agent, Malinovsky, to apprehend the relatively unimportant Elena Troyanovsky; such an act would have been contrary to Okhrana operational procedure.

An analysis of this affair requires that we become acquainted with the Troyanovskys.

Troyanovsky, who was born in Tula in 1882, was a somewhat unique bolshevik. He came from a military family and it was only natural that he entered the Voronezh Cadet Corps School. After graduation he completed the course at the Mikhailovsky Artillery School; posted to an artillery unit, he participated as an officer in the Russo-Japanese War, where revolutionary germs first infected him. He later recalled to friends during his tour as Soviet Ambassador in Washington (he had previously been the Soviet envoy to Japan) that he had been appalled at the poorly developed Russian artillery tactics in 1905. Evidence suggests that his family was financially well off and that he had inherited money. As an officer in the Kiev military garrison during 1907, he had joined mutinous troops. After temporarily avoiding arrest, he was tried and exiled to Siberia in 1908. Two years later he escaped from Siberia to Paris, where he apparently became affiliated with the bolsheviks.[602] He was above average in height, and his face, speech and manners suggested he might have had aristocratic antecedents. He spoke fluent German and English and played an expert hand of bridge. Although he survived Stalin's purges, his importance waned and in 1941 he was a minor employee of a Kuibyshev newspaper. During World War II he was seen in Moscow in tattered clothing and apparently suffering from Parkinson's disease.[603] On June 24, 1955, *Pravda* carried an obituary noting Troyanovsky's death the day before, after a "prolonged illness," and remarked that his last position had been as a teacher in the Higher Diplomatic Academy.[604] He had outlived Stalin by more than two years.

In 1913, however, Troyanovsky was a robust man of thirty-one in the prime of life, married to Elena Fedorova Rozmirovich, whom he would later divorce. Okhrana intercepts of their correspondence during this period strongly suggest that they were deeply in love. Elena, four years younger than her husband, combined good looks and mental alertness with devotion to Leninism. She was a lawyer. Born into the nobility, she had joined the Social-Democratic Party when she was nineteen, and Soviet records indicate she became a bolshevik in 1906. From 1904 to 1907 she had worked tirelessly and with great intensity as a propagandist of the Kiev social-democratic organization. She had been arrested in 1907 for the first time. A native of Kiev, she met and married her husband during the disorders of that year. A second arrest, in 1909, brought a one-year prison sentence followed by three years of exile in Narym, where Stalin was later in Siberian residence. Her sentence was commuted to exile outside Russia's borders from 1910 to 1912, when she and her husband maintained a residence in Vienna or Paris.[605]

During November and part of December, 1912, Elena was in St. Petersburg while her husband was in Cracow. Their letters at this time combine political matters and "love and many kisses." Troyanovsky wrote "Elochka," his wife, in late November that he was dissatisfied with the local group of people and their lack of interest and desire to work. He could only have been describing the Central Committee members and Lenin. On November 30th he wrote her, "Tomorrow the question will be decided in the information bureau [*spravochnoe biuro*]. I am mad that here they are so secretive about it. It is so stupid. But they love it. Yesterday I sent something for you. . . ." We are not told what was being decided, but one may agree with him that the secrecy of the bolsheviks was indeed stupid. Five days later he informed her of a report she should have received and expressed concern that it might have been lost. He inquired about her estimated time of arrival, apparently for the Cracow Conference, and discussed his belief that *Pravda* should be advertised in other St. Petersburg socialist publications. All this correspondence was intercepted and read by the Okhrana.[606]

Elena had attended the Cracow Conference with her husband and returned to Vienna about mid-January. In early February she made another trip to Cracow, met with Lenin, who entrusted her with secret documents, and proceeded to St. Petersburg. In a few days she was on her way to Kiev, the capital of the Ukraine, and the residence of her family, which also had a military background. But her mission had nothing to do with relatives. Rather, she was supposed to begin implementing plans for a Bolshevik Central Committee political school in Kiev. A few days after her arrival, the Okhrana arrested her. Incriminating and highly secret documents on her person were enough to cause her imprisonment. One month later she was mysteriously released and permitted to go abroad. She sped back to Vienna and to the open arms of her beloved husband, "Shurochka" (as she had addressed him in her letters). It is, unfortunately, impossible to find information in official Soviet works about her 1913 arrest, but Badaev, Shub and Samoilov all place it in February and in Kiev.[607] From March to September, 1913, Elena was in Vienna. At a conference of the Central Committee at Poronino, near Cracow, which Lenin convened in September, she was formally nominated secretary to the bolshevik Duma delegation. Earlier an argument had broken out between the bolsheviks and the mensheviks concerning the secretary of the social-democratic delegation in the Duma. The mensheviks, in order to overseer the correspondence and generally remain knowledgeable about party operations, had appointed S. M. Zaretskaya as the party's official secretary. Although the bolsheviks demanded the appointment of their own secretary, so that they could also remain in the know, they were temporarily unsuccessful. It was at this point—at the end of 1912—that the bolsheviks hired Vera Lobova as a private, unofficial secretary. But Lenin was not to be outdone in the matter of an official secretary. It is noteworthy, however, that Chkheidze, the venerable Georgian menshevik, who had long been wary of Stalin, testified before an official commission in 1917 that Malinovsky had insisted the bolsheviks needed a secretary, either Lobova or Elena Rozmirovich.[608] On October 27, 1913, at an official meeting of the bolshevik faction in St. Petersburg, Elena was installed as the first official secretary of the delegation. When she went on the payroll of the Duma, the split between bolsheviks and mensheviks in the legislature became irrevocable. To complete her story, in April, 1914, she was rearrested and again exiled abroad after residence in Kharkov. She returned to Moscow in the summer of 1915 and shortly thereafter an unknown police spy betrayed her and she was arrested and exiled to Siberia for a term of five years.[609] Nonetheless in 1917 she turned up in Petrograd as the editor of *Soldier's Truth* (*Soldatskaya Pravda*), a publication that was a propaganda outlet for the German General Staff and supported by its funds.[610] Some time afterward she married Nikolai Vasilevich Krylenko, who has been suspected of affiliation with both the Okhrana and the German intelligence service during World War I.[610a] He was to sit in judgment at Malinovsky's 1918 trial and later to send an untold number of Russians to death as People's Commissar for Justice until his demise in 1938.

We have noted Elena's solicitous greetings to the Malinovsky family. If Malinovsky had caused her arrest in Kiev and imprisonment, it is indeed ironic that after Troyanovsky's supposedly successful efforts to free his wife, she became the secretary of the bolshevik Duma faction. This would scarcely deserve a comment if it was not for the fact that she was then in the employ of a group headed by Malinovsky. Obviously, a person betrayed to the police does not select the betrayer as her employer! Yet this seems to be precisely what Elena considered reasonable and, we may assume, in her best interests—unless there was another, heretofore unexplained purpose for her action. At any rate, if Troyanovsky did threaten an exposé of Malinovsky, it seems unbelievable that she would whimsically have forgotten the assumed or real treachery and become Malinovsky's secretary.

The scene of our narrative must now leap from Vienna in 1913 to Paris in 1934, for it was there that the story of Troyanovsky, Elena Rozmirovich, her arrest, and her release was first published. Paul Miliukov and Alexander Kerensky, the ex-Prime Minister of Russia's Provisional Government, were in those days publishing and editing a Russian language newspaper, the *Latest News*. A certain S. Sumsky, a "correspondent" of the tiny newspaper, wrote the account of Elena's arrest in Kiev, Troyanovsky's letter to her father, and her subsequent release.[611] It was he who provided the titillating information that Vice-Director Beletsky of the Department of Police had informed Malinovsky of Troyanovsky's letter threatening a scandal. Sumsky would lead us to believe that as a result Elena was released after a month in prison. Though he provides no source for the information in his article, it may be surmised that he obtained his information from someone familiar with the case. This could have been Troyanovsky himself or a person who had heard the story from a participant in the affair.[612] Paris of 1934, and particularly its Russian émigré colony, was honeycombed with Stalin's secret police agents. Stalin himself was preparing the first of his dreadful purges. The assassination of Sergei Kirov, communist boss of Leningrad and a rival of Stalin's, was less than a year in the offing.

These factors entitle us to question why the Troyanovsky-Elena Rozmirovich-Malinovsky episode was reported in the *Latest News* at this juncture. It would seem that someone considered it useful to revive a series of events that were then more than twenty years old. But for the benefit of whom? Obviously Malinovsky, who died before a bolshevik firing squad in 1918, was not being rehabilitated in 1934. Elena had little to gain by the old yarn. Only Troyanovsky or Stalin stood to profit in some way by dredging up from pre-revolutionary history a story unlikely to interest more than a handful of people. Thus it could have been one of those subtle warnings with which the bolshevik scheme of events abounds. Troyanovsky was at this time the newly appointed Stalinist Ambassador to the United States. With his ear to the political ground, he could undoubtedly hear the initial rumblings that signalled the preparations for the first of Stalin's bloody purges in Soviet Russia. Thus he might well have leaked the story to the *Latest News* knowing that it would remind Stalin of bygone days in Vienna when he had been a guest of the Troyanovskys'. It might serve to make Stalin recall that Troyanovsky had suspected *him* of alerting the Okhrana to Elena on her trip.

If Elena Rozmirovich was apprehended with "secret" documents and instructions from Lenin on her person, they undoubtedly concerned the plans for the establishment of the Bolshevik Central Committee school in Kiev.[613] However, if Malinovsky betrayed Elena in order that the Okhrana obtain the documents, it was an unnecessary act on his part; sometime in February, 1913, Lenin wrote to Gorky:

Will write to Troyanovsky and his wife about your wish to get together. This really would be nice. They are good people. We haven't yet seen them at work, but everything we know about their past speaks in their favor. They also have money. They could go all out and do a lot of good for the journal. Mrs. Troyanovsky is going to Russia soon.[614]

When the Department of Police intercepted and read this letter, it was apparent that Elena was en route to Russia. Inasmuch as she had a record of previous arrests, the Okhrana had photographs and a description of her. It was a simple matter to alert Okhrana agents at St. Petersburg, Moscow, and Kiev and to place her under surveillance. There was no need, in other words, for Malinovsky's betrayal, although this does not exclude the possibility that he suggested she be arrested. But Lenin had already been an unwitting informer. Thus Badaev's remarks are of dubious validity. He wrote, in 1925:

When the Department of Police decided to arrest Rozmirovich in February, 1913, on Malinovsky's suggestion the arrest . . . was made in Kiev in order not to cast suspicion on Malinovsky. Also on his insistence a month later when Comrade Rozmirovich's arrest and imprisonment stirred up suspicions abroad, she was released from prison.[615]

Another Okhrana agent was involved in the Elena Rozmirovich affair. For operational reasons and in order to improve his bolshevik character, the Okhrana arrested its agent, Chernomazov, who had earlier been active in Baku and now was a principal figure in *Pravda,* in early February of 1913. He was quickly released. He later claimed, however, that on the fifth day after his arrest the Okhrana had tried to recruit him—a long-time Okhrana spy! He insisted that the Okhrana tried to prove to him that it was omniscient and that, in this connection, he had been told that "Galina" (Elena Rozmirovich) was in St. Petersburg and was planning to go to Kiev.[616] It is apparent that the arrest, imprisonment and release of Elena indicate unusual police behavior; as a matter of fact, there is no discernible reason why the Department of Police should have arrested her, since Okhrana could have obtained all the information in her possession from Malinovsky.

The arrest of Elena Rozmirovich, Toryanovsky's threatening letter to her father that fell into Okhrana hands and brought about her release, and Malinovsky's implication in the affair are puzzling enough. Now another figure, Nikolai Bukharin (whom Stalin executed as "an enemy of the people" in the purges of the nineteen-thirties), enters the Vienna picture. Stalin's letter to Malinovsky mentions several people but fails to name Bukharin, although he was in Vienna at this time.[617] In writing about the events of 1912, Shub has this to say about Bukharin and Malinovsky:

At this time Bukharin fled from exile, crossed the Russian frontier, and reached Lenin in Galicia. As soon as he arrived, he warned Lenin against Malinovsky. Lenin ordered Malinovsky to report to him in Poronino in order to meet Bukharin face to face. Bukharin sat waiting in a small room in Lenin's house. Malinovsky had not been told anything. When Malinovsky entered the room and saw Bukharin, he was terrified.

"I had the impression," Bukharin later wrote, "that he thought I would pounce upon him with a knife." But when Lenin entered the room, and Malinovsky realized he was in no immediate danger, he recovered his poise, walked over to Bukharin with outstretched arms, and said: "Ah, Nikolai. How did you get here?"

Despite Bukharin's suspicions, both Lenin and Zinoviev defended Malinovsky vigorously. They explained Malinovsky's swift conversion to Bolshevism on the ground that, as a real proletarian, he saw the harm the "liquidators" were doing. The accusations against Malinovsky were malicious, they insisted. Bukharin was not convinced. In the meantime Malinovsky had become the leader of the Bolshevik organization in Russia. He was, in fact, Lenin's deputy inside Russia. He sat in the fourth Duma as the leader of the Bolshevik faction of five deputies and as vice-chairman of the combined Social Democratic delegation, headed by Nikolai Chkheidze, an old Menshevik from the Caucasus. In the previous three Dumas the Social Democratic delegation had voted and acted as a unit, and had built up wide popularity among the Russian masses. At the opening of the Fourth Duma, the Social Democratic caucus picked Malinovsky to reply to the policy address of Prime Minister Kokovtzev.[618]

In 1913 the bolsheviks were a tightly knit coterie, and they all feared treachery—the insinuation of Okhrana agents into the party's operation. This matter of provocation, so well developed by the Department of Police, was always in the background of their thoughts. There was also inevitably a great deal of gossip within their small world. Thus when Nikolai Bukharin, only twenty-five years old at this time, went to Lenin and Zinoviev to warn them against Malinovsky, there must have been a basis for his dangerous act.[619] Stalin and the Troyanovskys could not have failed to get wind of the matter; Stalin in particular would have immediately understood Malinovsky's role as an Okhrana agent.

As for the Troyanovsky "revival" of the Vienna episode in 1934, at a troubled and critical moment within Russia, one can surmise that the motive behind it was one of self-protection.

Was it not possible that Troyanovsky's talent as a sleuth in the Malinovsky case made him suspect Stalin? This is not an easy question to answer, but it stands to reason that if Troyanovsky discovered Stalin's role, he might have told him bluntly in Vienna that he also had information about *his* Okhrana affiliation. If this interpretation is correct, Troyanovsky after Stalin had become dictator might have let Stalin know that the secret was securely cached abroad and that, in the event of his own arrest or demise, there would be a public disclosure of it. Giving support to this hypothesis is the fact that Trotsky and Bukharin, both of whom had also been in Vienna with Stalin, fell victims to his plans and were executed, whereas Stalin rewarded Troyanovsky in 1933 with the important position of first Soviet Ambassador to Washington. These mysteries defy solution except within the context of Soviet power-élite intrigues.

In 1913, however, a revolutionary such as Stalin would not hazard a letter like the one to Malinovsky without serious purpose and much thought. Stalin was not one to act foolishly or on the spur of the moment. He had always been—and was always to be—the consummate schemer and intriguer. With very few exceptions his life is free of impetuosity and of frivolous acts. Thus his one and only letter from abroad to Russia that we know about during his first thirty-three years is extremely important, the more so because he excluded it from his official autobiographical *Collected Works* and failed even to mention it. Nor has any Soviet work made reference to it except in a tangential fashion. For example, one Soviet source comments merely that "while in Vienna comrade Stalin continued to lead the work in Russia and in a letter to Petersburg on January 23, 1913, he demanded detailed information about the *Pravda* situation and the Duma faction." [620]

Not only had Stalin written to an Okhrana agent, but he also had shown concern for at least one, perhaps two, others. The publication of the full text of the letter would have revealed a thinly disguised criticism of Lenin and the very damaging admission that the subject matter on which his claim to prominence in the area of party theory—namely, "Marxism and the Nationality Question"—was, as he put it, "rubbish." The two are not unrelated. After all, he was in Vienna because Lenin wanted him to write the "rubbish."

There is a further inference in the letter that Lenin, because he did not know what was happening in the *Pravda* offices, was worried. On the contrary, Lenin was relieved, because Stalin was away from St. Petersburg, where he had, in the opinion of Ilich, hurt the newspaper. Reports of the *Pravda* situation were flowing more regularly to Lenin in Cracow now that Stalin was in Vienna. One detects in Stalin's admonition that Vera Lobova "write without delay" and "answer the following questions" an attempt to impress someone, some organization, with his importance. It would be easy to conclude that he was—even at that late date in 1913, a few weeks before his final arrest—attempting to demonstrate his authority among the bolshevik high command to the Department of Police. Perhaps he remained convinced that the tsarist government would triumph over the bolsheviks and, wanting to return to his status as a police agent, he was really writing to the Okhrana. It would certainly have been within his character to arrive at such a conniving course of action, undermining Lenin and the bolsheviks while just possibly advancing his own fortunes.

Stalin's letter to Malinovsky was evidently in response to one written by Vera Lobova. Thus, "The letter from B-na to Vienna received." It would appear that Malinovsky had instructed Vera to write Stalin, and the object of the letter had been to determine what had happened to a document Malinovsky had given to Elena Rozmirovich for Lenin, who was supposedly to return it to Malinovsky. An analysis of this complicated transaction is made more difficult by Stalin's grammar and syntax. Nonetheless, Elena *had* delivered a letter to Ilich; Malinovsky *had* expressed interest in retrieving it; Ilich *had* forgotten to return it to him. If all this is not sufficiently puzzling, Stalin's bold assertion that he would be with Lenin very soon and that he would try "to take it from him and send it" to Malinovsky confronts us with another of those riddles permeating the record of Stalin's early life. It also underscores the probability that Stalin had insufficient time to develop a meaningful study in Vienna.

The letter Stalin would try to take from Lenin may have had to do with *Pravda,* or with the organization of the party school in Kiev, but the urgency conveyed by Stalin's statement that he would try to take it from Lenin and send it to Malinovsky in St. Petersburg, gives it significance. It also indicates Stalin's eagerness to please Malinovsky. In any event, something of importance to the Okhrana, to its agent Malinovsky, and/or to Stalin had gone to Lenin and it was important to get it back. It is possible that the cryptic phrase, "the letter received from B-na," was an acknowledgment by Stalin of some sort of message, wittingly or not to induce his speedy return to St. Petersburg. Nor must we deduce from the tone of Stalin's letter to Malinovsky that he had decided Malinovsky was, as Lenin had decreed, a good bolshevik rather than a dedicated Okhrana spy.[621] Stalin characteristically softened his victims with sweet words before he moved in for the kill. Even if he only suspected Malinovsky's Okhrana status, Stalin could well have reckoned he could return to St. Petersburg and report to his contact in the Department of Police that Malinovsky was not performing as a good agent, and had come under Lenin's influence. If that were so, Malinovsky was not to be considered as an Okhrana agent among the bolsheviks, but a bolshevik agent in the Okhrana.

This could not fail to interest the Department of Police. With Malinovsky thus removed from the scene, Stalin might have entertained ambitions of taking his place as the chief bolshevik in Russia. Perhaps he saw a quick and easy method to power and vistas of great authority that were mutually compatible in regard to the bolsheviks and the Okhrana.

Finally it is interesting to have Stalin's personal testimony that Savelev, mentioned in the letter as "Vetrov," was working on the nationality problem. M. A. Savelev, a well-known bolshevik involved with *Pravda,* was later one of the editors of Lenin's *Collected Works.* He had earned a doctorate in economics in 1911 at the University of Liepzig.[622] He died in 1939 at the age of fifty-five under mysterious circumstances. In the letter under discussion, Stalin seemingly ordered Malinovsky to forbid the publication in *Pravda* of an article, already in preparation, on the subject of nationalities. It was to be sent to him to Vienna, although Stalin would be in Cracow in the near future with Lenin. "If possible send the article this very day," he says. Savelev had probably been at work on the nationalities question and had a finished or semi-finished manuscript ready for publication. The letter to Malinovsky indicates that Stalin's highly touted "Marxism and the National Question" was probably not exclusively of his own doing. Thus his attempt to foist it off as his major theoretical work would appear to be a hollow claim, one that falls into his familiar pattern of deception.

There had been many occasions in the short-lived history of the bolsheviks—and there were to be many more—when ambiguity and mystery reigned. It was almost as if the future dictator-leaders of Russia wanted to benumb history completely. Often they were successful. The Vienna letter from Stalin to Malinovsky in 1913 is a paradigm of this conspiratorial murkiness. Stalin wrote in a warm vein to Malinovsky, the bolshevik chieftain in Russia, a legislator in the Fourth Duma, and the principal Okhrana spy— later, as we know, executed by a bolshevik firing squad, but for the moment an important political figure in St. Petersburg. Rumors concerning Malinovsky's Department of Police affiliation had by this time begun circulating widely. Nonetheless Stalin's letter, ignoring elementary rules of security and conspiracy, displayed solicitude for at least one other Okhrana agent. His brazenness makes one wonder if the Lobovs, the Troyanovskys, and the Malinovskys were not involved, to some degree, in an Okhrana agent network, bizarre as it might seem.

Were Stalin and Malinovsky in some sort of agreement to undercut Lenin? This is most unlikely, although Stalin's remark that he will try to take the Malinovsky letter from Lenin is puzzling. The things that are evident, however, are the familiar and working relationship between Stalin and Malinovsky and the number of their mutual friends—some of whom were Okhrana agents. Perhaps most significant is the fact that Stalin's letter has only risen to the surface today. Had it been made available to Martov in 1918, when he charged that Stalin had been read out of the party, or had Lenin known about it, or had Trotsky been able to use the Stalin-Malinovsky correspondence, the history of our times might have been quite different.

13 | SIBERIAN YEARS

Wintry weather enveloped Vienna in the early days of February, 1913, when Stalin entrained at the North Railway Station for his return to Cracow.[623] He was on his way to see Lenin with the rough draft and notes of his essay on the nationalities' question. Even if Savelev had responded to Stalin's instruction to send his work on the subject to Vienna, the amount of Stalin's research accomplished there could not have been profound; three weeks had been sufficient for only a superficial consideration of the complex problem of the peoples of ancient and disparate ethnic, religious, and cultural patterns learning to live in a Russia governed by bolsheviks. Stalin probably departed Vienna before he had completed more than an outline of the work Lenin had assigned him.[623a]

In late January or early February Lenin had written Maxim Gorky, who had queried him about the nationalities' problem, "On the question of nationalities I am in complete agreement with you that we must pay more serious attention to it. We've got a wonderful Georgian here who has settled down to write a big article for *Proveshcheniye* (*Enlightenment*), bringing together *all the* Austrian and other material. We will really put our backs into this." [624] Lenin probably conferred with the "wonderful Georgian"—Stalin —in rewriting and revising the draft of the article, or, more likely in integrating Stalin's notes with Savelev's manuscript. Although Stalin deeply desired to become known as a theoretician of the party, he wisely deferred to "the old man" and his superior craftsmanship in language.

The most important aspect of the manuscript eventually published was that it in no way conflicted with Department of Police thinking or policy. That some copies of it were confiscated by the tsarist Ministry of the Interior in the spring of 1913 proves only that censors are often stupid; hundreds of publications had been confiscated because of a single remark that an inept censor considered deprecating to tsarism.[625] The article Stalin claimed as his own, "The National Question and Social Democracy," was published in the St. Petersburg Social Democratic journal *Enlightenment,* a legal periodical, in March and May of 1913 after Stalin had been arrested for the last time.[626] It was later published as a brochure and book, *Marxism and the National Question,* in millions of copies and in scores of languages after Stalin's rise to power in Soviet Russia.[627] The statement in his official record that claims he completed it before the end of January is highly doubtful.

"The National Question and Social Democracy" was wrongly titled. The article had less to do with marxism, social democracy, or the question of nationalities than it reflected concern with the Jewish Bund and the latter's adherence to the idea of national cultural autonomy. A more accurate title would have been "The Jewish Bund And Its Incorrect Ideas About National Cultural Autonomy." This is not meant to say that marxism, social democracy, and the nationalities' problem were ignored; rather that they were plainly subordinated to Lenin's concern with Jewish demands for cultural autonomy along the lines of the theory of the Austrian Social-Democrats, Springer and Bauer,[627a] and of Stalin's preoccupation with Jews and the question of Jewish autonomy and separatism.

The Bund (the Social Democratic Jewish Workers' Union of Lithuania, Poland and Russia) had been founded in 1897. Although it participated in the First Congress of the Russian Social Democratic Workers' Party in 1898, it decided to withdraw at the following Congress when it was denied recognition as the only Jewish workers' party. At the Stockholm Congress it again joined the party but, in opposition to Lenin, supported the mensheviks. Lenin had long been plagued with the Bund because it favored national cultural autonomy which he had denounced as early as 1903.

Nonetheless, what Stalin privately called "rubbish" has been since hailed as his coming-of-age as a theoretician and as a major pre-revolutionary contribution to Marxism-Leninism. One finds it, rather, an occasionally confusing and labored essay. It runs about eighty pages in his *Collected Works*. There are unmistakable marks of an editor or a collaborator who chopped away certain portions, added other passages, and tried to correlate them with Savelev's manuscript and render Stalin's Russian prose readable.[628]

Trotsky's belief that Lenin edited the essay was confirmed by Stalin himself at a Kremlin banquet in 1948. Milovan Djilas reported:

> I had long been interested in two questions—almost privately—and I wished to ask Stalin for his opinion. One was in the field of theory: neither in Marxist literature nor anywhere else could I ever find an explanation of the difference between "people" and "nation." Since Stalin had long reputed among Communists to be an expert on the nationalities question, I sought his opinion, pointing out that he had not treated this in his book on the nationalities question, which had been published even before the First World War and since then was considered the authoritative Bolshevik view.
>
> At my question Molotov first joined in: " 'People' and 'nation' are both the same thing."
>
> But Stalin did not agree. "No, nonsense! They are different!" And he began to explain simply: " 'Nation'? You already know what it is: the product of capitalism with given characteristics. And 'people'—these are the workingmen of a given nation, that is, workingmen of the same language, culture, customs."
>
> And concerning his book *Marxism and the National Question*, he observed: "That was Ilyich's-Lenin's view. Ilyich also edited the book." [629]

On February 12th, obviously after the essay had been completed, Lenin had indeed written the editors of *Social-Democrat* in St. Petersburg praising the work and criticizing Troyanovsky because of his suggestion that the nationalities' question be opened for discussion in the pages of *Enlightenment*.[630] This strengthens the idea that Lenin had a personal interest in the essay if, indeed, he had not re-written it.

The Bundists were attracted to the conception of "non-territoritality," which meant that the Jews could maintain cultural autonomy even though they were scattered over a wide area of a given nation. In the view of the Bund, a future socialist government in Russia would extend to each nationality the right to establish a sort of independent union that would act as a national legislature in cultural affairs. Lenin could see that if this idea took root among other national groups—Poles, Ukrainians, and Georgians, for example—it might jeopardize his political position. Thus he had declared, "The idea of a separate Jewish people is reactionary in its political meaning, prevents assimilation (of the Jews by the Russians), and promotes the 'mood of the ghetto.' " [631] And later, "Only clericals or bourgeois can speak of national culture," and "Only the unity and fusion of the workers of all nations in *all* workers' organizations in the struggle against capital can lead to the solution of the nationality question." [632] It now appears clear why Lenin wanted a non-Russian signature to "The National Question and Social Democracy," and why he wanted Stalin "saved" for this job. In the article the Bund, Jews, the Jewish people, and Jewish customs and traits are mentioned more than one hundred and eighty-five times, and not one comment about the Bund or Jews is favorable. The essay begins by defining the nation, the state, and the tribe and goes on to assert that "a nation is a historically constituted, stable community of people, formed on the basis of a common language, territory, economic life, and psychological make-up manifested in a common culture." This is hardly a world-changing contribution to knowledge, although it might have been an unusual definition in 1913. The essay upholds the right of all nations to autonomy and self-determination —but only under certain conditions that, one may assume, would be determined by a future bolshevik government in Russia. But the author considers the Jews' claim of nationhood for themselves to be absurd; after all, American and Georgian Jews have no common language. How can the Bund claim the right of self-determination and a workless Sabbath? Why does Bauer, the Austrian social democrat, claim that the Jewish people constitute a nation? "Of the five or six million Russian Jews, only three or four per cent are connected with agriculture in any way," Stalin and Lenin write.

"The remaining ninety-six per cent are employed in trade, industry, in urban institutions, and in general are town dwellers; moreover, they are spread all over Russia."

This essay's attempt to cope with the problem of nationalities and minorities in a supranational state such as Russia or Austro-Hungary was unsuccessful. As Stalin and Lenin groped for some key to the problem's complexities, they tacitly realized that the frustrating and ancient nationalities puzzle of Eastern Europe—indeed, of the whole planet—had no easy solution. The essay ended on a note of bafflement—albeit a Marxist point of view—with the statement, "There is no middle course: principles triumph, they do not 'compromise.' Thus, *the principle of international solidarity of the workers* is the essential element in the solution of the national question." This was hardly realistic, for the workers of Russia in 1913 certainly had few problems in common with those of Ireland or West Virginia.

"The Nationality Question and Social Democracy" identified the existence of a vexing nationalities problem, and tried to develop an approach. It was not surprising that Stalin had been unable to find a solution to this complex question in the three weeks he had resided in Vienna. However, after he became dictator of Soviet Russia, he discovered a neat solution: he forcibly crushed any manifestation of nationalism within the soviet empire. Under Stalin's dictatorship the Jews were hideously persecuted. On the other hand, Stalin was later to reorganize the Russian empire along the lines of ideas advanced in this brochure. His preoccupation with the establishment of autonomous national regions and areas perhaps stemmed from his own origins, as well as from what he had learned in his brief study of cultural and national autonomy in Vienna and his reading elsewhere before and after. In order to make the Jews in Soviet Russia conform to the definition provided in the essay, Stalin in 1928 established a national home for Russian Jews in a dreary and remote area of Siberia on the Manchurian frontier. He called it the Jewish Autonomous Oblast, or region, but it came to be known after the name of its capital, Birobidzhan. Russian Jews disliked the cold and forlorn area and it was thoroughly unpopular. Stalin tried to put his theory into practice with the whole power of the state behind him, and it did not work.[633]

It has been claimed that "The National Question and Social Democracy" was the reason Stalin was made Commissar of Nationalities in the first Soviet government. No one may be certain of that, but the most memorable and arresting statement in the essay is a pungent contribution to bolshevik cynicism: "Paper will put up with anything written on it!" [634]

While in St. Petersburg Stalin wrote one leaflet, "The Anniversary of the Lena Massacre," and a short and unimportant article, "The Situation in the Social-Democratic Group in the Duma" published in *Pravda* after his last arrest.[635] Meanwhile the situation at the *Pravda* offices in St. Petersburg had greatly improved. During the early days of February, while Stalin was in Cracow or Vienna, Lenin joyously pointed out "the tremendous improvement in all phases of managing the newspaper, noticeable in recent days." [636] To Sverdlov he wrote on February 8th, "Today we learned about the *Pravda* reforms. . . . A thousand congratulations, greetings and best wishes for success. . . . You cannot imagine how weary we are of working with a completely hostile editorial staff." [637] Sverdlov, then the real editor of *Pravda,* was living in illegal status, seldom emerging from the apartment of a Duma deputy supposedly immune to arrest, and busying himself all day with newspaper copy. Nonetheless he was arrested two days later, on February 10th, in the apartment of bolshevik Duma delegate G. I. Petrovsky by one account and in the apartment of Badaev by another.[638] Later he found himself again in exile with Stalin.

Stalin twisted the historical record once again by declaring in his official chronology that he returned to St. Petersburg in the "middle of February" and, with Sverdlov, proceeded to reorganize the editorial board of *Pravda* in conformity with Lenin's instructions.[639] In the first place, Sverdlov had been arrested several days before Stalin arrived in St. Petersburg; thus he was unable to do anything with Sverdlov. Sverdlov's widow, who should know, emphasized that "Stalin was not in Petersburg at that time, although until recently many works would have us believe that Sverdlov worked with Stalin. . . ." As a matter of fact, she maintains, "Stalin departed abroad before the arrival of Iakov (Jacob) Mikhailovich" and returned after his arrest.[640] Secondly, Lenin's instructions concerning *Pravda,* which paralleled Okhrana-Malinovsky strategy, were intended at least to circumvent and at best to eliminate Stalin's influence in the newspaper.

Stalin's new-found status as a budding theoretician immediately touched the already raw nerves of Malinovsky, who was cursed with an abundance of political problems and burdened with a conflict of conscience involving his dual role as a police agent and a bolshevik deputy in the Duma. At this juncture Stalin had to decide either for the bolsheviks or the Okhrana. Malinovsky, tortured by his double-agent status, had not yet made up his mind where his loyalty or future lay, but he and the Okhrana were certain that Stalin had to be removed, once and for all, from the St. Petersburg scene. Not only was he throwing his weight around in the offices of *Pravda,* but he had also become a kind of self-appointed emissary of Lenin's. In short, he was a troublemaker, quietly but definitely interfering with Okhrana plans.[640a]

Stalin on his part had no political stake in charging back to St. Petersburg into the clutches of the Okhrana, providing he was a valid and sound revolutionary. Logic thus suggests he had a mission to accomplish outside bolshevik objectives or Lenin's desires or orders. After all, Stalin had warmly written Malinovsky from Vienna as a friend, and it was to Malinovsky that Stalin was to turn in St. Petersburg. Somehow one wonders if Stalin's overly quick return to St. Petersburg perhaps had to do with his desire to settle both his Okhrana and party roles. Did he see a chance to advance his positions both in the Okhrana and the bolshevik faction, perhaps to take the place of Malinovsky?

After his return to St. Petersburg Stalin, nonetheless, hid in the apartments of bolshevik Duma delegates.[641] He visited the *Pravda* offices but generally maintained a cautious and secure posture befitting his status as a Party Central Committee member. He failed to visit the Alliluevs. He was understandably eager to begin open and active party work in St. Petersburg. When the *Pravda* management legally obtained police permission to organize a fund-raising musical evening in the hall of the Kalashnikov Grain Futures Exchange, it seemed an opportune occasion to renew party acquaintances and review the political situation as it had developed during the time he had spent abroad. "In the noisy crowd," one writer explained, "the comrades could discuss party matters." [642] However, his recent experiences with the Okhrana made him wary and he turned for advice to Malinovsky. Assured by Malinovsky that he would be safe, Stalin blundered into a trap carefully laid by the Okhrana, whose officials had decided his personal incursions into well-developed plans could no longer be tolerated. But there was more to it than that: Stalin must have been convinced that Malinovsky would not betray him to the Okhrana. His reasoning would have logically centered on his judgement that Malinovsky would not risk betraying Stalin, if Malinovsky personally gave him the appropriate reassurances. However, Stalin's interpretation of Malinovsky's attitudes and actions at Cracow and his letter from Vienna seem to have alarmed the intelligence officers in the Department of Police. They decided to act.

Badaev (who was not present) relates that a few days after Sverdlov's arrest, the bolshevik musicale to raise income for *Pravda* was held in St. Petersburg. Stalin and Malinovsky were present. Badaev continues:

> Before Stalin had time to warm his feet he found himself surrounded by police agents. The organizers of the concert took him into a dressing room to change his clothes and furnish him with a disguise, but agents of the secret police broke into the dressing room. One of them seized Stalin with the shout, "Dzhugashvili, we've finally got you!"
> "I'm not Dzhugashvili," said Stalin. "My name is Ivanov."
> "Tell these stories to your grandmother," the police operative told him. He was taken away to prison and again exiled to Siberia, where he remained until the revolution." [643]

One of the few actual witnesses who wrote about this last arrest was Shotman, whom, as we know, Stalin liquidated in the purges of the nineteen-thirties. Shotman's differing description of the arrest is obviously not contrived. He proudly recalled that earlier he had been designated the Helsinki foreign correspondent of *Pravda* and on a trip to St. Petersburg paid a visit at the *Pravda* editorial offices where he was received by V. M. Molotov. He related:

During April 1913 *Pravda* celebrated its anniversary jubilee.[644] To that end there was arranged a concert, on the premises of the Kalashinkov stock exchange. As a correspondent I was invited to the well-attended affair. All the bolshevik deputies of the State Duma, among them Malinovsky—the *agent provocateur*—were present.

Comrade Stalin, who had come in from abroad to Petersburg and led *Pravda* and the Bolshevik Duma faction, arrived when the evening was in full swing. As it later became known, Comrade Stalin . . . fully realized that there would be informers present who would recognize him. But Malinovsky guaranteed him complete security, describing the arrangements of the room and its extra exits through which one could depart with a minimum of risk. They arrested Comrade Stalin, if I am not mistaken, fairly close to an hour after his arrival. Comrade Stalin, who was talking with someone, sat at a table with his back to the hall. Grigory Ivanovich Petrovsky and I were standing not far away from him, say five or six steps. We did not immediately notice that a gendarme, approaching Stalin from the rear, had leaned forward to say something quietly to him.

The officer was without the usual rattles and jangles, and even his epaulets were not apparent. Comrade Stalin, not seeing the gendarme, but hearing his words, sharply turned around, and angrily uttered something we could not make out.

Then he peacefully went attended by the gendarme officer, surrounded by a host of informers. Malinovsky proceeded after Comrade Stalin "protesting" his arrest and giving the impression that he would take all measures to free him.

Now it is known that Comrade Stalin's arrest was organized and carried out by Malinovsky.

When they took Comrade Stalin away, Eino Rakhia whom I had taken to the evening celebration and I noted we were under surveillance. Thanks to our small cleverness we succeeded in getting away unnoticed.[645]

Shotman's account, while ommiting a few bizarre details, was essentially correct. Stalin's angry remark and his peaceful departure suggest he was surprised. Stalin's pre-revolutionary career ended with his seventh arrest on February 23, 1913, as he was chatting with several persons, including the wife of the orchestra conductor at the musicale. When the police swooped down on the concert hall, Stalin moved too slowly. Other accounts had an unidentified acquaintance throw a woman's coat over him and attempt to hustle him from the hall, but the police spotted his men's boots and promptly took him into custody. Soviet literature, while maintaining that Stalin was a genius at spotting and eluding the police, has insisted that in his final arrest Stalin was betrayed by an *agent provocateur*. Oddly, it has not always identified the agent as Malinovsky. But Stalin must have known that the Okhrana would have the *Pravda* festivities under adequate surveillance, and he went to the musicale feeling he would be safe from arrest.

A few days later Lenin learned of the arrest. The Department of Police intercepted a strange, unsigned letter from St. Petersburg to Lenin in Cracow that was dated February 25, 1913, and addressed to a certain Kobal, Lenartovich Street, No. 9.[646] The enclosed letter for "V. Ulyanov" (Lenin), Liubomirsk Street, No. 47, apparently including encoded portions, begins without a salutation:

I am writing to you as if I were in love: each time I include a picture. Oh, "dadya"! I was thrown into jail looking like this. They have probably written to you about it . . . day before yesterday our dear soul—the Georgian was captured.[647] Some fool brought him to our soirée. It was simply a lack of discretion to go there. I didn't even know about his presence in Petersburg, and was stunned to see him in a public place. "You won't get away with it," I said. He didn't. Now we are all left holding the bag, especially me. We already have begun to talk about my kind of reorganization, and we have set a date for a detailed discussion, now postponed. . . . I don't know what will happen. For God's sake, don't be angry with me for the words in my letters. We are both alike. I was very pleased to find out from Vasilii[648] that you like me. Let us be sincere—and we don't need anything else. In a moment of excitement I turned down the proofreading . . . [but] if necessary, I'll do it. But the situation is still the same. Someone is interfering. I cannot guess who it is. The situation is terrible. With all my willingness I can supply only the literary fruit . . . nothing else. I can work only when relations with the public have been established. And there is nobody to establish them.

It is hardly possible to clean up the mess. The Georgian's[649] arrest has shaken me. I feel I am on the path of misery, as would anybody who would help to renovate the editorial board. Someone is interfering, who is solidly embedded. All our "contemporaries" are united in one group . . . so closely united that it is impossible to penetrate this group not only for me. Roman is giving up. He is just getting upset, nothing else. Dearest [*golubchik*], console me with a kind word.

"Yours"

(Unsigned)

The unknown author of the letter confirms that Stalin was arrested on February 23, 1913. "Roman" obviously meant Malinovsky. Why he was unnerved by Stalin's arrest is puzzling. The text of the letter proves it emanated from someone on the *Pravda* staff, probably a person who had been recently arrested and released. However, there is a timbre of feminine vanity about the letter. Chernomasov, who, as we have seen, had been arrested and set free in early February, is a logical candidate for authorship of the letter, but he could scarcely have written in such a feminine style.

The *"golubchik"* letter from St. Petersburg was sent to Lenin on the same date, February 25, 1913, that he wrote Podvoisky in the capital and warned, "Vaska must be well protected. Of course he is unstable, he is too sick." "Vaska" was a diminutive of "Vasilii." Obviously Lenin was distressed that all his bolshevik adherents seemed to be disappearing into jail or exile. How could he function without party stalwarts in Russia? Vaska's (Stalin's) "sickness" perhaps meant that he was under intensive surveillance and would be arrested if appropriate precautions were not instituted.[650] On the other hand, Lenin's use of the word "unstable" could more reasonably have meant that Stalin was undependable. "Too sick" is a strong phrase indicating Lenin might have smelled a rat and was wondering about Stalin's reliability. After all, Stalin had returned from Vienna too soon and he was again muscling in on the *Pravda* operation. Three days later in a letter to N. I. Podvoisky for "No. 3" —the bolshevik code designation for Malinovsky—Lenin asked, "Why is there no news from Vasilii? What happened to him? We are worried. . . ."[651] This letter, and many others tediously written by Krupskaya, had a "chemical text," as secret writing was described in those days. Between the lines of a seemingly innocuous letter Krupskaya laboriously would use secret ink to convey Lenin's real instructions to the faithful in St. Petersburg. Her work was in vain. The Okhrana was able to raise the secret writing almost at once.

Lenin was delighted with the newly organized *Pravda,* and inferentially Malinovsky, as he revealed in a letter some weeks later. "I congratulate you heartily," he wrote, "on . . . the improvement. Let us hope it is final." [652] And after Stalin was in Siberian exile, Lenin wrote Kamenev, "Everybody is satisfied with the newspaper. I haven't heard a single word of criticism. . . . I myself am especially satisfied."

Also on the twenty-fifth of February, "No. 3" (Malinovsky), in St. Petersburg, wrote Troyanovsky at Schönbrunner Shlosstrasse, No. 30, Vienna. The letter read:

ESTEEMED COMRADES:
Today I received two transmittals of 50 rubles, one in my own name, the other in the name of Kalinsky [but] to transfer them according to the agreement was unnecessary because there had already been an advance of 100 rubles. . . . How is the trading—I don't know because I have had no time to be there. I beg you to ask Comrade Gala whether she has asked Keren . . . about the brother, I have asked and he said he himself will write. The materials will be sent tomorrow, I would be most appreciative were you to combine the materials on the military list . . . but it is not desirable to be quiet. There is no time to finish. All, all the best. Greetings to Gala. The day was 35 thousand.
                                                                R. MAL.[653]

This letter, intercepted by the Department of Police, definitely includes encoded portions. For example, the word "day" in the last sentence means *Pravda.* Other sentences are simply uncipherable. It is apparent that Malinovsky still had a fond regard for "Gala"— Mrs. Troyanovsky. However, most important is the absence of any reference in the letter to the arrest of Stalin, which had occurred two days before in the presence of Malinovsky; the police had already placed Stalin in the St. Petersburg Preliminary Detention Prison, which he knew from previous incarcerations. Meanwhile on March 1st, four days later, from Cracow, Lenin wrote Aleksander Efremovich Axelrod at his address in the Kalashnikov Branch of the Russian Bank for Foreign Trade in St. Petersburg. This letter, too, was in secret writing, or chemical ink, but the Okhrana soon made it unsecret and read it. Among other things the letter stated that "we have received the letter about the cooperative [decoded, this meant the Duma faction] with much delay. Also one letter from Vasilii, the other one was lost." [654] The contents of Stalin's letter are unknown.

There is no information about the circumstances of Stalin's imprisonment until he was sent from St. Petersburg "by stages" on July 2, 1913, more than four months after his final arrest. Gendarmes escorted him to the Turukhansk region, where he was sentenced to exile under open police surveillance for four years.[655] This was no light sentence. Nine days later, on July 11th, Stalin arrived in Krasnoyarsk, a city over twenty-five hundred miles from St. Petersburg situated on the Trans-Siberian railway.[656] He had travelled in the customary boxcars with other prisoners picked up on the way. He was already acquainted with Krasnoyarsk, a major assembly point for prisoners bound for Siberian exile. But on this occasion he was obliged to wait four days before he departed, on July 15th, for the Turukhansk region.[657] Although it was summer, the small boat he travelled in required a month to carry him up the Yenisei River some thirteen hundred miles farther to the initial point on his way to exile, the village of Monastyrskoye.[658] The mighty Yenisei was noted for its treacherous currents and awesome storms. Stalin and the other exiles (they have not been identified even though he spent almost seven weeks in their company) arrived at the Kostino Station, with a short stay at Miroedinskoye, on August 10th.[659] He was four months short of his thirty-fourth birthday.

Lenin had convened another conference in August at Poronino near Cracow.[660] Some evidence suggests that he tried to engineer Stalin's escape from exile in November.[661] But he coordinated his plans with Malinovsky—which, of course, meant that Malinovsky tipped off the Department of Police, which in turn informed its Siberian gendarmes. As a result, Stalin was placed under more careful security. Evidence that Malinovsky's word carried weight in St. Petersburg police circles during 1913 might be found in the fact that one of the two Vice-Directors of the Department of Police signed the order to transfer Stalin and Sverdlov from Kostino to Kureika, farther away from the vestiges of civilization.

This is an appropriate moment to return to the Special Section of The Department of Police which had dealt with Stalin's correspondence, his dossier, and had a hand in the orders taking him away to the Arctic Circle. At this point a character we know from former years, Alexander Mikhailovich Eremin, enters the story. In 1873 Eremin, a twenty-one-year-old cadet, had completed his preliminary military education in the Ural Cavalry Regiment and Orienburg Cadet Corps. He entered the Okhrana, the Separate Corps of Gendarmes, in 1901 and his career was brilliant from the start. Posted to Kiev in 1905, he was sent to headquarters of the Gendarme Corps (which meant special duty) in 1906, and appointed Chief of the Tiflis Gendarme Administration on January 12, 1908. Two years later, in January of 1910, he was ordered back to the St. Petersburg Headquarters of the Department of Police. Within seventeen years he had become a full Colonel in the Okhrana. In addition he received four decorations in 1901, 1906, 1910, and 1912. When he had arrived in St. Petersburg in 1910 the Colonel was placed in charge of the most secret *Osobyi Otdel* (The Special Section) in Department of Police Headquarters.[662] This inner sanctum gave direction to and oversaw most of the agents who penetrated revolutionary organizations prior to the abdication of Nicholas II in March 1917. Operating under control of one of two vice-directors of the Department of Police, the Special Section not only monitored all important security cases within the Empire but also practically controlled the very important Foreign Agency of the Okhrana located in the Imperial Russian Embassy in Paris. It is noteworthy that most all the police reports concerning Stalin emanating from the Special Section had been signed by Eremin, and that the Colonel was Chief of the Tiflis Okhrana from 1908 to 1910 when Stalin was a part-time resident of the Caucasus. Eremin's importance is indicated by the testimony of Beletsky, Director of the Department of Police from 1914 to 1917 and Vissarionov, a Vice Director, before a commission in 1917. Beletsky remembered:

> Malinovsky was an old collaborator. Colonel Martynov, chief of the Moscow Okhrana, arrived in St. Petersburg at the time of the elections to the Duma, and reported the possibility of Malinovsky being elected to the Duma. He also reported it to the Chief of the Special Section (*Osobyi Otdiel*), Eremin, and Vissarionov. They told me about it. We discussed it, and Eremin was against the admission of Malinovsky into the Duma, pointing out that this would be too dangerous . . . because, if the case were uncovered, there would be a big state scandal.[663]

For unexplained reasons, probably having to do with a decision in the Department of Police to groom him for the rank of general in the Gendarmes, Colonel Eremin was posted on June 24, 1913 to Helsinki as Chief of the Finland Gendarme Administration.[664] This was not, however, a minor responsibility. Under his command were twenty subdivisions throughout the Grand Duchy of Finland and scores of officers, noncommissioned officers and other ranks—forces that controlled the vital Russian-Finnish frontier from 1913 until the February Revolution. His duties included reporting on revolutionary movements and the surveillance of revolutionary personnel, supplies, and money that flowed from Europe through Finland to Russia.[665] He retained his post until February 1917 after which he disappeared, leaving no clue regarding his later whereabouts or his fate or that of his wife and three daughters; he was forty-four.

Colonel Eremin occupies a special place in the life of Stalin. It is not only that his section intercepted all his letters, including the "Dear Semyen" and "Iosif" letters and the "Vas" letter to Malinovsky, and compiled and signed many reports about him. It is also because of an event that took place many years after the Colonel had vanished. In the early nineteen-forties, however, a letter, or communication, ostensibly signed by Eremin made the rounds of the intelligence communities of the Western world— perhaps the Eastern as well. It was on the desks of many intelligence officers before anyone used it to suggest the possibility that Stalin had been an Okhrana agent. Dated July 12, 1913, the letter was on the stationery of the Special Section and seemed to be official enough. Eremin in July, 1913 was just about to leave for Helsinki and was winding up his duties at the Department of Police Headquarters. Addressed to the Chief of the Yeniseisk Okhrana Division, A. F. Zhelezhniakov, and classified "Top Secret" and "Personal," the letter bore the marks of authenticity. (Stalin had been exiled to the Turukhansk region over which the Yeniseisk Okhrana Division had jurisdiction.) The letter read:

Dear Alexei Fedorovich!

Iosif Vissarionovich Dzhugashvili-Stalin, who was administratively exiled to the Turukhansk Region upon his arrest in 1906, provided the Chief of the Provincial Gendarme Administration valuable denunciatory information.

In 1908 the Chief of the Baku Okhrana Division received from Stalin a series of intelligence reports and upon Stalin's arrival in Petersburg, Stalin became an agent of the Petersburg Okhrana Division.

Stalin's work was fragmentary but distinguished by accuracy.

After Stalin's election to the Central Committee of the Party in Prague, Stalin, upon his return to Petersburg, openly opposed the Government and completely broke off his Okhrana connection.

I inform you, dear sir, about this matter for your personal appreciation in operational matters.

Be assured of my high esteem.

[signed] EREMIN[666]

Eremin's demonstrated political and operational talent makes it difficult to believe that he would have written in 1913 the letter attributed to him.[666a] When a year earlier Lenin had brought Stalin into the first Bolshevik Central Committee, he became a person of some political importance; Eremin's purported letter therefore carried with it the possibility of a scandal à la Malinovsky. Furthermore, the letter includes several unlikely errors for an officer of Eremin's caliber. It is addressed to "Aleksei Fedorovich," although Captain Zhelezniakov's first name and patronymic were Vladimir Fedorovich, a fact ascertainable from the Gendarme officers' biographical register available in Eremin's office at the time. Moreover, the Special Section dossier on Stalin that Eremin himself had signed contained no information about an arrest of Stalin in 1906. The reference to "Iosif Vissarionovich Dzhugashvili-Stalin" is odd; in none of the previous Special Section reports was the pseudonym "Stalin" noted, although he had adopted it in late 1912—and "Stalin" recurs here seven times. The use of "Vissarionovich" is also curious; normally Okhrana letters and reports would drop the "ich," spelling the patronymic "Vissarionov." Stalin was in Baku during 1908 at the time Colonel Eremin headed the Tiflis Okhrana, and we have noted the curious dialogue during that period between the Baku and Tiflis Okhranas regarding Stalin. The Chief of the Baku Gendarme Administration was then Major General E. M. Kozinstov, who seems to have been an administrator and not directly involved in agent operations. Captain Fedor Vissarionovich Zaitsev was responsible for agent "intelligence reports"; Zaitsev joined the Gendarmes in 1903 and, in all likelihood, he and Eremin were in training together during that year. (Captain Zaitsev's name disappears, like so many others, and is not to be found in the Gendarme biographical register after 1909; for some unknown reason, his work in the Okhrana ceased when he was thirty-six.) The statement that upon Stalin's arrival in St. Petersburg he became an agent of the Okhrana Division there must refer to the period between June 24, 1909—when Stalin escaped from Solvychegodsk—and January 17, 1912, when he was co-opted by Lenin into the first Bolshevik Central Committee after the Prague Conference. If, as the letter goes on to say, Stalin completely broke off his Okhrana connection in 1912, it is curious that the information is being relayed for Zhelezniakov's "personal appreciation in operational matters." Having broken with the Okhrana, was it hoped that Stalin might be induced to renew his old relationship? If so, the letter could be expected to be more specific, particularly about the control factor previously used in

Stalin's case. Thus it is evident that Colonel Eremin neither wrote nor signed the letter *in 1913*.

The mystery of Colonel Eremin's disappearance from his post as Chief of Finland's Gendarme Administration after the February events of 1917 remains perplexing. Possibly he and his family perished, but this was not noted in the Finnish or Russian émigré press. We do not find Eremin in the rather detailed lists of officers who fought in the Civil War on the side of the White Armies.[666b] It may be that he decided to jettison his identity and disappear after the February events in Petrograd, when the Okhrana suffered disintegration; he had every plausible reason to do so. Eremin undoubtedly recognized the significance of the abdication of the Tsar and the establishment of the Provisional Government with its ministers— "the foolish virgins," as one observer dubbed them. It must have been clear to him that his knowledge of secret operations in revolutionary organizations would shortly mean that a number of former agents would be vitally interested in forever silencing him. It would have been only prudent for Eremin to go underground for the protection of his person and the safeguarding of his family. Perhaps he made his way abroad and, after adopting an alias, attempted to construct for himself a new career. Many former officers of the Department of Police in their diaspora of 1917 took with them official stationery, stamps, seals and, above all, their confidential knowledge of agents and operations. Wherever Eremin found himself, his need for money would not have lessened as he became older and he would have been well aware of the value of his knowledge of Stalin's affiliation with the Okhrana. It is easy to dismiss this letter as a fraudulent document produced in the nineteen-forties by one of the individuals specializing in this activity in many places from Harbin to Buenos Aires. Indeed, that is the conclusion of some reputable scholars acquainted with the crazy-quilt patterns of émigré forgeries. Others who regard the letter as completely authentic have attempted to explain away its obvious errors. Whatever version is correct, the letter in question was produced by someone (not a novice at operational intelligence matters) who had knowledge of Stalin's Okhrana dossier and who comprehended the interactions of the Okhrana and revolutionary organizations. Most important, he was convinced that Stalin had been an agent of the Okhrana.

Several persons in Siberian exile with Stalin wrote about this period, and a careful reading between the lines of their memoirs is revealing. Jacob Sverdlov, the nominal head of the future Soviet state, who had been arrested shortly before Stalin and who spent time in Turukhansk exile as his roommate, was an inveterate letter writer.[667] Anatol V. Baikalov, a social democrat, remembered Stalin from Siberia.[668] Because Sergo Alliluev and his family corresponded with Stalin, their recollections are also interesting.[669] Vera L. Shveitser, the wife of the Armenian revolutionary Suren Spandaryan, who joined her husband in the Turukhansk area during his exile there, wrote a great deal but obviously under Stalin's censors.[670] From these sources it is nonetheless possible to draw a composite picture of his final, four-year exile. Stalin publicly mentioned this period of his life only once, in a speech to a Moscow gathering of Red Army cadets on May 4, 1935. He waxed eloquent in his seeming concern for humanity:

I recall an incident in Siberia, where I was at one time in exile. It was in the spring, at the time of the spring floods. About thirty men went to the river to pull out timber which had been carried away by the vast, swollen river. Toward evening they returned, but with a man missing. When asked where the thirtieth man was, they replied that he had "remained there." To my question, "What do you mean?", they replied with unconcern, "Why ask?—drowned, of course." Thereupon one of them hurried off, saying, "I must go and water the mare." When I reproached them for having more concern for animals than for men, one said amid general approval, "Why should we worry about men? We can always make men. But a mare! Just try and make a mare!"[671]

Kostino, the small village to which Stalin was initially exiled and where he arrived about mid August, 1913,[672] was a world removed from European Russia. Malinovsky had made certain that he would not easily return. Nonetheless during the first part of March, 1914, some seven months after his arrival, he and Sverdlov, accompanied by two guards, were transferred to the small settlement of Kureika, near the Arctic Circle.[673] The Okhrana had two purposes in mind: Sverdlov, the able newspaper editor, was to be kept out of revolutionary circulation; Stalin, the disrupter of Lenin-Okhrana-Malinovsky plans, was to be placed in a deep Siberian freeze. No escape was to be possible during this exile.

Kureika was actually less than a village and more like an Alaskan outpost. It was not far from the mouth of the Kureika River, which emptied into the broad Yenisei River that cut across the Arctic Circle. At the time of Stalin's exile there, its population consisted of thirty-eight men and twenty-nine women, who, among other things, hunted and fished. All of them were illiterate.[674] Stalin then found himself in a territory larger than the combined area of Germany, France, and England and inhabited by only fifteen thousand people. The one route to Krasnoyarsk and Russia in winter and summer was along the Yenisei. During the short summer only one steamer navigated the river. Autumn travel was possible by sled over snow piled up to the height of a man. Winter frequently had temperatures of sixty-five degrees below zero. In spring the sled dogs were almost immobile in the slush. Under these circumstances escape was too complicated. "Comrade Stalin had to remain in exile this time," Vera Shveitser reported.[675]

That part of Siberia near the Arctic Circle was reserved for those persons considered undesirable but not highly dangerous. Yaroslavsky, Petrovsky, and Ordzhonikidze had been exiled further into Siberia to Yakutsk, closer to Alaska and far distant from European Russia. Nonetheless, only a few small villages, including Kureika, dotted hundreds of thousands of square miles of tundra in Stalin's exile area. During the nine long months of night, exiles and inhabitants of the area existed on a diet of fish and wild game. Vegetables, greens, and fruit were unobtainable. From a physical point of view, survival was exceptional for the political exile, particularly if he was from the Southern, subtropical part of Russia. From a psychological point of view, these excruciating Northern regions drove some exiles mad. But Stalin survived. In fact, he seems to have enjoyed good health through it all and his sturdy constitution served him well. Aloof, morose, and brooding about the fate that had taken him from the scene of important political developments in Russia and cursed him with these years of everlasting darkness, he apparently turned to hunting, fishing, and trapping to maintain his sanity.[676] Mail from European Russia was slow in arriving, letters from Western Europe even slower. The postman's delivery every month or so was erratic. Nonetheless, during 1913 Stalin had been able to keep in touch with Alliluev, in St. Petersburg, from whom he had received a hundred rubles for assistance in his plans for escape. The local gendarmes, informed by the Department of Police, cut off his allowance for a period of four months. The tsarist exile system provided its victims fifteen rubles per month, an adequate sum for living expenses.[677]

During the first part of his exile, Stalin shared a little house with Sverdlov.[678] Different from his roommate in almost every respect, Sverdlov, whom Lenin had sent to straighten out the *Pravda* mess, was a cosmopolitan in every sense of the word. He was a writer and a scholar, well read in several languages and well grounded in history and literature.[679] Yakov (Jacob) Mikhailovich Sverdlov was born May 23, 1885 in Nizhny Novgorod in the family of an engraver. He left the gymnasium in 1900 because of his mother's death and insufficient funds. He then became an apprentice in an apothecary shop and at age sixteen joined the Nizhny social-democratic Party, devoting himself to the study of marxist theory. Arrests, imprisonments and exiles interrupted his activities and travel on behalf of the party, but at the end of 1902 the Nizhny party entrusted him with the organization of an underground printing press that began operating the first part of 1903. Arrested and sentenced to a four-month prison term in February, 1903, he moved to Kostroma and until 1905 travelled widely, always with the police on his trail. Intensified police surveillance of his activities during January, 1906 forced him to move to Perm where, using his well-known underground pseudonym "Andrei," he organized party committees throughout the Ural mountain area. The police arrested him again on December 13, 1909. He was sentenced to exile in the Narym region of Siberia in March, 1910. He was refused permission to go abroad to cure the tuberculosis he had contracted in prison. At the end of March he left Moscow for Narym, escaping in August to join his wife in Ekaterinburg. Together they travelled to St. Petersburg, where he continued his revolutionary activities. Sverdlov and his wife were again arrested in November. After a three-month prison term she was released and banished from Moscow to Ekaterinburg. Sverdlov was sentenced to a four-year term of exile in the Narym region. His health, already bad, deteriorated as a result of the severe climate and poor food. He and Kuibyshev helped organize a 1912 May Day demonstration in Narym, after which he was again arrested and imprisoned in Tomsk prison for four months, returning to Narym in mid-August. A few days later he was caught trying to escape and was imprisoned in Tomsk and in September released from prison and sent to exile in Parabel, in the Narym region where his wife and son joined him in a room rented in a small village on the banks of the Ob river. In December of 1912 Sverdlov again escaped; he went again to St. Petersburg at the end of the year. From the end of December, 1912, to the beginning of February, 1913, Sverdlov lived in the apartment of Samoilov, a member of the Fourth Duma, rarely venturing out on the streets, although he was working as an editor of *Pravda.* It was Roman Malinovsky who presumably betrayed him to the Okhrana, and he and his wife and child were arrested and imprisoned in St. Petersburg's Kresty prison. Two months later they were banished to Ekaterinburg and forbidden to leave the town for two years. At the end of July, 1913, he arrived in Monastyrskoye, in the Turukhansk region and settled twenty miles north in the village of Seivanikha. After he went into exile with Stalin, the police in 1914 transferred them both to Kureika, a tiny village inside the polar circle. When Sverdlov discovered it was impossible to escape from exile in Turukhansk, he settled down to extensive reading, studying, and writing from which an entire volume emerged. He also acted as a leader of the local bolshevik exiles. Sverdlov moved back to the village of Monastyrskoye in 1915, where his wife and two children joined him. She obtained a job at the small local meterological station, and Sverdlov tutored students. Their small three-room house was a favorite meeting place for exiled friends. To complete his story, Sverdlov died on March 19, 1919 as a result of a virus infection which spread to his lungs. In contrast to Stalin, the sickly Sverdlov was an active participant in the October, 1917 revolutionary events, attending meetings, doing committee work, and generally being on the move.[680]

Now the gentle Sverdlov, a Jew, found himself in a tiny house with the crude, coarse, inerudite Stalin, whose hunting, fishing, and trapping accoutrements were spread at random about their modest dwelling. Even under the best of circumstances, two such diverse personalities would have clashed. Sverdlov was finally able to get away from Stalin and his sporting activities but, before he moved, he wrote his sister in St. Petersburg.

DEAR SARAH,
 . . . Dzhugashvili and I are being transferred 70 miles further north—55 miles north of the Arctic Circle. There will be only two of us. Surveillance is being increased and we are cut off from mail. The latter comes once monthly by a messenger on foot who is usually late. . . . Dzhugashvili has been deprived of his allowance for four months because he received money. Both he and I need money, but it cannot be addressed to us. . . .[681]

And later . . .

My arrangements in the new place are considerably worse. For one thing, I no longer live alone in the room. There are two of us. With me is the Georgian Dzhugashvili, an old acquaintance, for we had already met elsewhere in exile. He is a good chap, but too much of an individualist in everyday life, while I believe in at least a semblance of order. That's why I am nervous at times. But that is not so important. Much worse is the fact that there is no seclusion from our landlord's family. Our room is next to theirs, and has no separate entrance. They have children. Naturally, the youngsters spend many hours with us. Besides, grown-ups from the village drop in. They come, sit down, keep quiet for half an hour and suddenly rise: "Well, I've got to go, good-bye!" No sooner do they leave than someone else comes in, and it's the same thing all over again. They come, as if in spite, at the very best time for study, in the evening. That's understandable: in the daytime they work. We had to give up the habit of poring over a book until long after midnight. There is absolutely no kerosene. We use candles. Since that provides too little light for my eyes, I do all my studying in the daytime now. As a matter of fact, I don't study very much. We have virtually no books. . . .[682]

Vera Shveitser claims she observed Stalin's room in his Kureika exile. Her account, which was published in 1943 and so is understandably quite different, described a table piled high with books and newspapers, including all Marx's works and Rosa Luxemburg's book, which Stalin had presumably translated from German to Russian.[683] Sverdlov's statement, "We have virtually no books" gives the lie to this. Moreover, Stalin's knowledge of German—if, indeed, he had any—was presumably insufficient for translation. Shveitser's book bears the mark of Beria's or Stalin's editing.

Sverdlov, unable to live with Stalin, managed to move away from him. He wrote that "the moral atmosphere is not especially favorable. A number of encounters [personal conflicts], possibly only under the conditions of prison and exile, their pettiness notwithstanding, have had a pretty strong effect on my nerves." [684] Stalin's nerves, as we know, were extraordinarily cool.

"In May of 1914," Moskalev writes, "the Turukhansk police chief was obliged to change guards at Kureika after the urgent demands of I. V. Stalin." [685] The guard, a certain Laletin, had apparently been harassing Stalin. According to Moskalev, he was *grubyi* [crude] to Stalin. This is a classic case of the pot calling the kettle black. At any rate, Stalin had his way and Laletin was replaced by a new guard, Mikhail Merzliakov. We are not told what happened to Laletin.[686] Merzliakov was a quite different sort of guard. Before his departure from gendarme headquarters in Krasnoyarsk, he had been instructed, according to Moskalev, that he should make certain that Dzhugashvili not escape on one of the

Yenisei River steamboats, that he not be permitted to read magazines or newspapers, and that he be forbidden to assemble a group of people. He was also ordered to prevent Stalin from playing games with the young people of the settlement. Nor was Stalin to be allowed the use of a small boat for fishing. He was particularly cautioned to watch Dzhugashvili "in connection with firearms." [687] All of this is interesting, but doubtful. Why would the gendarmes be concerned if Stalin convened all sixty-nine of Kureika's residents for a political meeting? What could be gained by forbidding him to read periodicals? Anyhow, this objective could easily be accomplished by seizing the periodicals at Krasnoyarsk. Games with young people—what possible political significance could they have? And if Stalin possessed firearms, the most intelligent precaution was not to follow him through the tundra and the woods but to divest him of ammunition—or, better yet, the rifle. Moskalev writes:

Curiously when Merzliakov was excluded from a collective farm because he had been a guard, he wrote comrade Stalin, asking Stalin to verify the fact that Merzliakov's relationship to him was almost friendly and that Merzliakov was not a professional guard.

I. V. Stalin replied in the following letter . . . to Mikhail Merzliakov:

"I remember Merzliakov from my place of exile in the settlement of Kureika (*Turukh. krai*), where he was a guard from 1914-1916. At that time he had only one assignment from the police chief—to watch me (then there were no other exiles in Kureika). It is therefore understandable that I could not have been in a 'friendly relationship' with Mikh. Merzliakov. Nonetheless I must testify that whereas my relationship with him was not 'friendly,' it was not inimical, as was the usual relationship between exiles and guards. This may be explained, it seems to me, by the fact that Mikh. Merzliakov had a formal relationship to the objective of the police chief, without the usual policeman's zeal, he did not spy on me, he did not bait me, did not nag me and he looked through his fingers at my frequent absences and often insulted the police chief because of his annoying 'orders' and 'instructions.' To all this I consider it my duty to testify. . . .

"This happened in 1914-1916 when M. Merzliakov, being a guard, advantageously distinguished himself from the other police.

"What happened later to M. Merzliakov, how he conducted himself during the Kolchak period and the beginning of Soviet authority, and now—I, of course, do not know.

"With a communist greeting

I. STALIN

"MOSCOW, 27 II 1930g." [688]

This is Stalin's one letter to a gendarme. Because it appears in a book written in 1947 under Stalinist auspices, it must be regarded as authentic and Stalin must have given his express permission that it be published. At best it reveals a certain compassion for a distant guard in faraway exile. It also seems to indicate that Stalin had an understanding with the gendarmes in Turukhansk.

Germany declared war on Russia on August 1, 1914 (N.S.), roughly five months after Stalin's transfer to Kureika. News of the outbreak of hostilities reached Stalin some days later. Vera Shveitser writes that Krupskaya sent a letter, together with a copy of Lenin's "Theses on War," to a secret apartment address in Krasnoyarsk for transmission to Stalin. She found him in December visiting her husband. "You should have seen comrade Stalin at that moment," she wrote. He began to read the "Theses" of Lenin aloud. "We listened attentively. He read slowly and frequently exclaimed 'That's right!' " [689] Stalin, who had literally been out of touch with the world for more than a year, could hardly have been able to comment intelligently on Lenin's "Theses," which essentially called for the overthrow of the tsarist government by way of a Russian civil war to be undertaken in the midst of a world war.

On February 27, 1915, Stalin wrote Lenin from the village of Monastryskoye, where he was again visiting Spandaryan. It was his one letter to Lenin during the four years of the war that has been published:

My greetings to you, dear Ilich, warm, warm greetings. Greetings to Zinoviev, greetings to Nadezhda Konstantinovna. How are you? And your health. I am living as before, chewing my bread, completing half my term. It's rather dull, but can't be helped. How are things with you. It must be much livelier where you are. I recently read Kropotkin's articles—the old fool is completely out of his mind. I also read a short article by Plekhanov in *Rech*—an impossible old gossip. "Ekh-ma!" And the Liquidators with their deputies—agents of the Free Economic Society! Devil take me, there's no one to give them a whipping! Must they be allowed to go scot-free? We are supposed to rejoice that there will soon appear a newspaper which will hit them on the jaw and lay it on heartily with a vengeance.

In case you should want to write me the address is Turukhansk Territory, Yeniseisk Province, Monastyrskoye, for Suren Spandaryan.

Yours,

KOBA

P.S. Timofei [Spandaryan] asks that his most bitter regards be sent to Guesde, Sembat and Vandervelde in their glorious (ha! ha!) ministerial posts.[690]

Stalin and Spandaryan were so far out of touch with the outside world that they were commenting on events months old and of no particular importance to exiles in Northern Siberia. The tone and text of this letter suggest that it was composed during the darkness of the arctic winter after they had consumed a considerable amount of local spirits. Stalin's belligerence ("no one to give them a whipping" and "a newspaper which will hit them on the jaw") cannot be taken seriously. Lenin's reaction to this letter is unrecorded. As far as we know, he did not reply.

Stalin's official record states that during the summer of 1915—there is no precise date—he participated in a meeting in the village of Monastyrskoye attended by exiled members of the Central Committee and of the bolshevik deputies in the Fourth State Duma, at which time the February trial of the five bolshevik deputies was disclosed.[691] They had been exiled to the Turukhansk area during the summer of 1915, after their trial in February for anti-war agitation subversive activities. Kamenev alone seems to have had an attitude of pseudo-patriotism. Roman Malinovsky, with a handsome six-thousand-ruble honorarium from the Okhrana, had resigned his Duma position in 1914, gone off to Western Europe, joined the Russian Army, become a German prisoner of war, and was conducting bolshevik propaganda in prisoner-of-war camps.

The record is scrambled, with one Duma deputy, Samoilov, insisting that Stalin attacked Kamenev's position and with Petrovsky claiming that he defended it.[692] Vera Shveitser later wrote that he took a strong stand against the "traitor Kamenev." [693] Infinitely more believable is Mrs. Sverdlov's account that Stalin attended the meeting, but he sat silently smoking his pipe filled with the cheap Russian "makhorka" tobacco. He listened to a resolution of censure proposed by Sverdlov and Spandaryan and then, before a vote was taken, hurriedly returned to his Kureika home—perhaps to the mistress he was rumored to have.[694]

The official chronology claims that on November 10, 1915 Stalin wrote Lenin and Krupskaya from Turukhansk. This letter may not be found in the Lenin memorabilia and Stalin failed to produce it. However, for some unexplained reason Lenin did become concerned about Stalin in the late autumn of 1915. In a letter from Geneva to an old friend, V. A. Karpinsky, in Berne, Lenin revealed that he was unable to remember Stalin's name. "Big request: find out (from Stepko or Mikha, etc.) the last name of 'Koba' (Iosif Dzh. . . .?? We have forgotten). Very important!!" he wrote.[695] Mikha Tskhaya (Barsov) was a Georgian bolshevik resident in Berne who had known Stalin from the Caucasus. One wonders how it was possible for Lenin to forget the name of Dzhugashvili whom he had personally placed on the Party central committee at the 1912 Prague conference and who had collaborated on "The National Question and Social Democracy." In any event, he obviously had not forgotten the person. Apparently no one around Lenin (most of all Krupskaya) could remember Stalin's difficult last name. The precise reason for Lenin's need for this information at that time is unknown, but he called it "very important." The answer, probably lost to history, may possibly be found in Lenin's relations with the Germans who needed persons in Russia to carry out sabotage and other clandestine activities.[696]

Stalin's fondness for the Alliluev family was well known. From his Siberian exile he wrote a tender and revealing letter to his future mother-in-law, Olga Evgeievna, as a thank-you note for a parcel sent in 1915:

Many, many thanks to you, my dear Olga Evgeievna, for your kind and pure feelings toward me. I shall never forget your thoughtfulness. I await the moment when I will be free of prison and as soon as I am in Petersburg I shall thank you, and also Sergei, for everything you have done. But there are still two more years to wait.

I received the parcel. I appreciate it. I requested only one. Don't spend anything more on me—you need the money. I will be happy if now and then you send me a post card with a view of nature, etc. Nature is reduced to ugliness in this damned country,—in summer the river, in winter the snow, and no more nature than that. I am stupidly homesick for the sight of a landscape if only on paper.

My greetings to the boys and girls. All the best to them.

I live as before. I feel good. My health is fine. I am becoming accustomed to this place. Nature is severe here—three weeks ago we had 45° of frost.

Until the next letter.

Respectfully yours—

JOSEPH[697]

Mrs. Alliluev and Stalin had always enjoyed a particular rapport. As we know, she had helped him on occasion to elude the Okhrana when he was in St. Petersburg, and she had always seen to it that he had a place to sleep in the Alliluev apartment; she was also, of course, a mother looking after her daughter's suitor.

For the year 1916 there are four entries in Stalin's official chronology. On February 5th he presumably wrote a letter to the "Party Center" abroad concerning "his work on articles on the nationality question." On February 25th in a letter to the bolshevik center abroad, sent through Inessa Armand, he inquired about his article "Cultural-National Autonomy," which he had already forwarded. Then, on March 12th, he and Spandaryan (and other exiles) wrote a letter "to the journal *Voprosy Strakhovaniya* [*Insurance Questions*]." [698] Only the last letter has survived. Stalin claims he was completing the second volume of his work on the problem of nationalities, which he asked Sergei Alliluev to forward to Lenin. This manuscript has never been published although Moskalev, writing in 1947 under Stalinist censorship, claimed it had been intercepted by the Okhrana. At that time it supposedly could be found in the Krasnoyarsk regional state archives as part of the Eniseisk Gendarme Administration files, Report No. 1869.[699]

During his four years of exile Stalin produced nothing that was published. Even his letters were few and far between. Trotsky may be forgiven his caustic criticism of Stalin as a person who "remained on the sidelines . . ., sullen, and, as always, malevolent." [700] He was terribly lonely, yet there have been many historical examples in which loneliness developed purposeful literature. Stalin was occupied with his hunting, trapping, and fishing. One account has him acquiring a mistress who bore him a son; if this is true, he failed to mention it in later life and the son has never been identified. Nor is there any record of letters he sent to his son, Yasha, or his aging mother in Gori during this period.

By the end of 1916 the manpower shortage in the Russian armed forces was critical. Although fifteen million men had been inducted, almost two million had been killed in action and some three million were wounded or prisoners. More than a million ill soldiers crowded the inadequate hospitals. In view of this disastrous situation, an earlier law that exempted residents of the Turukhansk area from mobilization was replaced by an administrative decree that declared all able-bodied men subject to military draft even though "they are under investigation, being tried, or serving a sentence for a crime—provided it has not resulted in the loss of all civil rights, property and privileges." [701] Thus in October, 1916 the tsarist government drafted all administratively exiled persons, including Stalin, for military service. He had never been tried by a court of law. This call to the colors apparently surprised the Turukhansk Chief of Police, a certain Kibirov, who was responsible for convoying the exiles to the mobilization point at Krasnoyarsk, almost a thousand miles away. Autumn travel in the arctic regions being extremely difficult, the exiles reached Krasnoyarsk after two months—at the end of December, 1916—utilizing dog sleds, reindeers, and horses during a bitterly cold journey.[702] Stalin, according to Vera Shveitser, "conducted massive organizational work" at each stop of the column. This is easily discernible nonsense.

Stalin, Boris Ivanovich and others finally arrived in Krasnoyarsk at the end of December, 1916. The Tsarist bureaucrats wanted to send comrade Stalin off to the army, to the war, but they decided against it. They feared his influence, his revolutionary work among the troops. At that time it would have been difficult to send Stalin back to Turukhansk; the spring thaw would have complicated the return journey, and besides, comrade Stalin was to complete his exile term in several months.[703]

Yaroslavsky subscribed to this myth that Stalin himself partially dispelled in March, 1917, during a long conversation with the Alliluevs.[704] He explained that the authorities in Krasnoyarsk rejected him for military service because "they considered me an undesirable element, and later they found fault with my arm." [705] Stalin indulged himself in another half truth, for the Turukhansk Chief of Police had been ordered to dispatch *all* administratively exiled persons—desirable or undesirable—for induction. The official Russian handbook for military conscription included a list of diseases and injuries making a person unfit for military service. Three paragraphs pertain to Stalin's shortened left arm: No. 79, bent or shortened limbs; No. 80, limited mobility of large joints; and No. 81, atrophy of the limbs.[706] Stalin's left arm was inadequate to hold a rifle on target or to guide a bayonet. He was not an "undesirable element" but simply useless as a potential soldier. Anna Allilueva explains that Stalin's left arm was "shortened, crooked" from the elbow.[707] Contrary to the accounts of some biographers, Stalin did not take particular pains in later life to disguise the two- or three-inch difference in the length of his arms; photographs of Stalin at World War II conferences reveal this.

Once Stalin was found unfit for military duty, he was permitted to resettle in the small town of Achinsk, with its thousand residents, approximately eighty-five miles west of Krasnoyarsk.[708] The nearby Trans-Siberian railway made it much easier to slip back into the populated areas of Western Russia, an impossible feat from the edge of the Arctic Circle. In view of the few months remaining in his four-year term of exile, perhaps the gendarmes considered it illogical to send him back to Kureika. At any rate, he remained for a while in F. N. Samoilov's secret apartment at Krasnoyarsk, where many comrades had stayed and been fed by Samoilov's *"mamushka"* (mama), described as a real conspirator.[709] Stalin says that on February 20th he left Krasnoyarsk for Achinsk, "where he had received permission to reside until the expiration of his exile." [710] A number of bolsheviks, including Olminsky, Kamenev, and Muranov, had settled there. None of them had the foggiest notion that the Tsar was soon to abdicate or that Russia was about to have a short-lived democratic Provisional Government.

Vera Shveitser, whose husband, Suren Spandaryan, had died in 1916, became the principal chronicler of this brief interlude. Although her account is shot through with inaccuracies, she seems to have been closer to the Achinsk scene than the other revolutionaries residing there. According to her, Stalin spent three weeks in leading the group of bolsheviks in propaganda work at the local military garrison and in revolutionary agitation among soldiers bound for the front.[711] The official record fails to report these activities, and for good reason. The leadership of the bolshevik contingent in Achinsk was supplied by Kamenev, Trotsky's brother-in-law, or by Muranov, the exiled Duma delegate. If Stalin conducted propaganda among local troops or among those ordered to the front, it took place around a table over some beer or vodka at a tavern. He was not known to be outstanding as a propagandist. Vera Shveitser writes that "in the second part of January, 1917, Comrade Stalin arrived early one morning in Achinsk and came to my apartment," carefully pointing out that it was a conspiratorial, or secret, one.[712] Stalin lived there several days before he managed to obtain a "very ordinary room" on Irkutsk Street, No. 13. Strolling through the little town, Stalin once exclaimed, "If Achinsk was not on the railroad, it would be worse to live here than in Turukhansk." He obviously did not enjoy life among the other revolutionaries, but Petrograd and Moscow were no more than four days by express train from Achinsk.[713] Anatol N. Baikalov, who had wavered between menshevism, bolshevism, and the social revolutionaries, knew Stalin in Achinsk, which he described as a large-sized village and "not a city." [714] "The only brick buildings were a couple of churches and half a dozen houses belonging to the well-to-do merchants," he writes. Most dwellings were one-level homes of three or four rooms. There were two movies and a social club. "Nothing ever happened in this peaceful Siberian backwater, and life generally was dreary, drab, and cheap." Baikalov met Stalin several times there at Kamenev's, who lived "with his wife Olga Davidovna [Trotsky's sister], a pretty but somewhat vain and capricious woman, in a small warm and comfortably furnished house." He recalls:

There was nothing striking or even remarkable either in Stalin's appearance or in his conversation. Thick set, of medium height, with a swarthy face pitted by smallpox, a drooping moustache, thick hair, narrow forehead, and rather short legs, he produced the impression of a man of poor intellectual abilities. His small eyes, hidden under bushy eyebrows, were dull and deprived of that friendly humorous expression which forms such a prominent feature of his flattering post-revolutionary portraits. His Russian was very poor. He spoke haltingly, with a strong Georgian accent: his speech was dull and dry, and entirely devoid of any colour and witticism.

The contrast with Kamenev, a brilliant speaker and accomplished conversationalist, was striking. To chat with Kamenev was a real intellectual delight. . . .

Stalin usually remained taciturn and morose, placidly smoking his pipe filled with atrocious *makhorka* (Russian common tobacco). I remember how this poisonous smoke irritated Olga Davidovna. She sneezed, coughed, groaned, implored Stalin to stop smoking, but he never paid any attention to her.

Stalin's rare contribution to the conversation Kamenev usually dismissed with brief, almost contemptuous remarks. . . . He thought Stalin's reasoning unworthy of any serious consideration.

My general impression of Stalin was that his intellectual standard was much below that of an average "Party worker." . . . His education was very deficient and the main stock of his ideas was borrowed from popular two-pence half-penny Socialist pamphlets. It was equally plain to me that he was a narrow-minded fanatical man.

Poor education, insufficient knowledge of the Russian language, and incapacity for abstract theoretical cogitation prevented Stalin from becoming an effective writer, and as a public speaker he was no good at all. Neither was there any personal charm about him which sometimes gives a man a kind of magnetic power. His appearance was rather repellent; his manners were coarse; his general attitude towards other people was rude, provocative, and cynical.

This description of Stalin's personality reinforces what we already know about him.

When the news of the Tsar's abdication (March 2, 1917) reached Achinsk is unknown. It was probably no later than March 4th. Shortly thereafter the revolutionaries held a meeting in the town hall to hail the downfall of the Romanov regime and, incidentally, to send a telegram of congratulations to the venerated Grand Duke Mikhail Aleksandrovich for his refusal to accept the throne. Vera Shveitser says Stalin failed to attend this meeting because he was conducting propaganda meetings with the local troops.[715] He did attend the meeting, but his reason for later ignoring it had to do with the condemnation of Kamenev, who signed the congratulatory telegram to the Grand Duke. Somehow this was interpreted during the years of the purges as Kamenev's fawning before the royal family. That Stalin was soberly inculcating soldiers while joyous revolutionaries revelled in the unexpected, albeit partial realization of their objectives is a ridiculous invention. The Shveitser version is highly unlikely if for no other reason than that the electrifying knowledge of the abdication made every bolshevik worth his salt want to celebrate.

On March 8th Stalin joined a group of revolutionaries, including Vera Shveitser, for the triumphant return to St. Petersburg, renamed Petrograd. They travelled on the Trans-Siberian express that arrived in the capital four days later. At many stations along the way crowds turned out to welcome the hundreds of revolutionaries hurrying back to Petrograd and Moscow. Each stop, of course, required speeches from the townsfolk and the exiles. Muranov replied to the greetings. There is no evidence that Stalin spoke publicly during the trip to Petrograd.[716]

Midway on the journey, the bolshevik exiles stopped at Perm (a city later called Molotov), from which a telegram was dispatched to Lenin in Switzerland: FRATERNAL GREETINGS. STARTING TODAY FOR PETROGRAD. [SIGNED] KAMENEV, MURANOV, STALIN."[717]

This telegram is not found in the official record for the apparent reason that in later years Stalin denied any link with Kamenev. At that time, however, it was important that Lenin be informed that he was no longer in Siberia. No doubt, he shrewdly sensed that speechmaking and celebrations had little to do with the revolutionary turn of events or the seizure of political power.

As the express train clattered toward Petrograd, Stalin took wry pleasure in the auspicious turn of events. Four years of the black night of his arctic exile had ended. And though he was not aware of it, his rise to power was on the horizon. Unsurprisingly, when he returned to Petrograd on March 12th, he went at once to the Alliluevs' place.[718] He wanted to see Nadezhda and was certain he would be welcome there after his trip from Achinsk. But he discovered they had moved. A bit later he located them. As he arrived, with his pipe characteristically in one side of his mouth, he was greeted heartily: "Stalin, Iosif! You've come back!" [719] Indeed he had. Stalin had come in from the Siberian cold to end his career as an elusive revolutionary.

14 | THE GLOOMY
REVOLUTIONARY

Nicholas II—the last Tsar of the Romanov dynasty, which had ruled Russia for three hundred years—abdicated his throne in March, 1917, thus climaxing the events leading to what is known as the February Revolution. The pathetic Emperor, confused and dominated by his neurotic German-born wife, was replaced by a Provisional Government headed by the liberal Prince Lvov as Prime Minister, Professor Paul Miliukov as Minister of Foreign Affairs, and Alexander Kerensky, whom Lenin called a "loudmouth" and an "idiot," as Minister of Justice.[720] For a brief moment, history had provided all the Russians with freedom, perhaps too much of it. But it lasted only a short time and was abruptly overshadowed by the bolshevik *coup d'état* eight months later in October. The 1917 February Revolution, following in the steps of its 1905 predecessor, surprised, stunned, and exhilarated most of the revolutionary organizations and personalities. It caught Lenin napping in Switzerland, Trotsky in the United States, and Stalin, astonished, in the sleepy little Siberian town of Achinsk, twenty-five hundred miles from metropolitan Russia. The "three who made a revolution" were hardly in any position to take immediate advantage of the rapidly changing events in insurrectionary Petrograd and Moscow. Lenin required several days to collect his wits before he sent to Russia his now famous "Letter from Afar" on March 7th, which scorned the Provisional Government as a gang of "plunderers bound hand and foot by Anglo-French imperialist capital."[721] Even with the help of the Germans, weeks passed before his triumphal arrival in Petrograd on April 3rd.[721a] Trotsky reached Russia six weeks later, on May 17th, from a Canadian internment camp.[722] But when Stalin returned to the capital on March 12th, well ahead of the others, his actions and statements almost at once revealed how far out of touch with reality and Lenin he had been.

Trotsky described Petrograd in March of 1917 as one vast meeting.[723] More than that, the capital was a city of confusion on the edge of chaos. Unfortunately, Russia under the Provisional Government (which Lenin later voluntarily pronounced "the freest country in the world")[724] had made a serious error by emasculating the Department of Police. Mistakenly, the governmental authorities had failed to comprehend that freedom and democracy could not flower in disorder. While the war continued to exact its ghastly toll, councils (Soviets) of workers and soldiers mushroomed in the major urban areas and at the front, food shortages drove housewives in Petrograd to riot, and widespread looting was abetted by the release of political prisoners, among whom were more than a few criminals, rogues, and anarchists. Some weeks later a well-intentioned artillery colonel, B. V. Nikitin,[725] was appointed to establish a security and counterintelligence force in the capital, but the job was impossible. For the moment, political parties and groups of all shadings met separately in the best—or worst—Russian tradition to debate, haggle, bicker, and scheme. One observer noted that all of them seemed to have mandates from "God knows where." [726]

Anna Allilueva remembered that when she first saw Stalin at the door of their residence after four years of exile, he seemed older, more pensive, and more mature. She noticed that he was dressed simply in a dark suit and a blue Russian blouse, and he was wearing felt boots unlike those he wore the last time she had seen him. He had lost weight, which she judged was a result of fatigue. His mustache was the same, but his face and eyes "were older—significantly older." Shifting his pipe to the side of his mouth, Stalin had asked first about Sergei. And where was Mama Olga, the boys Pavel and Fedya, and his main interest, Nadezhda? Pavel was a soldier at the front, Fedya had been delayed somewhere, and Nadya was at a music lesson, she replied. When the others returned home, Anna recalls that they all gathered around Stalin in the dining-room. His description of Siberian life and his narrative of the four-day trip to Petrograd held them spellbound. The coals of the samovar had long since turned to ashes when Stalin asked, "When will you get up tomorrow? I must be at the *Pravda* offices early in the morning." [727] Nonetheless Stalin, who quite properly considered himself not only a member of the Bolshevik Central Committee but also the senior party member in the city, spent much of that night talking with the fifteen-year-old Nadezhda (whom he was to marry two years later) before hastening on the morning of March 13th to the offices of *Pravda*.

There is some confusion in dates here, but probably only of passing importance. Stalin's *Collected Works* claims that he left Achinsk on Thursday, March 8th.[728] The rail trip to Petrograd required four days and he, together with Kamenev and Muranov, arrived at the earliest March 12th. At any rate, Stalin had only a few hours of sleep, if any, before he was on his way to the party newspaper. Four years of sullen contemplation had made him relish this moment. He had not forgotten how Lenin had criticized his management of the bolshevik organ in 1913. He found two bolshevik workers, Shliapnikov and Zalutsky, running the paper with a "college boy," as Trotsky deprecatingly described Vyacheslav Mikhailovich Skriabin, whom the world knows as Molotov.[729] These three had also constituted the entire Russian Bureau of the Party Central Committee until March 7th, when nine members were added.[730] On Monday, March 12th, a dozen or so members of the Bureau met "in connection with the return of party workers from exile and considered the question 'Concerning the New People . . .'" They unanimously voted membership for Muranov, who had returned with Stalin. Then the sticky question of Stalin reared its head. The record is explicit:

Concerning Stalin, it was submitted that he was a Central Committee agent in 1912 and that it would therefore be desirable to have him in the Bureau of the Central Committee, but in view of certain personal traits characteristic of him the Bureau of the Central Committee expressed itself in favor of asking him to attend in a consultative capacity.[731]

Stalin was further humiliated when a Presidium of five persons was elected: Muranov, Olminsky, Stasova, Shliapnikov, and Molotov. He was excluded.[732] In the same resolution the Bureau allowed Kamenev the privilege of writing for *Pravda,* but decided that he could sign no journalistic articles in light of his questionable statements at the trial of the bolshevik deputies in 1915 and elsewhere. However, most important, the Bureau had dealt Stalin a political and personal blow that, practically coinciding with his return from four years of dreary exile, stunned and angered him. Ten years earlier at London he had been an obscure "consultative delegate," but had he not progressed in the party hierarchy during a decade? Had Lenin been in touch with these persons and, if not, who had outrageously suggested that his "personal traits" closed the Bureau of the Central Committee to him?

Crises of such dimensions usually made Stalin bide his time, calculate the true enemy, and then strike when it was least expected. This time, however, his anger made him indiscreet. He hurried off to the offices of *Pravda,* where, using his credentials as a Central Committee member co-opted in 1912 by Lenin himself, he began to clean house.[733] Undoubtedly out of pique after having been so long in Siberia, he acted in a highhanded and unwarranted fashion. He brought into the *Pravda* offices a new staff, which was, of course, subservient to his direction. Trotsky declares, probably correctly, that Stalin was in a hurry to show that he was boss.[734] On March 13th *Pravda's* staff, as confirmed by the Bureau, was composed of Olminsky, Stalin, Kalinin, Eremeyev, and Maria Ulyanov, Lenin's sister. But Stalin's petit purge was complete when, two days later, Kamenev, Muranov, and Stalin were listed as editors and the names of the others had been omitted.[735] Excluding Maria Ulyanov was an open slap at Lenin. Two more days brought forth another Bureau resolution aimed at investigating the matter of the Stalin-Kamenev-Muranov takeover of *Pravda,* which had been done in spite of the Bureau's admonition to the contrary.[736]

From Switzerland on March 6th Lenin had telegraphed to Petrograd his ideas concerning the beggarly, contemptible Provisional Government. A week later Stalin attended a Bureau meeting where

Evgeniya Bosh, recently returned from abroad, relayed Lenin's personal feelings to the assembly. Lenin denied any possibility of unification with the mensheviks and reminded his followers that the Kerenskys, Miliukovs, and Chkheidzes, and their adherents were thoroughly untrustworthy.[737] However, the time factor here is most significant. Stalin, directing *Pravda,* favored precisely the opposite: the Provisional Government might be "pressured" to do this or that but he seemed to find it dependable. He was not opposed to burying the hatchet with the mensheviks, and, rather than stop the war at once by calling on the Russian troops to lay down their arms, he favored a vague, general appeal for peace. Kamenev agreed with him.[738] According to a Soviet study completed in 1963, it is clear that Stalin's and Kamenev's "mistakes" cannot be explained by "ignorance" of Lenin's attitudes.[739] Further, before Lenin's return to Petrograd, Stalin began his distortion of history. Lenin's letters that appeared in *Pravda* were being twisted or "edited out" to conform more or less with Stalin's views, which were radically opposed to the leader now on his way back from Switzerland through Germany in the celebrated sealed railway car.[740] Four days after he had arrived in Petrograd and just over two weeks after the Tsar had abdicated, Stalin in a cocksure mood had signed an article in *Pravda* that once again seemed to doom his political future. Far from censuring the Provisional Government, he had called for "land for the peasants, security of labor for the workers, and a democratic republic for all citizens of Russia." [741] His viewpoint might well have qualified him as a member of the Provisional Government, but it clashed head on with Lenin's "Letter from Afar." A democratic republic ran counter to everything Lenin had been preaching. It was an élite of Lenin's chosen few that would lead Russia to the promised land, not a democratic rabble that could not, and did not, know how disgracefully the nobility, landowners, and bourgeoisie were exploiting them, and indeed failed to see the marvellous vistas a Leninist society would reveal after the capitalists and their kind had been deposed.

Stalin—almost unwittingly, it appears—had gone so far as to congratulate the Provisional Government in a *Pravda* article of

March 25th. He applauded its decree abolishing restrictions on non-Russian nationalities and its decision to forbid discrimination against persons who were not members of the Russian Orthodox Church. Of course, the Jews among others would have thus bene-fitted. And he had called on the Provisional Government to grant all non-Russian nations the right of secession.[742] When Lenin heard about these heresies, he was furious; his usually dyspeptic stomach became more upset and his insomnia more pronounced. After his return to Petrograd he lost little time in condemning those who had suggested conciliation with the mensheviks, the social revolutionaries, and the Kadets (a nickname of the Russian Constitutional Democratic Party taken from the initials of the party name K. D.), and above all anyone who sought sanction for the Provisional Government. Although Lenin never named Stalin as one of the culprits, he clearly had him in mind when he declaimed in early April: "We don't want a parliamentary republic, we don't want a bourgeois democracy, we don't even want any government except the Soviet of Workers', Soldiers', and Peasants' Deputies!" This was also part of Lenin's celebrated "April Thesis," in which he called for the bolshevik wing of the Social Democratic Workers Party to be renamed the Communist Party.[743]

A tumultuous reception greeted Lenin upon his return to Finland Station in Petrograd the night of April 3rd. There was a band playing the "Marseillaise," a makeshift guard of honor, a bouquet for the leader, and a welcoming speech by Chkheidze. Stalin was not present, but Kamenev was. As soon as Lenin was ushered into the formal Imperial waiting room at Finland Station, F. F. Raskolnikov, who was later a soviet ambassador, overheard him sharply question Kamenev: "What have you people been writing in *Pravda*? We saw several issues and were very angry with you." "You people" could only have meant Stalin, as a recent soviet version of the incident reveals.[744] Perhaps Stalin had anticipated Lenin's criticism and this was the reason he had absented himself from greeting Lenin upon his arrival. By this time Lenin's popularity in Petrograd was rising rapidly.[745] This criticism on the heels of the Bureau's condemnation must have been disheartening to Stalin.

For several weeks after the beginning of April, however, little is known or heard about Stalin, although he was in Petrograd.[745a] Like one of the Siberian animals he had hunted in Kureika, he seems to have vanished into the most convenient place to nurse his political wounds and to wonder if his career had reached an ignominious conclusion.

He turned up in early July as a sort of emissary from the bolsheviks to the militant sailors of the Kronstadt Fortress, in the Baltic Sea near Petrograd. During the "July days," as they are known, Lenin and most of his followers became involved in an abortive imbroglio aimed at seizing power in Petrograd. Their failure scared some of them, Zinoviev and Stalin included, almost out of their wits. Stalin, on July 4th, had summoned the sailors on behalf of the party to a "peaceful demonstration" in the streets of Petrograd. As the story goes—it may be unauthentic—the sailors wondered if they should carry their rifles in the peaceful demonstration. Stalin's advice was "Rifles? Comrades, it's up to you. We writers always carry our weapons—our pencils—with us. As regards your weapons, you can judge for yourselves." [746] The peaceful demonstration —actually an armed one—turned into a fiasco. Neither the civilian populace nor the armed forces were ready for Lenin's brand of revolutionary anarchy—which was, above all, essentially unpatriotic. To the masses Mother Russia was at war and the *mystique* of her sacred soil meant much more than Lenin's propagandistic utterances calling on the army to lay down its arms and fraternize with the German enemy. Although Kerensky, now the Minister of War, had issued a declaration two months previously, on May 9th, that sanctioned all forms of political agitation in the armed forces[747] (anyone with even a slight knowledge of military matters will recognize how this tended toward destructiveness of the army), the Russian soldier, usually a *muzhik*, still remained fervently Russian and quite uninterested in the idea of a proletarian revolution as enunciated by Karl Marx—whoever he was and whatever that meant. Nonetheless, the "peaceful demonstration" quickly degenerated into an uncontrollable mob.

Not surprisingly, during the night of July 4th-July 5th troops supporting the Provisional Government broke into the *Pravda* offices and demolished the bolshevik printing presses.[748] Lenin went into hiding.[749] There is irony in all this. *Pravda,* now under Lenin's firm control was, by its title, *The Truth.* Here it was, lucidly enlightening the exploited residents of Petrograd and the soldiers and sailors, who ungratefully had destroyed its capacity to help them. Well, the bolsheviks decided, there must be a rational explanation. So it turned out that almost anyone—mensheviks, Kerensky, tsarist officers—was responsible, but not "the people," although it was precisely the soldiers and the workers who had begun to distrust Lenin and his party. By this time, the public disclosure of Lenin's affiliation with the Germans was not a helpful development.[750]

The Central Committee, distraught by recent events, dispatched Stalin to the Petrograd Soviet the day after *Pravda* was smashed. He probably would not have undertaken this mission on his own, for he knew in advance that he would be obliged to talk with either Chkheidze or Tsereteli, both of whom had long known of his treachery in Transcaucasia. As it turned out, Tsereteli, then the dominant personality in the Soviet, received him the evening of July 5th in the Tauride Palace. Years later he wrote, "I particularly remember the meeting at this time with Stalin." The Provisional Government had decided to move against the bolshevik leaders and occupy their headquarters, the Kshesinskaya mansion, which the bolsheviks had sequestered from the Tsar's ex-mistress. Stalin knew from reliable sources that government troops were going to occupy the mansion and he wanted assurance that the bolsheviks would not be molested, that there would be no bloodshed. Tsereteli calmly replied that it was correct that the government would take over the Kshesinskaya mansion but there would be no bloodshed. "Stalin gave me a puzzled look and departed," he recalled.[751] The bolsheviks never lacked brazenness. Having instigated an abortive uprising in defiance of what order remained in the city, they now demanded governmental protection.

Stalin, as already noted, was accustomed to going to the Alliluev apartment. Upon his arrival in Petrograd when he learned that they were about to move again, he had asked Anna to reserve a

room in the new apartment for him. "Don't forget," he had emphasized, "a room for me!" [752] Anna and Nadezhda, responding to a
newspaper advertisement, had located a "comfortable and light"
apartment on the sixth floor of a building at No. 10 Rozhdestvenskaya Street, and in it they kept a separate room for Stalin. Anna
reports that she paid cash for the rent in advance.[753] Curiously,
although the room was Stalin's quarters, Lenin was the first occu-
pant, hiding from unknown and practically ineffectual security police of the government. When he moved in, on July 6th, he found
Zinoviev and his wife already there, occupying a room other than
Stalin's.[754] Of course, inasmuch as Stalin had Zinoviev shot in the
great purges, there is no mention of this episode in the Stalinist
literature of the late thirties and forties. Zinoviev, who was in a
highly nervous condition, was convinced that he would be arrested
at any moment. His fears were groundless. The rather weak poli-
cies of the Provisional Government made it almost certain that few,
if any, revolutionaries would be put under lock and key. However,
on July 7th the government issued a warrant for Lenin's and Zinoviev's arrest.[755]

After Lenin had spent five days in the Alliluev apartment, a
meeting of the bolshevik minds decided that he should not risk
arrest. One story claims that Stalin shaved off Lenin's beard and
whatever hairs remained on his balding head.[756] At any rate, he
donned a wig that must have provided more than a few comic moments as it slipped and slid about on his bald pate. On July 11th
Stalin and Alliluev escorted Lenin and Zinoviev nine kilometers to
the suburban Primorsky Railway Station, and they began two
months of hiding on the property of Emelyanov, close to the village
of Sestroretsk.[757] Lenin lived in a cold and damp sort of barn during these days. But a steady stream of visitors beat a pathway to his
bucolic location.[758] Stupidly, Lenin believed that by taking himself
away from the center of political events he would be more secure.
Actually, his visitors unwittingly could have led the authorities—
what there were of them—to his hideaway and he would probably
have been equally safe at the Alliluevs' in Petrograd. Two of his
frequent callers, if we may believe later Soviet sources, were Stalin

and Felix Dzerzhinsky, the ascetic Pole who was to be the first head of the dreaded Cheka, the communist political police that Lenin would create a few months later.

But toward the end of July matters went from bad to worse for the Provisional Government. A wave of peasant disorders again swept Russia. There were frequent seizures of land and property by various elements of the population. The Russian Army, largely composed of peasant youth, increasingly refused orders to attack. Russian soldiers were understandably influenced by German front-line propaganda that others were seizing their rightful share of land back in the villages, and in the absence of requisite discipline they deserted in droves. In the midst of all this, the Sixth Congress of the Social Democrats (purportedly representing some 150,000 members—an inflated figure) met in Petrograd from July 26th to August 3rd. This was the only bolshevik party Congress that Lenin did not attend. Stalin attended, had a certain role in the proceedings, and behaved with subdued respectability.[758a] He defended Lenin against the widespreading charges of connections with the German enemy. He commented on the publication of documents about "Lenin's treason" (made public by Alexinsky and Pankratov in the newspaper *The Living Word*). "They were intended" Stalin claimed, "to provoke the anger of the soldiers against the Bolsheviks. Obviously they calculated on playing on the soldiers' mentality who were to be influenced more than anything else by the news that Lenin was a German spy." [759]

Stalin gave two reports at the Congress, according to Trotsky, who grudgingly acknowledged that he spoke. Although he had been doing some thinking and writing, Stalin's remarks were, as usual, undistinguished. For example, he revealed:

Some comrades have argued because capitalism is poorly developed in our country to pose the question of a socialist revolution is utopian. Had there been no war, no collapse, had not the very foundations of the national economy gone to pieces they would have been correct. But today these questions of intervention are posed in all countries as imperative questions. . . . Nowhere is there such freedom in time of war as in our country.[760]

Significantly, the day the Congress ended, Kamenev (the only major bolshevik arrested during July) was released from prison and was accused in the press of having been an Okhrana agent. Kamenev, apparently convinced of his innocence, called for a full-fledged inquiry of the charges. The Central Committee appointed Stalin, now the editor of the party organ, to investigate the matter! In early August Stalin's articles defended Kamenev; he wrote that "the reptilian hissing of the counter-revolution is again becoming louder. The disgusting serpent of reaction thrusts its poisonous form around the corner. It will strike and slither back into its dark lair. . . ." [761] It was, of course, Stalin who would strike when, during the thirties, he had Kamenev executed.

Only when Lenin moved away was Stalin able to occupy his own room at the Alliluevs'. Where he had been residing in the interim is unclear; perhaps he had been sleeping at various places. At least, now he could afford a room—if he cared to rent one. When the first plenum of the Central Committee met on July 24th-25th, it included Stalin. The conferees lost no time in voting a salary of five hundred rubles a month for married committee members and four hundred for those unmarried.[762] For the first time since March, 1901, more than sixteen years earlier, there is an identifiable and certain source of Stalin's income. That it was a small portion of the subsidy being provided the bolsheviks by the German government was perhaps unknown to Stalin.[763]

From July and the Sixth Party Conference until roughly October, 1917, another of those mysterious periods of Stalin's life sets in. Careful, though somewhat incomplete, records have survived of Central Committee meetings from July, 1917, through February of the next year. Stalin, now a member of the power élite—if it may be called that—of the Communist Party might reasonably have been expected to attend committee meetings. Yet he failed to attend six meetings during August, September, and part of October. True enough, he was present at another eighteen sessions, but he seems to have frequently appeared and then, suddenly and curiously, departed without having made any impression on the other participants. Trotsky points out that a history of the party published in 1924 (before Stalin was in a favorable position for censorship) failed to mention him during August and September and that his name "is not even in the index of approximately five hundred proper names. In other words, throughout those two months the press did not take cognizance of anything he did or of a single speech he made and not one of the more or less prominent participants in the events of those days mentioned his name even once." [764] Trotsky failed to cite V. I. Nevsky's great work, *The History of the Russian Communist Party* (*Bolshevik*), published in 1926. Its four hundred and sixty-two pages included two very brief comments on Stalin, both of which pertained to 1917.[765]

While Stalin was doing some writing and thinking, there must have been something or someone sufficiently absorbing to make him miss Central Committee meetings, to speak rarely when he did attend, and generally to be not only, as N. N. Sukhanov described him, a "gray blur" but also a gray shadow. Suddenly arriving late at a meeting, he would listen a bit, perhaps say a few words, and depart. The someone was undoubtedly Nadezhda (Nadya) Allilueva, the youngest daughter (she was barely fifteen) of Sergo, his acquaintance from the Caucasus.[766] Stalin considered himself at home with them, and indeed seems to have known no other real home in 1917; the Alliluevs *were* his family.

Sergei Iakovlevich Alliluev was born in 1866, one of five children, in a small village of Voronezh Province. When he was seven, his father died and thereafter his mother worked as a seamstress to support the family. With money always a problem, an uncle cared for the elder brother, a childless shoemaker adopted a younger brother, and Sergei lived with an aunt. After beginning school at twelve, he soon left because his mother was unable to pay the tuition. A church deacon and a land surveyor taught him to read and write. He worked in a variety and grocery store in a village on the river Don for three years and then served five years of apprenticeship in a railroad repair shop. He joined a marxist workers' circle in late 1892, while working at the Tiflis railroad yard. He moved to the small railroad station of Mikhailovo in 1896, where his efforts to organize a labor union failed. Then he and his family, ill with malaria, were obliged to move to Yekaterinoslav. In 1900, again working at the Tiflis railroad yard, he participated in the May Day celebration organized by Stalin. Arrests and prison terms followed his political agitation, but his ever-present problem was to earn enough money to support himself and his family, which consisted of his wife, Olga, two sons, and a daughter. In February, 1902, he was arrested because of his connection with the social-democratic group that had staged the May Day demonstration in Tiflis two years before. After serving time in solitary confinement in Metekh prison, he was released at the end of May. He then worked in a printing plant supplying a Tiflis illegal printing press, which, he later learned, was the famous Avlabar underground printing operation that Stalin presumably betrayed. As an inmate of Metekh in 1930, he witnessed the murder of Lado Ketskhoveli, Stalin's hero, by a prison guard. The Okhrana banished him from the Caucasus in 1904, and he travelled to Moscow, then to nearby Serpukhov, and back to Moscow, always searching for steady employment, always living from hand to mouth, without sufficient funds to care for his family. In the meantime Nadya had been born in Baku in September of 1902. Three days after "Bloody Sunday" the Okhrana rearrested him and banished him to Rostov-on-Don. The Okhrana arrested him in Baku after a demonstration on September 11, 1905, and sent him to Kars prison. In the summer of 1906 he was arrested in connection with the assassination of an Okhrana *provocateur*. Sentenced to exile in the North of European Russia, he began his trek in October to a small village near Archangel. For the next ten years he lived and worked under an assumed name. From 1907-17 he apparently continued his revolutionary activity without excessive police harassment. In 1912 he began collecting contributions for Siberian exiles. Food and clothing parcels purchased with these funds were packed and addressed by Alliluev's two daughters, Anna and Nadezhda. Stalin was one of the many recipients.

Now, in 1917, Sergei Alliluev was fifty-one and had known Koba for fourteen years. So it was quite natural that Stalin should lick his wounds at the Alliluevs'. As already stated, Anna's book describing all this and more about Stalin's life was taken out of circulation by the dictator himself a year after it appeared, in the immediate post-World War II period. It obviously revealed too much personalia that was inadmissible in the making of a legend. Anna recalled, for example, that her mother had purchased clothes to replace Stalin's threadbare ones. She reported that he was absorbed with reading Chekhov's and Gorky's works, and she uncritically noted his comings and goings at rather bohemian hours. Mama Olga fed him well, as she did Lenin. But Anna's account falls flat when she describes Lenin's concern about Stalin during his stay with them and Stalin's benevolent attitude toward Vladimir Ilich.[767] From the record we know that Lenin deplored Stalin's actions and statements in the weeks after the February Revolution. Stalin had already declared a silent and patient vendetta against the man who had embarrassed and humiliated him in open sessions of party conferences. In the Caucasian tradition this was not easily forgotten, much less forgiven. It was one thing to shave Lenin, visit him, and defend him for pragmatic reasons: it was something else to tolerate Lenin's personal slights. Thus Stalin's faulty political sense in advocating measures and praising the Provisional Government in opposition to Lenin, his erstwhile patron, may be explained not only by his anger but also by his opportunism.

Upon his return to Petrograd, Stalin had good reason to doubt that mere shouting would tumble the Provisional Government.[767a] Just as he had previously cast his lot with the Okhrana, which appeared at one time to be the wave of the future, he estimated that the Provisional Government was likely to survive. Lenin was in faraway Zurich trying to get out of "this damned Switzerland," and Stalin had little knowledge of the ease and alacrity with which he would return—with the help of the German government, which was still at war with Russia. It must have occurred to him that Lenin might not return at all or, if he did, would be too late to have an appreciable impact on affairs in Russia proper. Moreover, even if the Provisional Government was not wholly stable, political parties other than the bolsheviks had impressive organization and considerable popular appeal. And how many bolsheviks were there?

Only a handful among the Russian masses. The fact that Chkheidze, who had assessed Stalin's treachery fifteen years earlier in Batum, was now Chairman of the Petrograd Soviet appeared as a bad omen. At any rate, Stalin decided to take himself off to get his bearings. Courting Nadezhda Allilueva and living now and then at the apartment of her family, he was in a somber mood. As in the spring of 1917, he withdrew in the late summer of this year of Russia's history, seemingly ignoring it or allowing it to pass him by, as he had the 1905 revolution. Anna Allilueva had seen him striding to and fro late at night in his bedroom, puffing away on a pipe gone cold, apparently immersed in deep, personal thoughts.[768] Perhaps he was reviewing his life, which had reached a critical juncture. Nine year later, in 1926, under very different circumstances, he provided a summation of his life before 1917 in the form of a speech he delivered in reply to toasts and greetings at a meeting of railway workers in Tiflis. This was two years after Lenin's death. Even with the expansiveness induced by the vodka he customarily mixed with Georgian red wine, his remarks were noteworthy for bravado and distortion. He said:

Let me turn to the past.

I recall the year 1898, when I was first put in charge of a study circle of workers from the railway workshops. That was some twenty-eight years ago. I recall the days when in the home of Comrade Sturua, and in the presence of Dzhibladze (he was also one of my teachers at that time), Chodrishvili, Chkheidze, Bochorishvili, Ninua and other advanced workers of Tiflis, I received my first lesson in practical work. Compared with these comrades, I was then quite a young man. I may have been a little better-read than many of them were, but as a practical worker I was unquestionably a novice in those days. It was here, among these comrades, that I received my first baptism in the revolutionary struggle. It was here, among these comrades, that I became an apprentice in the art of revolution. As you see, my first teachers were Tiflis workers.

Permit me to tender them my sincere comradely thanks [Applause].

I recall, further, the years 1907-1909 when, by the will of the Party, I was transferred to work in Baku. Three years of revolutionary activity among the workers in the oil industry steeled me as a practical fighter and as one of the local practical leaders. Association with such advanced workers in Baku as Vatsek, Saratovets, Fioletov and others, on the one hand, and the storm of acute conflicts between the workers and the oil owners, on the other, first taught me what it means to lead large masses of workers. It was there, in Baku, that I thus received my second baptism in the revolutionary struggle. There I became a journeyman in the art of revolution.

Permit me to tender my sincere comradely thanks to my Baku teachers [Applause].

Lastly, I recall the year 1917, when, by the will of the Party, after my wanderings from one prison and place of exile to another, I was transferred to Leningrad. There, in the society of Russian workers, and in direct contact with Comrade Lenin, the great teacher of the proletarians of all countries, in the storm of mighty clashes between the proletariat and the bourgeoisie, in the conditions of the imperialist war, I first learnt what it means to be one of the leaders of the great Party of the working class. There, in the society of Russian workers— the liberators of oppressed peoples and the pioneers of the proletarian struggle of all countries and all peoples—I received my third baptism in the revolutionary struggle. There, in Russia, under Lenin's guidance, I became a master workman in the art of Revolution.

Permit me to tender my sincere comradely thanks to my Russian teachers and to bow my head in homage to the memory of my great teacher—Lenin [Applause].

From the rank of apprentice (Tiflis), to the rank of journeyman (Baku), and then to the rank of a master workman of our revolution (Leningrad)—such, comrades, was the school in which I passed my revolutionary apprenticeship.

Such, comrades, is the true picture of what I was and what I have become, if one is to speak without exaggeration and in all conscience [Applause rising to a stormy ovation] [769]

We have no other autobiographical sketch of the man before 1917 than these few paragraphs of half truths. If Hitler was the master of the big lie, Stalin was the expert of the half lie—a much more effective device, it seems. Stalin, of course, had been a busy student in the seminary during 1898 and no one put him "in charge" of a railway workers' study circle. Dzhibladze, as we know, was not one of his "teachers," although it is interesting that he emphasized this lie; rather, he was a suspicious antagonist. Nor did Chkheidze instruct Stalin in "practical work," except in the sense that he advised him to leave Batum—not Tiflis—after having severely criticized him for the senseless shedding of workers' blood. Furthermore, Stalin was not transferred to Baku in 1907-1909 "by the will of the Party." Under suspicion as an Okhrana agent, he had been forced, as we know, to leave both Tiflis and Batum. Baku was the one city in Transcaucasia where his double-dealing was sufficiently unknown to allow him a fresh start. Nor did the will of the Party transfer him to Leningrad in 1917. He returned of his own free will and was not at all welcomed by his bolshevik associates. Lenin deplored his tactics on *Pravda* and criticized him roundly when he arrived in Petrograd during April of 1917.

Whether he realized it or not, Stalin differed from men whose ambition—fired by a family, a wife or lover, or the sheer desire to excel—carried them to high political office and power. He was conspicuously silent about this matter after he became dictator and, indeed, throughout his life. His regard for his first-born son and his "dearly beloved" first wife seems to be underscored by his massive silence about them in later life. He failed to mention his second wife, Nadezhda Allilueva, or their children Vassily and Svetlana, during his years of power in Soviet Russia. Although it appears to have been generally accepted in Soviet circles that his third wife was Rosa Kaganovich, the sister of Politburo-member Lazar, not a word can be found in Stalin's utterances or writings about the wedding or his wife.[770] And Soviet literature is devoid of information concerning her. Unsubstantiated and lurid accounts of Stalin's sex life have, understandably, crept into literature about him. Amba, his professed former bodyguard, has insisted that a Siberian woman in his last exile bore him a son. Various bits and pieces of information have suggested that he was rarely without women friends or a mistress, though no one has precise data.

A person rising to the pinnacle of political power without the assistance of friends or loyal lieutenants is a rarity in history. Such associations, usually made during the youth of the future leader, emerge from those among his acquaintances who are trustworthy, reliable, and dedicated. As we know, during the first half of his life.

Stalin had few, if any, friends or comrades. Uratadze, a menshevik, had known Stalin for many years in Georgia. His appraisal of him is summed up in an incisive passage:

> He was unable to co-operate with anyone. He had to be alone. From among all [my] numerous acquaintances—he was the only one who had no comrade, not one friend. He made the rounds of our organizations and nowhere was he able to remain for more than a short time. There was not one organization in which his stay had not been concluded by a party trial. First it was in Tiflis, later in Batum, and towards the end—in Baku. I say "towards the end" because after Baku he disappeared from the Caucasus party horizon and moved to Russia. Such a person was unable, of course, to gather anyone around himself. Therefore he had no chance to become a leader in his own [bolshevik] faction.[771]

Iremashvili, despite his knowledge of Stalin's treacherous nature, seems to have liked him simply because they grew up together in Gori and Tiflis, but by 1917 even he was completely disenchanted with his onetime friend, whom he described as bitter, vituperative, and soulless. Grigory Konstantinovich ("Sergo") Ordzhonikidze, a fellow Georgian, might be considered a pre-revolutionary friend, but the story goes that he, too, was finally disillusioned. His unexpected and mysterious death in 1937, at the height of Stalin's purges, has been explained by his realization that Stalin was totally evil.[772] Was he aware of Koba's affiliation with the Okhrana? He tried unsuccessfully to save some of those condemned in the purges. Many Russians of communist persuasion have somehow become convinced that Stalin poisoned him.[773]

Someone has remarked that a man is known best by his enemies. True or not, an overwhelming majority of those who came in contact with Stalin in the pre-1917 revolutionary milieu found him far from likable. The normal distaste of one competitive politician for another because of pushiness or ambition eventually—often quickly—gave way to a feeling that Stalin was thoroughly untrustworthy and treacherous. The list of contemporary revolutionaries who distrusted him is, as we know, distinguished and long: Dzhibladze, who suspected him of being an Okhrana agent; Shaumyan, who believed Stalin betrayed him to the Okhrana; Zhordania, who thought him insufficiently knowledgeable about marxism to participate in the social-democratic movement; Chkheidze, who deplored his inciting of poor unarmed workers into direct conflict with armed cossacks; Martov, who had proof of his murderous brigandage; Arsenidze, who considered him uncouth and a potential Okhrana agent; Vereshchak, who witnessed his savage and inexplicable denunciations of fellow prisoners and heard about his betrayal of fellow students; Sverdlov, who found him insufferable in Siberian exile; and Trotsky, who remembered only his "evil yellow eyes" from their brief initial meeting in Vienna. Generally speaking, Stalin was disliked by almost everyone of any political complexion who knew him prior to 1917. Uncensored writings prove this. Lenin was impressed with him, and Kamo seems to have shared the feeling. Kamo was not too bright and his attitude is understandable; Lenin, on the other hand, made a grievous error.

Consequently Stalin received little support from persons who knew him in the revolutionary movement prior to 1917. Most of them considered him a Judas. His overconfident, insolent manner was far from endearing. They avoided him whenever possible or tried to circumvent his activities when he persisted in losing workers' lives and retarding the process of revolutionary reform. One of the mildest appraisals of the man came from Nikolai Nikolaevich Himmer, better known as Sukhanov, a keen observer and journalist, who participated in the 1917 events. He had commented:

This man was one of the central figures of the Bolshevik Party and perhaps one of the few individuals who held (and hold to this day) the fate of the revolution and of the State in their hands. Why this is so I shall not undertake to say; "influence" in these exalted and irresponsible spheres, remote from the people and alien to publicity, is so capricious. But at any rate Stalin's role is bound to be perplexing. The Bolshevik Party, in spite of the low level of its "officers' corps," had a whole series of most massive figures and able leaders among its "generals." Stalin, however, during his modest activity in the Ex. Com. [the Executive Committee of the Petrograd Soviet in 1917] produced —and not only on me—the impression of a gray blur, looming up now and then dimly, not leaving any trace. There is really nothing more to be said about him.[774]

However, the "gray blur" enjoyed an uncanny stroke of good luck when Lenin decided he would be useful to his personal aims. Like others who had occasion to work with Stalin, Lenin failed to size up the true nature of the man until it was too late. He seems to have been cool with him during their first meetings in 1905 and 1906. Only when Stalin offered to deliver badly needed money by way of robbery and brigandage did Lenin presumably take an interest in him. Stalin entered the bolshevik inner circle not because of his political ability, theoretical knowledge, popularity as a leader, or writing. Nor is there evidence suggesting that Lenin was anticipating Stalin as a possible lieutenant, let alone a political heir, in the period before 1917. Had Lenin's treasury not been at such a low point in 1907 when Stalin presented, in Berlin, the Okhrana idea of the Tiflis "ex," he would doubtless have remained an isolated revolutionary. Had Lenin not spoken out in his favor at the 1907 London Congress and later co-opted him as a member of the first Bolshevik Central Committee in 1912, Stalin in all probability would have stayed in the role of a provincial functionary. One could speculate endlessly on the theme of what might have been. However, any review of Stalin's life before 1917 must emphasize that without Lenin's open support he would have amounted to little in the bolshevik movement. Oddly enough, the causal relationship of the Okhrana with the author of the Tiflis holdup, on the one hand, and Lenin's patronage of Stalin on the other, provides one of history's striking ironies. The Okhrana plan was meant to discredit the bolsheviks. So it did for the time being, but Stalin, the bearer of the supposedly lucrative plan, had impressed Lenin, who later rewarded him with elevation into the higher echelons of the bolshevik hierarchy.

Precisely for the reason that Stalinism had resulted from Lenin's pre-1917 approbation of him, de-Stalinization had to be stopped at a point where clinical examination would not reveal the damaging connection. If Lenin and Leninism were to remain the bedrock on which the Soviet system rested, then too much grubbing around in Stalin's pre-1917 life would conclusively lead to at least one unpleasant and devastating truth: Stalin and the Okhrana had duped the presumably infallible Lenin, and it was Lenin, therefore, who by his patronage bore the ultimate responsibility for the hideous excesses of the Stalinist period. Thus when Khrushchev's "secret speech" revealed Stalin's crimes and included Lenin's "last testament," in which Lenin proposed to get rid of Stalin, it went no further backward in time than 1924.[775] Not one word did Khrushchev utter about Stalin's pre-1917 life, nor has the commission that he insisted was to be established to examine Stalin's life issued a sentence of its findings. It will not do so until there is a radical change in the Soviet system which, of course, would mean a change of government. Stalin was a political creature of Lenin and the Okhrana.

In a letter to Maxim Gorky written from Cracow in 1913 Lenin had called Stalin a "wonderful Georgian." Lenin's word "wonderful," is one of the few favorable adjectives describing Stalin in the entire body of pre-1917 literature and correspondence. Incredibly enough, all statements or writings about Stalin in his early years point to his negative characteristics, and after the revolution only those persons under his control (with the understandable exception of his mother) spoke or wrote favorably about him during his first thirty-seven years. Others were uniformly critical, probably not from jealousy but from justifiable anger.

A treacherous nature combined with a high degree of native intelligence enabled him to become adept at deception. Even in childhood his will to power and his desire to be king of the hill was sullen, withdrawn, and vindictive. Although he later referred to himself more than once as an Oriental, he was a child of Western civilization.[775a] But in relation to both East and West he was totally amoral. Without loyalty to his most devoted companions, he was capable of betrayal—indeed murder—of friends and comrades. He never hesitated to waste the blood of good and honest workers simply to stir the revolutionary kettle. Bloodshed, as we have seen, pleased him.

There was no discernible benevolence in Stalin's character.[775b] His anti-Semitism, his deprecation of the peasantry, his disdain for intellectuals, his hatred of writers who failed to deify him—one could go on and on—indicate his incapacity to rule a great nation humanely. On his deathbed in 1924, Lenin belatedly recognized what should have been apparent to him long before 1917; namely, that Stalin was evil. Nonetheless, many statesmen, scholars, and, for that matter, associates of Stalin refused to recognize his unscrupulous nature even when they were face to face with him. It is painful to read in retrospect the opinion of the American Ambassador to Moscow (1937-38) Joseph E. Davies that Stalin's "brown eye is exceedingly kindly and gentle. A child would like to sit in his lap and a dog would sidle up to him. If you can picture a personality that is exactly opposite to what the most rabid anti-Stalinist anywhere could conceive, then you might picture this man." [776] Stalin was able to impress Churchill with his apparent grasp of military matters though Churchill did not like him; to impress Roosevelt, who thought he could "do business" with him; to impress Truman, who thought "Uncle Joe" was a prisoner of his own Politburo; and many others. Here we see Stalin's tremendous ability at dissimulation at work. He had frequently used the ability before 1917; indeed one of the reasons he was able to attain a position of political power was his remarkable ability to act, to play a given role necessary at a given time. In this connection we must recall how he "acted" as the leader of strikes and demonstrations, how he seemed to be faithful to Lenin, although the Okhrana owned his soul all the while.

"Certain personal traits" had initially kept Stalin from full membership in the Bolshevik Central Committee Bureau. This devastating blow to Stalin's political hopes had served to make his personal outlook even more depressing. He had hurried back to Petrograd, his fortunes low, with his morale buoyed up only by the knowledge that he had a position on the steering group of Lenin's organization. Now his past had shattered his future, and he reverted to the sullenness of his Siberian exile, when he had been rejected by both the Okhrana and the bolsheviks, knowing not where to turn. Those personal traits had apparently been closely considered by his bolshevik comrades. They had recognized his contempt for society, his hatred of authority, and his treacherous nature, marked by betrayal of friends and acquaintances, his cruelty, his instinct to bully and gain power for its own sake, his compulsion to control and dominate. In this respect, they realized, he had become a sort of Nechayev in reverse, with a complete lack of normative values induced, perhaps, by his religious training and his revulsion of it. They had observed his inability to make friends. His fantastic machine-like memory, his bravado, his deep and curious killer instinct, his joy at witnessing the flow of blood, and his lust for power and the wiles and craftiness to obtain it. The Petrograd bolsheviks of 1917 displayed more good sense in opposing Stalin than did Lenin or later statesmen. No revolutionary comrade came forward to endorse him. Having considered everything, it appeared to the Petrograd bolsheviks that it was better to keep Stalin outside their inner revolutionary organization. They wanted none of his treachery and they rejected his proved instinct for betrayal that often resulted in mayhem or murder. In their opinion, Stalin had excluded himself from their revolutionary enterprise.

15 | CHAOS BREEDS A COMMISSAR

October, 1917 holds a special and hallowed place in communist history. On a cold, misty, and rainy Wednesday, the twenty-fifth of that month, in Petrograd, there occurred the fabled replacement by the bolsheviks of the faltering Provisional Government. To communists, October is now imbued with a magic that conjures up the nobility of ideas and breadth of vistas that the revolution seems to represent. Like the fog from the Gulf of Finland that often rolls over the city of Peter the Great, the world has been enveloped in an overcast of Soviet propaganda that culminated, on October 25th, in the bolshevik revolution and seizure of power by Lenin. However, a successful revolution needs someone or some kind of authority against which to revolt, and a seizure of governmental influence means that a measure of identifiable power is somewhere in the vicinity to be taken over. Neither of these conditions can be discerned in the October events even though the bolsheviks have tried mightily to present the events as violent, evoking great heroism, and demanding detailed, decisive planning combined with the incomparable leadership of the general of the revolution, Lenin.

While October 25th and the preceding weeks comprise one of the most important periods in modern political history, there is little of a romantic nature about it, regardless of the spate of Soviet movies, books, paintings, and poems depicting it as a time in which justice and right overcame, against tremendous odds, the evil forces of reaction. For Petrograd in September and October was not the vast meeting Trotsky had earlier described, but one of real anarchy. The tens of thousands of criminals who had been released from the city's jails in February by the Provisional Government

would have represented an enormous problem to a municipal government with a normal or effective police force.[777] However, the
Petrograd Okhrana and Gendarme Administration had been abolished on February 27th.[778] Thenceforth, as Colonel Nikitin, a regular army officer and later head of a sometime security force in the
capital, put it, when the Provisional Government did away with the
forces of law and order, everyone who had worked for the police
"tried to forget his service." Former policemen were in virtual
hiding.[779]

Writing twenty-one years after the 1917 events, Colonel Nikitin
commented that "the March [February] Revolution had not only
totally destroyed the political police, but it had likewise wrecked
the machinery of state for protecting the public from the activities
of criminals, who are pursued and punished in every civilized
land." Although he was not particularly opposed to the Provisional
Government, he bitterly lamented:

> I leave it to the followers of Maxim Gorky to sing the praises of
> these "Heroes of the Revolution," tens of thousands of whom, released
> from the gaols of Petrograd, formed the vanguard of countless hordes
> who came from the convict prisons and penal settlements of Siberia
> and other places of banishment. All over Russia the whole of the old
> criminal fraternity were liberated and swelled the ranks of the scum
> of the population which boiled over in the tragic upheaval caused by
> the First Revolution. . . . It contributed far more to the subsequent
> issue than is generally realized.[780]

But history is not obliged to depend on the harassed Colonel
Nikitin for an appreciation of Petrograd in the days before October. The twentieth century seems to abound with bright young men
who observe, or participate in, the more monumental occurrences
of the century. So it was with this period. John Reed, Harvard-
educated, left-wing, in ill health, and confused, was on the spot. He
was a journalist with a keen eye for detail and mood. His descrip-
tive passages are noteworthy for their vividness in his *Ten Days That
Shook the World,* published in 1919. Reed, disillusioned by the
bolsheviks after he returned to Russia in 1919, died of typhus and
now reposes under the Kremlin Wall beside "Big Bill" Haywood

and a few other Americans. However, Lenin regarded Reed's book as one of the best on the October days (he wrote a short foreword to it), and he ordered a state funeral for the author.[781] Stalin suppressed the book, probably because Reed mentioned him only twice, and it reappeared in Soviet Russia only after Stalin's death in 1953. Reed writes (using the historical present tense):

> In the factories the committee rooms are filled with stacks of rifles, couriers came and went. . . . In all the barracks meetings every night, and all day long interminable hot arguments. On the streets the crowds thickened toward gloomy evening, pouring in slow voluble tides up and down the Nevsky [Petrograd's main thoroughfare] fighting for the newspapers. . . . Holdups increased to such an extent that it was dangerous to walk down side streets. . . . On the Sadovaya [another main street] one afternoon I saw a crowd of several hundred people beat and trample to death a soldier caught stealing. . . . Mysterious individuals circulated around the shivering women who waited in queue long cold hours for bread and milk, whispering the Jews had cornered the food supply—and while the people starved the Soviet members lived luxuriously. . . .
>
> Gambling clubs functioned hectically from dusk to dawn, with champagne flowing and stakes of twenty thousand rubles. In the center of the city at night prostitutes in jewels and expensive furs walked up and down, crowded the cafés.[782]

Petrograd was literally without government, and there was a mood of fear mixed with a devil-may-care attitude among its populace in autumn's depressing weather.

No one really knew what was going on in the capital or, for that matter, abroad. Of course, fighting continued on the Western Front, the Germans exerted great pressure against the demoralized Russian troops in the East, and the remaining effective military formations in Petrograd were fearful of joining the "death" battalions at the front, angry at Prime Minister Kerensky, or confused by the many different centers, or pockets, of propagandists attempting to disingregate further, if possible, the military units that remained under a modicum of discipline. Deserters from the front openly sold their sidearms and heavier weapons to German agents who, in turn, placed them in the hands of rebels, malcontents, thieves, bona-fide revolutionaries, or virtually anyone who could be expected to foment trouble, thus hastening Russia's disintegration and, it was hoped, withdrawal from World War I. Money, such as it was (there were at least three kinds of Provisional Government currency in circulation), had little value. Foreign currency was preferred in commerce.[783] Food and fuel were in short supply. Above all, a feeling of insecurity, a terrifying uncertainty of what the next hour or day would bring, gripped the inhabitants of the noble city.

In this grotesque setting the Provisional Government was headed by the volatile thirty-five-year-old Prime Minister Kerensky. Inexperienced, doctrinaire in a left-wing sort of way, he was, however, honest. In this respect he was quite different from a great majority of the bolsheviks, and especially Stalin. Some military-school cadets and formations of fierce cossacks were supposedly ready to restore order, and other units of equal unreliability were armed but at the moment docile in their barracks or drunk on the streets. The troops and the government were in no way effective. Kerensky was contemplating a boat trip down the Volga. The situation could not have been more confused. Under the menacing skies of Petrograd, shortly to be in the throes of winter, a virtually nonexistent government was about to be finished off by its own apathy.

In early September, after weeks of rumors that officers and troops were moving into Petrograd to restore order, General Lavr Kornilov, an ambitious Siberian cossack who was Supreme Commander of all Russian ground forces, made a decision to crush the Soviets and the bolsheviks "not later than the morning of September 1." [784] His effort failed ignominiously and, in an action typical of those mad days, Kerensky personally arrested Kornilov, whom he had earlier appointed to his post. But the wretched and bungled effort served to frighten and rally left-wing parties and groups, who were apprehensive that someone might succeed in ending the disorder that racked Petrograd which, they clearly saw, might result in firing squads for some socialist leaders. Thus bolsheviks, mensheviks, and social revolutionaries who had been at dagger points now entered into an uneasy alliance.[785] It remained for Lenin, still in hiding, to provide a formula brilliant in its slickness. "We will fight with Kornilov," Lenin wrote, "but will not support Kerensky." [786]

Stalin characteristically remained in the shadows during this period and continued editing or working on the editorial board of *Rabochy* [*The Worker*], the bolshevik central press organ. It is difficult to determine the extent of his editing and writing. Many of the editorials found in his *Collected Works* are unsigned. Nonetheless, his familiar liturgical cadence easily identifies an editorial in *Rabochy* No. 5, of August 28th, entitled "The Conspiracy Continues." Thus:

> *It is a fact* that General Headquarters are the headquarters of the counter-revolution.
> *It is a fact* that the general staff of the counter-revolution consists of "certain public men. . . ."
> *It is a fact* that the plot has been organized and is being directed by "representatives of the Kadet Party." [787]

He proceeds to imply that Kornilov and the Germans were working hand in glove, that their collaboration, if successful, would doom the Russian Revolution. In an interesting forewarning of things to come he concludes, ". . . You don't confer with enemies, you fight them." [788] During the following nine days he claims to have written three short editorials, all unsigned. Then from September 6th to October 24th, on the eve of the revolution, his official account includes twenty-five articles or editorials he wrote for *Rabochy Put* (*Workers Way*).[789] He signed only four, using "K. St.," "K. Stalin," or simply "K." The remaining twenty-one, largely editorials, are suspect. Altogether these take up some hundred and thirty pages of the *Collected Works* and are brief, usually from one to two hundred words. Most of them are definitely not of his manifest style, and the only possible conclusion is that someone, whom Stalin in later years denied recognition, authored them. Many sound suspiciously like Lenin's or Trotsky's or Kamenev's prose. Perhaps Stalin was receiving manuscripts and, as an "editor," running them as his own work after changing the punctuation.

However, he was intermittently appearing at the newspaper offices at Kalvalergardskaya Street, No. 40,[790] during September and October, and at least we know his whereabouts during a portion of this two-month period. (The main party newspaper or party propaganda organ had three names from August through October: *Proletary, Rabochy,* and *Rabochy Put.*) Lenin indirectly confirmed this when, on September 30th, he complained that the "central organ," of which Stalin was the editor, had ignored his disenchantment with party tactics. He wrote that he detected a "hint of gagging me"—of forcing him into retirement. Lenin's threat to resign from the Central Committee because of his conviction that if the party "let the present moment pass, we shall ruin the revolution" came to naught.[791] Earlier, on September 12th, Lenin had written that inasmuch as the bolsheviks were gaining substantial majorities in the Petrograd and Moscow Soviets, action was of the essence. "History will not forgive us if we do not assume power now," he declared.[792]

The Central Committee reaction to this recommendation, or call for action, was far from enthusiastic. It was thought that "the old man" might be out of his senses.[793] Assume power with what? It seemed an appropriate question. Kamenev and Zinoviev were adamantly opposed to the Lenin proposition, and when someone suggested that Lenin's letter be destroyed by burning, only two votes out of sixteen (there were six abstentions) made it mandatory that one copy be retained for party files.[794] We do not know how Stalin voted on this subject. When Lenin discerned that Kamenev and Zinoviev were opposed to his idea of imminent seizure of power, he demanded that they be expelled from the party. Stalin protested that "expulsion from the party is not a cure. . . ." However, Stalin's *Collected Works* includes this spurious item:

> September 15—At a meeting of the Central Committee of the Party, J. V. Stalin opposes Kamenev's demand that V. I. Lenin's letters, "The Bolsheviks Must Assume Power" and "Marxism and Insurrection," should be burned, and recommends that they should be circulated for discussion among the bigger party organization.[795]

As we have had reason to learn, Stalin was no fool. He fully recognized from the fact of Petrograd's chaos that Kamenev made more sense than Lenin at this moment. Stalin could well have reckoned that there was no need for the bolsheviks to assume power at once: a few more weeks of the disorder would give it to the disciplined bolsheviks with little effort. He was thus in favor of "evolutionary revolution." [796] Since Stalin did not have Lenin's broad and strategic concept and probably did not know about Lenin's connections with the Germans, he judged that the bolsheviks could scarcely afford to begin expelling members of the party.

In the meantime, most of the various political parties and groups in Petrograd had decided to convoke a "pre-parliament" in advance of a Constituent Assembly. There was little the party could do to ameliorate the plight of the worker, who had witnessed since 1914 an increase in food prices of 566 per cent, 51 per cent above his wages.[797] However, the pre-parliament idea enraged Lenin. Dutifully Stalin's *Collected Works* echoes Lenin's idea with an entry:

> September 21—At a meeting of the Bolshevik group at the Democratic Conference, J. V. Stalin insists on the observance of V. I. Lenin's directive to boycott the Pre-parliament.[798]

October 25th, the celebrated date of the bolshevik coup, was only a month away. Almost all the old and famous bolsheviks—or, for that matter, the old mensheviks, social revolutionaries, kadets, and members of other political parties—recalled their whereabouts and activities in later years or someone remembered for them. John Reed, for example, describes the harsh voice of the menshevik Martov as he participated in debates and discussions; portrays Chkheidze as the "old eagle"; notes Tsereteli, who "poured out beautiful eloquence for a lost cause;" and regards Trotsky and others as rushing hither and yon, exhorting workers, organizing and participating in party activities and, in general, plunging full strength into the chaos—attempting to bring forth something in the bolshevik favor.[799] Their activities were not without chroniclers, but all the torrent of literature about October and the previous weeks before Stalin's rise to power, there are only a few brief remarks about him. For example, N. N. Sukhanov in his detailed, eyewitness account of this period mentions Stalin only a few times. But about Trotsky he wrote:

Trotsky, tearing himself away from work, personally rushed from the Obukhovsky plant to the Trubochny, from the Putilov to the Baltic works, from the riding school to the barracks; he seemed to be speaking at all points simultaneously. His influence, both among the masses and on the staff, was overwhelming. He was the central figure of those days and the principal hero of this remarkable page of history.[799a]

Undoubtedly, Stalin was out on the streets witnessing or participating in the wild celebrations of Petrograd. His salary of four hundred rubles a month was sufficient for a bit of recreation and squiring Nadezhda about. (As a matter of fact, the Bolshevik Central Committee members had voted themselves a remuneration about twice that of Petrograd's master craftsmen. It was at this point that the origins of the "new class" might have been recognized.) His journalistic work occupied some of his time, and his thinking even more. But there is a void in these two months that even his official account is unable to fill. For example, the *Collected Works* indicate that on September 28th Stalin delivered a speech on the "Democratic Conference at a meeting of bolsheviks of the Vasilyevsky-Ostriov district." (The Democratic Conference had been convened by the Central Executive Committee of the Soviets in Petrograd. It was a coalition of left wing organizations that met from September 1st to 9th.) On the following day the official record claims, "The party Central Committee decided to publish a list of candidates to the constituent assembly. J. V. Stalin was nominated for the Petrograd, Yekaterinoslav, Transcaucasian and Stavropol electoral areas." [800] Then on October 5th, at a meeting of the Central Committee and upon his motion, a conference of members of the Central Committee and Petrograd and Moscow party functionaries was, according to the record, called to take place at the time of the Congress of the Soviets of the Northern Region.[801] On October 8th he supposedly discussed preparations for an armed uprising with Lenin, who by that time had secretly returned from Finland to Petrograd. On October 10th he and Lenin presumably attended a meeting of the Party Central Committee, where Lenin's resolution on armed insurrection was approved and a seven-man political bureau of the Central Committee headed by Lenin and Stalin was set up to direct the uprising.[802] (Regardless of the truth of the latter statement Stalin, it should be noted, was made a member of the original politburo that was abolished by Khrushchev and reinstituted in 1966 by Brezhnev.)

The *Collected Works* states that in those days immediately preceding the bolshevik *coup d'état* he headed "a Party Center . . . elected to direct the uprising." [803] Trotsky, the real organizer of whatever insurrection took place during the October days, exposed the "party center" as he wrote:

That at the October 16 conference of the Central Committee with the leading Petrograd party organizers it was decided to organize a "military revolutionary center of five Central Committee members." "This center," states the resolution hastily written by Lenin in a corner of the hall, "will become a part of the revolutionary soviet committee." Thus, in the direct sense of a decision "the center" was not designed for independent leadership of the insurrection but to complement the Soviet staff. However, like many improvisations of those feverish days this idea was fated never to be realized. During the very hours in my absence the Central Committee was organizing a new center on a piece of paper, the Petrograd Soviet, under my chairmanship, definitely launched the military revolutionary committee, which from the moment of its origin was in complete charge of all the preparations for the insurrection. Sverdlov, whose name appeared first (and not Stalin's name as is falsely recorded in recent Soviet publications) on a list of the "center" members, worked before and after the resolution of October 16 in close contact with the chairman of the military revolutionary committee. Three other members of the center, Uritsky, Dzerzhinsky and Bubnov, were drawn into work for the military revolutionary committee each of them individually, as late as October 24 as if the resolution of October 16 had never been passed. As for Stalin, in line with his entire policy of behavior at that period, he stubbornly kept from joining either the executive committee of the Petrograd Soviet or the military revolutionary committee and did not appear at any of its sessions. All of the circumstances are easily established upon the basis of officially published protocols.[804]

So much for the "party center." Trotsky points out, somewhat inaccurately, "The biographer, no matter how willing, can have nothing to say about Stalin's participation in the October Revolution. Nowhere does one find mention of his name—neither in documents nor the numerous memoirs." [805] Trotsky was unnecessarily bitter: it would have been more correct to recognize simply that of all those bolsheviks who were later to achieve prominence, Stalin's role in the pre-October events was the least important and most unknown. We do know that he attended some Central Committee meetings and that he did talk with Lenin now and then during September and October. But indeed it was Trotsky and Sverdlov—most of all Trotsky—whose Bureau of the Military Revolutionary Committee provided the leadership, the planning, and the required military muscle (very little was needed) to replace the Provisional Government with the bolshevik cabal under Lenin. Even the mild-mannered Sverdlov, who would later become Soviet chief of state, played a more active role in the October days than did Stalin, who later arrogated to himself many of Sverdlov's accomplishments of this period.

Astonishingly enough, Stalin in his later life was unable to create a credible legend for the days before October. From the month of July, when he moved in to occupy Lenin's room (or to reoccupy his own room), he was a lodger at the Alliluevs', Rozhdestvenskaya Street No. 10, not far from Smolny, a former school for aristocratic girls that had been converted into bolshevik headquarters. Although we know from Anna's observations that his hours were irregular, this might easily be explained by his attendance at meetings or his work at the offices of the party newspaper. However, we also know that he was not noted for his attendance at the never-ending conferences, and his writing during September and October was not prolific.

In the absence of definite information, a reconstruction of his life in the days and weeks before October must be based on his past behavior patterns and must include what he would logically have wanted to do in disorderly Petrograd. At the top of the list of his desires, perhaps, was that of courting the teen-aged Nadezhda Allilueva. Stalin married her in March, 1919. It is not too much to imagine that she felt honored to be escorted by Stalin—who was almost thirty-eight years old—from one proletarian gathering to another. Sergo Alliluev, always a good family man, must have insisted that Stalin get Nadya home at an early hour, certainly before dark, when looting and lawlessness ruled the streets. Darkness descends in late afternoon during October in Petrograd and this left little time for daylight courtship. Nadya was in school weekdays. But Stalin undoubtedly whiled away a goodly portion of the hours of darkness in the comfortable Alliluev apartment, enjoying the food prepared by Mama Olga, who constantly complained that Stalin was too thin. As a Caucasian woman, she could be depended upon to discourage and ultimately forbid any premarital activity beyond mere hand-holding, even though Stalin's room was adjacent to that of Nadya and her sister Anna.[806]

After night settled in Petrograd, Stalin on the streets was as good prey for the cutthroat gangs as any bourgeois or aristocrat unless he had managed to ingratiate himself with certain criminal elements, as he had previously done in Tiflis, Batum, and Baku. Was he looting and stealing? Was he drinking with the influential few of the thousands of criminals who frequented all-night establishments? It is not untoward to ask these questions, because Stalin was perfectly capable, as his past record reveals, of indulging in these activities.

From what we know of his past it may be surmised that Stalin's life during this period included activities in the area of secret operations. If true, Stalin found himself in the midst of potential recruits for conspiratorial matters. The criminals released from the Petrograd jails were still at large, their ranks swelled by others from all over Russia. He had previously consorted with underworld characters in the Caucasus and Siberia.

Stalin was certainly not an orator, and scarcely talented as a writer, but his aptitude at expropriation and intelligence are a matter of record before and after 1917. In this catastrophic year we find no examples, publicly acknowledged, of his conspiratorial actions. Yet we do know that, even though he was in opposition to Lenin during this period on at least three occasions, Lenin sufficiently valued his services to place him on the first politburo of the party and make him a member of the first bolshevik government in much the same manner as he had allegedly co-opted him into the first bolsheviik central committee five years earlier at the Prague conference and ten years earlier sponsored him at the London Congress of 1907.

Thus Lenin must have recognized Stalin's great usefulness. But, in what way? Certainly not in the field of marxist theory and evidently not in military insurrectionary planning or tactics. However, as early as 1906 Stalin had exclaimed to Arsenidze in Tiflis, "Yes, if it is necessary, we will be the gendarmes of the revolution." As Stalin understood the term "gendarmes of the revolution," it included not only law enforcement personnel but also, and more important, conspiratorial and clandestine operations in which the Okhrana had been engaged. If Stalin had gathered about himself a group of hoodlums or fellow-conspirators from among party sympathizers who were possibly engaged in robbery, but who also functioned as an embryonic clandestine intelligence service throughout Petrograd, Stalin's value to Lenin assumes a quite different, more significant, dimension. We may not conclude that these persons, Stalin's operatives, were of monumental importance to the revolution, but they might have been extremely important in Lenin's view. Having been appropriately bribed, Stalin's low level agents might have reported on the mood of the city, the attitudes and loyalty of military formations, and, most significant to Lenin, the process of his own indictment of treason for collusion with the Germans. Kerensky and Krasin, together with the German social democrat, Edward Bernstein and the French minister of munitions, Albert Thomas, revealed Lenin's "treachery." Lenin, who had been involved in complex dealings with the Germans, may have wanted to know just how much information the Provisional Government had accumulated for his forthcoming trial. Stalin's *petit* intelligence service might have tried to penetrate the Department of Justice on Lenin's behalf.

We know that Lenin had dispatched Karl Radek on just such a mission to Germany about this time. In any event, the possibility that Stalin was in some way working for Lenin in the area of clandestine operations is more credible than the mere acceptance of the blank period in Stalin's official *Collected Works,* or in adopting Trotsky's bitter accusation that Stalin did nothing in the October days. Two points are clear: Stalin, a doer, was involved in something other than his newspaper work (which might have been a blind for his other activities), his squiring about of Nadya, and his attendance at party meetings. Lenin was aware of this activity, whatever it was. He was not a political philanthropist; his placing of Stalin on the original politburo and the later appointment of him as a member of the first bolshevik government was based on services Stalin rendered to Lenin's objectives at that time. Any other explanation would seem to fall outside the well developed behavioral patterns of both Stalin and Lenin. Although most former Okhrana officers and men were in hiding and had managed to flee the country, or were in prison, it is probably not farfetched to imagine Stalin trying to get in touch with his old superiors in the Department of Police. Did his days include a search for those persons who had invaded Department of Police Headquarters and destroyed many of the Okhrana files? [807] Was he quietly seeking through underworld acquaintances the whereabouts of those Okhrana personalities who had knowledge of his past police connections? Stalin's taciturnity raises these questions to which, unfortunately, there are no readily available answers. Boswell reminds us, "If a man could say nothing against a character but what he can prove, history could not be written." Certainly such endeavors would have suited Stalin's character and personality.

In Petrograd, with two weeks remaining before the twenty-fifth of October, the Party Central Committee convened under odd circumstances on the evening of October 10th. The meeting took place in the apartment of N. N. Sukhanov, the outstanding chronicler of those days. That he was not present is unfortunate for history but understandable in view of his political differences with his tubercular wife: he was not a party member and she was a devoted follower of Lenin. Sukhanov was working far across the city on Maxim Gorky's newspaper, *New Life.* As winter drew closer, there were fewer hours of daylight and unreliable transportation facilities made travel not at all easy within the metropolis; Mrs. Sukhanov seized on the bad weather and the uncertainty of the trolleys to suggest that her husband spend the night at the offices of *New Life*. When he agreed, she made her apartment available to Lenin and the Bolshevik Central Committee. Sukhanov, who abhorred any kind of violent action, slept in his office on a makeshift bed while in his own home the bolsheviks gathered to plot armed uprising.[808] He wrote about this episode:

> Oh, the novel jokes of the merry Muse of History! This supreme and decisive session took place in my own home, still at Karpovka. But—without my knowledge. As before, I would very often spend the night somewhere near the office or Smolny—that is, about eight versts [about five miles] from the Karpovka. This time special steps were taken to have me spend the night away from home: at least my wife knew my intentions exactly and gave me a piece of friendly, distinterested advice—not to inconvenience myself by a further journey after work. In any case the lofty assemblage had a complete guarantee against my arrival.
>
> For such a cardinal session not only did people come from Moscow, but the Lord of Hosts himself, with his henchmen, crept out of the underground. Lenin appeared in a wig, but without his beard. Zinoviev appeared with a beard, but without his shock of hair. The meeting went on for about ten hours, until about 3 o'clock in the morning. Half the exalted guests had to sleep somehow in the Karpovka.[809]

How and by what means Lenin notified the Central Committee members to assemble on this day remains unclear. He was not very successful, because only ten of the twenty-two members appeared. Besides Lenin, there were in attendance Bubnov, Dzerzhinsky, Kamenev, Mme. Kollontai, Sokolnikov, Sverdlov, Trotsky, Uritsky, Zinoviev, and Stalin. Hovering in the background was Galina Flakherman Sukhanov, silently and respectfully providing tea, cookies, and sandwiches to the bolsheviks who had secretly made their way to the meeting. For some of them it had been an arduous trip, and as misty evening became pitch-black night and night grew into the sunless morning, they napped to ease their fatigue.

A group of eleven would decide Russia's fate that night. There were many interesting characters among them, but none more fascinating than Alexandra Mikhailovna Kollontai, the only female committee member present. At this time she was forty-five but still one of those remarkably striking women whose good looks seem to improve with age. Daughter of a tsarist general, she had rebelled in her youth against the old order and had become a bolshevik agitator. Although she had briefly rejected bolshevism and Lenin, she had returned to the fold in 1915 after residence in the United States, when she had militantly crusaded for pacifism. As a novelist, she was a pioneer in favoring free love. Before her death in 1952 she served in a number of diplomatic posts, most notably as Soviet envoy in Sweden. Even before 1917 she had been a subject of gossip among the bolsheviks.[810] One of the few encounters Trotsky had with Stalin in 1917 concerned Alexandra. He wrote that when he arrived in Petrograd he scarcely remembered Stalin's name. "I probably ran across it in the bolshevik press," he recalled later, "signed to articles which hardly held my attention." However, he clearly remembered:

After the Revolution the first session of the Bolshevik Government took place in Smolny, in Lenin's office, where an unpainted wooden partition segregated the cubbyhole of the telephone girl and the typist. Stalin and I were the first to arrive. From behind the partition we heard the thick basso of Dybenko. He was speaking by telephone with Finland, and the conversation had a rather tender character. The twenty-nine-year-old black-bearded sailor, a jolly and self-confident giant, had recently become intimate with Alexandra Kollontai, a woman of aristocratic antecedents who knew a half dozen foreign languages and was approaching her forty-sixth year. In certain circles of the Party, there was undoubtedly a good deal of gossip about this. Stalin, with whom until then I had not carried on a personal conversation, came up to me with a kind of unexpected jauntiness and, pointing with his shoulder toward the partition, said, smirking: "That's he with Kollontai, with Kollontai!" His gestures and his laughter seemed to me out of place and unendurably vulgar, especially on that occasion and in that place. I don't remember whether I simply said nothing, turning my eyes away, or answered drily, "That's their affair." But Stalin sensed that he had made a mistake. His face changed, and in his yellow eyes appeared the same glint of animosity that I had noticed in Vienna. From that time on, he never again attempted to engage me in conversation on personal themes.[811]

Of the others present at the meeting of the Central Committee, the reader is acquainted with the Pole, Felix Dzerzhinsky, soon to become the first chief of Lenin's secret political police, the Cheka. Both Trotsky and Sverdlov are well known. Kamenev (John Reed described him as "a little man with reddish pointed-beard and Gallic gestures) had been in exile with Stalin, as had Zinoviev.[812] Andrei Sergeyevich Bubnov, a revolutionary since 1900 and always a supporter of Lenin, had worked on *Pravda*. (He was purged by Stalin in the nineteen-thirties.) Grigory Yakovlevich Sokolnikov (Brilliant) was ten years younger than Stalin; well-educated with a doctoral degree in law and economics, he had suffered imprisonment and exile, had been with Lenin in Paris, and had returned with him in the sealed train across Germany to Russia. Moisei Solomonovich Uritsky, six years older than Stalin, had been exiled to Siberia and, as a friend and supporter of Trotsky, had joined the bolsheviks only in July of 1917. He was an important member of the Military Revolutionary Council who figured in the October days. Afterward Lenin appointed him head of the Petrograd Cheka. A member of the Social Revolutionary Party assassinated him, in August of 1918.

These were the persons who met their leader, Lenin, still wearing his wig, which, though it was slipping this way and that, remained atop his head. Lenin of course was subject to arrest on the basis of a warrant issued by the Provisional Government. Stalin's deeply irrational anti-Semitism must have been aroused as he realized that Jews constituted a large part of the membership of the meeting. Furthermore, the brainpower and intellectual prowess was largely theirs: Trotsky, Kamenev, Zinoviev, Sverdlov, Sokolnikov and Uritsky were providing an important contribution to the bolshevik push for power.[813] Stalin was directly responsible for the deaths of five of them.

Electric lights were turned off at darkness in Petrograd because of the target they presumably offered German zeppelins. Candles (kerosene was hard to come by) dimly lit the stuffy apartment, its windows calked, as Stalin, puffing his pipe, listened to Lenin in one of his uncompromising moods. "The old man" violently advanced the false and absurd argument that France, England and Russia were about to arrange a separate peace with Germany; therefore an immediate armed uprising in Petrograd was absolutely essential.[814] Debate was long and heated. The thirteen persons attending, besides Mrs. Sukhanov (there were two alternates), took turns munching sausage sandwiches and dozing off. Uritsky, Kamenev and Zinoviev had serious reservations about armed uprising.[815] As far as can be determined, Stalin said nothing. Anna Allilueva writes that during the days before October he "often spoke about the remarkable, simple people of Petrograd. . . . He had seen in them marks of humane courage, simplicity, modest heroism." He said, "With such people you can do everything." [816]

Nonetheless, silly as it may then have appeared (toward the small hours of the morning Lenin insisted that the Provisional Government was about to deliver Petrograd to the Germans), a resolution was adopted—Stalin concurring, with only Kamenev and Zinoviev in opposition—that called for an armed uprising:

> The Central Comittee recognizes that both the international position of the Russian Revolution (mutiny in the fleet in Germany as an extreme manifestation of the growth all over Europe of the world socialist revolution, then the menace of a separate peace between the imperialists with the object of strangling the Revolution in Russia) and the military situation (the unquestionable decision of the Russian bourgeoisie and of Kerensky and Comany to surrender Peter [Petrograd] to the Germans), and the gaining of a majority by the proletarian party in the Soviets—all this, taken in connection with the peasant uprising and with the turn of popular confidence toward our Party (elections in Moscow), finally, the clear preparation of a second Kornilov affair (removal of troops from Peter, bringing up of Cossacks to Peter, surrounding of Minsk by Cossacks, etc.)—all this places armed insurrection on the order of the day.
>
> So, recognizing that armed insurrection is inevitable and that the time is quite ripe for it, the Central Committee proposes to all Party organizations to be guided by this and from this standpoint to consider and solve all practical problems (the Congress of Soviets of the Northern Region, the withdrawal of troops from Peter, the demonstrations of the Moscow and Minsk people, etc.).[817]

Barbara Yakoleva, an alternate or candidate member of the

Central Committee, had acted as secretary to the proceedings. She provides a comic touch to their ending as she describes Lenin, heavily bespectacled and wearing his wig, groping about for the exit of the apartment and slinking back in the darkness to his hiding place. He had accomplished his purpose. Some of the conferees stayed to sleep. We do not know if Stalin remained or risked the dangerous, although not lengthy, trip back to his room at the Alliluevs'.

Before the committee members had dispersed, Dzerzhinsky proposed that a bureau be established to guide the insurrection which as of that moment Lenin considered imperative. His proposal was accepted and the bureau members, seven in all, were Lenin, Kamenev, Zinoviev, Trotsky, Stalin, Sokolnikov and Bubnov.[818] But, as Trotsky has pointed out, "This important decision led nowhere. . . ."[819] With Lenin and Zinoviev in hiding and fearful of imminent arrest and with Kamenev and Zinoviev in implacable opposition to the resolution passed in the long night at Sukhanov's apartment, the "bureau" disappeared into oblivion before it began to function.[820]

Nearly another week went by with no mention of Stalin's whereabouts or activities. His *Collected Works* claims that his article "The Counter-Revolution Is Mobilizing—Prepare To Resist!" appeared in *The Workers' Way,* No. 32, on October 10th and that his "A Study in Brazenness" and "Blacklegs of the Revolution" appeared in the same paper on October 15th.[821] These two editorials and one article, less than ten pages in total length, add up to a few hundred words. On October 16th we have an unusual agreement of Stalin's records and other literature. As we have seen, Lenin had tried to read Kamenev and Zinoviev out of the party for their refusal to endorse his call for an immediate armed uprising. Other Central Committee members had also wavered, unsure of Lenin's idea. History would prove the correctness of Lenin's idea, but for the moment he was obliged to whip his disciples into line.

Accordingly he convoked another meeting of the Central Committee, the city committee, and other labor unions to take place the evening of October 16th.[822] By this time conditions in Russia had become incredibly chaotic. The number of deserters from the army ran into the hundreds of thousands. More and more peasants fired the homes on the estates and beat their owners to death. In the capital, food was growing scarce and fuel to warm houses for the fast-approaching winter was practically nonexistent. Sukhanov reported, "Disorders were taking on absolutely unendurable, really menacing proportions in Russia. Anarchy was really getting under way. The city and the countryside were both in revolt. The first was demanding bread, the second land." [823] The meeting convened by Lenin was attended by only twenty-five persons, among whom was Stalin, in the offices of Kalinin, the municipal head, a sort of deputy mayor, of the Lesnoi district of Vyborg, the most militantly Red part of Petrograd's suburbs.[823a]

This meeting seems to have had a sort of *Götterdämmerung* quality. Lenin was determined to follow the pathway of armed uprising: he orated loudly in competition with a deafening downpour of rain swept in from the Gulf of Finland, and he expounded in his belief that the "masses have expressed their confidence in the Bolsheviks." They had done no such thing. An experienced old bolshevik with many years in conspiratorial matters, Shliapnikov, chief of the metalworkers' union, reminded the meeting that his union was not at all in favor of a bolshevik uprising.[824] Another factory committeeman, Skrypnik, confirmed this.[825] Lenin's finely honed political and historical instinct told him that the Provisional Government might just pull out of this, given a bit of time. If he were to win, it would have to be soon. Trotsky later acknowledged that this viewpoint was the only valid one, given the circumstances at that time.[826]

Stalin's *Collected Works* states that on October 16th, "V. I. Lenin and J. V. Stalin direct an enlarged meeting of the Central Committee of the Bolshevik Party. J. V. Stalin sharply criticizes the speeches of the traitors Kamenev and Zinoviev on the question of armed insurrection . . ." Indeed, Stalin spoke at this meeting but Lenin's hand-picked delegates heard something quite different from a criticism of the two doubting Thomases. The minutes of the meeting reveal that Stalin was concerned not with the "traitors" but with "expediency."

> The date for the insurrection must be chosen with expediency. The revolution may only be understood in this sense.
> They maintain that we must wait for the government to attack, but we must be clear what an attack means. The raising of the price of bread, the dispatch of Cossacks to the Don Basin . . . this already means an attack. How long do we wait in the absence of an armed attack? Objectively, what Kamenev and Zinoviev are proposing would enable the counter-revolution to prepare and organize its forces. We would be retreating endlessly and we would lose the revolution. Why should we not ensure for ourselves the possibility of choosing the date of the uprising and the conditions, thus depriving the counter-revolution of the possibility of organizing.[827]

The glorious revolution was now a little more than a week away.

Nothing is known of Stalin's whereabouts for the next four days. Even his *Collected Works,* usually good for some sort of padded alibi, picks up his traces only on October 20th as it proclaims, "At a meeting of the Party Central Committee, J. V. Stalin proposes that V. I. Lenin's letters on Kamenev's and Zinoviev's blackleg actions be discussed at a plenary meeting of the Central Committee. J. V. Stalin takes part in the first meeting of the Revolutionary Military Committee of the Petrograd Soviet . . . [and] at a meeting of Petrograd trade union representatives in the Smolny . . . speaks on the preparations for armed insurrection." Here Stalin tried unsuccessfully to perpetrate a great piece of fiction. At this session he did not, as his official autobiography suggests, support Lenin. According to Trotsky, he defended Kamenev and Zinoviev and decided to submit his resignation from the editorial board of the party newspaper.[828] All this was bluster, but significant nonetheless: Kamenev returned to the Central Committee before October 25th and Stalin did not resign his "editorial" responsibilities. Stalin would have us believe that on October 21st the Party Central Committee appointed "him and Dzerzhinsky to the Executive Committee of the Petrograd Soviet in order to strenghen the influence of the Bolsheviks in it. It adopts Stalin's proposal that reports and theses should be prepared for the Second All-Russian Congress of Soviets. . . . Stalin and Sverdlov are appointed to direct the Bolshevik group at the Congress." [829] Stalin did attend this meeting, but nothing happened. According to Trotsky's description, "At this session . . . it was decided to put ten more prominent Bolsheviks, among them Stalin, onto the Executive Committee of the Petrograd Soviet for the purpose of improving its activity. But that was just another resolution that remained on paper." [830]

The following day, Sunday, had been proclaimed "The Day of the Petrograd Soviet." Petrograd was again a city of meetings. However, at the last minute the authorities cancelled a solemn "Procession of the Cross" by the cossacks, since the Provisional Government did not want to exacerbate the situation. The following day (Monday, the 23rd), Trotsky—in his best rhetorical and histrionic form—went to the dreary ancient Peter and Paul Fortress. By means of his forceful arguments the soldiers and sailors were converted, at least for the time being, to the bolshevik cause: the Provisional Government was from this moment practically without military resources in and around Petrograd.[831]

Kerensky and his Ministers finally realized that Russia was faced with disaster and that an unparalleled crisis confronted freedom. Early the next day, Tuesday, with the minutes ticking away in the final hours of the Provisional Government, the Cabinet again decided to shut down the bolshevik newspapers and arrest the party leaders.[832] Their action was pathetically tardy. In a sort of tragicomedy troops were summoned to Petrograd and proved to be thoroughly ineffectual. At about six o'clock in the morning of October 24th a detachment of military cadets invaded the party's printing presses, smashed their typesettings and confiscated over eight thousand copies of the newspaper.[833] Had there been anyone with military sense in the Kerensky entourage, he would have observed that the confiscation of newspapers was unimportant compared to the investing of bolshevik headquarters at defenseless Smolny. Ruefully aware of their weak position, the bolsheviks managed belatedly to gather a pitiful collection of small-caliber artillery, armored cars, and machine guns, most of which were in unusable condition, to protect their place of power and political headquarters.[834] Both sides agreed later that a determined and disciplined battalion could have overwhelmed Smolny and nipped Lenin's *coup d'état* in the bud.

It was now Tuesday, October 24th, the eve of the day when the course of human events would be irrevocably fixed by a small group of open conspirators. John Reed recalled that "a chill damp wind came from the west, and the cold mud underfoot soaked through my shoes. . . . Yunkers [military cadets] passed swinging up the Morskaya, tramping stiffly in their long coats and singing an old time crashing chorus, such as soldiers used to sing under the Tsar. . . . Along the sidewalk a row of deserters in uniform sold cigarettes and sunflower seeds." [835]

That night Kerensky, belatedly deciding to use force, called upon the 1st, 4th, and 14th Don Cossack Regiments: "In the name of freedom, honor, and the glory of the fatherland, come to the aid of the Central Executive Committee, the revolutionary democracy, and the Provisional Government." Because he incorrectly considered the cossacks loyal to the Provisional Government, Kerensky was now astonished to learn that they would go into action against the bolsheviks only under certain conditions: they required a written order from the commander-in-chief, which Kerensky immediately signed and dispatched by courier; they wanted infantry support which, although unavailable, Kerensky promised; they wanted a guarantee that if they moved into action their sacrifices would not "be in vain as in July, when the Bolsheviks were captured, and then released without punishment." Kerensky gave them his word. Frenzied telephone calls throughout the night to the quarters of the cossacks produced only the information that they were about to saddle their horses, were saddling them, or had saddled them. But the Cossacks failed to move.[836]

If there is one constant and identifiable thread running through Stalin's pre-revolutionary life, it is his curious absence from places at which important events took place. He had walked all night around the streets of Tiflis on March 21-22, 1901, while the

Okhrana arrested the Georgian social-democratic leaders and raided his quarters in the observatory; he had evaded the post-May Day arrests in the same city in 1901 (according to Iremashvili, the Okhrana could not locate him); he had been absent from Tiflis at the time of the Okhrana raid on Avlabar; and he had absented himself from the scene of the 1907 Tiflis Erevan Square robbery. His absence from the proceedings of the Central Committee on October 24th, however, is the most incredible one. That body had convened on Tuesday morning, and Kamenev's proposal at the very beginning that "no member of the Central Committee may absent himself from Smolny today without special dispensation" was immediately adopted.[837] Certain committee members were assigned to oversee various elements in the fast-moving situation. Trotsky's assertion is incontestable: he wrote, "Most amazing of all is the fact that Stalin was not even present at this decisive session. Central Committee members obliged themselves not to leave Smolny. But Stalin did not even show up in the first place. This is irrefutably attested to by the protocols published in 1929. Stalin never explained his absence, either orally or in writing. No one made any issue of it, probably in order not to provoke unnecessary trouble. All the most important decisions on conducting the insurrection were made without Stalin, without even the slightest indirect participation by him." [838]

Stalin was nowhere to be found. Although his official account states otherwise: ("In the evening V. I. Lenin arrives at Smolny. J. V. Stalin informs him of the political developments"),[839] the records prove that Stalin was elsewhere. If true, this statement lends support to the theory that Stalin had been engaged in clandestine intelligence-gathering on behalf of Lenin, but no one has even suggested what he was doing on this fateful date. Perhaps he felt that Lenin would fail in his attempt to assume power, or perhaps he was simply waiting, as Trotsky suggests, so that if something went wrong he could absolve himself of all blame. Only Anna Allilueva remembers him on the eve of the revolution.[840] Perhaps this is another reason Stalin found her recollections so unpleasant and banned them.

"I remember," she writes, "how he arrived home on the eve of the great day. . . . All of us were at home.

" 'Iosif!,' we welcomed him. Mama scurried about to feed him. Over a glass of tea, Stalin discussed with Sergei what had happened in the city, calmly explaining that everything was in bolshevik hands, that they would seize power." [841] The details of this dialogue may well be apocryphal but what matters is Anna's assurance that Stalin was at the Alliluev apartment "on the eve of the great day," as she put it. To a member of a bolshevik family, that momentous evening was as unforgettable as Pearl Harbor or D-Day later were to a citizen of the United States. No one forgot his associates of that night. Thus Stalin absented himself from Smolny and all the frenetic activity going on in preparation for the next day's uprising.[842] Anna has nothing more to say about him on October 24th.

There was no dawn and no sunlight on Wednesday, October 25th. It was a typical autumn day in Petrograd—damp, cold, dark, thoroughly unpleasant. Lenin had sneaked into Smolny during the night disguised under a facial bandage and his wig.[843] He was afraid that his forces would lose their nerve, but when he arrived, he found that orders for the revolution had already been issued.[844] During the morning the Ministers of the Provisional Government remained at their desks protected by a few military cadets and members of the women's battalions.[845] The so-called attack on the Winter Palace was a farce, with the bolshevik detachments gradually convincing the youngsters that resistance was futile. The women's battalions went docilely to other quarters, some claiming they had been raped. Throughout the early morning hours, forces loyal to Lenin and the bolsheviks assumed control of the central communication and financial centers.

Kerensky now faced a desperate situation. In a car flying the American flag, borrowed from Secretary Whitehouse of the American Legation, he made off to obtain troops to quell the insurrection[846] but, too late, he failed to stop the October events. Kerensky, young and vain, had underestimated the infinite damage that a conspiratorial minority can do to a great nation state. The operations against the Winter Palace, begun at approximately 9 P.M., were crowned with success the morning of October 26th. At 11 P.M. on October 25th, however, the Second All-Russian Congress of the Soviets opened in Smolny while the Winter Palace remained under an almost make-believe state of siege.[847]

"The massive façade of Smolny blazed with lights as we drove up," John Reed wrote, "and from every street converged upon it streams of hurrying shapes dim in the gloom." [848] Inside Lenin was writing innumerable memorandums and dictating orders and instructions. So intense had he become that he threatened to court-martial and shoot Podvoisky, one of the major figures of October. Podvoisky later recalled that moment as one when he realized there was a dictatorship. By then it was too late.[849]

Lenin prematurely announced the fall of the Provisional Government at ten o'clock the morning of October 25th.[850] In the meantime there was desultory firing from the Peter and Paul Fortress and from warships in the Neva River. Some shots were blank cartridges. Such was the great bolshevik revolution. Five sailors and one soldier lost their lives in the bolshevik takeover of Petrograd, the capital of a sixth of the land surface of the globe. True enough, a civil war was soon to engulf Russia and claim millions of dead and wounded, but for the moment Lenin had come to power over the bodies of six dead and a few wounded militants.

Until the early morning of October 26th, Stalin was still unaccounted for in the "faint unearthly pallor stealing over the silent streets, dimming the watch-fires, the shadow of a terrible dawn grey-rising over Russia. . . ." [851] Anna Allilueva recalled that it was "already known the majority of the delegates to the [2nd] congress would be Bolsheviks." She was at Smolny that evening mingling with the "workers and peasants." She learned that the Congress was to be an "open" one and she was determined to obtain a permit for Nadya and then run home and bring her to witness the proceedings.[852]

Nadya was alone in the apartment when Anna arrived. They left almost at once, walking along the trolley tracks because there were no street lights and the darkness was complete. Fog and rain made their trip back to Smolny more difficult. En route the rain turned into mushy snow. Finally, they found themselves in the hall and saw Stalin enter surrounded by his comrades. He stopped and looked at the girls. "Ah, there you are," he said. "It's good that you came! Have you heard? We have just now taken the Winter Palace! . . ." [853] It had fallen at 2 A.M. on October 26th.[854]

After he became dictator of Soviet Russia, Stalin wrote falsely in his *Collected Works:* "October 24-25—V. I. Lenin and J. V. Stalin direct the armed uprising." [855] Whatever armed uprising there had been was of Trotsky's doing. We have little knowledge of Stalin's activities during October 24th and 25th, but we know Lenin was not directing an armed uprising—nor was Stalin. As a matter of fact it was neither "armed" nor an "uprising." Lenin later said it was "easier than lifting a feather" to assume power. However, Stalin gave the lie to his own claim that he and Lenin directed an armed uprising in 1917. On the first anniversary of the October days, in 1918, he wrote that "all the work of practical organization of the insurrection was conducted under the direct leadership of the President of the Petrograd Soviet, Comrade Trotsky. It may be said with certainty that the swift passing of the garrison to the side of the Soviet and the bold execution of the work of the Military Revolutionary Committee, the Party owes principally and above all to Comrade Trotsky. Comrades Antonov and Podvoisky were Comrade Trotsky's chief assistants." [856]

"Extraordinary historical circumstances invested his ambition with a sweep startling even to himself," Trotsky wrote about Stalin. "In one way he remained invariably consistent: regardless of all other considerations, he used each concrete situation to entrench his own position at the expense of his comrades—step by step, stone by stone, patiently, without passion, but also without mercy! It is in the uninterrupted weaving of intrigues, in the cautious doling out of truth and falsehood, in the organic rhythm of his falsifications that Stalin is best reflected as a human personality and as the leader of the new privileged stratum, which, by and large, has to concoct fresh biographies for itself." [857] However, this day Stalin had no need to concoct a role for himself.

John Reed described Lenin, now in his element:

A short, stocky figure, with a big head set down in his shoulders, bald and bulging. Little eyes, a snubbish nose, wide generous mouth and heavy chin; cleanshaven now, but already beginning to bristle with the well known beard of his past and future. Dressed in shabby clothes, his trousers much too long for him.[858]

In the early hours of October 27th, he announced through Kamenev (returned to the fold) that Russia had a new government, completely bolshevik. There were to be fifteen Cabinet members. Lenin had decided the term "Minister" was too suggestive of tsarism; thus the title "Commissar" was adopted. The fifteenth Commissar, Kamenev intoned at 2:30 A.M., was Commissar for Nationalities I. V. Dzhugashvili.[859]

Stalin had finally arrived; he was now a member of the government, however ephemeral, of Russia. From Gori to Petrograd had been a long, tortuous journey for him, through a maze of Okhrana and party functionaries, fending off both police and comrades. The road had often seemed creviced and impassable. He had outguessed the Department of Police, had enchanted Lenin, and now found himself named as a Commissar in the capital. In his youth, a pious mother and the monks in the religious schools he had attended had explained to him that all good things came from God and tsar. He had never believed that, and now he had proof it was absurd. The proof had come from the appalling disorder in the city of Peter. Neither God nor tsar but chaos and crime had bred a Commissar.

After he became dictator of Soviet Russia, however, Stalin would kill off the majority of the old bolsheviks, and others who had tirelessly worked for revolution and a classless society; he would establish a rigid two-caste system in which there were only the new class of communist exploiters and the masses they exploited. He would establish a new autocracy with himself as its head that would be vastly more ruthless and heartless than that of the Romanovs. He would use Russian nationalistic fervor, and even the Russian Orthodox Church, in waging war. He would create a monstrous intelligence-security-conspiratorial service that would murder and terrorize not only in Russia, but throughout the world. The Siberian exile system during his years of power would have been the envy of the old Okhrana. Basically he would restore an unholy and terribly cruel tsarism in Russia, and thus it may be said that within two decades the Okhrana had won the fight against the revolutionaries after all. There was merely a new tsar.

SOURCES AND NOTES

1. BACKGROUND AND EARLY LIFE

1. "Georgia," *The Encyclopedia Britannica*, 1911, vol. XI, pp. 758-761.
2. G. I. Uratadze, *Obrazovanie i konsolidatsiya Gruzinskoi Demokraticheskoi Respubliki* (Munich: Institute for the Study of the USSR, 1956).
3. D. M. Lang, *The Last Years of the Georgian Monarchy, 1658-1832* (New York: Columbia University Press, 1957).
4. P. P. Nadezhdin, *Kavkazsky krai, priroda i liudi* (Tula: Tip. V. N. Sokolova, 1901).
5. Aleksandr Kazbegi, "Otseubiytsa," *Izbrannoe* (Tbilisi: Zaria Vostoka, 1948), vol. I.
6. *Entsiklopedichesky slovar* (S.-Peterburg: Brokgauz i Efron, 1893), vol. IX, pp. 224-5, has a description of Gori; its population was 7,247.
7. *Spisok No. 1 lits, podlezhashchikh rozysku po delam politicheskim*, issued by the Ministry of Internal Affairs, Department of Police, Special Section, dated May 1, 1904. On file at The Hoover Institution.
8. H. R. Knickerbocker, "Stalin Mystery Man Even to His Mother," *New York Evening Post*, Dec. 1, 1930, p. 2. *Pravda* (October 27, 1935, p. 3) published an interview by a Tass correspondent with Stalin's mother on October 22, 1935, concerning his visit to Georgia five days before. Her rambling account included the information that she was about seventy-five years of age; she expressed concern about Stalin's graying hair, and said he had assured her that he was feeling well. She had inquired about her grandchildren she loved so much—Svetlana, Yasha, and Vaso—and Stalin had passed on to her Svetlana's request for some walnut preserves. On this occasion she stated that she had had *two* other sons who had died early. She said that though she had sent Stalin to school, her husband Vissarion took him out to teach him the cobbler's trade; she succeeded in bringing Soso back to school, where he was the best student.
9. Vladimir Kaminsky and Ivan Vereshchagin, "Detstvo i iunost vozhdia," *Molodaya gvardiya*, 1939, no. 12, pp. 22-101.
10. The American journalist, Margaret Bourke-White, visited Didi-Lilo in the 1930's and discovered scores of persons named Dzhugashvili. The speculation that Stalin was born there was demolished by Keke Dzhugashvili when she declared to H. R. Knickerbocker in 1930: "I want you to correct one thing. They talk a lot about Soso's [Stalin's] being born in [Didi] Lilo, but that's entirely wrong. Lilo

was only the place where his grandfather was born. Soso was born in Gori. I could show you the place. I know he was born there. I'm his mother and I ought to know." See H. R. Knickerbocker, *op. cit.*

11. Josef Iremashvili, *Stalin und die Tragödie Georgiens* (Berlin: Volks-blatt-Druckerei, 1932), p. 11.

12. Eugene Lyons, *Stalin: Czar of all the Russias* (Philadelphia: J. B. Lip-pincott Co., 1940), p. 27. Stalin's mother died in 1937 at the age of seventy-eight.

13. V. Kaminsky and I. Vereshchagin, *op. cit.*, p. 25. Also see J. Iremash-vili, *op. cit.*, p. 8.

14. Stalin publicly mentioned his childhood and parents only once in his seventy-four years. Long after his rise to power—in December, 1931 —he gave an interview to Emil Ludwig, who asked questions of Stalin that had apparently been appropriately checked beforehand with the leader. The dialogue as published in Stalin's *Collected Works* is revealing:

> Ludwig: "What impelled you to become an oppositionist? Was it perhaps bad treatment by your parents?"
> Stalin: "No. My parents were uneducated, but they did not treat me badly by any means . . ."

See Iosif Vissarionovich Stalin, *Sochineniya* (Moscow: Gospolitizdat, 1951), vol. XIII, p. 113. Also see Emil Ludwig, *Stalin* (New York: G. P. Putnam, 1942), p. 19.

15. TASS interview with Stalin's mother in *Pravda*, October 27, 1935, p. 3.

16. V. Kaminsky and I. Vereshchagin, *op. cit.*, pp. 28, 36-7.

17. *Ibid.*, pp. 30-3.

18. J. Iremashvili, *op. cit.*, p. 5.

19. Jerome Davis, "Josef Stalin—Russia's Ruler Today," *Current History*, vol. XXIX (March 1929), p. 961.

20. V. Kaminsky and I. Vereshchagin, *op. cit.*, p. 34.

21. *Ibid.*

22. *Ibid.*

23. *Ibid.*, p. 35.

24. *Ibid.*, pp. 35-6.

25. *Ibid.*, p. 38.

26. *Ibid.*

27. Dorimedont Gogokhiya, "Na vsiu zhizn zapomnilis eti dni," *Rasskazy starykh rabochikh o velikom vozhde* (Tbilisi: Zaria Vostoka, 1937), pp. 7-8.

28. J. Iremashvili, *op. cit.*, p. 18.

29. V. Kaminsky and I. Vereshchagin, *op. cit.*, p. 53.

30. *Ibid.*, p. 42.

31. Emelyan Yaroslavsky, *Landmarks in the Life of Stalin* (Moscow: Foreign Languages Publishing House, 1940).

32. J. Iremashvili, *op. cit.*, p. 8 ff.

33. V. Kaminsky and I. Vereshchagin, *op. cit.*, p. 43.

34. T. H. Rigby., ed., *Stalin* (Englewood Cliffs, N.J.: Prentice Hall, 1966), p. 8.

35. V. Kaminsky and I. Vereshchagin, *op. cit.*, p. 37.

36. Anna Sergeevna Allilueva, *Iz vospominanii* (Moscow: Sovetsky Pisatel, 1946), p. 36.

37. V. Kaminsky and I. Vereshchagin, *op. cit.*, p. 44.

38. TASS interview with Stalin's mother, *op. cit.*

39. V. Kaminsky and I. Vereshchagin, *op. cit.,* p. 44.

40. *Ibid.,* pp. 43-4.

41. Circular issued by the Ministry of Internal Affairs, Department of Police, dated August 19, 1909, signed by S. Vissarionov, *Spisok A. Litsa, podlezhashchiya nemedlennomu obysku i arestu.* On file at The Hoover Institution.

42. No photograph of Stalin's father or, for that matter, of any of his paternal relatives has survived. While this may be simply explained by the fact that none existed, there are several photographs of the youngster Soso and of his mother, Keke, Vissarion's wife.

43. V. Kaminsky and I. Vereshchagin, *op. cit.,* p. 45.

44. J. Iremashvili, *op. cit.,* p. 8.

2. THE EDUCATION OF A REBEL

45. After Stalin's rise to power these initials became part of Soviet jargon. They stand for the All-Union Communist Party (bolshevik).

46. Three dates have been provided by Kremlin historians for Stalin's entry into the Tiflis Theological Seminary: 1892, 1893, and 1894. As with so many other events, Stalin never clarified this innocuous matter, thoroughly devoid of political implication. The correct date is 1894. Ironically, in 1939 this information was on a marble plaque on what was then the Hotel Palace, located on Beria Square.

47. V. Kaminsky and I. Vereshchagin, *op. cit.,* p. 62.

48. J. Iremashvili, *op. cit.,* p. 15.

49. V. Kaminsky and I. Vereshchagin, *op. cit.,* p. 64.

50. *Ibid.,* p. 66.

51. J. Iremashvili, *op. cit.,* p. 16.

52. V. Kaminsky and I. Vereshchagin, *op. cit.,* p. 66.

53. *Ibid.,* p. 67.

54. *Iz vospominany russkago uchitelia Pravoslavnoi Gruzinskoi Dukhovnoi Seminarii* (Moscow: Tip. "Russkaya Pechatnia," 1907).

55. J. Iremashvili, *op. cit.,* p. 16.

56. *Ibid.,* p. 12.

57. V. Kaminsky and I. Vereshchagin, *op. cit.,* p. 67.

58. *McGraw-Hill Encyclopedia of Russia and the Soviet Union,* ed. by Michael T. Florinsky (New York: McGraw-Hill, 1961), p. 334. Also see William Henry Chamberlin, *The Russian Revolution* (New York: Grosset & Dunlap, 1965), vol. I, p. 33-6.

59. The famous Czech patriot Thomas Masaryk, first president of Czechoslovakia was probably history's youngest conscious socialist. See Emil Ludwig, *Stalin* (New York: G. P. Putnam, 1942), p. 19, and I. V. Stalin, *Works,* Vols. I-XIII (Moscow: Foreign Languages Publishing House, 1949-1955, v. 13, p. 113.

60. J. Iremashvili, *op. cit.,* p. 17.

61. *Ibid.,* p. 22.

62. V. Kaminsky and I. Vereshchagin, *op. cit.,* p. 67.

63. *Ibid.,* p. 68.

64. *Ibid.*

65. *Iz vospominanii russkago uchitelia . . . , op. cit.,* p. 18-9.

66. V. Kaminsky and I. Vereshchagin, *op. cit.,* p. 71.

67. N. Nikolaishvili, "Stikhi yunogo Stalina," *Zaria Vostoka*, December 21, 1939.
68. Robert Payne, *The Rise and Fall of Stalin* (New York: Simon and Schuster, 1965), pp. 49-51. Payne claims that this was written on October 29, 1895 on the anniversary of Eristavi's death. However, Eristavi died six years later on April 3, 1901. See *Bolshaya Sovetskaya Entsiklopediya* (Moscow: Sovetskaya Entsiklopediya, 1933), vol. 64.
69. M. Kelendzheridze, "Stikhi yunogo Stalina," *Rasskazy o velikom Staline* (Tbilisi: Zaria Vostoka, 1941), pp. 67-70.
70. V. Kaminsky and I. Vereshchagin, *op. cit.*, pp. 69-70.
71. R. Payne, *op. cit.*, p. 51.
72. *Iz vospominanii russkago uchitelia* . . . , *op. cit.*, pp. 11, 19.
73. *Okhrana Collection*, Index IIIf, Folder 1, "Deep Cover Agents." On file at The Hoover Institution.
74. *Stalin i o Staline: ukazatel literatury* (Leningrad: Lenpartizdat, 1940), p. 218.
75. James H. Billington, *The Icon and the Axe* (New York: A. A. Knopf, 1966), p. 535.
76. V. Kaminsky and I. Vereshchagin, *op. cit.*, p. 70.
76a. *Ibid.*, p. 71.
77. *Ibid.*, p. 73.
78. *Ibid.*, p. 72.
79. *Iz vospominanii russkago uchitelia* . . . , *op. cit.*, p. 23, 33 ff.
80. V. Kaminsky and I. Vereshchagin, *op. cit.*, pp. 72-3.
81. *Ibid.*, p. 73.
82. *Ibid.*, pp. 63 and 84.
83. R. Payne, *op. cit.*, p. 85.
84. See G. I. Uratadze, *op. cit.*
85. Lavrenty Beria, *K voprosu ob istorii bolshevistskikh organizatsy v Zakavkazye* (Moscow: Partizdat, 1937) p. 6 ff. Also see Emelyan Yaroslavsky, *op. cit.*, p. 19 ff.
86. P. Kapanadze, "Ya dolzhen uvidet Lenina," *Raskazy starykh rabochikh Zakavkazya o velikom Staline* (Moscow: Molodaya gvardyia, 1937), p. 26.
87. V. Kaminsky and I. Vereshchagin, *op. cit.*, p. 84.
88. J. Iremashvili, *op. cit.*, p. 21 ff.
89. L. Beria, *op. cit.*, p. 14. Also see V. Kaminsky and I. Vereshchagin, *op. cit.*, p. 76.
90. *Ibid.*, p. 77.
91. J. Iremashvili, *op. cit.*, p. 19.
92. V. Kaminsky and I. Vereshchagin, *op. cit.*, p. 75.
93. G. I. Uratadze, *op. cit.*, p. 112.
94. V. Kaminsky and I. Vereshchagin, *op. cit.*, p. 77.
95. *Ibid.*, p. 78.
96. *Ibid.*, p. 79.
97. *Ibid.*, p. 84.
98. *Ibid.*, p. 84-5.
99. *Ibid.*, p. 84.
100. *Ibid.*, p. 67.
101. N. Vakar, "Stalin po vospominaniyam N. N. Zhordania," *Posledniya Novosti*, Paris, December 16, 1936, p. 2.

102. E. Yaroslavsky, *op. cit.*, p. 17.
103. V. Kaminsky and I. Vereshchagin, *op. cit.*, p. 86.
104. H. R. Knickerbocker, *op. cit.*, p. 2.
105. J. Iremashvili, *op. cit.*, p. 23.
105a. Victor Serge, *Portrait de Staline* (Paris: B. Grasset, 1940), p. 14.

3. THE MAKING OF A SECRET AGENT

106. I. V. Stalin, *Sochineniya*, v. 1-13 (Moscow: Gospolitizdat, 1946-1951).
Also see Henri Barbusse, *Stalin* (New York: Macmillan, 1935). Barbusse appears to have been semi-officially commissioned by the Kremlin to do a biography of Stalin.

L. Beria, *op. cit.*, Lavrenty Beria, a fellow Georgian whom Stalin later elevated to a position of power second only to his own in Soviet Russia, was the leader of all historical falsifiers concerning Stalin's pre-revolutionary life. It is possible that Beria's rise to power as chief of Stalin's omnipotent police-intelligence services was directly attributed to his mutilation of history. He was police chief of Soviet Russia from 1939 until he was shot in 1953.

107. V. Kaminsky and I. Vereshchagin, *op. cit.*, p. 62.
108. L. Shaumyan, *Kamo* (Moscow: Gospolitizdat, 1959), p. 9, writes that in 1901 when the nineteen-year-old revolutionary Kamo decided to enter the army, Stalin prepared him for the necessary examinations and advised him to become an officer. While this account may be true, Shaumyan's footnoted source is the Georgian Communist Party Archives, long pawed over and distorted by Stalin and his lieutenants. See also S. Medvedeva Ter-Petrosyan, "Tovarishch Kamo," *Proletarskaya revoliutsiya*, 1924, No. 8-9 (31-2), p. 120.
109. J. Iremashvili, *op. cit.*, p. 24.
110. I. V. Stalin, *op. cit.*, v. I., p. 417.
111. E. Yaroslavsky, *op. cit.*, p. 17.
111a. Leo Yaresh, "Ivan the Terrible and the Oprichnina," *Rewriting Russian History* (New York: Vintage Books, 1962), pp. 216-232. This article reviews Stalinist attitudes toward the *Oprichniki* and shows that he had high regard for Ivan the Terrible and his security forces.
112. See Anatole G. Mazour, *The First Russian Revolution, 1825* (Berkeley: University of California Press, 1937).
113. Sidney Monas, *The Third Section; Police and Society in Russia Under Nicholas I* (Cambridge: Harvard University Press, 1961), p. 48.
114. Boris Nicolaevsky, *Aseff, the Spy, Russian Terrorist, and Police Stool* (Garden City: Doubleday, Doran and Co., 1934), pp. 161-2.
115. "Kak Department Politsii otpustil Lenina zagranitsu dlia bolshevistkoi propagandy," *Byloe*, 1926, No. 2, pp. 85-92. Okhrana agent reports show that after Lenin was released from his 1900 term of exile he promptly went to the house of an Okhrana agent. Later he was detained for nine days in St. Petersburg by the Department of Police. An agent report states he had fourteen hundred rubles in his pockets. After his detention, he was given a passport for foreign travel and he subsequently departed from Russia.
116. Mrs. Lenin used her maiden name, Krupskaya, in revolutionary circles and in her writing.
117. The Special Section (*Osoby Otdel*), sometimes abbreviated ("O.O.,") is

not to be confused with the several component Security Divisions (*Okhrannoe Otdelenie*), also sometimes referred to as "O.O."

118. B. K. Erenfeld, "Delo Malinovskogo," *Voprosy istorii*, 1965, No. 7, pp. 106-116.

119. M. G. Fleer, "Revoliutsiya 1905-1906 gg. v. doneseniyakh diplomatov," *Krasny arkhiv*, 1926, No. 3(16), pp. 220-4. In 1904 a "top secret office" headed by gendarme Colonel Komissarov was established in Department of Police Headquarters for the surveillance of "foreign ambassadors, ministers, and military attachés." It employed servants to filch secret correspondence from foreign diplomatic premises, it opened diplomatic mail, and it intercepted diplomatic telegrams.

120. Circular No. 1, classified "secret," dated December 29, 1906, and issued by the Registration Section of the Department of Police, outlined the proper procedure for the registering of all persons detained or arrested. Three photographs were necessary in accord with the Bertillon system: one full-face view, one in profile, and one standing up, dressed in the same clothes as at the moment of arrest or detention. A detailed instruction guide for photography and registry was attached. Twenty-eight pages of instructions consisted of three parts: (1) general information; (2) photography; and (3) completion of the registration form. On file at the Hoover Institution.

121. From 1895 on, there was published annually (with a few exceptions) a complete biographical register of gendarme officers, the "List of the Staff of the Separate Corps of Gendarmes." It included the complement of each local Gendarme Administration. No listing for the Department of Police Headquarters, the Special Section, or the Foreign Agency in Paris was provided. However, a bit of detective work reveals that officers assigned to the latter organizations could be located, much the same as C.I.A. operatives are discernible in today's Department of State biographical registers. Establishing deep cover for intelligence personnel represented an almost insoluble problem even then. See *Spisok obshchago sostava chinov Otdelnago Korpusa Zhandarmov* (St. Petersburg: Tip. Otd. Korp. Zhand., 189?-   ).

122. This *esprit de corps* is an obvious feature of the F.B.I. On the other hand, the C.I.A. and the Soviet service, to mention only two contemporary intelligence organizations, have been unable to avoid intramural feuds, backstabbing, "one-upmanship," and general politicking to the detriment of operations.

123. *McGraw-Hill Encyclopedia of Russia, op. cit.,* p. 80.

124. A. E. Badaev, *Bolsheviki v Gosudarstvennoi Dume* (Moscow: Gospolitizdat, 1954), p. 278.

125. Semen Vereshchak, "Stalin v tiurme," *Dni*, January 22, 1928, p. 2; January 24, 1928, p. 3.

126. V. Kaminsky and I. Vereshchagin, *op. cit.,* p. 97.

127. Both the Okhrana and the revolutionaries called these secret meeting places "conspiratorial apartments" (*konspirativnye kvartiry*). The term remains in Soviet police-intelligence jargon.

128. V. Kaminsky and I. Vereshchagin, *op. cit.,* p. 88. During the autumn of 1899 some fifty students in the Tiflis Theological Seminary were required by a special order to quit the seminary forever, according to Vano Ketskhoveli. From what is known of Soso's denunciations

he might well have figured in this extraordinary expulsion of seminarians.

129. Boris Souvarine, *Staline* (Paris: Plon, 1935), p. 1. Also see A. I. Spiridovich, *Istoriya bolshevizma v Rossii ot vozniknoveniya do zakhvata vlasti* (Paris: Tip. "Franko-russkaya pechatnia," 1922), p. 239.

130. V. Kaminsky and I. Vereshchagin, *op. cit.*, p. 89.

131. *Ibid.*, p. 88.

132. J. Iremashvili, *op. cit.*, p. 24.

133. V. Kaminsky and I. Vereshchagin, *op. cit.*, p. 89.

134. Department of Police Document No. 101145, dated March 31, 1911, signed by Vissarionov and Eremin, and serving as a cover letter for the report submitted by the Chief of the Tiflis Police Department, Colonel Pastriulin, No. 53-s, dated March 4, 1911, and classified "top secret." On file at The Hoover Institution.

135. V. Kaminsky and I. Vereshchagin, *op. cit.*, p. 91-2.

136. The *Narodnaya Voliya*, the party of the People's Will or the party of the People's Freedom was a terroristic group responsible for the assassination of Alexander II on March 1, 1881. Lenin felt the group courageous, but attacked its utopian and liberal democratic theories. See Stefan T. Possony, *Lenin: the Compulsive Revolutionary* (Chicago: Regnery, 1964), pp. 128-133. Also see *Pisma P. B. Axelroda i Yu. Martova* (Berlin: Russky Revoliutsionny Arkhiv, 1924), pp. 291-2.

137. V. Kaminsky and I. Vereshchagin, *op. cit.*, p. 93.

138. L. Beria, *op. cit.*, p. 15.

139. V. Kaminsky and I. Vereshchagin, *op. cit.*, p. 93.

140. I. V. Stalin, *op. cit.*, p. 417.

141. L. Beria, *op. cit.*, p. 11.

142. V. Kaminsky and I. Vereshchagin, *op. cit.*, p. 90.

143. L. Beria, *op. cit.*, p. 13-14.

144. V. Kaminsky and I. Vereshchagin, *op. cit.*, p. 91.

145. R.S.D.R.P. (sometimes also R.S.D.L.P.) are the initials of the Russian Social-Democratic Workers Party organized at Minsk in March, 1898.

146. I. V. Stalin, *op. cit.*, p. 417.

147. H. Barbusse, *op. cit.*, p. 18.

148. S. T. Arkhomed, *Rabochee dvizhenie i sotsial-demokratiya na Kavkasye* (Moscow/Petrograd: Gos. izd-vo, 1923), p. 74.

149. Iremashvili, who visited Stalin's quarters, remembers "piles of books and brochures" there.

150. V. Kaminsky and I. Vereshchagin, *op. cit.*, p. 95.

151. *Ibid.*, p. 96.

152. Irina Guro, *Ozarennye* (Moscow: Gospolitizdat, 1963). Also see G. Volchek and V. Voinov, *Viktor Kurnatovsky* (Moscow: Molodaya gvardiya, 1961).

4. BLOODSHED AT TIFLIS AND BATUM

153. *Obshchy sostav upravleny i chinov Otdelnago Korpusa Zhandarmov po 20 iyulia 1903 g.* (St. Petersburg: Tip. Otd. Korp. Zhand., 1903).

154. L. Beria, *op. cit.*, p. 15.
155. V. Kaminsky and I. Vereshchagin, *op. cit.*, p. 97.
156. On call to quell the demonstration were the 10th Police Division, the 3rd Caucasian Rifle Battalion, a company of the 2nd Sapper Battalion, and a company of the 1st Rifle Battalion, in addition to regular police forces. Available troops were more than five times as strong in numbers as the demonstrators. Unarmed workers clashing with this force in the name of the "revolution" were obviously helpless. See V. Kaminsky and I. Vereshchagin, *op. cit.*, p. 97.
157. *Ibid.*
158. *Iskra*, No. 6, July 1901.
159. J. Iremashvili, *op. cit.*, p. 28.
160. *Ibid.*, p. 27.
161. E. Yaroslavsky, *op. cit.*, p. 24.
162. I. V. Stalin, *op. cit.*, pp. 393 and 418.
163. L. Beria, "Lado Ketskhoveli," *Lado Ketskhoveli; sbornik* (Moscow: Partizdat, 1938), pp. 12-3.
164. I. V. Stalin, *op. cit.*, p. 393.
165. *Ibid.*, p. 26 ff.
166. Conversation in 1923 with Dzerzhinsky and Kamenev. See E. Lyons, *op. cit.*, p. 37.
167. E. Yaroslavsky, *op. cit.*, p. 25.
168. L. Beria, *K voprosu ob istorii bolshevistskikh organizatsy v Zakavkazye* (Moscow: Partizdat, 1937), p. 16.
169. N. Vakar, *op. cit.*, p. 2.
170. *Brdzolis Khma*, Paris, No. 3, 1930.
171. N. Vakar, *op. cit.*, p. 2.
172. J. Iremashvili, *op. cit.*, p. 64.
173. *Ibid.*, pp. 63-4.
174. S. T. Arkomed, *Rabochee dvizhenie i sotsial-demokratiya na Kavkazye* (Geneva: Impr. Chaumontel, 1910), p. 74.
174a. B. N-skii [Boris Nicolaevsky], "Pamiati G. I. Uratadze," *Sotsialisticheskii Vestnik* No. 4 (728) (April, 1959), pp. 75-76.
174b. G. Uratadze, *Moi vospominaiya* (unpublished manuscript on file at The Hoover Institution), pp. 56-7.
175. See *Obshchy sostav . . . , op. cit.*
176. I. V. Stalin, *op. cit.*, p. 418.
177. *Batumskaya demonstratsiya 1902 goda* (Moscow: Partizdat, 1937), p. 152.
178. *Ibid.*
179. I. V. Stalin, *op. cit.*, p. 418.
180. E. Yaroslavsky, *op. cit.*, p. 26.
181. *Batumskaya . . . , op. cit.*, p. 153.
182. *Ibid.*
183. David Shub, *Lenin* (Garden City: Doubleday, 1948), p. 186.
184. S. T. Arkomed, *op. cit.*
185. E. Yaroslavsky, *op. cit.*, p. 25. Also see L. Beria, *op. cit.*, pp. 36-38.
186. *Ibid.* Also see L. Beria, *op. cit.*, pp. 42-43. Beria writes: "It should be noted that Karlo Chkheidze and Isidor Ramishvili, who were in Batum at the time, not only took no hand in the revolutionary struggle of the Batum workers but sent their friends to Stalin time and again and came in person to urge him to leave Batum, giving as their

reason that he, *i.e.*, Stalin, would not be able to found an illegal Social-Democratic organization or rouse the Batum workers to a political struggle. But their main reason for doing this was their fear of trouble and persecution for themselves as a result of Comrade Stalin's underground work.

"Finding that their urging was in vain, I. Ramishvili and K. Chkheidze tried direct attacks, provocative, slanderous thrusts at Comrade Stalin, calling him 'madcap' and 'disrupter.' They even tried to dissuade individual workers from listening to Comrade Stalin, to intimidate them with statements to the effect that Comrade Stalin was putting the workers in mortal peril. But the future Mensheviks suffered utter defeat in their efforts to disrupt the enormous political work of Comrade Stalin and the leading workers of Batum."

187. I. V. Stalin, *op. cit.*, p. 419.
188. E. Yaroslavsky, *op. cit.*, p. 26.
189. I. V. Stalin, *op. cit.*, p. 419.
190. E. Yaroslavsky, *op. cit.*, p. 27.
191. L. Trotsky, *Stalin* (New York: Grosset & Dunlap, 1941), p. 33.
192. E. Yaroslavsky, *op. cit.*, p. 27.
193. I. V. Stalin, *op. cit.*, p. 419. According to Soviet accounts his pseudonym at this time was *Bedny Rabochy* (Poor Worker). However, authentic Department of Police reports assert that he was known as *Chopur*, a vulgarization of the Georgian word, *chopura*, meaning "pockmarked."
194. B. Souvarine, *op. cit.*, p. 46.
195. *Izvestia*, April 28, 1937, p. 3.
196. Louis Fischer in his *The Life and Death of Stalin* (New York: Harper and Brothers, 1952) wrote on page 8: "Struggle fascinates Stalin. Competition sharpens his wits. The Bolshevik party, born to fight, bound to be persecuted by the Czar's government, was Stalin's natural home. He rose in its ranks quickly. The police was on his trail. In 1902, on a visit to St. Petersburg, he rented a furnished room. In the early hours of the morning, there was a loud knock on the door. 'Why don't you let me sleep?' he groaned, half-awake. The reply was Russia's traditional night call: 'Open up, it's the police.' This was one of his many arrests."

Because Soviet sources placed Stalin in Baku during 1902, and not in St. Petersburg, I wrote Mr. Fischer: "It would be most helpful and I would be very appreciative were you to inform me where I might locate the source materials on which the aforementioned statements were made." Mr. Fischer, then at the Woodrow Wilson School of Public and International Affairs at Princeton University, promptly replied that: "You will find the data on Stalin in the *Large Soviet Encyclopedia* and in several biographies published during his rule. The facts about Stalin which you mention are common knowledge and easily verifiable from many sources. Sincerely yours, Louis Fischer."

Mr. Fischer's statement about Stalin's sojourn in St. Petersburg can not be found in the *Large Soviet Encyclopedia* nor are these "facts" verifiable anywhere.

197. N. Vakar, *op. cit.*, p. 2.
198. "Stalin i Khashim," *Batumskaya demonstratsiya 1902 goda* (Moskva: Partizdat, 1937), p. 150 ff.

199. He was appropriately concerned. The Batum Gendarme Administration in 1902 was composed of a staff of more than twenty officers headed by the experienced Lieutenant Colonel Sergei Petrovich Shabelsky. See *Obshchy sostav* . . . , *op. cit.,* p. 292.

200. "Stalin i Khashim" *op. cit.*

201. E. Yaroslavsky, *op. cit.,* p. 28. Also see H. Barbusse, *op. cit.,* pp. 21-2, and *Batumskaya* . . . , *op. cit.,* p. 167.

202. A fantastic version has him arrested by a Captain Lavrov in the cottage of Stefan Malenkov, a distant relative of Georgy M. Malenkov, Premier of the U.S.S.R. after Stalin's death. See Yves Delbars, *The Real Stalin* (London: Allen & Unwin, 1953), p. 38.

203. N. Vakar, *op. cit.*

203a. G. Uratadze, *op. cit.,* p. 56. Uratadze was in Kutais prison when Stalin arrived: "Koba (Stalin) I saw for the first time. . . . He was insignificant looking. His face pitted with small pox that did not particularly give him a clean appearance. Right here I must note that all the portraits which I saw later—after he became dictator were absolutely not like the Koba whom I saw in prison the first time and not like the Stalin whom I knew many years later. . . . In prison he had a beard, long hair brushed back. His gait was smooth—small steps. He never laughed with an open mouth, but only smiled. And the measure of his smile depended upon the measure of his emotion. . . . We were together in Kutais prison more than six months, and not once did I see him become upset . . . get angry, shout, argue, in a word—conduct himself other than in complete tranquility. And his voice precisely corresponded to his 'icy character' . . ."

204. B. Souvarine, *op. cit.,* p. 46.

205. *Obshchy sostav* . . . , *op. cit.,* p. 292.

206. A. S. Alliluyeva, *op. cit.,* p. 167.

207. R. Payne, *op. cit.,* p. 81.

208. A. Weingart, *Ugolovnaya taktika* (St. Petersburg: [n.p.] 1912). On page 6 is a sketch that graphically shows the steps to be taken in drawing up a report such as the one on Stalin that Shabelsky signed. Also see M. V. Lebedev, *Note concernant l'organisation de la Police de recherches criminelles et Service d'identification des recidivistes* (Paris: Wolff, 1914).

209. L. Trotsky, *op. cit.,* p. 33. Note that this contradicts Iremashvili.

210. J. Iremashvili, *op. cit.,* p. 28.

211. L. Trotsky, *op. cit.,* pp. 33-4.

212. *Batumskaya* . . . , *op. cit.,* p. 120.

213. L. Trotsky, *op. cit.,* p. 34.

214. *Batumskaya* . . . , *op. cit.,* p. 120.

215. *Ibid.*

216. *Ibid.,* p. 122.

217. *Ibid.,* pp. 134-6.

218. *Ibid.*

5. SIBERIAN EXILE AND ESCAPE: A POLICE RUSE

219. *Batumskaya* . . . , *op. cit.,* p. 199.

220. *Ibid.,* p. 203 ff.

221. *The Life of Stalin; a Symposium* (London: Modern Books, 1930), p. 3.
222. "Ot redaktsii," *Izvestia*, April 28, 1937, p. 3.
223. *Batumskaya* . . . , *op. cit.*, p. 200.
224. *Vostochnoe Obozrenie*, Irkutsk, November, 1903-April, 1904. On file at The Library of Congress.
225. John Foster Fraser, *The Real Siberia* (London: Cassell, 1912), p. 27.
226. I. Guro, *op. cit.*, p. 44 ff. Also see G. Volchek and V. Voinov, *op. cit.*, p. 125 ff.
227. I. V. Stalin, *O Lenine* (Moscow: Partizdat, 1934), pp. 22-3.
228. "Vtoroi syezd i raskol partii," *Krasny arkhiv*, No. 1 (62), 1934, pp. 155-72. This article, concerning Lenin during 1903-1904, is largely comprised of letters from abroad to Russia intercepted by the Department of Police. Most of them were in secret writing to Lenin's colleagues and raised by Okhrana specialists.
229. *Batumskaya* . . . , *op. cit.*, pp. 195-6.
230. *Iosif Vissarionovich Stalin; kratkaya biografiya* (Moskva: Gosizdatpolit, 1953), p. 20.
231. G. Volchek and V. Voinov, *op. cit.* Also see I. Guro, *op. cit.*
232. B. Ivanov, "V Novoi Ude," *Pravda*, December 25, 1939.
233. M. Vetoshkin, "V Sibirskoi ssylke," *Istorichesky zhurnal*, 1940, No. 1, p. 64.
234. I. V. Stalin, *Sochineniia*, v. 1 (Moscow: Gospolitizdat, 1946), p. 420.
235. Sergei Alliluev, *Proidennyi put* (Moskva: OGIZ, 1946), p. 108.
236. A. S. Allilueva, *op. cit.*, pp. 37-38. Later, on p. 110, Anna writes that "Koba escaped in 1903. In 1909, in the summer, he again escaped from Solvychegodsk."
237. Joseph Hutton, *Stalin, the Miraculous Georgian* (London: Spearman, 1961), pp. 28-9.
238. I. V. Stalin, *op. cit.*, p. 420.
239. S. Alliluev, *op. cit.*, p. 108. Also see A. S. Allilueva, *op. cit.*, p. 37.
240. Y. Delbars, *op. cit.*, p. 44.
241. E. Yaroslavsky, *op. cit.*, p. 31.
242. L. Beria, *op. cit.*, p. 335.
243. Department of Police Document No. 101145, *op. cit.*
244. H. Barbusse, *op. cit.*, p. 23.
245. Avel Enukidze, *Nashi podpolnye tipografii na Kavkazye* (Moscow: Novaya Moskva, 1925), p. 33.
246. David M. Cole, *Josef Stalin—Man of Steel* (London: Rich and Cowan, 1942), p. 20.
247. Department of Police Document No. 101145, *op. cit.*
248. I. V. Stalin, *op. cit.*, p. 421.
249. *The Life of Stalin, op. cit.*, p. 3.
250. L. Beria, *op. cit.*, p. 335.
251. L. Trotsky, *op. cit.*, pp. 37-38.
252. Y. Delbars, *op. cit.*, p. 20.
253. E. Yaroslavsky, *op. cit.*, p. 31.
254. Radzen Arsenidze, "Iz vospominanii o Staline," *Novy zhurnal*, no. 72, 1963, pp. 218-37.
255. L. Trotsky, *op. cit.*, p. 45.
256. I. V. Stalin, *op. cit.*, pp. 420-1.
257. Filip E. Makharadze, *Ocherki revoliutsionnogo dvizheniya v Zakavkazye* (Tiflis: Gosizdat Gruzii, 1927).

258. V. I. Nevsky, *Istoria RKP(b)*, ed. 2 (Leningrad: Priboi, 1926).

259. I. V. Stalin, *op. cit.*, p. 421.

260. *Iz proshlogo; stati i vospominania iz istorii Bakinskoi organizatsii i rabochego dvizhenia v Baku* (Baku: Bakinsky rabochy, 1923). Also see Solomon M. Schwarz, *The Russian Revolution of 1905* (Chicago: The University of Chicago Press, 1967), pp. 301-314. This account, appropriately entitled "The Baku Strike of December, 1904: Myth and Reality," forever lays to rest the idea that Beria and Stalin tried to propagate about Stalin's role in the Baku strike. As late as 1950, for example, *The Big Soviet Encyclopedia* (2nd ed., Vol. IV, pp. 62-63) was insisting that Stalin and Dzhaparidze directed the strike. Schwarz conclusively proves Stalin had nothing to do with it.

261. L. Trotsky, *op. cit.*, p. 43.

262. J. Iremashvili, *op. cit.*, p. 30.

262a. On July 24, 1941, Goebbels' Berlin daily *Volkischer Beobachter,* the official organ of the Nazi party, carried a page-one story and photograph concerning Yasha's capture on July 16, 1941. This account claimed that he surrendered at Liosno, near Vitebsk, on July 16, 1941, regarding further resistance to the German forces as senseless. He claimed that he was born March 16, 1908, in Baku (strangely, this would have been one year after his mother's death, from what we know from other sources), that he had attended a technical school and later had decided to become an officer, completing the five-year course of the Moscow Artillery Academy in two and a half years. When captured, he was a lieutenant in the 14th Artillery Regiment of the 14th Tank Division.

263. *Ibid.*, pp. 30-39.

264. *Ibid.*, pp. 31-2.

265. *Ibid.*, p. 40.

266. R. Arsenidze, *op. cit.*, p. 220.

267. S. T. Possony, *op. cit.*, p. 86.

268. Department of Police Document No. 101145, *op. cit.*

6. A REVOLUTIONARY IGNORES A REVOLUTION

269. L. Trotsky, *op. cit.*, p. 64.

270. Department of Police Document No. 101145, *op. cit.*

271. D. Shub, *op. cit.*, p. 84.

272. L. Trotsky, *op. cit.*, p. 65.

273. R. Arsenidze, *op. cit.*, p. 231.

274. For a more detailed treatment of the 1905 events see Sidney Harcave, *First Blood; the Russian Revolution of 1905* (New York: Macmillan, 1964), p. 69 ff. Also see S. Schwarz, *op. cit.*

275. Nicholas II, *Dnevnik Imperatora Nikolaya II* (Berlin: Russky Revoliutsionny Arkhiv, 1923), p. 194.

275a. G. Uratadze, *op. cit.*, p. 60 ff. Uratadze, who was also born in Guria, describes the events of 1905 in that area.

276. "Revoliutsiya 1905-1907 gg.," *Krasnyi Arkhiv,* No. 1 (62), 1934, pp. 173-214. Department of Police documents comprise the main part of this article. All pertain to Lenin and many are intercepted letters he or Krupskaya wrote from abroad. There is also some information

from surveillance agents revealing the concern of Okhrana officers in St. Petersburg about Lenin's activities and associates.

277. R. Arsenidze, *op. cit.,* p. 221. Also see Stanislaw Kot, *Conversations with the Kremlin and Dispatches from Russia* (London: Oxford University Press, 1963), pp. 140-153. At a meeting in the Kremlin on December 3, 1941, attended by Polish General Sikorski, Professor Kot, the Polish Ambassador, General Anders, Commander of the Polish Armed Forces in the USSR, and Molotov, Stalin remarked: "The Jews are rotten soldiers."

278. See J. Fishman and J. B. Hutton, *The Private Life of Josif Stalin* (London: W. H. Allen, 1962), p. 114 ff.

279. I. V. Stalin, *op. cit.,* p. 422.

280. V. I. Nevsky, *op. cit.*

281. R. Arsenidze, *op. cit.,* p. 220.

282. "The Proletarian Class and the Proletarian Party" published on January 1 was followed by "Workers of the Caucasus—It is Time to Take Revenge." In early February he produced a leaflet entitled "Long Live International Fraternity!" Then on February 15, he wrote "To Citizens, Long Live the Red Flag!" and almost three months later his first pamphlet "Briefly About Disagreements in the Party" was published. Another two months preceded his article in *The Proletarian Struggle,* No. 10. "Armed Insurrection and Our Tactics," a scarcely camouflaged reproduction of something Lenin had written previously. Another month went by before his subsequent article "Reaction to a Social Democrat" appeared in "Proletarian Struggle," No. 11. When *Proletarian Struggle,* No. 12 published his articles "Reaction is Growing" and the "Bourgeoisie is Laying a Trap" another two months had passed by. Later on, "in connection with the October all-Russian political strike" he wrote a leaflet "Citizens!" and "To All the Workers!" Then on November 20, in No. 1 of the "Caucasian Workers News Sheet" he had a lead article entitled "Tiflis November 20, 1905." See I. V. Stalin, *op. cit.,* pp. 422-3.

283. R. Arsenidze, *op. cit.,* p. 225.

284. *1905; materialy i dokumenty,* ed. by M. N. Pokrovsky (Moscow: Gos. izd-vo, 1925-   ).

285. F. Makharadze, *op. cit.*

286. S. Maglakelidze and A. Iovidze, compilers, *Revoliutsiya 1905-1907 gg. v Gruzii; sbornik dokumentov* (Tbilisi: "Sakhelgami," 1956).

287. I. V. Stalin, *op. cit.,* p. 130.

288. *Ibid.,* p. 422.

289. *Ibid.*

290. R. Arsenidze, *op. cit.,* p. 230. Almost sixty years later, in 1963, Khrushchev posed a similar question. Had Stalin been a true Marxist? "Da," he answered. See *Pravda,* March 10, 1963.

291. R. Arsenidze, *op. cit.,* p. 231.

292. I. V. Stalin, *op. cit.,* p. 423.

293. R. Arsenidze, *op. cit.,* p. 229.

294. *Ibid.,* p. 231.

295. B. M. Volin, *12 biografy* (Moscow: Rabochaya Moskva, 1924).

296. L. Trotsky, *op. cit.,* p. 65.

297. I. M. Dubinsky-Mukhadze, *Shaumyan* (Moscow: Molodaya gvardiya, 1965). At this writing Shaumyan's son is active in Moscow. He de-

livered a eulogy in Moscow on the occasion of Mrs. Mikoyan's funeral that was outspokenly anti-Stalinist (See N.Y. *Times,* Nov. 10, 1962, p. 2). Perhaps the young Shaumyan had learned of Stalin's betrayal of his father almost sixty years earlier in Tiflis.

298. N. Vakar, *op. cit.*

299. Department of Police Document No. 101145, *op. cit.*

300. A. Piaskovsky, *Pervaya (Tammersforskaya) konferentsiya RSDRP* (Moscow: Gospolitizdat, 1951).

301. V. I. Lenin, *Polnoe sobranie sochineny* (Moscow: Gospolitizdat, 1961), ed. 5, Vol. XXII, p. 558.

302. *Kommunisticheskaya partiya Sovetskogo Soiuza v rezoliutsiakh, i resheniakh syezdov, konferentsy i plenumov TSK,* Vol. 1 (Moscow: Gospolitizdat, 1954).

303. *Listovki Kavkazskogo Soiuza RSDRP. 1903-1905* (Moscow: Gospolitizdat, 1955).

304. *Revoliutsionnoe proshloe Tbilisi* (Tbilisi: Izd-vo "Metsniereba," 1964), p. 79.

305. S. Alliluev, *op. cit.,* p. 157. Also see A. S. Allilueva, *op. cit.,* p. 63.

306. I. V. Stalin, *op. cit.,* Vol. 3, p. 27.

307. L. Trotsky, *op. cit.,* p. 63.

308. See B. Krugliakov, "Pravitelstvo i zheleznodorozhnye zabastovki v Peterburge v 1905 godu," *Krasnaya letopis,* No. 2(13), 1925, pp. 64-89. Numerous Department of Police reports stress the degree of police concern with the 1905 railway strikes in this article.

309. N. K. Krupskaya, *Reminiscences of Lenin* (Moscow: Foreign Languages Publishing House, 1959), p. 139.

310. M. N. Pokrovsky, ed., *op. cit.*

311. E. Yaroslavsky, *op. cit.,* p. 31.

312. I. V. Stalin, *op. cit.,* Vol. 1, p. 424.

313. I. V. Stalin, *O Lenine,* pp. 23-5.

314. N. K. Krupskaya, *op. cit.,* p. 141.

315. E. Yaroslavsky, *op. cit.,* p. 47; L. Trotsky, *op. cit.,* p. 69, citing B. I. Gorev.

316. N. K. Krupskaya, *op. cit.,* p. 141.

317. E. Yaroslavsky, "Tri vstrechi," *Pravda,* December 23, 1939, p. 4.

318. I. V. Stalin, *Sochinenia,* Vol. 1 (Moscow: Gospolitizdat, 1946) pp. 206-213.

319. E. Yaroslavsky, *op. cit.*

320. E. Yaroslavsky, *Landmarks in the Life of Stalin,* p. 47.

321. N. K. Krupskaya, *op. cit.,* p. 141.

322. Isaac Deutscher, *Stalin, a Political Biography* (London, New York: Oxford University Press, 1949), p. 81. Deutscher provides no source.

322a. See *Malaya Sovetskaya entsiklopediya,* Vol. 6, 1959, 3rd. ed., pp. 1292-1293, for a partial list of the confreres.

323. I. V. Stalin, *O Lenine,* pp. 22-23.

7. THE AVLABAR AFFAIR

324. S. T. Possony, *op. cit.,* p. 95.

325. See F. Matasova "Nabliudenie za V. I. Leninym v dekabre 1905 g.—yanvare 1906 g.," *Krasnaya letopis,* No. 1(12), 1925, pp. 123-5. The authoress exhumed from Okhrana files the notebook of a surveillance

agent assigned to shadow Lenin during the period. It shows how closely Lenin's movements and contacts were observed by the Department of Police. See also I. Deutscher, *op. cit.,* p. 81.

326. L. Trotsky, *op. cit.,* p. 72.

327. K. T. Sverdlova, *Yakov Mikhailovich Sverdlov* (Moscow, Molodaya gvardiya, 1957), p. 40. Jacob Sverdlov, a delegate to the conference, was delayed by the railway strike until January.

328. B. Souvarine, *op. cit.,* p. 98.

329. I. V. Stalin, *Sochinenia,* Vol. 1 (Moscow: Gospolitizdat, 1946), pp. 196-205.

330. *Ibid.,* p. 213.

331. *Ibid.,* p. 217.

332. B. Souvarine, *op. cit.,* p. 85.

333. *Avlabarskaya nelegalnaya tipografiya Kavkazskogo soyuznogo komiteta RSDRP (1903-1906 gg.); sbornik materialov i dokumentov* (Tbilisi: Gosizdat, 1954), p. 6 ff.

334. S. Maglakelidze, compiler, *Revoliutsya 1905-1907 gg. v Gruzii; sbornik dokumentov* (Tbilisi: "Sakhelgami," 1956), p. 774.

335. I. Bas, "Muzei bolshevistskogo pechatnogo slova," *Istorichesky zhurnal,* No. 11, November 1937, pp. 109-11.

336. See R. Arsenidze, *op. cit.*

337. See *Avlabarskaya . . . , op. cit.,* pp. 8-12.

338. *Ibid.,* p. 91.

339. *Ibid.,* p. 74.

340. *Ibid.,* pp. 12-3.

341. *Ibid.*

342. *Ibid.,* pp. 74-5.

343. There was no Yulipets in the Separate Corps of Gendarmes. See *Spisok obshchago sostava chinov Otdelnago Korpusa Zhandarmov* (St. Petersburg: Tip. Otd. Korp. Zhand., 1913), pp. 12, 82, 380. There was a Captain Petr Dmitrievich Yulinets who had become chief of the Batum Gendarme Police Administration of the Transcaucasian Railways on February 24, 1906. At this time he was thirty-one. He had served exclusively in the Caucasus from 1903, the date of his first post, and was transferred to the position of Chief of the Granitsk Division of the Warsaw Gendarme Police Administration of Railways on May 8, 1910. His career was not particularly distinguished.

The fact that the Rostomashvili "home" [Avlabar] was alongside the railway probably explains Captain Yulinets' jurisdiction in leading the raid and search of Avlabar. And, a typographical error would explain the misspelling of his name.

344. S. Maglakelidze, *op. cit.,* p. 780.

345. *Novoye vremia,* St. Petersburg, April 22, 1906, p. 3.

346. S. Maglakelidze, *op. cit.,* p. 773 ff. Document No. 572 of August 15, 1911 concerns an indictment in the case of the Avlabar printing press of the Caucasian Union Committee of the RSDRP uncovered by the gendarmerie 15 April, 1906, that presumably reposes in "TsGIA Gruz. SSR (State Central Historical Archives of the Georgian SSR), f.23-S, d.289, l.l. 2-11" in its "original typewritten" form.

347. "Shkola filerov," *Byloe,* 1917, No. 3(25), pp. 66-7. *Byloe (The Past)* was at this time published in Petrograd and edited by V. Burtsev.

348. The late Charles Malamuth who was the translator and editor of

Trotsky's biography of Stalin had been unable to locate the document on which Trotsky based his assertion on p. 447 of *Stalin, an Appraisal of the Man and His Influence.* A letter to this effect from Charles Malamuth is in author's possession.

349. R. Arsenidze, *op. cit.,* p. 220.
350. *Ibid.,* pp. 221-2.
351. See the account of David Rostomashvili in *Avlabarskaya . . . , op. cit.,* p. 42. Also see *Vtoroi period revoliutsii, 1906-1907; chast pervaya: yanvar-aprel 1906 goda, kniga vtoraya* (Moscow: Gospolitizdat, 1959), p. 662. Also see *Novoye vremia,* St. Petersburg, April 20, 1906. It announced that the arrestees were to be tried by a "military tribunal."
352. *Avlabarskaya . . . , op. cit.,* p. 63.
353. *Ibid.,* p. 91.
354. *Ibid.,* p. 60 ff.

8. STOCKHOLM AND LONDON

355. *Chetverty (obyedinitelny) syezd RSDRP, aprel (aprel-mai) 1910 goda; protokoly* (Moscow: Gospolitizdat, 1959), p. 10.
356. *Svod zakonov Rossiiskoi Imperii,* Vol. XIV, "Ustav o passportakh" (St. Petersburg, 1903).
357. *Chetverty . . . , op. cit.,* p. 540.
358. Letter from Det Forenede Dampskibs-Selskab, Copenhagen, dated Jan. 10, 1966, in author's possession.
359. M. Liadov, *Iz zhizni partii* (Moscow: Gospolitizdat, 1956), pp. 159-61.
360. *Chetverty . . . , op. cit.,* p. 537 ff.
361. M. Futrell, *Northern Underground* (New York: Praeger, 1963), p. 47.
362. *Ibid.*
363. A copy of the Stockholm City Police document confirming this is in the author's possession.
363a. See G. Uratadze, *op. cit.,* p. 140. Uratadze, who was present, claims that 111 voting delegates and 22 consultative delegates attended the Stockholm Congress. He adds: "The bolshevik historians are lying when they write that Stalin was at this congress as a delegate. True, Stalin went to the congress, but he was not among the number of elected delegates. He attended as a delegate of the 'Borchalo social-democratic organization,' [from Tiflis] but because no such organization existed, the mandate commission of course did not accept his mandate [credentials] and he had to leave the congress. But the bureau of the bolshevik faction requested our delegation not to object to his admittance with a consultative vote and only after our agreement, Stalin was admitted to the congress with a consultative vote. He was registered under the pseudonym of *Ivanovich.*" In other words, Stalin registered at the *Congress* as Ivanovich: his passport was in the name of Vissarionovich.
364. *Chetverty . . . , op. cit.,* pp. 490-94 and 481 ff.
365. I. V. Stalin, *Sochinenia,* Vol. I (Moscow: Gospolitizdat, 1946), pp. xi-xiv, 214-40.
366. *Chetverty . . . , op. cit.*
367. See S. T. Possony, *op. cit.,* p. 98.
368. I. V. Stalin, *O Lenine,* p. 22 ff.

369. Report No. 165, dated 17 (30) May, 1906, from the Chief of the Okhrana Foreign Agency to the Director of the Police Department. On file at The Hoover Institution. Also see "K 35-letiyu IV (Obyedinitelnogo) syezda RSDRP," *Krasny arkhiv*, No. 3(106), 1941, pp. 3-39. Department of Police reports (some signed by Eremin, Klimovich and Garting) indicate the extent of Okhrana knowledge of the Congress.

370. M. Futrell, *op. cit.*, p. 47.

371. I. V. Stalin, *Sochinenia*, Vol. 1 (Moscow: Gospolitizdat, 1946), p. 424.

372. *Ibid.*, p. 246 ff.

373. B. Souvarine, *op. cit.*, p. 99.

374. I. V. Stalin, *op. cit.*, p. 425.

375. *Ibid.*, Vol. 2, p. 408. See G. Uratadze, *op. cit.*, p. 159. Stalin attended the London Congress as a "delegate" from the Borchalo district of Tiflis. The crude alteration of his "mandate," or credentials, was noted by other delegates from the Tiflis committee, which had not approved the "election" of Stalin, who in any event produced no records of the election. This was understandable in view of the fact that no party organization existed in the Borchalo district.

375a. See Report No. 148 [unsigned] dated May 1, 1907 (N.S.) from Paris. On file at The Hoover Institution.

375b. See Report No. 152 dated April 24, 1907 (N.S.) from Paris. Report 145 of April 17, addressed to the Director of the Department of Police and referred to above, is unfortunately handwritten, partially torn, and completely illegible.

376. Letter from Det Forenede Dampskibs-Selskab, Copenhagen, *op. cit.*

377. V. I. Lenin, *Polnoe sobranie sochinenii*, ed. 5, Vol. 15 (Moscow: Gospolitizdat, 1961), p. 571.

378. M. Liadov, *op. cit.*, p. 207. Also see *Vospominaniya o V.I. Lenine* (Moscow: Izdatelstvo Ts.K VLKSM, 1953), pp. 14-15.

379. *Piatyi (Londonsky) syezd RSDRP, aprel-mai 1907 goda; protokoly* (Moscow: Gospolitizdat, 1963), p. 630.

380. Letter from Det Forenede Dampskibs-Selskab, *op. cit.*

381. *Daily Express*, London, May 10 and 11, 1907.

382. *Justice*, London, June 8, 1907.

383. *Daily Express*, London, May 11, 1907.

384. *Ibid.*

385. *Daily Mirror*, London, May 10 and 11, 1907.

386. Bobrovskaya, Tsetsilia S. (Zelikson), *Provocateurs I Have Known* (London: Modern Books, 1931), pp. 13-6.

387. Report no. 225, classified "top secret" submitted by the Chief of the Okhrana Foreign Agency to the Director of the Department of Police, dated May 26, 1907. On file at The Hoover Institution.

388. J. Iremashvili, *op. cit.*, p. 31.

389. See L. Trotsky, *op. cit.*, p. 90.

390. *Ibid.* Shaumyan complained, according to Trotsky, that "The Caucasian mensheviks taking full advantage of their crushing numerical weight and official dominance in the Caucasus, do everything in their power to prevent bolsheviks from getting elected." Also see *Piatyi . . . op. cit.*, p. 241.

391. The bolshevik members of the new Central Committee were Meshkovsky, Rozhkov, Teodorovich, Nogin, and Lenin. Bogdanov, Krasin,

Zinoviev, Rykov, Shantser, Sammer, Leiteisen, Taratuta, and A. Smirnov were alternates. But Stalin was neither a member nor an alternate. See *Piaty . . . , op. cit.,* p. 590 ff.

392. L. Trotsky, *op. cit.,* p. 92.
393. I. V. Stalin, *op. cit.,* p. 382.
394. *Ibid.,* p. 50.
395. *Ibid.,* p. 52.
396. I. V. Stalin, *O Lenine,* p. 22 ff.
397. I. P. Tovstukha, *Iosif Vissarionovich Stalin* (Moscow: Gos. izd-vo, 1927), p. 9. S. Alliluev, *op. cit.,* p. 134. Alliluev claimed that in July 1907 Koba and Keke lived in Baku in a small one story house.

9. THE EREVAN SQUARE ROBBERY

398. *Piaty (Londonsky) syezd, op. cit.,* pp. 121, 241, 349, 350.
399. *Ibid.,* p. 241.
400. V. I. Lenin, *op. cit.,* ed. 5, Vol. XV, p. 571.
401. *Ibid.*
402. N. K. Krupskaya, *op. cit.,* p. 159.
403. *Ibid.,* p. 162.
404. R. Payne in his *The Rise and Fall of Stalin,* p. 121, is mistaken in writing that Lenin was not in Germany during 1907. He was there on three different occasions. See V. I. Lenin, *op. cit.,* ed. 5, Vol. XVI, pp. 680-6, and Vol. XV, p. 571.
405. I. V. Stalin, *Sochinenia,* Vol. 2 (Moscow: Gospolitizdat, 1946), pp. 408-409.
406. H. Barbusse, *op. cit.,* p. 40.
407. E. Ludwig, *op. cit.,* p. 38.
408. R. Payne, *op. cit.,* p. 121. I am unable to locate Payne's source.
409. L. Trotsky, *op. cit.,* p. 108.
410. *Ibid.*
411. M. Futrell, *op. cit.,* p. 58 ff. Also see S. T. Possony, *op. cit.,* p. 94, for an account of these financial transactions.
412. S. T. Possony, *op. cit.,* p. 97 fn.
413. *Ibid.,* p. 97.
414. *Ibid.,* p. 101. See also *Piaty (Londonsky) syezd . . . , op. cit.,* facsim. pp. 688-9.
415. V. I. Lenin, *Sochinenia,* ed. 3, Vol. XII (Moscow: Gospolitizdat, p. 566.
416. E. Ludwig, *op. cit.,* pp. 42-3.
417. *Le Petit Temps,* Paris, June 27, 1907.
418. S. F. Medvedeva Ter-Petrosyan, "Tovarishch Kamo," *Proletarskaya revoliutsiya,* 1924, No. 8-9 (31-2), p. 120. See also L. Shaumyan, *Kamo* (Moscow: Gospolitizdat, 1959), p. 9.
419. Report No. 490 from the Chief of the Okhrana Foreign Agency to the Director of the Department of Police, dated October 31, 1907. On file at The Hoover Institution.
420. See N. K. Krupskaya, *op. cit.,* p. 155.
421. *Ibid.*
422. S. F. Medvedeva Ter-Petrosyan, *op. cit.,* p. 130.
423. *Ibid.,* p. 130 ff.

424. Frank Owen, *The Three Dictators* (London: Allen & Unwin, 1940), p. 114.
425. L. Trotsky, *op. cit.*, pp. 107-8.
426. D. Shub, *op. cit.*, p. 100.
427. Report No. 490, *op. cit.* It claims that "forty Cossacks and policemen were killed."
428. L. Trotsky, *op. cit.*, p. 110.
429. N. K. Krupskaya, *op. cit.*, p. 174.
430. Report No. 490, *op. cit.*
431. *Ibid.*
432. L. Shaumyan, *op. cit.*, p. 268.
433. Report No. 490, *op. cit.*
434. S. T. Possony, *op. cit.*, p. 102.
435. *Spisok obshchago sostava* . . . , *1907*, p. 442.
436. Report No. 490, *op. cit.*
436a. Arsenidze maintained that Stalin was in the Tiflis Railway Station during the Erevan Square robbery and that sometime later the Georgian social democrats excluded him from their organization. See page 59 of an unpublished interview with Razden Arsenidze on file at The Hoover Institution.
437. Bertram D. Wolfe, *Three Who Made A Revolution* (New York: Dial Press, 1948), p. 395.
438. R. Arsenidze, *op. cit.*, p. 233.
439. L. Martov, "Artilleriskaya podgotovka," *Vpered*, Petrograd, March 18, 1918.
440. B. D. Wolfe, *op. cit.*, p. 471.
441. *Zarya Rossii*, Petrograd, April 17, 1918. Also see Grigory Aronson, "Stalinsky protsess protiv Martova," *Sotsialistichesky Vestnik*, Paris, No. 7-8, 1939, pp. 84-89.
442. B. D. Wolfe, *op. cit.*, p. 471.
443. J. Iremashvili, *op. cit.*, p. 37.

10. THE BLACK CITY

444. I. V. Stalin, *Sochinenia*, Vol. II (Moscow: Gospolitizdat, 1946), p. 410. There is unconfirmed information that the Rothschild archives in France include information that Stalin was on the payroll of the Baku Rothschild Works in Baku during this period.
445. *Dvadtsat piat let Bakinskoi organizatsii bolshevikov* (Baku: Bakinsky rabochy, 1924).
446. B. Souvarine, *op. cit.*, p. 107.
447. I. V. Stalin, *op. cit.*, p. 410. The strike was ineffectual but it moved Lenin to write in virtual desperation from abroad that the strikers were "the last of the Mohicans." See V. I. Lenin, *Polnoe sobranie sochineny*, ed. 5, Vol. XIX (Moscow: Gospolitizdat, 1961), p. 385.
448. "Arkhivnye materialy o revoliutsionnoi deiatelnosti I. V. Stalina, 1908-1913 gg.," *Krasny arkhiv*, 1934, No. 2, p. 3.
449. S. Vereshchak, "Stalin v tiurme," *Dni*, January 22, 1928, p. 2; January 24, 1928, p. 3.
450. I. Vatsek, "Stalinskaya shkola revoliutsionnoi borby," *Rasskazy o velikom Staline* (Tbilisi: Zarya Vostoka, 1941), Vol. 2, p. 22.

451. B. Souvarine, *op. cit.*, p. 108. Also see Demyan Bednyi, "S podlinnym verno!" *Pravda*, December 20, 1929, p. 2.

452. S. Vereshchak, *op. cit.*, p. 3.

453. Vereshchak meant he wanted a guarantee from the Bolshevik member that Koba could be trusted as a genuine revolutionary.

454. V. I. Lenin, *Polnoe sobranie sochinenie*, ed. 5, Vol. XLV, pp. 345-6.

455. S. Vereshchak, *op. cit.*

456. L. Trotsky, *op. cit.*, p. 119.

457. The possibility that homosexuality was a factor in this brutal murder has been implied but not clarified. See Isaac Don Levine, *Stalin's Great Secret* (New York: Coward-McCann, 1956), p. 40.

458. I. Dubinsky-Mukhadze, *Ordzhonikidze* (Moscow: Molodaya gvardiya, 1963), p. 377.

459. Most of his biographers repeat an entry in his official chronology that he departed November 9, 1908. Authentic Department of Police documents disagree. See Department of Police Document 101145.

460. I. V. Stalin, *op. cit.*, p. 412.

460a. See "Politseiskoe dielo," in *Katorga i ssylka*, No. 1 (22), Moscow, 1926, p. 285.

461. E. Yaroslavsky, *op. cit.*, p. 66.

462. N. K. Sarkisov, *Borba Bakinskogo proletariata v period pervoi russkoi revoliutsii* (Baku: Azerbaidzhanskoe gos. izd-vo, 1965), p. 8 ff.

463. Lavrenty Beria, *On the History of the Bolshevik Organization in Transcaucasia* (Moscow: Foreign Languages Publishing House, 1949). The original, *K voprosu ob istorii bolshevistskikh organizatsy v Zakavkazye*, was published in Moscow by Partizdat in 1935.

464. This is Beria's footnote: "From the report of the chief of the Tiflis Gubernia Gendarmerie Department, October 24, 1909, No. 13702. Material from the Central Party Archives of the Central Committee of the Communist Party (b.) of Azerbaijan. File No. 430." The original document has not been published.

465. Another Beria footnote reads: "From the report of Captain Galimbatovsky on the arrest of Joseph Vissarionovich Dhugashvili, March 24, 1910. Material from the Central Party Archives of the Central Committee of the Communist Party (b.) of Azerbaijan, File No. 430." See L. P. Beria, *op. cit.*, pp. 224-5. In the original 1935 edition these passages may be found on p. 90.

It was standard operating procedure for the Okhrana in its official reports to omit the "ich" from "Vissarionovich" leaving "Vissarionov", the patronymic. That Vissarionovich appears here is evidence that the report had been doctored by someone unfamiliar with the form of Okhrana reporting.

466. I. V. Stalin, *op. cit.*, p. 412.

467. A. S. Allilueva, *op. cit.*, pp. 110-2.

468. B. Souvarine, *op. cit.*, p. 112.

469. On his trips to and from the Caucasus when he journied to Tammerfors (1905), Stockholm (1906), and London (1907).

470. *Spisok obshchago sostava chinov Otdelnago Korpusa Zhandarmov*, 1909, pp. 59 and 192.

471. "Shkola filerov," *Byloe*, 1917, No. 3(25), pp. 40-67.

472. David Cole's biography of Stalin has an unsubstantiated story that late in 1909 "following the usual escape, this time from Solvychegodsk

. . . Stalin arrived in St. Petersburg and spent a busy month renewing old contacts and collecting information from this clearing house between the Caucasus and Krassin." See David Cole, *op. cit.,* p. 32.

473. I. V. Stalin, *op. cit.,* p. 412.

474. Y. Delbars writes that on June 24, "Koba was on the move again, under the name of Movradiantz. . . . He spent a couple of days in Moscow with Lialin, a party comrade." Yaroslavsky writing in 1940 relates that on June 24, Stalin left Solvychegodsk and returned to Baku under the name of Oganes Totomyants." Both accounts are incorrect. See Yves Delbars, *op. cit.,* p. 57, and E. Yaroslavsky, *op. cit.,* p. 66.

475. I. V. Stalin, *op. cit.,* p. 412.

476. L. Trotsky, *op. cit.,* p. 124, quoting Ordzhonikidze.

477. I. V. Stalin, *op. cit.,* p. 146-96.

478. *Ibid.,* p. 413.

479. M. D. Bagirov, *Iz istorii bolshevistskoi organizatsii Baku i Azerbaidzhana* (Moscow: OGIZ, 1946), pp. 101-02.

480. *Ibid.,* p. 115.

481. I. V. Stalin, *op. cit.,* p. 414.

482. Captain Martynov received a decoration in Baku on December 6, 1910. He had been on hand—figuratively—to greet Stalin when he returned to Baku in 1909. See *Spisok obshchago sostava chinov Otdelnago Korpusa Zhandarmov, 1911,* p. 613.

483. Department of Police Document No. 101145, *op. cit.*

484. L. Beria, *op. cit.,* p. 224-5.

485. Document No. 97373 (classified Top Secret), dated January 10, 1911, from the Special Section of the Department of Police to the Chief of the Okhrana Foreign Agency. On file at The Hoover Institution.

486. Kamenev's name is omitted in the reprinted copy of the letter in Stalin's *Collected Works.* See I. V. Stalin, *op. cit.,* p. 215.

487. In Stalin's *Collected Works* this is translated as "vexed questions." See I. V. Stalin, *Collected Works,* Vol. 2, p. 215.

11. LENIN REDISCOVERS DZHUGASHVILI

488. I. V. Stalin, *Sochinenia* (Moscow: Gospolitizdat, 1946), Vol. 2, pp. 209-12. Also see N. Anisimov, "I. V. Stalin v gody Solvychegodskoi i Vologodskoi ssylok," *Istorik-marksist,* 1940, No. 9, pp. 3-26.

489. Aleksei E. Badaev, *Bolsheviki v Gosudarstvennoi Dume* (Moscow: Gospolitizdat, 1954), ed. 8, p. 98.

490. Top secret document No. 98570, dated February 7, 1911, from the Special Section of the Department of Police to the Chief of the Okhrana Foreign Agency in Paris has Stalin's letter as an enclosure. On file at The Hoover Institution.

491. S. T. Possony, *Lenin: the Compulsive Revolutionary* (London: Allen & Unwin, 1966), p. 405.

492. Department of Police Document No. 101145, *op. cit.*

493. Department of Police document No. 101375, dated April 6, 1911 classified "secret," signed by Vissarionov and Eremin, serving as a cover letter for a report submitted by Captain Plotto of the Vologda Gendarme Administration, No. 147, dated March 30, 1911, and classified "top secret." On file at The Hoover Institution.

494. I. V. Stalin, *op. cit.,* p. 415.
495. I. Dubinsky—Mukhadze, *op. cit.,* pp. 91-6.
496. Pavel G. Kurlov, *Gibel imperatorskoi Rossii* (Berlin: Otto Kirchner, 1923).
497. N. Anisimov, *op. cit.*
498. Report No. 217, from the Chief of Vologda Province Gendarme Administration, dated May 18, 1911. On file at The Hoover Institution.
499. I. V. Stalin, *op. cit.,* p. 415.
500. *Ibid.*
501. *Ibid.*
502. N. Anisimov, *op. cit.*
503. S. I. Todriya (1880-1936) joined the Social Democratic Party in 1901. A professional typesetter and printer he had plied his trade in Batum, Baku, Moscow, and St. Petersburg. Apparently he died during Stalin's purges.
504. A. S. Allilueva, *op. cit.,* p. 107-110.
504a. *Ibid.*
505. L. Trotsky, *op. cit.,* p. 135, quoting S. Alliluev.
506. Department of Police report No. 102383, dated June 11, 1912, classified "secret," from the Special Section of the Department of Police, signed by Vissarionov and Eremin. On file at The Hoover Institution.
507. I. V. Stalin, *op. cit.,* p. 416.
508. *Ibid.*
509. S. T. Possony, *Lenin: the Compulsive Revolutionary* (Chicago: Regnery, 1964), p. 125.
510. I. V. Stalin, *op. cit.,* p. 415.
511. S. T. Possony, *op. cit.,* p. 126.
512. "K istorii Prazhskoi konferentsii," *Krasny arkhiv,* 1939, No. 6(97), pp. 91-123. This indicates Okhrana knowledge of the conference in Prague.
513. A. E. Badaev, "Russkie bolsheviki do revoliutsii," *Byloe,* 1926, No. 1, pp. 70-119. Badaev comments that Lenin continually worked with the unwitting aid of agents-provocateurs, that police agents attended the bolshevik 1912 conference in Prague, that Lenin's 1912 trip from Paris to Austria was with the agreement of the Germans, and that there Lenin prepared the revolution in Russia "under the protection of the Department of Police and the Germans."
514. See V. Zhilinsky, "Organizatsiya i zhizn Okhrannogo Otdeleniya vo vremiya tsarskoi vlasti," *Golos minuvshago,* 1917, no. 9/10, p. 278.
515. N. K. Krupskaya, *op. cit.,* pp. 228-9.
516. B. D. Wolfe, *op. cit.,* p. 538. Also see S. T. Possony, *op. cit.,* p. 131.
517. A. E. Badaev, *Bolsheviki v Gosudarstvennoi Dume* (Moscow: Gospolitizdat, 1954), ed. 8, p. 278.
518. See T. S. Bobrovskaya, *op. cit.,* pp. 26-30.
519. N. K. Krupskaya, *op. cit.,* p. 216.
519a. See N.. Valentinov, "O liudiakh revoliutsionnogo podpolia," *Novyi Zhurnal,* No. 73, September 1963, pp. 244-58. This account reveals how Lenin misjudged the Okhrana agent I. Konovalov, whom he praised in 1913 as "honorable and intelligent." He wanted to honor Konovalov by securing him a place in the Duma.
520. G. Walter, *Lénine* (Paris: Julliard, 1950), p. 225. Also see B. D. Wolfe, *op. cit.,* p. 542.

521. Vladimir Burtsev, "Lenine and Malinovsky," *Struggling Russia,* Vol. I, No. 9/10, May 17, 1919, pp. 138-40.

522. V. I. Lenin, *Sochinenia* (Moscow: Gospolitizdat, 1937), ed. 3, Vol. XV p. 653.

523. S. T. Possony, *Lenin: the Compulsive Revolutionary* (London: Allen & Unwin, 1966), p. 151. The conference cost about 10,000 francs.

524. V. I. Lenin, *op. cit.,* p. 653.

525. See D. Shub, *op. cit.,* pp. 98 ff.

526. I. V. Stalin, *Politichesky otchet Tsentralnogo komiteta XV syezdu VKP(b)* (Moscow: Partizdat, 1936), p. 63. Also see M. Moskalev, *Biuro tsentralnogo komiteta RSDRP v Rossii* (Moscow: Izd-stvo Pol. Lit., 1964), p. 197. Moskalev writes that in early 1912 "I V. Stalin, a member of the Central Committee and the Russian bureau conducted much work for the Party. But then he did not understand the principal character of the Prague conference decisions about the complete organizational break with the mensheviks."

527. I. V. Stalin, *Sochinenia,* Vol. 2 (Moscow: Gospolitizdat, 1946), p. 416.

528. *Iosif Vissarionovich Stalin: kratkaya biografiya* (Moscow: Institut Marksa-Engelsa-Lenina, 1953), ed. 2, pp. 50-1.

529. *Krasnyi arkhiv,* 1936, No. 5(78), p. 21. Also see M. Moskalev, *op. cit.,* p. 194. The Russian Bureau of the Central Committee "for practical leadership of party work in Russia" was also created at Prague. Its members were Ordzhonikidze, Spandariyan, Goloshchekin, Stalin, and Stasova—in that order.

530. I. V. Stalin, *op. cit.,* p. 417.

531. B. D. Wolfe, *op. cit.,* p. 541.

532. *Ibid.,* p. 542. Also see S. T. Possony, *op. cit.,* p. 141. G. Uratadze, *op. cit.,* pp. 214 ff. Several months later, in August, there was a conference of Trotsky's followers, bundists, mensheviks, and others in Vienna. Uratadze was a menshevik delegate from Tiflis. He remarks that from the first day of the conference rumors were current that Okhrana agents acting as delegates were in attendance. The fear of being spied upon disconcerted the delegates and delayed the work of of the conference. Then the delegate from Svastopol, who had been suspected as an Okhrana agent, left. Before his departure he caused some consternation by his statement, "I will go, but watch him." He pointed to Uritsky, the delegate from Odessa who was then Trotsky's secretary. It was later proven that another Okhrana agent, Polyakov, attended the conference as the delegate from Moscow.

533. I. V. Stalin, *op. cit.,* p. 417.

534. *Ibid.*

534a. Ladis K. D. Kristof, "Boris I. Nicolaevsky, 1887-1966," *The Russian Review,* Vol. 25, No. 3, July, 1966, pp. 324-27.

535. *Dvadtsat piat let Bakinskoi organizatsii, op. cit.,* p. 229.

535a. After 1917 Nicolaevsky learned that a secretary of the party in Baku from 1907 to 1917 had been an Okhrana agent. This person—a certain Seregin—had "betrayed everyone who had fallen into his orbit." But, curiously he had protected the bolsheviks—among them Stalin —betraying only mensheviks to the Okhrana. Thus in 1962 Nicolaevsky concluded Stalin had informed Seregin who, in turn, brought about Nicolaevsky's arrest. See Interview—January 19, 1962, *Interviews No. 10-18 With B. I. Nicolaevsky November 1961—November*

1962. Inter-University Project on the History of The Menshevik Movement—430 West 116th Street, New York. On file at The Hoover Institution.

536. Among the materials about Nicolaevsky at the Hoover Institution is a detailed autobiography which Nicolaevsky dictated—but did not edit —in the early nineteen-fifties. This account was reconstructed by Ladis K. D. Kristof, Research Fellow at The Hoover Institution.

537. Harry S. Truman in his speech in Eugene, Oregon, on June 11, 1948. See *Facts on File,* Vol. VIII, 1948, p. 183.

538. Ilya Mgeladze, "Nachalo podyema," *Dvadtsat piat let Bakinskoi organizatsii, op. cit.,* p. 229.

539. *Ibid.*

540. I. V. Stalin, *op. cit.,* p. 417.

541. S. T. Possony, *op. cit.,* p. 142.

542. Clara Zetkin was a favorite of both Lenin and Stalin. See Sandor Korosi-Krizsan, "Rumania and the Comintern," *East Europe,* Vol. XV, December 1966, No. 12, pp. 13-5. The author, a Rumanian, active in the international communist movement, went to Soviet Russia in 1923 to confer with communist leaders in regard to the Rumanian nationality question. He found Clara Zetkin ensconced in an apartment in the right wing of the Kremlin. Clara, Piatnitsky, and Bukharin conferred with the Rumanian communists. Stalin never talked with them.

543. I. V. Stalin, *op. cit.,* p. 417.

544. See F. Drabkina, "Tsarskoe pravitelstvo i Pravda," *Istorichesky zhurnal,* Vol. VII, No. 3/4, March/April 1937, pp. 115-23. Several reports of the Department of Police Special Section from 1910 to 1913 show intelligence reporting about *Pravda* and personalities associated with it.

545. *Pravda, 1912-1914, 1917 gg.* (Moscow: Gospolitizdat, 1962).

546. See S. T. Possony, *op. cit.,* p. 162 ff. for an excellent account of the birth of *Pravda.* Also see *Pisma P. B. Axelrod i Y. O. Martov. Materialy po istorii russkogo revoliutsionnogo dvizheniia, Vol. I* (Berlin: Russky Revoliutsionnyi Arkhiv, 1924), pp. 291-92. Martov wrote Axelrod on June 2, 1914: "We must hurry. All our affairs have now come to the one [issue]—the case of Malinovsky. As long as this abscess remains unopened we won't be able to move forward. We all are convinced without any doubt that M. is a provocateur, and we are practically sure that 'Pravda-ism' was directed by the Okhrana. But whether we shall succeed to prove it *ad oculos* is another question because we are handcuffed by our own people and the allies who are afraid of the horror of the fight with the *Pravdists.*"

547. Moisei A. Moskalev, *Russkoe biuro TsK bolshevistskoi partii, 1912-mart 1917 g.* (Moscow: Gospolitizdat, 1947), p. 56.

548. Department of Police report No. 102383, *op. cit.*

549. I. V. Stalin, *op. cit.,* p. 418.

550. S. Vereshchak, *op. cit.*

551. E. Pesikina, "V Naryme," *Pravda,* December 26, 1939, p. 4.

552. B. Souvarine, *op. cit.,* p. 128. Also see N. Karganov "Iz proshlogo Stalina," *Vozrozdenie,* Paris, January 13, 1929, p. 3.

553. I. V. Stalin, *op. cit.,* p. 418.

554. A. S. Allilueva, *op. cit.,* p. 114.

555. E. Gorodetsky, *Yu. Sverdlov; zhizn i deiatelnost* (Moscow: Gospolit-izdat, 1961), p. 85.
556. I. V. Stalin, *op. cit.,* p. 418.
557. S. T. Possony, *op. cit.,* p. 163.
558. I. V. Stalin, *op. cit.,* p. 420.
559. *Ibid.*
560. *Ibid.*
561. A. Shotman, *Kak is iskry vozgorelos plamia,* ed. 2 (Leningrad: Molo-daya gvardiya, 1935), p. 166 ff.
562. A. Shotman, *op. cit.,* pp. 169-176.
562a. See A. S. Allilueva, *Iz vospominanii,* pp. 19-20. Also see Stanislaw Kot, *op. cit.,* pp. xxi-xxvi. Stalin told essentially the same yarn at a Kremlin banquet in December 1941. He added a few details missing in the Allilueva account. As recalled by the Polish Ambassador Kot, Stalin related: "I reached Trzebinia and saw a large restaurant. I was terribly hungry. I ordered some food and sat down at a table. The waiter carted a lot of food around, but he continually gave me a miss, and then I heard a bell. Some of the people got up and ran to a train going westward. I went up to the buffet and said sharply: 'This is scandalous; everybody else has been served except me.' The waiter filled a plate with soup and handed it to me. Then there was another bell, a train for Cracow arrived and everybody rushed to get in. In my fury I threw the plate on the floor, flung a ruble at the waiter and flew out. I arrived at Cracow. . . . A few moments later I was with Lenin. We had hardly greeted each other when I burst out: 'Lenin, give me something to eat at once, for I'm half dead; I've had nothing since yesterday evening.' Lenin replied: 'Why didn't you eat at Trzebinia; there's a good restaurant there?' 'The Poles wouldn't give me anything to eat.' And I told him the whole story. 'But what language did you order the food in?' he asked. 'Why, in Russian of course, I don't know any other.' 'What a fool you are, Stalin. . . . Don't you know that the Poles think of Russian as the language of their persecutors?' "
563. Letter from Lenin to Axelrod dated December 6 (N.S.), 1912 for Vasiliev (Stalin). See *Iz epokhi "Zvezdy" i "Pravdy",* Vol. 3 (Mos-cow: Gos. izd-vo, 1923), p. 199. A footnote explains that Lenin was concerned about a passport which Stalin had used for foreign travel. See also Circular No. 108622 issued by the Special Section of the De-partment of Police, dated March 27, 1910, signed by Colonel Eremin, classified "secret," concerning 21 illegal passports in pos-session of RSDRP. The list with names, dates and places of issue is attached. Most of the passports are copies of originals still in possession of their owners. None pertain to Stalin. The document is on file at The Hoover Institution.

12. THE CRACOW-VIENNA EPISODE

564. I. V. Stalin, *op. cit.,* p. 436.
565. L. Trotsky, *op. cit.,* pp. 147-148.
566. I. V. Stalin, *op. cit.,* p. 436.
567. See letter classified "top secret" dated December 13, 1912, from the Special Section of Department of Police to the Chief of the Foreign

Agency, covering a copy of an intercepted letter from Nadezhda Krupskaya in Beuthen, Germany, dated December 14 [N.S.], 1912, to A. E. Axelrod in St. Petersburg. On file at The Hoover Institution.

568. I. V. Stalin, op. cit., p. 436.

569. Iz epokhi . . . , op. cit., p. 199-201.

570. V. I. Lenin, Polnoe sobranie sochineny, ed. 5, Vol. 22 (Moscow: Gospolitizdat, 1961), p. 582.

571. Report from the Special Section of the Department of Police, No. 96322, dated March 12, 1913, signed by Colonel Eremin, classified "secret." On file at The Hoover Institution.

572. N. K. Krupskaya, op. cit., p. 244.

573. I. V. Stalin, op. cit., p. 421.

574. It is curious that according to Lenin, op. cit., Vol. XXII, the conference began on December 28th.

575. See A. E. Badaev, op. cit., p. 106.

576. Ibid., p. 95 ff.

577. Lobov's police agent status was proved after the revolution and he was shot on June 30, 1918. See S. B. Chlenov, Moskovskaya Okhranka i ee sekretnye sotrudniki (Moscow: Otdel pechati Moskovskogo sovieta R. i K.D., 1919), p. 69.

578. F. N. Samoilov, Po sledam minuvshego (Moscow: Gospolitizdat, 1940), p. 200. Samoilov writes that a Department of Police report states its agent lost Koba at the railway station because of the great number of travellers. On November 11, 1912, the St. Petersburg Police reported Koba left for Finland. Police agents were sent to follow him to Abo and Hangö, but in vain. They had to be recalled.

579. A. Shotman, op. cit., p. 176.

580. M. A. Tsiavlovsky, ed., Bolsheviki . . . (Moscow: Zadruga, 1918), p. 210.

581. A. Tolmachev, Kalinin (Moscow: Molodaya gvardiya, 1963), p. 226.

582. D. Shub, op. cit., pp. 218-9.

583. A. Tolmachev, op. cit., p. 226.

584. I. V. Stalin, op. cit., p. 421.

585. Padenie tsarskogo rezhima (Leningrad: Gos. izd-vo, 1924), Vol. III, p. 255 ff.

586. I. V. Stalin, op. cit., p. 437.

587. Ibid.

588. Its original title was Natsionalny vopros i sotsial-demokratiya. See Prosveshchenie, 1913, No. 3-5. Also see I. V. Stalin, op. cit., p. 367.

589. V. I. Lenin, op. cit., p. 584.

590. I. V. Stalin, op. cit., p. 437.

591. Ibid.

592. See K. T. Sverdlova, Yakov Mikailovich Sverdlov (Moscow: Molodaya gvardiya, 1957), p. 210. Lenin wrote Sverdlov at the beginning of February, 1913 about the "Day"—code word for Pravda.

592a. See V. I. Lenin, Sochinenia, 3rd ed. (Moscow, 1935), Vol. XVI, pp. 720-9 ff. Lenin had become particularly annoyed at a speech that Akaki Chkhenkeli, a Georgian Menshevik deputy, had made in the Duma on December 10, 1912. In it he had called for institutions to be created "for the free development of each nationality."

593. S. T. Possony, op. cit., p. 149.

593a. Richard Pipes, The Formation of The Soviet Union—Communism *and Nationalism 1917-1923* (Cambridge: Harvard University Press, 1964), p. 21. The author correctly observes that "Marx and Engels left their followers little guidance in matters of nationality and nationalism. In Western Europe, whence they drew the bulk of the source material for their economic and political studies, the minority problem presented no serious issue: most of the states were naturally homogeneous, without significant minority populations."

594. Otto Bauer, *Die Nationalitätenfrage und die Sozialdemokratie* (Wien: I. Brand, 1907). Also see Karl Renner, *Das Selbstbestimmungsrecht der Nationen in besonderer Anwendung auf Oesterreich* (Leipzig und Wien: F. Deuticke, 1908).

595. N. K. Krupskaya, *op. cit.,* pp. 261-2.

595a. Most of the footnotes for "Marxism and the National Question" refer, at any rate, to Russian translations of Bauer, Renner, and Springer made by members of the Bund. The references made to German-language source materials might have been supplied by Troyanovsky, Bukharin, or Lenin.

596. I. V. Stalin, *op. cit.,* pp. 179-201.

597. L. Trotsky, *op. cit.,* p. 158.

598. The plaque installed on December 21, 1949 (Stalin's 70th birthday) is maintained by the Vienna city authorities. During the 1956 Hungarian revolution it was smeared with red paint, but it has been restored.

599. "Top secret" report No. 94182, dated January 25, 1913, to the Chief of the Okhrana Foreign Agency in Paris from the Special Section of the St. Petersburg Department of Police Headquarters. On file at The Hoover Institution.

600. For the party cover names of Lobov, Lobova, Rozmirovich, and Sverdlov see M. A. Tsiavlovsky, *op. cit.,* pp. 210, 211, 227, 228, and 230.

601. Bertram D. Wolfe, *op. cit.,* p. 548. Also see D. Shub, *op. cit.,* Chapter VI.

602. *Bolshaya Sovetskaya Entsiklopediya,* ed. 2, Vol. XLIII (Moscow: Izd-vo "Bolshaya Sovetskaya Entsiklopediya," 1956), pp. 303-4.

603. Eddy Gilmore, the veteran American correspondent for the Associated press in Russia during World War II, recalls: "I met him first at the Republican National Convention in Cleveland that nominated Alf Landon. He was the Soviet Ambassador in Washington and I found him on the final night sitting in the box of the guest of honor—as any ambassador would have been.

"The next time I saw him was in Kuibyshev in November, 1941. There was a hell of a row in the Grand Hotel barbershop—where I had gone when I had a legitimate excuse for entering a barbershop. Anyhow, I saw a Red Army sergeant demanding that a civilian be emptied from a barber chair so he could be barbered. The civilian, with soap on his face, protested, but the sergeant won the argument, for that was the rule in those days—Red Army men first. The guy with the lather came and sat down beside me. I recognized him as Troyanovsky and he admitted it. This was highly embarrassing for us both—that switch from the guest of honor's box at a big national convention in America, to being hurled out of a chair in a third-rate barbershop in a fourth-rate Soviet city by a sergeant! T. was then writing for the *Volga Tribune.*

"I saw him often, the last time in Moscow. Then he was almost in tatters. We talked near the Central Telegraph Office. I think he was suffering from Parkinson's disease." Letter in author's possession.

604. Troyanovsky's son was one of Khrushchev's translators-interpreters.

605. *Malaya Sovetskaya Entsiklopediya*, Vol. VII (Moscow: Izd-vo "Sovetskaya Entsiklopediya," 1930), pp. 386-7.

606. Reports No. 107704, dated December 11, 1913; No. 17805, dated December 12, 1913; and No. 107926, dated December 17, 1913, all from the Special Section of the Department of Police to the Okhrana Foreign Agency in Paris, enclosing copies of intercepted letters from Troyanovsky in Cracow to his wife, Elena Rozmirovich in St. Petersburg. See also report No. 165718, dated January 15, 1914 with the copy of the intercepted letter from Rozmirovich to Troyanovsky. On file at The Hoover Institution.

607. A. E. Badaev, *op. cit.*, p. 280. The most believable account is that of F. N. Samoilov, *Vospominaniya*, Vol. III (Moscow-Leningrad: Gos. izd-vo, 1925), pp. 27-8. It was written before Stalin had assumed total power in Soviet Russia.

608. A. E. Badaev, *op. cit.*, p. 168. See also F. N. Samoilov, *op. cit.*, pp. 27-8 and the testimony of Chkheidze in *Padenie tsarskogo rezhima*, Vol. III (Leningrad: Gos. izd-vo, 1924), pp. 484 ff.

609. M. A. Tsiavlovsky, *op. cit.*, pp. 227-8.

610. S. T. Possony, *op. cit.*, p. 245.

610a. *Ibid.*, p. 295.

611. S. Sumsky, "Troyanovsky," *Posledniya novosti*, January 1, 1934, p. 3.

612. S. Sumsky, *op. cit.*

613. M. A. Tsiavlovsky, *op. cit.*, pp. 130-1.

614. V. I. Lenin, *Sochinenia*, ed. 2, Vol. XVI (Moscow: Gospolitizdat, 1931), p. 327.

615. A. E. Badaev, *op. cit.*, p. 280.

616. M. A. Tsiavlovsky, *op. cit.*, p. 131.

617. D. Shub, *op. cit.*, pp. 119 ff. Also see N. Bukharin, "Pamiati Ilycha," *Pravda*, January 21, 1925, p. 3.

618. D. Shub, *op. cit.*, pp. 119-123, quoting A. E. Badaev. This story cannot be verified.

619. *Ibid.*, p. 121.

620. M. Moskalev, *Russkoe biuro bolshevistskoi partii, 1912 g.—mart 1917 g.* (Moscow: Gospolitizdat, 1947), p. 129.

621. D. Shub, *op. cit.*, p. 121. Shub claims that Bukharin and Troyanovsky wrote the Central Committee demanding that Malinovsky appear before a party court. "In reply, they received a severe rebuke from Lenin, who, speaking for the Central Committee, forbade them to spread these rumors about Malinovsky. Lenin called their action worse than treason, and threatened to have them expelled from the Party if they persisted. Bukharin obeyed, but Troyanovsky soon parted company with Lenin and did not rejoin the Bolsheviks until 1921."

622. George Wolfgang Felix Hallgarten, *Imperialismus vor 1914*, ed. 2, Vol. II (Munich: C. H. Beck, 1960), p. 448.

13. SIBERIAN YEARS

623. I. V. Stalin, *op. cit.*, p. 421.

623a. V. I. Lenin, *Sochineniya*, 3rd ed., Vol. XXX, pp. 7-90. Also see Lenin, *op. cit.*, XVI, p. 328. Pipes comments that "Lenin expected Stalin to go through all the Austrian and other socialist writings in order to refute the ideas which were gaining prevalence among Russian Marxists. The product of Stalin's efforts, however, hardly fulfilled these expectations." See Richard Pipes, *op. cit.*, p. 37.

624. Lenin's letter, dated February 1913, is found in *V. I. Lenin i A. M. Gorky: Pisma, vospominaniya, dokumenty*, Ed. 2 (Moscow: Izd-vo Akademii nauk SSSR, 1961), p. 98.

625. Moisei L. Lurye, *Bolshevisktskaya pechat v tiskakh tsarskoi tsenzury* Leningrad: Gazetno-zhurnalnoe izd-vo, 1939).

626. K. Stalin, "Natsionalny vopros i sotsial-demokratiya," *Prosveshchenie*, March-May, 1913, No. 3-5.

627. I. V. Stalin, *Marksizm i natsionalny vopros* (Moscow: Gospolitizdat, 1946, 1949, 1950, 1952, and 1953).

627a. See Richard Pipes, *op. cit.*, pp. 24-5. "The national problem first came up for discussion at the Bruenn Congress of the Austrian Social Democrats, held in 1899." Bauer later—in 1907—wrote that nationalistic feeling was increasing.

628. I. V. Stalin *Sochinenia*, Vol. II (Moscow: Gospolitizdat, 1946), pp. 290-367.

629. L. Trotsky, *op. cit.*, p. 158. Milovan Djilas, *Conversations With Stalin*, trans. Michael B. Petrovich (New York: Harcourt, Brace and World, 1962), pp. 156-7. Also see Richard Pipes, *op. cit.*, pp. 36-41. In a detailed analysis Pipes correctly draws attention to many errors made by the author—or authors—of "Marxism and the National Question." However, in my estimation he insufficiently evaluates the anti-Bund, hence anti-Jewish, thrust of the work. He concludes: "The character of the work and the ideas expressed in it indicate that in the main it was a work of Stalin's . . . which long ago would have been relegated to total oblivion, were it not for the author's subsequent career."

630. V. I. Lenin, *Polnoe Sobranie Sochineny*, Ed. 5, Vol. XXII (Moscow, Gospolitizdat, 1961), p. 588.

631. V. I. Lenin, *Sochinenia*, Ed. 2, Vol. I (Moscow: Partizdat, 1931), p. 84 fn.

632. V. I. Lenin, *op. cit.*, Ed. 2, Vol. XVI, p. 618.

633. *Birsko-Bidzhansky Raion Dalne-Vostochnogo Kraya* (Moscow: Komitet po zemelnomu ustroistvu trudiashchikhsia evreev, 1928-30), 2 Vols.

634. I. V. Stalin, *op. cit.*

635. I. V. Stalin, *op. cit.*, pp. 373-6.

636. V. I. Lenin, *Sochinenia*, Ed. 2, Vol. XXIX (Moscow: Partizdat, 1932), p. 89.

637. *Ibid.*

638. M. Moskalev, *Russkyoe* . . . , p. 135.

639. I. V. Stalin, *op. cit.*, p. 421.

640. K. T. Sverdlova, *op. cit.*, p. 209.

640a. M. Moskalev, *Biuro* . . . , pp. 222-3. It is clear that Stalin was exerting a negative role on *Pravda* as late as February 1913: "As a member of the Russian bureau of the Central Committee he had not fulfilled Lenin's orders. In an article 'The Situation in the Social-

Democratic Faction' published in *Pravda* on February 26, 1913, Stalin wrote about the necessity to preserve the 'integrity of the s.-d. faction which is in danger of a split.'

"And only under the decisive influence of Lenin was the correct line in relation to the Duma bolshevik faction maintained."

641. K. Sharikov, "Vazhneishie mesta prebyvaniya i revoliutsionnoi deiatelnosti I. V. Stalina v Peterburge-Petrograde-Leningrade (1909-1934)," *Propaganda i agitatsiya*, 1939, No. 32, p. 60.

642. M. Moskalev, *op. cit.*, p. 137.

643. D. Shub, *op. cit.*, p. 122 quoting A. E. Badaev. This cannot be verified.

644. It was February, not April.

645. A. V. Shotman, *op. cit.*, pp. 175 ff.

646. Report No. 95691, dated February 27, 1913, classified "top secret," from the Chief of the Special Section of the Department of Police to the Okhrana Foreign Agency in Paris, with copy of the *"Golubchik"* letter. On file at The Hoover Institution.

647. Stalin.

648. *Ibid.*

649. *Ibid.*

650. Report No. 96088, dated March 6, 1913, from the Special Section of the Department of Police to the Chief of the Okhrana Foreign Agency in Paris with a copy of the intercepted letter from Nadezhda Krupskaya in Cracow, dated March 10, 1913 [N.S.], to N. I. Podvoisky in St. Petersburg. On file at The Hoover Institution.

651. Report No. 95796, dated February 28, 1913, classified "secret," from the Special Section of the Department of Police to the Okhrana Foreign Agency in Paris with a copy of an intercepted letter from Krupskaya. On file at The Hoover Institution.

652. *Leninsky Sbornik*, Vol. XXV (Moscow: Part. izd-vo, 1933), p. 334.

653. Report No. 95677, dated February 26, 1913, classified "top secret," from the Special Section of the Department of Police to the Okhrana Foreign Agency in Paris, with a copy of Malinovsky's letter. On file at The Hoover Institution.

654. Report No. 96395, dated March 13, 1913, from the Special Section of the Department of Police to the Okhrana Foreign Agency in Paris, with a copy of the letter from Lenin to Axelrod. On file at The Hoover Institution.

655. I. V. Stalin, *op. cit.*, p. 421.

656. I. V. Stalin, *op. cit.*, p. 422.

657. *Ibid.*

658. M. Moskalev, *op. cit.*, p. 149.

659. I. V. Stalin, *op. cit.*, p. 422.

660. *Ibid.*

661. M. Moskalev, *op. cit.*, p. 150.

662. *Spisok obshchago sostava* . . . , *op. cit.*, 1913, p. 263.

663. *Padenie Tsarskogo Rezhima*, *op. cit.*, Vol. III, p. 281.

664. *Spisok* . . . , *op. cit.*

665. See M. Futrell, *op. cit.*, for a scholarly and detailed account of these activities.

666. By the use of this document and by way of intuitive methodology, Isaac Don Levine was a pioneer in providing a new dimension in the study of Stalin's pre-revolutionary life. See I. D. Levine, *op. cit.*

666a. See G. M. Derenkovsky, ed., *Vtoroi period revoliutsii, 1906-1907 gody. Chast pervaya; yanvar—aprel 1906 goda; kniga vtoraya.* (Moscow: Izdat-stvo akademii nauka SSSR, 1959), pp. 57, 59, 60, 64, 68, 69, 88, 89, and 92. This compendium reproduces numerous reports made by Captain Eremin that reveal his professional expertise and knowledge of revolutionaries.

666b. This signature is found on Report No. 97784 classified "top secret" and dated April 10, 1913, from the Special Section of The Department of Police to the Chief of the Foreign Agency. On file at The Hoover Institution. General Alexander I. Spiridovich, an important police official and Eremin's superior in the Kiev Okhrana from 1903 to 1904, wrote a long letter on this subject dated January 13, 1950 (in possession of the author). Spiridovich reveals that Eremin was a Cossack and a protégé of the famous Zurbatov, an Okhrana official who founded "police-socialism," and that Eremin performed brilliantly in his assignments, bringing professionalism and expertise to secret agent operations. It is Spiridovich's opinion that Eremin's letter is authentic, his signature genuine, and that Stalin was an Okhrana agent. See, for example, the von Lampe and Markov Collections at The Hoover Institution.

667. Yakov M. Sverdlov, *Izbrannye proizvedeniya,* Vols. I-IV, (Moscow: Gospolitizdat, 1957).

668. Anatoly V. Baikalov, *I Knew Stalin,* (London: Burns Oates, 1940).

669. A. S. Allilueva, *op. cit.*

670. Vera Shveitser, *Stalin v Turukhanskoi ssylke* (Moscow: Molodaya gvardiya, 1943).

671. I. V. Stalin, *Address to the Graduates From the Red Army Academies* (Moscow: Co-op Publishing Society, 1935).

672. I. V. Stalin, *Sochinenia,* Vol. II (Moscow: Gospolitizdat, 1946), p. 422.

673. *Ibid.* See also Y. M. Sverdlov, *op. cit.,* p. 266.

674. M. Moskalev, *op. cit.,* pp. 158 ff.

675. V. Shveitser, *op. cit.,* p. 16.

676. M. Moskalev, *op. cit.,* pp. 160 ff. V. Shveitser, *op. cit.,* p. 36.

677. *Ibid.,* pp. 18-20. Vera Shveitser indicates Stalin often wrote Alliluev for funds and to maintain contact with Lenin. If true, the letters have not yet been published.

678. E. Gorodetsky and Yu. Sharapov, *op. cit.,* p. 85.

679. Yakov M. Sverdlov, *op. cit.*

680. K. T. Sverdlova, *op. cit.,* p. 558.

681. Y. M. Sverdlov, *op. cit.,* Vol. I, p. 266.

682. *Ibid.,* pp. 268-9.

683. V. Shveitser, *op. cit.,* p. 31.

684. Y. M. Sverdlov, *op. cit.,* p. 267 ff.

685. M. Moskalev, *op. cit.,* p. 165.

686. *Ibid.*

687. *Ibid.*

688. *Ibid.,* p. 165-6.

689. V. Shveitser, *op. cit.,* pp. 22-3.

690. L. Abramyan, *S. Spandaryan—pobornik i propagandist proletarskogo internatsionalizma* (Erevan: Armgiz, 1955), p. 13. Also see V. Shveitser, *op. cit.,* 40-1.

691. A. E. Badaev, "Arrest Dumskoi Piaterki," *Krasny Arkhiv,* No. 3 (64),

1934, pp. 31-51. Department of Police and Okhrana Documents concerning the 1914 arrest of the bolshevik Duma faction in Finland show the professional expertise of tsarist security-intelligence organs.

692. F. N. Samoilov, *Po sledam minuvshego* (Moscow: Gospolitizdat, 1940), p. 306.

693. Vera Shveitser, *op. cit.*, p. 44.

694. K. T. Sverdlova, *op. cit.*, p. 266. Also see Achmed Amba, *I Was Stalin's Bodyguard* (London: F. Muller, 1952), p. 125-6.

695. *Leninsky Sbornik*, ed. 2, Vol. XI (Moscow-Leningrad: Institut Lenina Pri Ts.K. V.K.P.(b), 1931), p. 193.

696. S. T. Possony, *op. cit.*, pp. 197-209 includes a detailed account of Lenin's contacts with Germany during this period.

697. A. S. Allilueva, *op. cit.*, pp. 117-8.

698. I. V. Stalin, *op. cit.*, p. 423.

699. *Ibid.* Also see M. Moskalev, *op. cit.*, p. 186.

700. L. Trotsky, *op. cit.*, p. 182.

701. O. I. Averbakh, *Zakonodatelnye akty, vyzvannye voinoiu, 1914-1916 g.g.*, Vol. III (Vilno/Petrograd, [n.p.], 1915-18, pp. 655-6.

702. A. Allilueva, *op. cit.*, p. 35.

703. V. Shveitser, *op. cit.*, p. 56.

704. E. Yaroslavsky, *op. cit.*, p. 81.

705. A. S. Allilueva, *op. cit.*, p. 167.

706. *Voinskaya povinnost: nastavlenie, instruktsiya, bolezni i nedostatki* (Moscow: "Yurist," 1941). Also see *Kakie bolezni prepiatstvuiut postupleniu na voennuiu sluzhbu* (Moscow: Moskovskoe izd-vo, 1915).

707. A. S. Allilueva, *op. cit.*, p. 167.

708. I. V. Stalin, *op. cit.*, p. 423.

709. V. Shveitser, *op. cit.*, p. 56.

710. I. V. Stalin, *op. cit.*, p. 423.

711. V. Shveitser, *op. cit.*, p. 64.

712. *Ibid.*, p. 61.

713. *Ibid.*, p. 62.

714. A. Baikalov, *op. cit.*, p. 27 ff.

715. V. Shveitser, *op. cit.*, p. 65.

716. *Ibid.*, p. 67. Also see F. N. Samoilov, *op. cit.*, p. 324.

717. *Leninsky Sbornik*, Vol. XIII (Moscow: Partizdat, 1933), p. 271.

718. A. S. Allilueva, *op. cit.*, p. 165.

719. *Ibid.*, p. 166.

14. THE GLOOMY REVOLUTIONARY

720. V. I. Lenin, *Sochinenii*, ed. 2, Vol. XXI (Moscow/Leningrad: Gosiz-vo, 1928), p. 72.

721. V. I. Lenin, *op. cit.*, Vol. XXXI, p. 634.

721a. George Katkov, *Russia; 1917—The February Revolution* (New York: Harper & Row, 1967). Katkov's brilliant analysis of the February revolution refutes the idea that it was spontaneous. Like Possony he has concluded from a study of the German Foreign Office archives that the Germans had more to do with it than is generally realized. The thought that the Germans had a hand in the February revolution and the Bolshevik *coup d'état* was considered far-fetched and, of course, anti-Lenin. Now with the knowledge derived from original source materials, scholars like Katkov are appreciated, but far less than they deserve. The thesis of Okhrana complicity in revolutionary events will undoubtedly need some years before it is acceptable, even though the source materials are available for research.

722. L. Trotsky, *op. cit.*, p. 455.
723. L. Trotsky, *op. cit.*, p. 187.
724. V. I. Lenin, "The Tasks of Our Revolution," *op. cit.*, Vol. XXXI, pp. 151-186.
725. B. V. Nikitine, *The Fatal Years, Fresh Revelations on a Chapter of Underground History* (London: William Hodge & Co., 1938), p. 1.
726. N. N. Sukhanov, *The Russian Revolution, 1917; An Eyewitness Account* (New York: Harper & Brothers, 1962), p. 59.
727. A. S. Allilueva, *op. cit.*, pp. 165 ff.
728. I. V. Stalin, *op. cit.*, Vol. II, p. 423.
729. L. Trotsky, *op. cit.*, p. 186.
730. Moisei A. Moskalev, *Biuro tsentralnogo komiteta RSDRP v Rossii* (Moscow: Izdatelstvo politicheskoi literatury, 1964), p. 284.
731. A. V. Snegov, "Neskolko stranits iz istorii partii," *Voprosy istorii KPSS*, 1963, No. 2, p. 19.
732. The Soviet record explains that on March 15th, at the next session of the Bureau it was decided to admit Zalutsky and Stalin, but only because Molotov and Shliapnikov had become members of the Presidium. Stalin was the lowest ranking person in the Bureau. See "Protokoly i resoliutsii Biuro Tsk RSDRP (b) (mart 1917 g)," *Voprosy istorii KPSS*, No. 3, 1962, pp. 134-57.
733. A. V. Snegov, *op. cit.*, p. 19.
734. L. Trotsky, *op. cit.*, p. 187.
735. M. Moskalev, *op. cit.*, pp. 288-9.
736. A. V. Snegov, *op. cit.*, p. 20.
737. A. V. Snegov, *op. cit.*, p. 22.
738. K. Stalin, "O sovdepakh rabochikh i soldatskikh deputatov," *Pravda*, No. 8, March 14, 1917. Also see A. V. Snegov, *op. cit.*, p. 21.

    M. Moskalev, *Biuro . . .* , *op. cit.*, pp. 287-9. In the words of this Soviet author, Stalin during March was giving an "erroneous interpretation" to many deep-rooted questions about the development of the revolution. Moskalev also suggests that Stalin actually supported the Provisional Government during March 1917.

    Kamenev's apparent support for the Provisional Government is suggested by his articles in *Pravda* on March 14 and 15, 1917.
739. *Ibid.*
740. A. V. Snegov, *op. cit.*, pp. 22-25. The author juxtaposes examples of Lenin's writings with the versions appearing in *Pravda* during this period. There is no doubt that Stalin was distorting Lenin's views. Also see M. Moskalev, *Biuro . . .* , 1964, pp. 289-90. "On March 18th A. M. Kollontai brought to Petrograd the first two of Lenin's 'Letters From Afar.' But, on March 21st and March 22nd, *Pravda* printed only the first letter." This account goes on to prove that *Pravda*, under Stalin's editorship, was distorting Lenin's views, and worse, altering his writings.
741. K. Stalin, "O voine," *Pravda*, No. 10, March 16, 1917.

742. K. Stalin, "Ob otmene natsionalnykh ogranichenii," *Pravda,* No. 17, March 25, 1917.

743. V. I. Lenin, *op. cit.,* Vol. XXXI, pp. 113-118.

744. F. Raskolnikov, *Kronshtadt i Piter v 1917* (Moscow/Leningrad: Gosiz-vo, 1925), p. 54. Raskolnikov's account of Lenin's question to Kamenev is repeated in another edition of the same book. See F. Raskolnikov, *Na boevykh postakh* (Moscow: Voennoe Iz-vo, 1964), p. 63 and fn. pp. 63-4. A footnote explains that Lenin was explicitly referring to Stalin and his anti-Leninist views expressed in *Pravda.*

    Raskolnikov served as soviet envoy to Afghanistan, Estonia, Denmark, and Bulgaria. Stalin recalled him to Moscow in April 1938, but Raskolnikov, fearing for his life, took refuge in Belgium. He died in September 1939 in Southern France under circumstances that strongly suggest Stalin had him murdered.

745. S. T. Possony, *op. cit.,* pp. 241-252.

745a. See M. A. Moskalev, *op. cit.,* p. 296. "At a meeting of the Bureau of the Central Committee on April 6, 1917 Kamenev, Bogdatev, and Teodorovich came out against Lenin's thesis [the April thesis]. Stalin also was not at once aware of the genius-like thought of Lenin's thesis . . ."

746. F. Raskolnikov, "V yulskie dni," *Proletarskaya Revoliutsiya,* 1923, No. 5, pp. 55-101.

747. Adam B. Ulam, *The Bolsheviks* (New York: The Macmillan Company, 1965), p. 339.

748. *Pravda 1912-1914, 1917* (Moscow: Gospolitizdat, 1962), p. 8. Also see I. V. Stalin, *op. cit.,* Vol. III, p. 177. See N. N. Sukhanov, Vol. II, *op. cit.,* pp. 454-5.

749. S. T. Possony, *op. cit.,* p. 252.

750. *Ibid.,* p. 254.

751. I. G. Tsereteli, *Vospominaniya o Fevralskoi Revoliutsii,* (2 vols.), (Paris: Mouton & Co., 1963), p. 344.

752. A. S. Allilueva, *op. cit.,* p. 38.

753. *Ibid.*

754. *Ibid.,* p. 45. Also see A. B. Ulam, *op. cit.,* p. 348.

755. A. B. Ulam, *op. cit.,* p. 348.

756. A. S. Allilueva, *op. cit.,* p. 51.

757. N. K. Krupskaya, *op. cit.,* p. 368.

758. A. B. Ulam, *op. cit.,* p. 352.

758a. See "The Personality Cult," *Survey,* No. 63, April, 1967, p. 163. At a recent conference of old bolsheviks and soviet historians that had been convened at the request of "34 Old Bolsheviks" (p. 164), a certain old party member, Sedugina, insisted, "None of the congresses suffered such distortion as the sixth. There is no stenographic record, while as regards minutes the same questions are interpreted in different ways. . . . Persistent attempts are made to show that Stalin led the congress."

    This and other passages clearly show that considerable differences of opinion about the Sixth Congress still exist among communist historians.

759. L. Trotsky, *op. cit.,* p. 218.

760. I. V. Stalin, *op. cit.,* Vol. 3, p. 185.

761. L. Trotsky, *op. cit.*, p. 221.

762. K. T. Sverdlova, *op. cit.*, p. 329.

763. S. T. Possony, *op. cit.*, p. 261.

764. L. Trotsky, *op. cit.*, pp. 222-225.

765. V. I. Nevsky, *Istoriya RKP(b)*, ed. 2 (Leningrad: "Priboi," 1926), pp. 406 and 423.

766. S. Alliluev, "Moi vospominaniya," *Krasnaya Letopis*, No. 5, 1923, p. 171. Nadezhda was born in September 1902 in Baku.

767. A. S. Allilueva, *op. cit.*, p. 60. Anna recalls Lenin's return from Finland to the Alliluev apartment. He had knocked on the door:
"Puzzled I asked, 'Who's there?'
"Is Stalin here?
"And, by his voice I recognized Lenin.
"My God! It is you. Vladimir Ilich, a real Finn!
"Well done, right?", Ilich laughed. "Is Stalin home?", he asked again.

767a. See "The Personality Cult," p. 160. At a recent meeting held in the Institute of Marxism-Leninism, as reported by the editors of *Survey*, a certain Borisov (identified only as an old Bolshevik) related: "Together with Bolshevik delegates I visited Stalin after the February revolution. We asked: 'Why is the question of the Soviets' seizing power not being considered?' Stalin replied: 'The Provisional Government is not all that weak; it is about the same as the Soviets.' That was his statement."

768. A. S. Allilueva, *op. cit.*, p. 52.

769. *Zarya vostoka*, Tiflis, June 10, 1926, VIII, pp. 171-5.

770. See N. B. Basseches, *Stalin* (London: Staples Press, 1952), p. 231. "The sister of Lazar Kaganovich is regarded as his wife, but she seems to be rather the superintendent of his household than a wife. After the death of Nadezhda Allilueva the party was concerned with the question how Stalin's private life should be arranged for in the future. As little change was to be made as could be helped. The household should be managed in the way he had been used to. Stalin cannot endure new people around him. Someone had therefore to be found whom he had long known, and who was also to be trusted. These conditions were satisfied by the sister of his loyal supporter Kaganovich. The lady was already of middle age." No source is supplied for this information.

771. G. Uratadze, *op. cit.*, p. 184.

772. See Alexander Orlov, *The Secret History of Stalin's Crimes* (New York: Random House, 1953, pp. 188-9).

773. See Bertram D. Wolfe, *Khrushchev and Stalin's Ghost* (New York: Praeger, 1957), p. 212. Khrushchev reported that "Stalin allowed the liquidation of Ordzonikidze's brother and brought Ordzhonikidze himself to such a state that he was forced to shoot himself. (Indignation in the hall.)"
This is doubtful. Stalin's secret police probably murdered Ordzhonikidze.

774. N. N. Sukhanov, *op. cit.*, pp. 229-30.

775. B. D. Wolfe, *op. cit.*

775a. See Eugene Lyons, *op. cit.*, p. 114. "In later years he would greet a Japanese newspaperman with the statement: 'I, too, am an Asiatic.' There would be an occasion when someone remarked about his conspicuous politeness to some visitors; and he would comment: 'What else, except our politeness, have we Asiatics to meet you Europeans with?' "

775b. See "The Personality Cult," *Survey*, pp. 178-9. In a recent discussion of A. M. Nekrich's book, *22 June 1941*, held in the Institute of Marxism-Leninism, a certain Petrovsky of the Institute of Historical Archives stated that "Stalin is a criminal." Another old Party member, Snegov, who has written about Stalin's pre-1917 career, in commenting about World War II stated, "Stalin ought to have been shot. Instead of which, people are now trying to whitewash him."

Later, Snegov maintained, "How can one be a communist and speak smoothly about Stalin—who betrayed and sold communists, who eliminated nearly all the delegates of the eighteenth congress and nearly all the central committee members elected. . . ."

776. Joseph E. Davies, *Mission to Moscow* (New York: Simon & Schuster, 1941), pp. 230-1.

15. CHAOS BREEDS A COMMISSAR

777. B. V. Nikitine, *op. cit.*, p. 24 ff.
778. *Izvestia*, February 27, 1917.
779. B. V. Nikitine, *op. cit.*, p. 5.
780. *Ibid.*, p. 24.
781. John Reed, *Ten Days That Shook the World* (New York: Random House, 1960), p. xli.
782. *Ibid.*, p. 49.
783. S. T. Possony, *op. cit.*, p. 274.
784. John Reed, *op. cit.*, p. 23. Also see A. B. Ulam, *op. cit.*, pp. 375-58, S. T. Possony, *op. cit.*, p. 265 ff., and L. Trotsky, *op. cit.*, p. 225.
785. N. N. Sukhanov, *op. cit.*, Vol. II, p. 522.
786. William Henry Chamberlin, *The Russian Revolution, 1917-1921* (New York: Grosset and Dunlap, 1965), p. 217. Chamberlin quotes Sukhanov.
787. I. V. Stalin, *op. cit.*, Vol. III, p. 261-263.
788. *Ibid.*, pp. 272-390.
789. *Rabochy's* name had been changed to *Rabochy Put*. See Whitman Bassow, "The Pre-Revolutionary *Pravda* and Tsarist Censorship," *American Slavic and East European Review*, February, 1954, No. 1, p. 63.
790. K. Sharikov, *op. cit.*, p. 63.
791. V. I. Lenin, *op. cit.*, Ed. 4, Vol. XXVI, pp. 61 fn.
792. V. I. Lenin, *op. cit.*, Vol. VI, p. 217.
793. See Leon Trotsky, *The History of the Russian Revolution* (Ann Arbor: The University of Michigan Press, 1932), p. 152. About this time it was rumored that Lenin had lost his mind. Trotsky unsympathetically reports that an old bolshevik worker, Kisselev, wrote: "The workers' part of the party, with the exception of certain individuals, went with Lenin. Against Lenin, however, was a small group of party intellectuals and solitary workers . . . in private arguments . . . they went so far as to say that 'Lenin is a crazy man; he is pushing the working class to certain ruin. From this armed insurrection we will get nothing; they will shatter us, exterminate the party

and the working-class, and that will postpone the revolution for years and years, etc.' Such was the attitude of Frunze in particular, a man of great personal courage but not distinguished by a wide outlook."

794. W. H. Chamberlin, *op. cit.*, p. 288. The author quotes Protocols of the Bolshevik Central Committee. Trotsky wrote that Stalin wanted to send the letters to important party organizations for discussion. See L. Trotsky, *op. cit.*, p. 226.

795. I. V. Stalin, *op. cit.*, p. 421.

796. S. T. Possony, *A Century of Conflict* (Chicago: Henry Regnery, 1953), p. 212.

797. John Reed, *op. cit.*, pp. 18-9. These were official statistics.

798. I. V. Stalin, *op. cit.*, p. 421.

799. John Reed, *op. cit.*, p. 40 ff.

799a. N. N. Sukhanov, *op. cit.*, p. 578.

800. I. V. Stalin, *op. cit.*, p. 421.

801. *Ibid.*, p. 422.

802. *Ibid.*

803. *Ibid.*

804. L. Trotsky, *Stalin, op. cit.*, p. 232.

805. *Ibid.*

806. A. S. Allilueva, *op. cit.*, pp. 184 ff.

807. E. H. Wilcox, "The Secret Police of Old Regime," *The Fortnightly Review,* Vol. CVIII, December 1, 1917, pp. [826]-836. Wilcox, on the scene in Petrograd, writes that "During the disorders of the Russian Revolution a mob broke into the offices of the Okhrana . . . at Petrograd and wrecked the contents of the building with thoroughness . . . the destruction was general, but the rioters paid special attention to the records, large quantities of which were burnt."

808. N. N. Sukhanov, *op. cit.*, p. 556.

809. *Ibid.*, pp. 556-7.

810. L. Trotsky, *op. cit.*, pp. 243-4. See also Isabel de Palencia, *Alexandra Kollontay; Ambassadress from Russia* (New York: Longmans, Green and Co., 1947), pp. 174-5. Although Kollontai could not speak her real mind during Stalin's regime of terror it is still interesting to learn of her impressions of Stalin—"in the early days of the Revolution"—as told to de Palencia:

"The power of Stalin lay in his strong will, quick thinking and rapid decisions. If Stalin undertook a task, the Party could be sure it would be accomplished to perfection. Although he belonged to the younger generation, Lenin liked to have him around and consult him. At the meetings of the Cabinet, Lenin used to be rather impatient with other members of the Cabinet and in giving any of us the turn to speak would almost always say: 'Be brief, time is valuable.' But if Stalin asked to speak, Lenin would put aside the documents he might be considering and give all his attention to what Stalin might have to say. . . . Stalin spoke very little and only if he had something clear and practical to propose. He was silent and attentive to what was going on but if he gave an order it was a command that must be obeyed.

"Stalin at that time had a slender figure, and wore a black Russian blouse with a belt around his waist, the typical costume of

Caucasians. His movements had the grace usual in mountaineers and he would walk with light quick steps down the long corridors of the Smolny, seeking for Lenin in his provisional and very modest office or hurrying back to the room where the Revolutionary Committee sat. I never saw him excited or nervous even at moments when dangers were surrounding us from all sides and when some of the leading members of the Party would lose their heads and be ready to compromise. Above all things he valued courage and initiative."

811. L. Trotsky, *op. cit.*, pp. 242-4.
812. John Reed, *op. cit.*, p. 44.
813. Milovan Djilas, *op. cit.*, p. 154. Stalin's anti-semitism was still strong twenty years later in 1947. Djilas reports that toward the end of a dinner in the Kremlin,

> ". . . Stalin unexpectedly asked me why there were not many Jews in the Yugoslav Party and why these few played no important role in it. I tried to explain to him that there were not many Jews in Yugoslavia to begin with, and most belonged to the middle class. I added, 'The only prominent Communist Jew is Pijade, and he regards himself as being more of a Serb than a Jew.'
> "Stalin began to recall: 'Pijade, short, with glasses? Yes, I remember, he visited me. And what is his position?'
> "He is a member of the Central Committee, a veteran Communist, the translator of *Das Kapital*," I explained.
> "In our Central Committee there are no Jews!" he broke in, and began to laugh tauntingly. "You are an anti-Semite, you too, Djilas, you, too, are an anti-Semite!"
> Djilas goes on: "I took his words and laughter to mean the opposite, as I should have—as the expression of his own anti-Semitism and as a provocation to get me to declare my stand concerning the Jews, particularly Jews in the Communist movement."

814. A. B. Ulam, *op. cit.*, p. 364. Ulam refers to "The Protocols of the Central Committee."
815. *Ibid.*
816. A. S. Allilueva, *op. cit.*, p. 194.
817. W. H. Chamberlin, *op. cit.*, p. 292.
818. L. Trotsky, *op. cit.*, p. 229.
819. *Ibid.*
820. *Ibid.*
821. I. V. Stalin, *op. cit.*, p. 422.
822. L. Trotsky, *op. cit.*, p. 229.
823. N. N. Sukhanov, *op. cit.*, p. 533.
823a. See A. Tolmachev, *Kalinin* (Moscow: Molodaya gvardiya, 1963), pp. 130-4. Lenin, Shotman, and Rakhia approached Kalinin's offices from an alley. When Lenin arrived he joked about his appearance because a strong wind had toppled his hat and wig into the mud. Both were filthy. It was dawn when the meeting ended. The ever faithful Shotman and Rakhia accompanied Lenin who was the first to depart. Also see I. V. Lenin, *op. cit.*, ed. 5, Vol. XXXIV, p. 576.

Also see N. Zubov, *F. E. Dzerzhinsky, biografiya* (Moscow: Gospolizdat, 1963), p. 131. Soviet historians remain confused about what happened at this meeting. Lenin and Stalin attended an expanded gathering of the bolshevik central committee, representatives of the Petrograd Committee, the Military Organization, the Petrograd Soviet, the Petrograd district committee, factory committees, and trade unions. "This second historical meeting of the Central Committee took place on the Vyborg side [of Petrograd] at No. 13/17 Bolotnaya Street on the premises of the Lesnoi-Udelinsk regional duma, the chairman of which was M. I. Kalinin." Lenin again declared for an immediate armed uprising. Kamenev and Zinoviev wanted to wait for the convocation of the Constituent Assembly. This account asserts that Lenin's resolution about the uprising was warmly supported by Dzerzhinsky, Kalinin, Krylenko, Rakhia, Sverdlov, Skrypnik, Stalin, "and others."

824. W. H. Chamberlin, *op. cit.,* Vol. I, p. 295.
825. *Ibid.*
826. L. Trotsky, *op. cit.,* p. 230.
827. I. V. Stalin, *op. cit.,* p. 450.
828. See Leon Trotsky, *The History of the Russian Revolution,* pp. 163-4. "Stalin spoke out against the acceptance of Kamenev's resignation, arguing that 'our whole situation is self contradictory.' . . . Kamenev's resignation was accepted by five votes against three. By six votes, again with Stalin opposing, a decision was adopted forbidding Kamenev and Zinoviev to carry on a struggle against the policy of the Central Committee. The minutes read: 'Stalin announces that he withdraws from the editorial board.' In order not to complicate an already difficult situation, the Central Committee refused to accept Stalin's resignation."

Trotsky's statement is confirmed by a recent soviet work. See N. Zubov, *op. cit.,* pp. 132-3. By October 20th Stalin had once more switched to an anti-Leninist position. Lenin did not attend a meeting of the central committee on that date. However, he sent letters demanding that Kamanev and Zinoviev, who had opposed his call for an immediate armed uprising, be expelled from the party. The record shows that "The majority of the members who participated (Stalin, Sverdlov, Sokolnikov, and others) did not support Lenin's proposition. Stalin (he was supported by Miliutin and Uritsky) came out against the demand of Vladimir Ilich. . . . By five votes against two the Central Committee decided 'to accept the resignation of Kamenev' from the Central Committee and by six votes charged Kamenev and Zinoviev not to come forth with any pronouncement against decisions of the Central Committee. . . ."

829. I. V. Stalin, *op. cit.,* p. 451.
830. L. Trotsky, *Stalin,* p. 233.
831. N. N. Sukhanov, *op. cit.,* p. 596.
832. *Ibid.,* p. 602. Also see John Reed, *op. cit.,* pp. 89-90. W. H. Chamberlin, *op. cit.,* p. 308.
833. See A. B. Ulam, *op. cit.,* pp. 367-8.
834. *Ibid.*
835. See John Reed, *op. cit.,* pp. 86-7. The same day Lenin wrote to the central committee, "It is impossible to wait!! . . . The government is

wavering. It must be *beaten to death* [Lenin's italics] at all costs. To delay the move is similar to death." See V. I. Lenin, *Polnoe sobranie sochinenii* (ed. 5), Vol. XXIV, p. 436.

836. W. H. Chamberlin, *op. cit.*, pp. 314-5.
837. L. Trotsky, *op. cit.*, pp. 233-4.
838. *Ibid.*
839. I. V. Stalin, *op. cit.*, Vol. 3, p. 451.
840. A. S. Allilueva, *Iz vospominanii, op. cit.*, p. 61.
841. *Ibid.*
842. *Ibid.*
843. A. B. Ulam, *op. cit.*, p. 369.
844. S. T. Possony, *op. cit.*, p. 276.
845. W. H. Chamberlin, *op. cit.*, pp. 318-20.
846. *Ibid.*, p. 314.
847. *Ibid.*, p. 321.
848. John Reed, *op. cit.*, p. 120.
849. S. T. Possony, *op. cit.*, p. 277 quoting Podvoisky.
850. V. I. Lenin, *Sochineniya*, 4th ed., Vol. 26, p. 207.
851. John Reed, *op. cit.*, p. 150.
852. A. S. Allilueva, *op. cit.*, p. 62.
853. *Ibid.*, p. 63.
854. S. Melgunov, *Kak bolsheviki zakhvatili vlast* (Paris: Editions "La Renaissance," 1953), pp. 125-36. Melgunov's scholarly and extensively researched account of the events of October 25th and 26th includes a detailed chronicle of the happenings during this period. He notes, for example, that although Lenin had prematurely announced the fall of the Provisional Government at 10 A.M., Trotsky sent a radio-telegram to the army at 2:35 P.M. declaring the Provisional Government had ceased to exist. Actually his declaration was almost twelve hours too soon: the Winter Palace fell at 2:10 A.M. on October 26th.
855. I. V. Stalin, *op. cit.*, p. 451.
856. L. Trotsky, *op. cit.*, p. 236. Also see *Pravda,* November 6, 1918, p. 2.
857. *Ibid.*, p. 237.
858. John Reed, *op. cit.*, p. 170.
859. *Ibid.*, p. 186.

BIBLIOGRAPHY

1. WESTERN LANGUAGES

Adamlari, H. M., *Berühmte Männer des Krieges: Josif Wissariono-witsch Stalin* [n.p., n.d.], unpublished ms. From the archives of the Anti-komintern Sowjetabteilung, on file at The Hoover Institution.

Albrecht, K. I., *Der verratene Sozialismus*. Berlin: Niebelungen-Verlag, 1939.

Amba, A., *I Was Stalin's Bodyguard*. London: F. Muller, 1952.

Aronson, G., "Was Stalin a Tsarist Agent?" Review of *Stalin's Great Secret* by I. D. Levine, *New Leader,* August 20, 1956.

Avtorkhanov, A., *The Reign of Stalin*. London: Bodley Head, 1953.

Backer, G., *The Deadly Parallel: Stalin and Ivan the Terrible*. New York: Random House, 1950.

Badaev, A. E., *Bolsheviks in the Tsarist Duma*. New York: International Publishers, 1932. London: Martin Lawrence, 1932.

Baedeker, K., *Russia with Teheran, Port Arthur, and Peking: Handbook for Travellers*. Leipzig: Karl Baedeker, 1914.

Baikalov, A. V., *I Knew Stalin*. London: Burns, Oates, 1940.

Balabanova, A., *My Life As a Rebel*. New York: Harper & Brothers, 1938. London: Hamish Hamilton, 1938.

Barbusse, H., *Stalin*. New York: Macmillan, 1935. London: John Lane, 1935.

Basseches, N., *Stalin*. London: Staples Press, 1952.

Bassow, W., "The Pre-Revolutionary *Pravda* and Tsarist Censorship," American Slavic and East European Review, February, 1954, No. 1.

Bauer, O., *Die Nationalitätenfrage und die Sozialdemokratie*. Wien: I. Brand, 1907.

Bazhanov, B. G., *Avec Staline dans le Kremlin*. Paris: Editions de France, 1930.

Beria, L., *On the History of the Bolshevik Organization in Transcaucasia*. Moscow: Foreign Languages Publishing House, 1949.

Besedovsky, G. Z., *Stalin, "L'Homme d'acier."* Paris: Librarie de la Revue Française, A. Redier, 1932.

Billington, J. H., *The Icon and the Axe.* New York: A. A. Knopf, 1966.

Bissonette, G. A. A., *Moscow Was My Parish.* New York: McGraw-Hill, 1956.

Bloch, J. R., *L'homme du communisme; portrait de Staline.* Paris: Editions sociales, 1949.

Bobrovskaya [Zelikson], T. S., *Provocateurs I Have Known.* London: Modern Books, 1931.

Bordeaux, A. F. J., *Sibérie et Californie.* Paris: Plon-Nourrit, 1903.

Borkenau, F., "Stalin im Schafspelz. Zu einer neuen Biographie von Isaac Deutscher," *Der Monat,* 1949, No. 14.

Bronstein, J., *The Politics of Murder.* New York: W. Sloane, 1950.

Burtsev, V., "Lenine and Malinovsky," *Struggling Russia,* Vol. I, No. 9/10, May 17, 1919.

Butenko, F., *Enthüllungen über Moskau.* Berlin/Leipzig: Niebelungen-Verlag, 1938.

Chamberlin, W. H., *The Russian Revolution, 1917-1921.* 2 Vols. New York: Grosset and Dunlap, 1965.

Cole, D. M., *Josef Stalin—Man of Steel.* London: Rich & Cowan, 1942.

Coudenhove-Kalergi, R. N., *Stalin & Cie.* Vienna: Editions Paneuropéenes, 1932.

Daily Express, London, May 10, 11, and 25, 1907.

Daily Mirror, London, May 10 and 11, 1907.

D'Astier de la Vigerie, E. R., *Sur Staline.* Paris: Plon, 1963.

Davies, J. E., *Mission to Moscow.* New York: Simon and Schuster, 1941. London: Victor Gollancz, 1942.

Davis, J., "Josef Stalin—Russia's Ruler Today," *Current History,* Vol. XXIX, October, 1928-March, 1929.

Delbars, Y., *The Real Stalin.* London: Allen & Unwin, 1953.

Deutscher, I., *Stalin, a Political Biography.* London/New York: Oxford University Press, 1949.

Deutscher, I., *The Prophet Armed: Trotsky, 1879-1921.* New York, London: Oxford University Press, 1954.

Dewar, H., *Assassins at Large.* Boston: Beacon Press, 1952. London: Allan Wingate, 1951.

Djilas, M., *Conversations With Stalin.* New York: Harcourt, Brace and World, 1962. London: Rupert Hart-Davis, 1962.

Donovan, R. J., *The Assassins.* New York: Harper & Bros., 1955. London: Elek Books, 1956.

Duranty, W., "Stalin: Man, Mouthpiece, Machine." New York *Times Magazine,* January 18, 1931.

Eastman, M., *Leon Trotsky: the Portrait of a Youth.* New York: Greenberg, 1935. London: Faber & Gwyer, 1926.

The Encyclopedia Britannica. New York: The Encyclopedia Britannica Company, 1910.

Essad-Bey, pseud., *Stalin: The Career of a Fanatic.* New York: Viking Press, 1932. London: John Lane, 1932.

Fischer, L., *The Life and Death of Stalin.* New York: Harper, 1952. London: Jonathan Cape, 1953.

Fischer, L., *The Life of Lenin.* New York: Harper & Row, 1964. London: Weidenfeld & Nicolson, 1965.

Fishman, J., and Hutton, J. B., *The Private Life of Josif Stalin.* London: W. H. Allen, 1962.

Fraser, J. F., *The Real Siberia.* London: Cassell, 1912.

Futrell, M., *Northern Underground: Episodes of Russian Revolutionary Transport and Communications through Scandinavia and Finland 1863-1917.* New York: Praeger, 1963. London: Faber & Faber, 1963.

Garnett, D., *The Golden Echo.* New York: Harcourt Brace, 1954. London: Chatto & Windus, 1953, 1955.

Gerasimov, A. V., *Der Kampf gegen die erste russische Revolution.* Frauenfeld/Leipzig: Huber & Co., 1934.

Graham, S., *Stalin—an Impartial Study of the Life and Work of Joseph Stalin.* London: Ernest Benn, Ltd., 1931.

Granier, L., *Staline.* Lyon: Gutenberg, 1945.

Guide to the Great Siberian Railway. S.-Petersburg: Artistic Printing Society, 1900.

Gunther, J., "Stalin," *Harper's* magazine, 1935, No. 12.

Gurko, V. I., *Features and Figures of the Past.* Stanford: Stanford University Press, 1939. London: Oxford University Press, 1939.

Harcave, S., *The First Blood; The Russian Revolution of 1905.* New York: Macmillan, 1964.

Hallgarten, G. W. F., *Imperialismus vor 1914,* ed. 2, Vol. II. Munich: C. H. Beck, 1960.

Hilger, G., *Stalin—Aufstieg der UdSSR zur Weltmacht.* Goettingen: Musterschmidt-Verlag, 1959.

History of the Communist Party of the Soviet Union. Moscow: Foreign Languages Publishing House, 1960. London: Lawrence & Wishart, 1960.

History of the Communist Party of the Soviet Union (Bolsheviks) Short Course. New York: International Publishers, 1939.

Hutton, J., *Stalin, the Miraculous Georgian*. London: Neville Spearman, 1961.

Iremashvili, J., *Stalin und die Tragödie Georgiens*. Berlin: Volksblatt-Druckerei, 1932.

Joseph Stalin, a Short Biography. Moscow: Foreign Languages Publishing House, 1942.

Just, A., *Josef Wissarionowitsch Stalin*. Lübeck: Colemans Verlag, 1932.

Just, A., *Stalin und seine Epoche*. München: W. Heine, 1953.

Justice, London, May 25, June 1, and 8, 1907.

Katkov, G., *Russia 1917; The February Revolution*. New York: Harper & Row, 1967.

Klimov, G., *The Terror Machine*. New York: Praeger, 1953. London: Faber & Faber, 1953.

Knickerbocker, H. R., "Stalin, Mystery Man Even to His Mother," New York *Evening Post,* December 1, 1930.

Kokovtsov, V. N., *Out of My Past; The Memoirs of Count Kokovtsov*. Stanford: Stanford University Press, 1935. London: Oxford University Press, 1935.

Kolarz, W., *Stalin und das ewige Russland*. London: Lincolns-Praeger, Ltd., 1942. *Stalin and Eternal Russia*. London: Lindsay Drummond, 1944.

Kommoss, R., *Juden hinter Stalin*. Berlin/Leipzig: Niebelungen-Verlag, 1938.

Korosi-Krizsan, S., "Rumania and the Comintern," *East Europe,* Vol. XV, December, 1966, No. 12.

Kot, Stanislaw, *Conversations with the Kremlin and Dispatches from Russia*. Translated and arranged by H. C. Stevens. London: Oxford University Press, 1963.

Kristof, L. K. D., "Boris I. Nicolaevsky, 1887-1966," *The Russian Review,* Vol. XXV, No. 3, July, 1966.

Krivitsky, W. G., *In Stalin's Secret Service*. New York: Harper & Bros., 1939. *I Was Stalin's Agent*. London: Hamish Hamilton, 1939.

Krupskaya, N. K., *Reminiscences of Lenin*. Moscow: Foreign Languages Publishing House, 1959. London: Lawrence & Wishart, 1959.

Lang, D. M., *The Last Years of the Georgian Monarchy, 1658-1832*. New York: Columbia University Press, 1957. London: Oxford University Press, 1957.

Laporte, M., *Histoire de l'Okhrana*. Paris, Payot, 1935.

von Laue, T. H., *Why Lenin? Why Stalin? A Reappraisal of the Revolution, 1900-1930*. Philadelphia-New York: J. B. Lippincott Co., 1964.

Lebedev, M. V., *Note concernant l'organisation de la Police de recherches criminelles et Service d'identification des récidivistes*. Paris: Impr. Wolff, 1914.

Lehmann, J., *Prometheus and the Bolsheviks*. New York: Knopf, 1938. London: Cresset Press, 1938.

Lenin, V. I., *The Letters of Lenin*, ed. by E. Hill and D. Mudie. New York: Harcourt, Brace & Co., 1937. London: Chapman & Hall, 1937.

Lescure, J., *Le bolchevisme de Staline*. Paris: Ed. Domat-Montchestien, 1934.

Levine, I. D., *Stalin*. New York: Cosmopolitan Book Corp., 1931. London: Jonathan Cape, 1931.

Levine, I. D., *Stalin's Great Secret*. New York: Coward McCann, 1956.

Levine, I. D., *The Man Lenin*. New York: Seltzer, 1924.

Levine, I. D., *The Mind of an Assassin*. New York: Farrar, Straus & Cudahy, 1959. London: Weidenfeld & Nicolson, 1960.

The Life of Stalin, a Symposium. London: Modern Books, Ltd., 1930.

Lomonosov, M. V., *Memoirs of the Russian Revolution*. New York: Rand School of Social Science, 1919.

Ludwig, E., *Stalin*. New York: G. P. Putnam, 1942.

Ludwig, E., "Staline, Maître Absolu de la Russie des Soviets," *Le Mois*, 1932, No. 21.

Lyons, E., *Stalin; the Czar of All the Russias*. Philadelphia / New York: J. B. Lippincott Co., 1940. London: George Harrap & Co., 1940.

McGraw-Hill Encyclopedia of Russia, ed. by Michael T. Florinsky. New York: McGraw-Hill, 1961.

McNeal, R. H., "Caveat Lector—a Preface to Stalin's Sochineniia," *Survey*, October, 1963, No. 49.

McNeal, R. H. (compiler), *Stalin's Works—An Annotated Bibliography*. Stanford: The Hoover Institution On War, Revolution and Peace, 1962.

Martynov, A. P., *My Service in the Separate Corps of Gendarmes, 1898-1917*, unpublished ms. on file at The Hoover Institution.

Mazour, A. G., *The First Russian Revolution, 1825*. Berkeley: University of California Press, 1937. Cambridge: Cambridge University Press, 1937.

Monas, S., *The Third Section; Police and Society in Russia Under Nicholas I.* Cambridge: Harvard University Press, 1961. London: Oxford University Press, 1961.

Montagu, I. G. S., *Stalin, a Biographical Sketch of the Man Who Leads the USSR.* London: Communist Party of Great Britain, 1942.

Murphy, J. T., *Stalin, 1879-1944.* London: John Lane, 1945.

Nikitine, B. V., *The Fatal Years, Fresh Revelations on a Chapter of Underground History.* London: William Hodge and Co., 1938.

Nicolaevsky, B. I., *Aseff, the Spy, Russian Terrorist, and Police Stool.* Garden City: Doubleday, Doran & Co., 1934. *Aseff, the Russian Judas.* London: Hurst & Blackett, 1934.

Norman, H., *All the Russias.* New York: Charles Scribner's Sons, 1904. London: William Heinemann, 1902.

Oblenskaia, R., *Kamo: The Life of a Great Revolutionist.* Moscow/Leningrad: Co-op Publishing Society of Foreign Workers in the USSR, 1933.

O'Neill, H. C., *Men of Destiny; Being Studies of the Four Who Rode the War and Made This Precarious Landfall.* London: Phoenix House, 1953.

Orlov, A., *The Secret History of Stalin's Crimes,* New York: Random House, 1953.

Orlov, A., "The Ghastly Secrets of Stalin's Power," *Life,* Vol. XXXIV, April 6, 13, 20, and 27, 1953.

Orlov, V., *The Secret Dossier.* London: George Harrap & Co., 1932.

Owen, F., *The Three Dictators: Mussolini, Stalin, Hitler.* London: Allen & Unwin, 1940.

de Palencia, I., *Alexandra Kollontay; Ambassadress from Russia.* New York: Longmans, Green and Co., 1947.

Payne, R., *The Rise and Fall of Stalin.* New York: Simon & Schuster, 1965. London: W. H. Allen, 1966.

Le Petit Temps, June 27 and 28, 1907.

Pipes, Richard, *The Formation of the Soviet Union—Communism and Nationalism 1917-1923.* Cambridge: Harvard University Press, 1964.

Possony, S. T., *A Century of Conflict.* Chicago: Henry Regnery, 1953.

Possony, S. T., *Lenin: The Compulsive Revolutionary.* Chicago: Regnery, 1964; London: Allen and Unwin, 1966.

"The Personality Cult," *Survey,* No. 63, April, 1967.

Price, M. P., *Siberia.* London: Methuen & Co., 1912.

Raffalovich, S., "The Youth of Stalin," Condensed from *Miroir du Monde,* July 20, 1935.

Raguza, I. (pseud.), *La vie de Staline.* Paris: A. Fayard, 1938.

Randall, F., *Stalin's Russia.* New York: Free Press, 1965. London: Macmillan & Co., 1965.

Reed, J., *Ten Days That Shook the World.* New York: Random House, 1960. London: Lawrence & Wishart, 1962.

Renner, K., *Das Selbstbestimmungsrecht der Nationen in Besonderer Anwendung auf Osterreich.* Liepzig und Wien: F. Deuticke, 1908.

Rigby, T. H. (ed), *Stalin.* Englewood Cliffs, N. J.: Prentice Hall, 1966.

Schapiro, L., *The Communist Party of the Soviet Union.* New York: Random House, 1960.

Scheffer, P., "Stalin's Power," *Foreign Affairs,* July, 1930, No. 4.

Schwarz, Solomon M., *The Russian Revolution of 1905; The Workers' Movement and the Formation of Bolshevism and Menshevism.* Translated by Gertrude Vakar. Chicago and London: The University of Chicago Press, 1967.

Serge, V., *Destiny of a Revolution.* London: National Bank Association, Hutchinson & Co., 1937. London: Jarrolds, 1937.

Serge, V., *From Lenin to Stalin.* New York: Pioneer Publishers, 1937. London: Martin Secker & Warburg, 1937.

Serge, V., *Portrait de Staline.* Paris: B. Grasset, 1940.

Serge, V., *Vie et mort de Trotsky.* Paris: Amoit, Dumont, 1951.

Seton-Watson, H., *The Decline of Imperial Russia, 1855-1914.* New York: Praeger, 1960.

Seydewitz, M., *Stalin oder Trotski.* London: Malik-Verlag, 1938.

Shub, D., *Lenin.* Garden City: Doubleday, 1948.

Smith, E. E., *The Department of Police, 1911-1912; From the Recollections of N. V. Veselago* [by] *Ellis Tennant* [pseud.], unpublished ms. on file at The Hoover Institution.

Souvarine, B., *Staline. Aperçu historique du bolchevisme.* Paris: Plon, 1935.

Spring-Rice, C., *A Record.* Boston: Houghton Mifflin & Co., 1929. London: Constable & Co., 1929.

Stalin, I. V., *Address to the Graduates from the Red Army Academies.* Moscow: Co-op Publishing Society, 1935.

Stalin, I. V., *Interviews with Foreign Workers' Delegations.* New York: International Publishers, 1935.

Stalin, I. V., *Marxism vs. Liberalism,* an Interview by H. G. Wells. New York: International Publishers, 1935. *Stalin-Wells Talk.* London: New Statesman, 1934.

Stalin, I. V., *Stalin's Kampf; Joseph Stalin's Credo, Written by Himself,* edited by M. R. Werner. New York: Howell, Soskin & Co., 1940. London: Jarrolds, 1940.

Stalin, I. V., *Works*, Vols. I-XIII. Moscow: Foreign Languages Publishing House, 1949-55.

Stalin—a Short Biography. London: Grant Publishing Co., 1939.

"Stalin et ses ennemis," *Le Monde Slave* [n.s.], 1933, No. 6.

Sukhanov, N. N., *The Russian Revolution, 1917; Eyewitness Account*, 2 Vols. New York: Harper and Brothers, 1962. London: Oxford University Press, 1955.

"Sur la biographie politique de Staline," *Bulletin de l'opposition russe*, 1930.

Taft, M. L., *Strange Siberia*. New York: Eaton & Mains, 1911.

Tetzlaff, H., "Stalin," *Frankfurter Zeitung*, April 20, 1930.

Treadgold, D. W., *Lenin and His Rivals*. New York: Praeger, 1955. London: Methuen & Co., 1955.

Trotsky, Leon, *The History of the Russian Revolution*. Translated by Max Eastman. Ann Arbor: The University of Michigan Press, 1932.

Trotsky, L., *Lenin*. New York: Minton, Balch & Co., 1925.

Trotsky, L., *My Life*. New York: Charles Scribner's Sons, 1930. London: Thornton Butterworth, 1930.

Trotsky, L., *Stalin, an Appraisal of the Man and His Influences*. (New York: Harper & Bros., 1941). London: Hollis & Carter, 1947.

Turner, S., *Siberia*. London: T. Fisher Unwin, 1911.

Ulam, A. B., *The Bolsheviks; The Intellectual and Political History of the Triumph of Communism in Russia*. New York, The Macmillan Company, 1965.

Usmani, S., *I Met Stalin Twice*. Bombay: K. Kurian, 1953.

Walter, G., *Lenine*. Paris: Julliard, 1950.

Wenyon, C., *Four Thousand Miles Across Siberia on the Great Post-Road*. London: C. H. Kelly, 1909.

Wilcox, E. H., "The Secret Police of the Old Regime," *Fortnightly Review*, Vol. CVIII, December 1, 1917.

Windecke, C., *Der Rote Zar*. Leipzig: Quelle & Meyer, 1932.

Windecke, C., *Wie Stalin wurde*. Bern: A. Scherz, 1943.

Wolfe, B. D., *Khrushchev and Stalin's Ghost*. New York: Praeger, 1957. London: Atlantic Press, 1957.

Wolfe, B. D., *Three Who Made a Revolution*. New York: Dial Press, 1948.

Wright, R. L., and Digby, B., *Through Siberia*. New York: McBride, Mast & Co., 1913. London: Hurst & Blackett, 1913.

Yaresh, Leo, "Ivan the Terrible and the Oprichnina," in Black, Cyril E., ed., *Rewriting Russian History*. New York: Vintage Books, 1962.

Yaroslavsky, E., *Landmarks in the Life of Stalin*. Moscow: Foreign Languages Publishing House, 1940. London: Lawrence & Wishart, 1942.

2. SLAVIC LANGUAGES

Abramyan, L., S. *Spandariyan-pobornik i propagandist proletarskogo internatsionalizma*. Erevan: Armgiz, 1955.

Abramovich, R., "Chingiz-Khan 20-go veka," *Sotsialistichesky vestnik*, December 30, 1949, No. 12.

Agafonov, V. K., *Zagranichnaiya Okhranka*. Petrograd: Izd-vo "Kniga," 1918.

Albom nagliadnykh posobii po istorii VKP(b). Moscow: Gospolitizdat, 1951.

Aleksandrov, pseud., *Diktator-li Stalin?* Paris: Knizhnyi magazin "Vozrozhdeniye," 1932.

Alfavitnyi spisok lits, rozyskivaemikh tsirkuliarami Departamenta Politsii ot 16 marta 1907 goda po i ianvaria 1910 goda. St. Petersburg: Tip. shtaba Otd. Korp. Zhand., 1910.

Alliluev, S., "Moi vospominaniya," *Krasnaya letopis*, No. 5, 1923.

Alliluev, S., *Proidennyi put*. Moscow: OGIZ, 1946.

Alliluev, S., "Vstrechi s tovarishchem Stalinym," *Proletarskaya revoliutsiya*, 1937, No. 8.

Allilueva, A. S., *Iz vospominanii*. Moskva: Izd-vo "Pravda," 1946.

Allilueva, A. S., *Vospominaniya*. Moskva: Sovetsky pisatel, 1946.

Anisimov, N., "I. V. Stalin v gody solvychegodskoi i vologodskoi ssylok," *Istorik-marksist*, 1940, No. 9.

"Arkhivnye dokumenty k biografii V. I. Lenina. Nachalo podema rabochego dvizheniya (1910-1914)," *Krasnyi arkhiv*, 1934, No. 1.

"Arkhivnye materialy o revoliutsionnoi deiatelnosti I. V. Stalina, 1908-1913 gg.," *Krasnyi arkhiv*, 1934, No. 2.

Arkomed, S. T., *Rabochee dvizhenie i sots.-demokratiia na Kavkazye*. Geneva: Impr. Chaulmontet, 1910.

Arkomed, S. T. *Rabochee dvizhenie i sotsial-demokratiia na Kavkazye (s 80-kh godov po 1903)*. Moscow/Petrograd: Gos. izd-vo, 1923.

Aronson, G., "Stalinsky protsess protiv Martova," *Sotsialistichesky Vestnik*, Paris, No. 7-8, 1939.

Arsenidze, R., "Iz vospominanii o Staline," *Novyi zhurnal*, June, 1963, No. 72.

Arsenidze, R., "L. Beria: K voprosu ob istorii bolshevistskikh organizatsii v Zakavkazye," *Caucasian Review,* 1955, No. 1.

Arutiunian, A. B., *Narody Zakavkazia v borbe protiv tsarizma v gody pervoi russkoi revoliutsii.* Erevan: Izd-vo Erevanskogo univ., 1957.

Averbakh, O. I., *Zakonodatelnye akty, vyzvannye voinoiu, 1914-1916 gg.* [n.p.] Vilna/Petrograd: 1915-18.

Avlabarskaya nelegalnaya tipografiya Kavkazskogo soyuznogo komiteta RSDRP (1903-1906 gg.); sbornik materialov i dokumentov. Tibilisi: Gosizdat, 1954.

Badaev, A. E., "Arest dumskoi 'piaterki' v 1914 g." *Krasnyi arkhiv,* 1934, No. 3(64).

Badaev, A. E., *Bolsheviki v Gosudarstvennoi Dume.* Moscow: Gospolitizdat, 1954.

Badaev, A. E., "O Staline," *Pravda,* December 19, 1939.

Badaev, A. E., "Russkie bolsheviki do revoliutsii," *Byloe,* 1926, No. 1.

Bagirov, M. D., *Iz istorii bolshevistskoi organizatsii Baku i Azerbaidzhana.* Moscow: OGIZ, 1946.

Bakai, M. E., "Iz vospominanii M. E. Bakaia o chernykh kabinetakh v Rossii," *Byloe,* 1908, No. 7.

Bas, I., "Muzei bolshevistskogo pechatnogo slova," *Istorichesky zhurnal,* November 1937, No. 11.

Batumskaya demonstratsiya 1902 goda. Moscow: Partizdat, 1937.

Bediia, E., "Pervoe maia 1901 goda v Tbilisi," *Izvestia,* April 27, 1937.

Bednyi, D., "S podlinnym verno!" *Pravda,* December 20, 1929.

Bega, F. F., and Aleksandrov, V. G., *Petrovsky.* Moscow: Molodaya gvardiya, 1963.

Beria, L., *K voprosu ob istorii bolshevistskikh organizatsy v Zakavkazye.* Moscow: Partizdat, 1937.

Beria, L., *K voprosu ob istorii bolshevistskikh organizatsy v Zakavkazye,* ed. 5. Moscow: Gospolitizdat, 1939.

Beria, L., "Lado Ketskhoveli," *Lado Ketskhoveli; sbornik.* Moscow: Partizdat, 1938.

Bialik, B., "Stalin i Gorky," *Krasnaia nov,* 1939, No. 12.

Bibineishvili, V. E., *Za chetvert veka.* Moscow: Molodaya gvardiya, 1931.

Birsko-Bidzhansky Raion Dalne-Vostochnogo Kraya. Moscow: Komitet po zemelnomu ustroistvu trudiashchikhsia Evreev, 1928-1930, 2 Vols.

Bokov, I., "Sila Stalina," *Pravda,* December 24, 1939.

Bolshaya sovetskaya entsiklopediya. Moscow: "Sovetskaya entsiklopediya," 1926-47.

Bolshaya sovetskaya entsiklopediya, ed. 2. Moscow: "Sovetskaya entsiklopediya," 1950-60.

Bukharin, N., "Pamiati Ilicha," *Pravda,* January 21, 1925.

Burenin, N. E., *Pamiatnye gody.* Leningrad: Lenizdat, 1961.

Butrina, P., "Iz zhizni bolshevika v tsarskom podpolye," *Krasnaya letopis,* 1936, No. 1.

Chernov, V. M., *Rozhdenie revoliutsionnoi Rossii.* Paris: Iubileinyi komitet po izdaniiu trudov V. M. Chernova, 1934.

Chetverty (obyedinitelny) syezd RSDRP, aprel (aprel-mai) 1910 goda; protokoly. Moscow: Gospolitizdat, 1959.

Chlenov, S. B. *Moskovskaya Okhranka i ee sekretnye sotrudniki.* Moscow: Otdel pechati Moskovskogo soveta R. i K. D., 1919.

Dadiani, S., "Istoricheskie mesta Tbilisi," *Pravda,* December 17, 1939.

Dan, F., *Iz istorii rabochego dvizheniya i sotsial-demokratii v. Rossii, 1900-1904.* Rostov na Donu: Izd. "Donskoi rechi," [n.d.]

Deiateli revoliutsionnogo dvizheniya v Rossii. Vol. V. Moscow: Vsesoyuznoye obshchestvo politicheskikh katorzhan; i ssylno-poselenstev, 1931-33.

"Deiatelnost t. Kirova v Tomskoi s.-d organizatsii," *Krasnyi arkhiv,* 1939, No. 6(97).

Derenkovsky, G. M. (ed.), *Vtoroi period revoliutsii, 1906-1907 gody. Chast pervaya; yanvar—aprel 1906 goda; kniga vtoraya.* Moscow: Izdat-stvo akademii nauk SSSR, 1959.

Dmitrievsky, S. V., *Stalin.* Berlin: "Strela," 1931.

Doklad Komissii izbrannoi obshchim sobraniem prisiazhnykh poverennykh 16 ianvaria 1905 goda po povodu sobytii 9-11 ianvaria. St.-Petersburg: Tip. I. N. [n.d.].

"Dokumenty iz biografii G. K. Ordzhonikidze," *Istorichesky zhurnal,* 1937, No. 2.

Drabkina, F., "Tsarskoe pravitelstvo i 'Pravda,'" *Istorichesky zhurnal,* 1937, No. 3-4.

Dubinsky-Mukhadze, I. M., *Orzhonikidze.* Moscow: Molodaya gvardiya, 1963.

Dubinsky-Mukhadze, I. M., *Shaumyan.* Moscow: Molodaya gvardiya, 1965.

Dvadstat piat let Bakinskoi organizatsii bolshevikov. Baku: Bakinsky rabochy, 1924.

Dvevnik Imperatora Nikolaya II. Berlin: Russky Revolutsionny Arkhiv, 1923.

Ebanoidze, L., *Aleksandr Tsulukidze*. Tbilisi: Zariya Vostoka, 1950.

Entsiklopedichesky slovar. S.-Peterburg: Brokgauz i Efron, 1893-1906.

Entsiklopedichesky slovar Russkago bibliograficheskago instituta Granat., ed. 7 (11th stereotyped ed.). Moscow: 1933-1937.

Enukidze, A. S., *Nashi podpolnye tipografii na Kavkazye*. Moscow: "Novaya Moskva," 1925.

"Epokha reaktsii (1908-1910)," *Krasnyi arkhiv*, 1934, No. 1(62).

Erenfeld, B. K., "Delo Malinovskogo," *Voprosy istorii*, 1965, No. 7.

Fleer, M. G., "Revoliutsiya 1905-1906 gg. v. doneseniyakh diplomatov," *Krasnyi arkhiv*, 1926, No. 3(16).

Garvi, P., *Revoliutsionnye siluety*. New York: Inter-University Project on the History of the Menshevik Movement, 1962.

"Gazeta Departamenta Politsii," *Byloe*, 1908, No. 7-8.

Gegeshidze, Z. T., *Lado Ketskhoveli*. Moscow: Gospolitizdat, 1959.

Gertik, D. (Gerb), "Pravda 1912-14 godov," *Pravda*, May 6, 1927.

Golubovich, V., "Molodoi Stalin," *Istorik-marksist*, 1940, No. 1.

Gorodetsky, E., and Sharapov, Yu., *Sverdlov, zhizn i deiatelnost*. Moscow: Gospolitizdat, 1961.

Gruziia v datakh. Khronika vazhneissikh politicheskikh ekonomicheskikh i kulturnykh sobytii. Tbilisi: Izd-vo TsK KP Gruzii, 1961.

Guro, I. R., *Ozarennye*. Moscow: Gospolitizdat, 1963.

Interviews No. 10-18 with B. I. Nicolaevsky, November 1961-November 1962. [n.p.]

"Iosif Vissarionovich Stalin-biograficheskaya spravka," *Komsomolskaya pravda*, December 21, 1929.

Iosif Vissarionovich Stalin, kratkaya biografiya, ed. 2. Moscow: Gospolitizdat, 1947, 1949, and 1953.

Ivanov, B., *Stupeni zhizni-borby*. Moscow: Molodaya gvardiya, 1931.

Ivanov, B., "V Novoi Ude," *Pravda*, December 25, 1939.

Ivanov, R. V., *Tiurmy i ssylki*. New York: Izd-vo im. Chekhova, 1953.

Iz epokhi "Zvezdy" i "Pravdy" (1911-1914 gg.). Moscow: Gos. izd-vo, 1921-23.

"Iz otcheta o perliustratsii Dep. politsii za 1908 g," *Krasnyi arkhiv*, 1928, No. 2(27).

"Iz perepiski TsK RSDRP s mestnymi partiinymi organizatsiiami, 1912-1914," *Istorichesky arkhiv*, 1960, No. 2.

Iz proshlogo; stati i vospominaniya iz istorii Bakinskoi organizatsii i rabochego dvizheniya v Baku. Baku: Bakinsky rabochy, 1923.

"Iz revoliutsionnoi deiatelnosti G. K. Ordzhonikidze," *Krasnyi arkhiv*, 1938, No. 1(86).

Iz vospominanii russkago uchitelia Pravoslavnoi Gruzinskoi Dukhovnoi Seminarii. Moscow: Tip. "Russkaya pechatnia," 1907.

"Ot redaktsii," *Izvestia,* April 28, 1937.

"K istorii Prazhskoi konferentsii," *Krasnyi arkhiv,* 1939, No. 6(97).

"K istorii vseobshchei stachki na iuge Rossii v 1903 g.," *Krasnyi arkhiv,* 1938, No. 3(88).

"K 35-letiyu IV (Obedinitelnogo) syezda RSDRP," *Krasnyi arkhiv,* 1941, No. 3(106).

"Kak Departament Politsii otpustil Lenina zagranitsu dlia bolshevistskoi propagandy," *Byloe,* [n.s.] 1926, Vol. II.

Kakie bolezni prepiatstvuiut postupleniiu na voennuiu sluzhbu. Moscow: Moskovskoe izd-vo, 1915.

Kalinin, M., *K shestidesiatiletiiu so dnia rozhdeniya tovarishcha Stalina.* Moscow: Gospolitizdat, 1939.

Kaminsky, V., and Vereshchagin, I., "Detstvo i iunost vozhdia: dokumenty, zapisi, rasskazy," *Molodaya gvardiya,* 1939, No. 12.

Karganov, N., "Iz proshlago Stalina," *Vozrozhdenie,* January 13, 1929.

"Karl Marx i tsarskaya tsenzura," *Krasnyi arkhiv,* 1933, No. 1(56).

Kazbegi, A., *Izbrannoe.* Tbilisi: Zariya Vostoka, 1948.

Kazbegi, A., *Izbrannye proizvedeniia.* Tbilisi: "Zariya Vostoka," 1957.

Kelendzheridze, M., "Stikhi iunogo Stalina" *Rasskazy o velikom Staline.* Tbilisi: "Zariya Vostoka," 1941.

Keller, B. A., "Na putiakh mirovoi istorii," *Oktiabr,* 1939, No. 12.

Khachapuridze, G. V., and Makharadze, F. E., *Ocherki po istorii rabochego i krestianskogo dvizheniya v. Gruzii.* Moscow: Zhurnalno-gazetnoe obedinenie, 1932.

Khachapuridze, G., "Pobeda velikoi sotsialisticheskoi revoliutsii v Zakavkazye," *Istorichesky zhurnal,* 1937, No. 10.

Kikoin, V. G., " 'Zvezda' i 'Pravda,' " *Krasnaya letopis,* 1920, No. 2 (35).

Kniazeva, G. V., *Borba bolshevikov za sochetanie nelegal'noi i legal' noi partiinoi raboty v gody reaktsii 1907-1910.* Leningrad: Izd-vo Leningradskogo Univ., 1964.

Kommunisticheskaya partiya Sovetskogo Soiuza v rezoliutsiakh i resheniakh syezdov, konferentsy i plenumov TSK, Vol. I. Moscow: Gospolitizdat, 1954.

Krivtsov, S., "I. V. Stalin," *Pod znamenem marksizma,* 1930, No. 2-3.

Krugliakov, B., "Pravitelstvo i zheleznodorozhnye zabastovki v Peterburge v 1905 godu," *Krasnaya letopis,* 1925, No. 2(13).

Kurlov, P. G., *Gibel imperatorskoi Rossii.* Berlin: Otto Kirchner, 1923.

Kuznetsov, I. D., *Natsionalnye dvizheniya v period pervoi revoliutsii v Rossii (sbornik dokumentov iz arkhiva byv. Departamenta Politsii)*. Cheboksary: Gos. izd-vo, 1935.

Lado Ketskhoveli; sbornik pod red. L. Beriya i G. Broido. Moscow: Partizdat TsK VKP(b), 1938.

Landau, M. A., *Sovremenniki,* M. A. Aldanova [pseud.], ed. 2. Berlin: "Slovo," 1932.

Lenin, V. I., *Polnoe sobranie sochinenii,* ed. 5. Moscow: Gospolitizdat, 1961.

Lenin, V. I., *Sochineniia,* ed. 3. Moscow: Partizdat, 1935-37.

Leninsky sbornik, Vol. XI, ed. 2. Moscow: / Leningrad: Institut Lenina pri TsK VKP(b), 1931.

Leninsky sbornik, Vols. XIII, and XXV. Moscow: Part. izd-vo, 1933.

Lepeshinsky, P., "Vtoroi sezd partii," *Istorik-marksist,* 1933, No. 4 (32).

Liadov, M., *Iz zhizni Partii.* Moscow: Gospolitizdat, 1956.

Listovki Kavkazskogo soiuza RSDRP, 1903-1905 gg. Moscow: Gospolitizdat, 1955.

Lomonosov, Iu. V., *Vospominaniya o martovskoi revoliutsii 1917 g.* Stokgolm/Berlin, 1921.

Londonsky sezd Rossiiskoi Sots.-demokr. Rab. Partii (sostoiavshiisia v 1907 g.) Polnyi tekst protokolov. Paris: Impr. Gnatovsky, 1909.

Lurye, M. L., *Bolshevistskaya pechat v tiskakh tsarskoi tsenzury.* Leningrad: Gazetno-zhurnalnoye izd-vo, 1939.

Lurye, M., *Stalin v Peterburge v gody revoliutsionnogo podema, 1911-1913.* Leningrad: Lenizdat, 1939.

Maevsky, E., *Massovoe dvizhenie s 1904 po 1907 gg.* S.-Peterburg: 1910.

Maglakelidze, S. and Iovidze, A., comp., *Revoliutsiya 1905-1907 g.g. v Gruzii; sbornik dokumentov.* Tbilisi: "Sakhelgami," 1956.

Maisky, I. M., *Vospominaniya sovetskogo poslannika.* Moscow: Izd-vo "Nauka," 1964.

Makharadze, F. E., *Ocherki revoliutsionnogo dvizheniya v Zakavkazi.* Tiflis: Gosizdat Gruzii, 1927.

Malaya sovetskaya entsiklopediya. Moskva: "Sovetskaya entsiklopediya," 1930-31.

Malaya sovetskaya entsiklopediya, ed. 2. Moscow: "Sovetskaya entsiklopediya," 1933-47.

Malaya sovetskaya entsiklopediya, ed. 3. Moscow: "Sovetskaya entsiklopediya," 1958-61.

Markov, E. L., *Ocherki Kavkaza,* ed. 3. S.-Peterburg / Moscow: T-vo M.O. Volf, 1904.

Martov, L., "Artilleriskaya podgotovka," *Vpered*, Petrograd, March 18, 1918.

Martov, L., *Spasiteli ili uprazdniteli?* (Kto i kak razrushal RSDRP). Parizh, Izd.: "Golosa Sotsial demokrata," 1911.

Masanov, I. F., *Slovar psevdonimov.* Moscow: Vsesoiuznaya knizhnaya palata, 1956-60.

Matasova, F., "Nabliudenie za V. I. Leninym v dekabre 1905 g.-yanvare 1906 g.," *Krasnaya letopis*, 1925, No. 1(12).

Materialy po peresmotru ustanovlennykh dlia okhrany gosudarstvennago poriadka iskliuchitelnykh zakonopolozhenii. S.-Peterburg: [n.p.] 1905.

Medvedeva Ter-Petrosyan, S. F., *Geroi revoliutsii* (*"Tovarishch Kamo"*). Moscow: Gos. izd-vo, 1925.

Medvedeva Ter-Petrosyan, S. F., "Tovarishch Kamo," *Proletarskaya revoliutsiya*, 1924, No. 8-9(31-2).

Melgunov, S., *Kak bolsheviki zakhvatili vlast.* Paris: Editions "La Renaissance," 1953.

Melgunov, S. P., *Na putiakh k dvortsovomu perevorotu.* Paris: "Rodnik," 1931.

Ministerstvo Vnutrennikh Del, 1802-1902; istorichesky ocherk. S.-Peterburg: M.V.D., 1901.

Moskalev, M. A., *Biuro tsentralnogo komiteta RSDRP v Rossii.* Moscow: Izdatelstvo politicheskoi literatury, 1964.

Moskalev, M., "K 25-letiiu Prazhskoi konferentsii RSDRP," *Istorichesky zhurnal*, 1937, No. 1.

Moskalev, M., *Russkoe biuro Tsk Bolshevistskoi partii, 1912-mart 1917.* Moscow: Gospolitizdat, 1947.

Nadezhdin, P. *Kavkazsky krai, priroda i liudi.* Tula: Tip. V. N. Sokolova, 1901.

"Neopublikovannye materialy iz biografii tovarishcha Stalina," *Antireligioznik*, 1939, No. 12.

Nevsky, V. I., *Istoriya RKP(b)*, ed. 2. Leningrad: "Priboi," 1926.

Nevsky, V., *Materialy dlia biograficheskogo slovaria sotsial-demokratov,, vstupivshikh v rossiiskoe rabochee dvizhenie za period ot 1880 do 1905 g.* Moscow / Petrograd: Gos. izd-vo, 1923.

Nikolaishvili, N., "Stikhi yunogo Stalina," *Zariya Vostoka*, December 21, 1939.

Nikulin, L., "Domik v Serpukhove," *Pravda*, December 19, 1939.

Nord, L. A., "Marshal M. N. Tukhachevsky," *Vozrozhdeniye*, Paris, 1957, No. 63-69.

"Novye dannye ob ubiistve Lado Ketskhoveli," *Krasnyi arkhiv*, 1938, No. 6(91).

Obshchestvennoe dvizhenie v Rossii v nachale ZZ-go veka. S.-Peter-
burg, Tip.: "Obshchestvennaia pol'za," 1909-14.
Obshchy sostav upravleny i chinov Otdelnago Korpusa Zhandarmov.
St.-Peterburg, Tip.: Otd. Korp. Zhand., 18??-1903.
Ocherki istorii Kommunisticheskoi partii Azerbaidzhana. Baku: Azer-
baidzhanskoe gos. izd-vo, 1963.
Okhrana Collection at The Hoover Institution on War, Revolution and
Peace, Stanford University, Stanford, California.
Ordzhonikidze, Z. G., *Put bolshevika.* Moscow: Gospolitizdat, 1945.
Osnovnye vekhi zhizni i deiatelnosti I. V. Stalina," *Propaganda i agi-
tatsiya,* 1939, No. 23.
Ozerov, I. K., *Politika po rabochemu voprosu v Rossi za poslednie
gody.* Moscow: Izd-vo I. D. Sytina, 1906.
"P. A. Moiseenko v arkhangelskoi ssylke," *Krasnyi arkhiv,* 1939,
No. 1(92)
Padenie tsarskogo rezhima. Leningrad: Gos. izd-vo, 1924-1927.
"Pamiati 26 bakinskikh komissarov," *Krasnyi arkhiv,* 1938, No. 4-5
(89-90).
*Partiya bolshevikov v revoliutsii 1905-1907 godov; dokumenty i ma-
terialy.* Moscow: Gospolitizdat, 1961.
Pesikina, E., "V Naryme," *Pravda,* December 26, 1939.
Piaskovsky, A., *Pervaya (Tammersforskaya) konferentsiya RSDRP.*
Moscow: Gospolitizdat, 1951.
Piatnitsky, O. A., ed., *Prazhskaya konferentsiya RSDRP.* Moscow:
Molodaya gvardiya, 1937).
Piatyi (Londonsky) sezd RSDRP, aprel-mai 1907 goda; protokoly.
Moscow: Gospolitizdat, 1963.
Pisma P. B. Axelroda i Yu Martova. Berlin: Russky Revoliutsionny
Arkhiv, 1924.
Pitersky, A., "Zhizn Iosifa Vissarionovicha Stalina v materialakh
Muzeia revoliutsii SSSR," *Istorichesky zhurnal,* 1949, No. 1.
Pokrovsky, M. N. (ed.), *1905; materialy i documenty.* Moscow: Gos.
izd-vo, 1925.
Poletaev, N., "Piatnadtsat let nazad," *Pravda,* May 6, 1927.
Polevoi, Y., "Chto chitat o zhizni i deiatelnosti tovarishcha Stalina,"
V pomoshch marksistsko-leninskomu obrazovaniiu, 1939
No. 9.
"Politseiskoe delo o Staline," *Katorga i ssylka,* 1926, No. 1(22).
Pravda 1912-1914, 1917 g.g.; bibliografichesky ukazatel. Moscow:
Gospolitizdat, 1962.
Radus-Zenkovich, V. A., *Stranitsy geroicheskogo prochlogo; vospomi-
naniya i stati.* Moscow: Gospolitizdat, 1960.

Raskolnikov, F., *Kronshtadt i Piter v 1917.* Moscow/Leningrad: Gosiz-vo, 1925.

Raskolnikov, F., *Na boevykh postakh.* Moscow: Voennoe Iz-vo, 1964.

Raskolnikov, F., "V yulskie dni," *Proletarskaya Revoliutsiya,* 1923, No. 5.

Rasskazy o velikom Staline. Tbilisi: "Zariya Vostoka," 1941.

"Rasskazy krestian s. Kureiki o tovarishche Staline," *Pravda,* December 18, 1939.

Rasskazy starykh rabochikh o velikom vozhde. Tbilisi: "Zariya Vostoka," 1937.

Rasskazy starykh rabochikh Zakavkazya o velikom Staline. Moscow: Molodaya gvardiya, 1937.

"Revoliutsiya 1905-1907 gg," *Krasnyi arkhiv,* 1934, No. 1(62). Molodaya gvardiya, 1937.

Revoliutsionnoe proshloe Tbilisi. Tbilisi: Izd-vo "Metsniereba," 1964.

Rozkanov, F., *Zapiski po istorii revoliutsionnago dvizheniia v. Rossii (do 1913 goda).* S.-Peterburg: Izd. Departamenta Politsii, 1913.

Rudnev, D., "V Solvychegodske," *Pravda,* December 16, 1939.

Sagirashvili, D., "Stalin (iz vospominanii i razmyshlenii)," *Vestnik Instituta po izucheniiu SSSR,* 1954, No. 2.

Samoilov, F. N., *Po sledam minuvshego.* Moscow: Gospolitizdat, 1940.

Samoilov, F. N., *Vospominaniyia.* Moscow / Leningrad: Gos. izd-vo, 1923-27.

Sarkisov, N. K., *Borba Bakinskogo proletariata v period pervoi russkoi revoliutsii.* Baku: Azerbaidzhanskoe gos. izd-vo, 1965.

Savinov, V., "Za Narvskoi zastavoi," *Pravda,* December 19, 1939.

[*Sbnornik sekretnykh tsirkuliarov, obrashchennykh k Nachalnikam gubernskikh zhandarmskikh upravlenii, gubernatoram i pr. v techenie 1902-1907 g.g.*]

Sharikov, K. G., and Shidlovsky, G. L., *Lenin v Peterburge.* Leningrad: Lenizdat, 1940.

Sharikov, K. G., comp., "Vazhneishie mesta prebyvaniya i revoliutsionnoi deiatelnosti I. V. Stalina v Peterburge-Petrograde-Leningrade (1909-1934 gg.)," *Propaganda i agitatsiya,* 1939, No. 32.

Shaumyan, L., *Kamo: zhizn i deiatelnost professionalnogo revoliutsionera S. A. Ter-Petrosyana.* Moscow: Gospolitizdat, 1959.

Shaumyan, L., "Plamennoe serdtse," *Izvestia,* December 15, 1962.

Shaumyan, L., "Stoikii bolshevik. K 85-letiiu so dnia rozhdeniia A. S. Enukidze," *Pravda,* May 19, 1962.

Shaumyan, L., "Vernyi boets leninskoi partii. K. 80-litiiu so dnia rozhdeniia M. D. Orakhelashvili," *Pravda*, June 10, 1963.

Shaurov, I. V., *1905 god. Vospominaniya uchastnika revoliutsii 1905-1907 godov*. Moscow: Izd-vo "Mysl," 1965.

Shengelaya, D., "V Gori," *Pravda*, December 14, 1939.

"Shkola filerov," *Byloe*, 1917, No. 3(25).

Shotman, A., *Kak iz iskry vozgorelos plamia*, ed. 2. Leningrad: Molodaya gvardiya, 1935.

Shub, D., "Noveishaya falsifikatsiya istorii KPSS," *Novogve Russkoe Slovo*, December 24, 1963.

Shumiatsky, Ya., Iosif Vissarionovich Stalin, biograficheskaya spravka," *Komsomolskaya pravda*, December 21, 1929.

Shumiatsky, Ya., *V Sibirskom podpolye; ocherki 1903-1908 gg*. Moscow/Leningrad: Moskovsky rabochy, 1926.

Shumiatsky, Ya., *Po tiurmam*. Moscow: "Katorga i ssylka," 1925.

Shumiatsky, Ya., "Za poliarnym krugom," *Komsomolskaya pravda*, December 21, 1929.

Shveitser, V., "Nelegalno v Pitere," *Komsomolskaya pravda*, December 21, 1929.

Shveitser, V., *Stalin v Turukhanskoi ssylke*. Moscow: Molodaya gvardiya, 1943.

Snegov, A. V., "Neskolko stranits iz istorii partii," *Voprosy istorii KPSS*, 1963, No. 2.

Sobranie uzakonenii i rasporiazhenii Pravitelstva, Otd. 1-2, Petrograd: [n.p.] 1914-17.

Solomon, G. A., *Lenin i ego semiya*. Paris: Impr. des Travailleurs intellectuels, 1931.

Spiridovich, A. I., *Istoriia bolshevikzama v Rossii ot vozniknovenya do zakhvata vlasti, 1883-1903-1917*. Paris, Tip.: "Franko-Russkaya pechat," 1922.

Spisok obshchago sostava chinov Otdelnago Korpusa Zhandarmov. St.-Peterburg, Tip.: Otd. Korp. Zhand., 189?-.

"Stachka rabochikh zheleznodorozhnykh masterskikh v Tiflise (1900 g.)," *Krasnyi arkhiv*, 1939, No. 3(94).

Stalin—biografichesky ocherk [n.p., n.d.], unpublished ms. from the archives of the Antikomintern Sowjetabteilung. On file at The Hoover Institution.

Stalin, I. V., "K desiatiletiiu 'Pravdy,' " *Pravda*, May 5, 1922.

Stalin, I. V., *Marksizm i nationalny vopros*. Moscow: Gospolitizdat, 1946, 1949, 1950, 1952, and 1953.

Stalin, I. V., *O Lenine*. Moscow: Partizdat, 1934.

Stalin, I. V., *O Lenine*. Moscow: Gospolitizdat, 1951.

Stalin, I. V., *Politichesky otchet Tsentralnogo komiteta XV syesda VKP(b)*. Moscow: Partizdat, 1936.

Stalin, I. V., *Sochineniya*, Vols. I-XIII. Moscow: Gospolitizdat, 1946-1951.

Stalin i Khashim; nekotorye epizody iz Batumskogo podpolia. Moscow: Partizdat TSK(b), 1935.

Stalin i o Staline; ukazatel literatury. Leningrad: Lenpartizdat, 1940.

Stalin, K., "Natsionalny vopros i sotsial-demokratiya," *Prosveshchenie*, March-May, 1913, No. 3-5.

Stalin, K., "Ob otmene natsionalnykh ogranichenii," *Pravda*, March 25, 1917.

Stalin, K., "O sovdepakh rabochikh i soldatskikh deputatov," *Pravda*, No. 8, March 14, 1917.

Stalin, K., "O voine," *Pravda*, No. 10, March 16, 1917.

"Studencheskie volneniya v 1901-1902 gg," *Krasnyi arkhiv*, 1938, No. 4-5 (89-90).

Sumbadze, L. Z., *Gori*. Moscow: Gos. izd-vo arkhitekt. lit-ry, 1950.

Sumsky, S., "Troyanovsky," *Poslednia novosti*, January 1, 1934.

Sverdlov, Ya. M., *Izbrannye proizvedenia*, Vols. I-IV Moscow: Gospolitizdat, 1957.

Ya. M. Sverdlov, sobornik vospominanii. Moscow: Izd-vo Znanie, 1959.

Sverdlova, K. T., *Yakov Mikhailovich Sverdlov*. Moscow: Molodaya gvardiya, 1957.

Svod zakonov Rossiiskoi Imperii, Vol. XIV, "Ustav o passportakh." St. Peterburg, [n.p.], 1903.

Teknika bolshevistskoga podpolia. Sbornik statei i vospominanii, ed. 2. Moscow: Gos. izd-vo, 1925.

Tolmachev, A., *Kalinin*. Moscow: Molodaya gvardiya, 1963.

Tovarishch Stalin—vozhd narodov, otets trudiashchikhsia [n.p., n.d.], unpublished ms. from the archives of the Antikomintern Sowjetabteilung. On file at The Hoover Institution.

Tovstukha, I. P., *Iosif Vissarionovich Stalin*. Moscow: Gos. izd-vo, 1927.

Tsereteli, I. G., *Vospominaniya o Fevralskoi Revoliutsii*, (2 Vols.). Paris: Mouton and Co., 1963.

Tsiavlovsky, M. A., ed., *Bolsheviki. Dokumenty po istorii bolshevizma s 1903 po 1916 gody byvsh. Moskovskogo Okhrannogo Otdeleniya*. Moscow: Zadruga, 1918.

Ugriumov, A. L., *Partiya bolshevikov v period pervoi russkoi revoliutsii (1905-1907 gg.)*. Moscow: Gos. izd-vo "Sovetskaya nauka," 1957.

Uratadze, G. I., *Moi vospominaniya.* [n.p.] [n.d.]. On file at The Hoover Institution.

Uratadze, G. I., *Obrazovani i konsalidatsiya Gruzinskoi Demokraticheskoi Respubliki.* Munich: Institute for the Study of the USSR, 1956.

"Ustav o pasportakh" in *Svod zakonov Rossiiskoi Imperii,* Vol. XIV. Sanktpeterburg: [n.p.] 1903.

"Ustav o ssylnykh" in *Svod zakonov Rossiiskoi Imperii,* Vol. XIV. Sanktpeterburg: [n.p.] 1903.

Ustav o voinskoi povinnosti. S.-Peterburg, Tip: "Selskogo vestnika," 1913.

V. I. Lenin i A. M. Gorky; pisma, vospominaniya, dokumenty, ed. 2. Moscow: Izd-vo Akademii nauk SSSR, 1961.

"V. I. Lenin v gody imperialisticheskoi voiny," *Krasnyi arkhiv,* 1939, No. 1(92).

Vakar, N., "Stalin po vospominaniyam N. N. Zhordania," *Posledniya Novosti,* Paris, December 16, 1936.

Valentinov, N., "O liudiakh revoliutsionnogo podpolia," *Novyi Zhurnal,* No. 73, September 1963.

Vatsek, I., "Stalinskaya shkola revoliutsionnoi borby," in *Rasskazy o velikom Staline.* Tbilisi: "Zarya Vostoka," 1941.

Veidenbaum, E., *Putivoditel po Kavkazu.* Tiflis, Tip.: Kants. Glavnonach. grazhd. chastiu na Kavkaze, 1888.

Vereshchak, S., "Stalin v tiurme; vospominaniya politicheskogo zakliuchennogo," *Dni,* January 22 and 24, 1928.

Vetoshkin, M., "V sibirskoi ssylke," *Istorichesky zhurnal,* 1940, No. 1.

Vinogradov, L., *Fedor Samoilov.* Moscow: Gospolitizdat, 1961.

Voennaya entsiklopediya, Vol. XI. S.-Peterburg-T-vo Sytina, 1913.

Voinskaya povinnost: nastavlenie, instruktsiya, bolezni i nedostatki. Moscow, Izd.: "Yurist," 1914.

Volchek, G., and Voinov, V., *Viktor Kurnatovsky.* Moscow: Molodaya gvardiya, 1961.

Volin, B. M., *12 biografy.* Moscow: "Rabochaya Moskva," 1924.

Vospominaniya o V. I. Lenine. Moscow: Izdatelstvo Ts.K VLKSM, 1955.

Vostochnoe Obozrenie, Irkutsk, November, 1903-April 1904.

Vpered, Moscow, March 18, 1918.

Vrochinskaya, K., "Doma-muzei I. V. Stalina v s. Kureika i g. Achinske," *Sovetskii muzei,* 1939, No. 4.

Vtoroi period revoliutsii, 1906-1907; chast pervaya: yanvar-aprel 1906 goda, kniga vtoraya. Moscow: Gospolitizdat, 1959.

"Vtoroi syezd i raskol partii (1903-1904)," *Krasnyi arkhiv,* 1934, No. 1(62).

Vtoroi vserossiskii sovetov rabochikh i soldatskikh deputatov; sbornik dokumentov. Moscow: Gospolitizdat, 1957.

Weingart, A., *Ugolovnaya taktika.* St.-Peterburg: [n.p.] 1912.

Yaroslavsky, E., "Tri vstrechi," *Pravda,* December 23, 1939.

Yaroslavsky, E., "Vazhneishie vekhi zhizni i deiatelnosti tovarishcha Stalina," *V pomoshch marksistsko-leninskomu obrazovaniiu,* 1939, No. 10, 13-14.

Zarya vostoka, Tiflis, June 10, 1926, VIII.

Zhilinsky, V., "Organizatsiya i zhizn Okhrannogo Otdeleniya vo vremya tsarskoi vlasti," *Golos minuvshago,* 1917, No. 9/10, p. 278.

Zhordania, N. N., *Bolshinstvo ili menshinstvo.* Geneva, Izd.: "Iskry," 1905.

Zhukov, Y. "Gori-Tbilisi," *Novyi mir,* 1939, No. 12.

Zhvania, G., *Bolsheviki Zakavkazia v borbe za leninskie idei druzhby narodov.* Tbilisi: Inst. istorii partii pri TsK KP Gruzii, 1963.

Zubov, N., *F. E. Dzerzhinsky, biografiya.* Moscow: Gospolitizdat, 1963.

APPENDICES

1879	December 9	Birth of Joseph Vissarionovich Dzhugashvili.
1888	September 1	Stalin enters the Gori theological school.
1890-93		Stalin run over by carriage. Resulting illness leaves left arm permanently shortened.
1894	July	Stalin graduates from the Gori theological school.
1894	September 1	Stalin enters Tiflis Theological Seminary.
1898	March 1-3	First Congress of the Russian Social-Democratic Workers Party held in Minsk.
1899	May 29	Stalin leaves the Tiflis Seminary.
1899	December 28	Begins work at the Tiflis Geophysical Observatory.
1900	April 23	Speaks publicly for first time at Salt Lake, near Tiflis.
1901	March 21-22	Stalin apartment in observatory raided by Okhrana in general dragnet while he is absent.
1901	April	Stalin incites demonstrations in Tiflis.
1901	November	Stalin, forced to leave Tiflis by its social-democratic organization, goes to Batum.
1902	March	Provokes riots in Batum.
1902	April 5	Arrested for the first time, in Batum.
1903	April 19	Transferred to Kutais prison.

1903	August 4	Lado Ketskhoveli killed in prison.
1903	July 17- August 10	Second Congress of the Russian-Social-Democratic Workers Party held in Brussels and London.
1903	November 1-15	Stalin "exiled" for three years in Siberia.
1904	January 5(?)	Stalin claims he escaped from Novaya Uda, Irkutsk Province.
1904(?)	June	Stalin marries Ekaterina Svanidze, his first wife.
1904	December 13-31	Strike of oil workers in Baku.
1905	January 9	"Bloody Sunday" in St. Petersburg.
1905	April 12- April 27	Third Congress of the Russian Social-Democratic Workers Party held in London.
1905(?)	(date unknown)	Stalin's second arrest. Place unknown. Escape from prison.
1905	December 12-17	Stalin attends bolshevik conference at Tammerfors, Finland.
1905(?)		Stalin's first son, Yasha, born.
1906	April 10-25	Stalin attends Fourth Congress of the Social-Democratic Workers Party in Stockholm.
1906	April 15	Okhrana raid on Avlabar printing press in Tiflis. Stalin already in Stockholm.
1907	April (?)	Death of Ekaterina Svanidze.
1907	April 24-28	Stalin meets Lenin in Berlin. Reveals plan for Tiflis robbery.
1907	April 30- May 19	Fifth Congress of the Russian Social-Democratic Workers Party held in London, the last until the revolution of 1917. Stalin attends the conference, takes no part, but is proposed as consultative delegate by Lenin.
1907	June 12	Kamo in charge of Tiflis (Erevan Square) expropriation planned by Stalin.
1907	August 15	Murder of Prince Ilya Chavchavadze in Georgia.
1907	December 22-25	Stalin meets with Lenin in Berlin.
1908	March 25	Stalin arrested for third time, in Baku.
1908	September 29	Leaves Bailov prison (Baku) under guard for exile in Solvychegodsk.

1909	February 27	Arrives in Solvychegodsk after illness en route.
1909	June 24	Escapes from Solvychegodsk and goes to St. Petersburg.
1910	March 23	Arrested for fourth time, in Baku. Transferred to Bailov prison on March 26th.
1910	September 23	Again exiled to Solvychegodsk.
1910	October 29	Arrives in Solvychegodsk.
1910	Decmber 31	Stalin writes Lenin in Paris ("Comrade Semyen" letter).
1911	January 24	Stalin writes "Iosif" letter to Moscow bolshevik organization.
1911	June 27	Stalin released from Police surveillance at expiration of his term of exile. Chooses Vologda as place of residence.
1911	July 16	Arrives in Vologda.
1911	September 6	Illegally leaves Vologda for St. Petersburg.
1911	September 9	Arrested for fifth time, in St. Petersburg.
1911	December 14	Deported to Vologda for three years.
1912	January	After the Prague Conference Lenin co-opts Stalin, still in exile, as a member of the first Central Committee of the Bolshevik Party.
1912	February 29	Escapes from Vologda and goes to St. Petersburg, then to the Caucasus.
1912	April 1	Departs from Baku for St. Petersburg.
1912	April 22	Arrested for sixth time, in St. Petersburg. First issue of *Pravda* appears.
1912	July 2	Deported under escort to Narym territory for three years.
1912	September 1	Escapes from Narym.
1912	September 12	Claims he arrives in St. Petersburg.
1912	*Ca.* October 1	Stalin actually arrives in St. Petersburg.
1912	October	Travels to Helsinki and obtains false Finnish passport. Departs Abo, Finland, by ship en route to Cracow.
1912	mid-November	In Cracow to receive instructions from Lenin and attend meeting of Central Committee.

1912	end of November	Returns to St. Petersburg.
1912	December 1	Lenin writes letter from Cracow to St. Petersburg: "get rid of Stalin."
1912-13	December 26-January 1	Stalin attends "February" Conference at Cracow.
1913	Latter part of January	Visits Vienna and works on "Marxism and the Nationality Question."
1913	January 20	Writes warm letter to Malinovsky in St. Petersburg from Vienna, where Stalin says he is writing "rubbish."
1913	February	Returns to Cracow, confers with Lenin.
1913	mid-February	Returns to St. Petersburg.
1913	February 23	Arrested for seventh and last time at fund raising musicale organized legally by *Pravda* in St. Petersburg.
1913	February 23-July 2	Incarcerated for last time in St. Petersburg Detention Prison.
1913	March-May	"The National Question and Social Democracy" (later *Marxism and The National Question*) signed K. Stalin published in Nos. 3-5 of *Prosvescheniye* (*Enlightenment*) in St. Petersburg.
1913	July 2	Deported for four years to Siberia.
1913	July 11	Arrives in Krasnoyarsk, Siberia.
1913	July 25	Leaves Krasnoyarsk for Turukhansk, Siberia.
1913	August 10	Arrives in Turukhansk.
1914	Early March	Transferred to village of Kureika near Arctic Circle.
1914	July 19	Germany declares war on Russia.
1915	June 5	Five bolshevik deputies, exiled to Turukhansk, arrive at village of Monastyrskoye. Stalin attends meeting at Monastyrskoye.
1916	December 14	Arrives in Krasnoyarsk to report for military service.
1917	January-February	Rejected for military service because of left arm. Resettles in Achinsk, a village near Trans-Siberian railway.
1917	February 23	February (March) Revolution begins in Petrograd.

1917	March 2	Tsar Nicholas II abdicates.
1917	March 8	Stalin leaves Achinsk for Petrograd.
1917	March 12	Arrives in Petrograd.
1917	March 12	Russian Bureau of Bolshevik Central Committee meets in Petrograd. Decides in view of "certain personal traits" to deny Stalin full membership in Bureau.
1917	March 15	Stalin permitted to enter Bureau as lowest ranking member—on temporary basis.
1917	March 16	Stalin writes article in *Pravda,* which he now heads, conciliatory toward Provisional Government.
1917	April 1-3	Attends All-Russian Party Conference in Petrograd. Declares conditional support for Provisional Government.
1917	April 3	With help of Germans Lenin arrives at Petrograd's Finland Station from Switzerland. Stalin not present to greet Lenin.
1917	April 4	Lenin calls for establishment of Communist Party. Formulates celebrated "April Thesis."
1917	April 6	Stalin attends meeting of Bureau of Bolshevik Central Committee. According to record "fails at first to understand the genius-like idea" of Lenin's April thesis.
1917	April 24-29	All-Russian Conference of Bolsheviks meets in Petrograd. Stalin elected member of Central Committee for first time.
1917	May 4	Trotsky arrives in Petrograd from Canada.
1917	May 5	Kerensky becomes Minister of War in Provisional Government.
1917	June 3	Stalin attends First All-Russian Congress of Soviets.
1917	July 4-6	Abortive mass insurrection in Petrograd. The so-called "July Days." Lenin accused in press of being German agent.

1917	July 7	Kerensky becomes Prime Minister.
1917	July 11	Stalin and Sergo Alliluev help Lenin to escape from Petrograd to Sestroretsk, Finland.
1917	July 12-15	Stalin moves into Alliluev home at Rozhdestvenskaya Street No. 17.
1917	July 24	Trotsky, Kamenev, and others arrested. Orders issued for Lenin's arrest.
1917	July 26- August 3	Stalin attends and speaks at Sixth Congress of Social Democratic Party in Petrograd.
1917	September 1-3	Lenin, still in hiding, calls for armed uprising.
1917	September 15	Central Committee, Stalin in attendance, narrowly decides not to burn Lenin's letter calling for armed uprising.
1917	October 7	Lenin secretly arrives in Petrograd from Vyborg.
1917	October 10-11	Stalin attends bolshevik Central Committee meeting at apartment of N. N. Sukhanov in Petrograd. Dzherzhinsky proposes that first Political Bureau be created. Stalin among seven men chosen.
1917	October 16	Stalin attends expanded Central Committee meeting led by Lenin in Lesnoi suburb of Petrograd. Lenin again calls for an armed uprising.
1917	October 21	Stalin attends meeting of Central Committee. Lenin calls for expulsion from Party of Kamenev and Zinoviev. Stalin's offer to resign from editorial board of party central organ in support of Kamenev not accepted.
1917	October 24	Bolshevik Central Committee meets at Smolny Institute in Petrograd. Eleven members present. Stalin absent. Lenin comes out of hiding and appears at Smolny.
1917	October 25	Premature announcement by Lenin that Provisional Government overthrown

		at 10 a.m. Operations to seize head-quarters of Provisional Government begin at 9 p.m. Second All-Russian Congress opens at 11:30 p.m.
1917	October 26	Provisional Government arrested by Military Revolutionary Committee at 2:10 a.m. in Winter Palace.
1917	October 27	Lenin appoints Stalin Commissar of Nationalities in first Bolshevik Government. Announcement made by Kamenev at 2:30 a.m.

2. P S E U D O N Y M S ,   A L I A S E S ,   A N D   C O V E R   N A M E S   O F
I O S I F   V I S S A R I O N O V I C H   D Z H U G A S H V I L I

Bednyi Rabochy	party cover name (?)
I. Besoshvili	pseudonym used in writing
Petr A. Chizhikov	alias used in passport
Chopur	party cover name
David	pseudonym used in writing
Dzh-shvili	pseudonym used in writing
Ivanov	pseudonym used in writing
Ivanovich	alias used in passport for travel abroad
K.	pseudonym used in writing
K . . . b . . . a	pseudonym used in writing
K. Kato	pseudonym used in writing
K. Ko	pseudonym used in writing
Ko.	pseudonym used in writing
Koba	used for writing and as a revolutionary nickname
Koba Ivanovich	pseudonym used in writing
Koba-K.	pseudonym used in writing
Zakhar Grigorian Melikiants	alias used in passport
Kaios (or Gaioz) Vissarionov Nizheradze	alias used in passport
Riaboi	("the Pockmarked One") name used by Okhrana to identify him in reports
S.	pseudonym used in writing
K.S.	pseudonym used in writing
K.S-n	pseudonym used in writing

K. St.	pseudonym used in writing
K. Salin	pseudonym used in writing
K. Solin	pseudonym used in writing
Iosif Vissarionovich Stalin	
K. Stalin	pseudonym used in writing
K. Stefin	pseudonym used in writing
Soso	Georgian affectionate nickname meaning "Little Joe"
Soselo	Georgian nickname (diminutive of "Little Joe")
Molochny	("Milky") name used by Okhrana to identify him in reports
Oganess Vartanovich Totomyants	alias used in passport issued by Tiflis police
Tovarishch K.	pseudonym used in writing
Vas . . .	party cover name
Vasilii	party cover name
Vasiliev	party cover name
Vaska	party cover name
Ivan Ivanovich Vissarionovich	alias used in passport for travel to Stockholm

3. A NOTE ABOUT DATES AND TRANSLITERATION

Two problems invariably vex the author of a book that deals with pre-1917 events in Russia. The first concerns dates. Before the revolution Russia's Old Style Julian calendar differed from the Gregorian New Style used in the West by twelve days during the nineteenth century and by thirteen days during the twentieth century. Accordingly, Stalin's birthday, December 9, 1879, now falls on December 21. The date of the bolshevik assumption of power in Petrograd, October 25, 1917, now is celebrated on November 7. I have used the Old Style calendar throughout this book. When, infrequently, it was necessary to make reference to a New Style date, I have so indicated by (N.S.) after the date.

The second problem involves transliterating Russian words and proper names into English. Unfortunately there is no universally accepted system for transliteration and I have used what may be called a modified Library of Congress system. Those names such as Trotsky and Troyanovsky with which the reader should be familiar and whose pronunciation is roughly equivalent I have retained, although by the Library of Congress rules they would be "Trotskii" and "Troianovskii," respectively. Similarly, I have rejected the spelling of Krupskaia in favor of the less cumbersome and more familiar Krupskaya. Russian place-names generally conform to spellings in commonly accepted usage. I have also omitted the "soft" sign from transliterated Russian words. Hopefully, this will make reading easier for those unacquainted with the Russian language. For the same reason, I have utilized English-language translations of Russian source materials when I was able to determine that the translation did not differ substantially from the original.

INDEX